As I was saying

C. H. ROLPH

LONDON
Police Review
1985

First published in the United Kingdom
in 1985
by Police Review Publishing Co. Ltd.
14 St. Cross Street, London EC1N 8FE.

Made and printed in the United Kingdom
by
Heffers Printers Limited, Cambridge

ISBN 0 85164 016 8

As I Was Saying

By the same author

Police Duties (1936). Police Review Publishing Co.
An ABC for Special Constables and Police War Reserves (1943). Police Review Publishing Co.
A Licensing Handbook (1947). Police Review Publishing Co.
Crime and Punishment (1950). Bureau of Current Affairs.
Towards my Neighbour (1950). Longmans Green.
On Gambling (1951). Bureau of Current Affairs.
Personal Identity (1956). Michael Joseph.
The Human Sum (1957). Heinemann.
Mental Disorder (1958). National Association for Mental Health.
Commonsense About Crime and Punishment (1961). Gollancz.
The Trial of Lady Chatterley (1961). Penguin Books.
Hanged by the Neck (with Arthur Koestler) (1961). Penguin Books.
All Those in Favour? (The E.T.U. Trial) (1962). Deutsch.
The Police and the Public (1962). Heinemann.
Homeless from Prison (1966). Carnegie United Kingdom Trust.
Law and the Common Man (1967). Charles C. Thomas, Illinois.
Books in the Dock (1969). Deutsch.
What is the Purpose of Punishment? (1969). New Zealand Univ. Press.
Kingsley (1973). Gollancz.
Believe What you Like (1973). Deutsch.
Living Twice (autobiography) (1974). Gollancz.
Mr Prone (1977). Oxford University Press.
The Queen's Pardon (1978). Cassells.
London Particulars (autobiography) (1980). O.U.P.
The Police (a child's history) (1980). Wayland Publishers.

Preface

I forget whose idea this originally was, but it gradually came to be regarded as a kind of *Festschrift*, the *Fest* being the survival of a weekly columnist for fifty years, and the *Schrift* a collection of the articles by reason of which, or in spite of which, he had thus carried his bat. Nonetheless I forbear to wave my bat in the direction of the pavilion, since I do not really know whether anyone in it is applauding. I have come to suspect that usually, if anyone is, he is applauding survival as if it were some praiseworthy achievement instead of a fantastic run of good luck.

The series of bread-and-butter articles by which the more indulgent ones in this book have really been sustained, the indulgent ones being in *Punch, The Spectator, The New Statesman*, etc, began in the *Police Review* fifty years ago at the suggestion of its then editor Mr David Harris, an elderly lecturer in English at Aberystwith, University of Wales – a 'fine old Liberal' who sometimes took me to lunch at the National Liberal Club. It took its origin, I believe, from a letter of protest about something or other from myself to an editor I didn't know, somewhere about 1933. The series was to run for an experimental three months. Then we extended it to twelve months. After which we began pretending to each other that it might go on for ever.

Mr. Harris's son Rowland, a barrister who had found that he didn't really like the Bar, succeeded to the editorship almost at the same time (though I noticed the paternal hand for some time after that). Rowland lasted thirty years and became a close friend of mine. Counting in these two, I can confess to having worn out five *Police Review* editors in my fifty years; all of whom, plus Miss Doreen May the sixth and present incumbent who is young enough to outdo them all, have been amazingly tolerant, giving me a free hand with which I have taken – I think – more and more liberties as time went on.

So I want to explain, or excuse, some changes in style. In the mid-Thirties, when I was writing editorially, the phrases 'we think' and 'it is our opinion' inevitably surrounded themselves with pomposity. In this selection I have rather skated over that period, merely including a few articles from then to show that they really were happening. I've tarried a little through the war years, when the weekly stint was often done (like many other people's more perilous stints) during heavy air raids on the City; and felt glad to arrive at March 27, 1970, the week when I was first invited to begin writing in the first person singular. To me it seems that the articles then come alive; indeed the texture and simplicity, plus a bit of fun are, I diffidently think, so much better at the end that I would almost like to think that everyone would read the book backwards and not really finish it.

There seemed no logical or helpful way of grouping the articles according to subject or even period. I gave up trying. Here they are, in strict chronological order as they appeared – with but one exception. From June 1975 I have winkled out the one called *Anyone Bored?*, and brought it to the front of the book. This is because, if I had such a thing as a philosophy of experience, this is what it would be, and I like starting the book with it.

Some of the opinions, pleas, grouses and pronunciamentoes have been Outdated by Events (my personal O.B.E.), but you are invited to look upon those, if you happen to notice them, as a form of history. After all, nearly all history is wrong. I have to thank the editors of *Punch*, The *Spectator*, the *New Statesman*, *The Observer Magazine, The Listener, The New Law Journal, The Radio Times*, and The *Justice of the Peace* for their kind permission to reproduce pieces first published by them. I am happy to thank also two old friends: Brian Hilliard of *The Police Review*, without whose never-failing sympathy and encouragement (as P.G. Wodehouse so memorably said of his daughter) this book would have been finished in half the time; and Roger Levy, for compiling a better Index than I should have got from anyone else, anywhere.

C.H.R.

Contents

CONTENTS

CONTENTS

CONTENTS

CONTENTS

CONTENTS

CONTENTS

Anyone Bored?

I ask myself, how is it possible for anyone to be *bored* at University? I do not see that it is possible. Then I ask my friends who went to universities (as I did not), and they say 'That's why you can't understand - you never went there, you see it as an ideal world you never lived in'. During the French student revolt of May 1968 someone wrote on the wall of a Paris urinal: 'The prospect of being pleased tomorrow will never console me for the boredom of today'. How should a student, a volunteer learner, be brought to the pitch of recording his boredom on walls? And do you remember that Tolstoy, in *Anna Karenina*, said 'boredom is the desire for desires'?

I've never been bored in universities, because I have been admitted to them only as a kind of prison visitor, to talk briefly to the inmates, sign a book and go away. And the inmates have always seemed to me lively rather than bored. If I was lecturing and they were there (notionally anyway) to listen, they never fell asleep: they talked animatedly among themselves or threw paper darts. It is only an alert and dissident man, not a bored man, who makes and throws a paper dart during a lecture. And yet it is only those who have enjoyed the university culture who run it down. 'You will hear more good things on the outside of a stage-coach from London to Oxford,' wrote Hazlitt, 'than if you were to pass a twelvemonth with the undergraduates, or heads of colleges, of that famous university.'

And it is only the heads of colleges, the professors, and the dons who have any right to such boredom as may be available at our seats of learning. For some reason, people of that academic eminence are no longer regarded, and no longer regard themselves, as students. When Albert Einstein revisited Princeton in middle age and was asked to sign the visitors' book, he hesitated at the 'Occupation' column and then wrote 'student'. This was regarded as so extraordinary, so painstakingly droll, that it is known throught the world, as I have wretchedly discovered when trying to tell the story in far-flung common-rooms. The fact that so many heads of colleges, professors and dons *do* seem to find their lives boring, whispering and muttering about each other at high table and teaming up with each other's wives, is to me one of the mysteries of university life, already mysterious and exciting beyond description. It must, I sadly admit to myself, be boredom. They see, more clearly and fearfully than most men, how much there is to learn. And they cover their eyes.

Perhaps it could be prevented by the ideological separation of studies from learning - 'I didn't begin to learn anything,' wrote Anatole France, 'until after I had finished my studies'; and I suppose he meant he was too busy stacking his mind to have time to use it. Still, he couldn't have been bored at any time? A bored mind takes in nothing; but only a mind of the highest quality can ever know the true mystical experience of total boredom. I've always said that my most unfavourite philosopher is Nietszche, but I almost bow in the direction of Bonn and Leipzig when I read what he said about boredom: 'Only the finest and most active animals are capable of it. A subject for a great poet - God's boredom on the seventh day of creation'. Are you sure you know enough to be bored?

FUSS [Journal of the University of Kent at Canterbury] June, 1975.

Reading from the Wrong Note-book

When a Police officer enters the witness-box in a Court to give evidence as to his personal recollection of facts which happen also to be recorded in his official note-book, it is undoubtedly his safest and wisest course to leave the note-book in his pocket. The other day a Constable, giving evidence in a Court of Assize, entered the witness-box note-book in hand and laid the book on the ledge in front of him. While he was being cross-examined by counsel for the prisoner (and indeed throughout the whole of his evidence) he repeatedly glanced down at his open pocket-book. At last a point was reached which the defending counsel thought vital to his case, and the inevitable happened. "Are you reading your evidence from a note-book?" the Constable was asked; "don't you know the answers to these perfectly simple questions without referring to something you have written down? When did you write all this down? Please hand me that note-book a moment and keep it open at the page you are reading from." And so on. At the Judge's direction the Constable handed in his note-book. After an impatient search the prisoner's counsel was unable to find the relevant entry. The note-book passed to and fro, and it was discovered that the book was one used for recording entries of a quite different character, containing nothing bearing in any way on the trial then proceeding. The Constable explained that he did not know it was the wrong book; the proper one was still in his pocket. The Judge remarked that the Constable's frequent glances at his book must have been made with unseeing eyes, and betokened nothing more than a mere nervous gesture; the Constable drew some comfort or reassurance from the presence of a note-book before him, but never once did he read anything in it, or he would have known that it was useless to him at the moment. It is probable that this is more often than not the explanation of a Constable's addiction to his note-book; at the moment of giving evidence it seems his only friend. This illustration may serve, however, to show that it is unreliable even though it be void of entries, since it may occasion more embarrassment than it saves. Perhaps a pebble in each hand would be safer and equally effective.

Police Review April 8, 1935.

Waiting Defendants Allowed in Court

Now that it is becoming the common lot of the citizen to find himself in a criminal court as a consequence of an act of mere forgetfulness, particularly in regard to the lighting of his house, there is a growing tendency to seek methods of evading conviction. The art of self-defence is actually learned in Court, in many cases. There are still many Courts at which the only accommodation for waiting defendants is in the Court-room itself, so that sometimes twenty or thirty persons separately accused of lighting offences can sit and hear the trial of cases exactly similar to their own, making mental notes and planning their own defences according to the fortunes of those called before them. To any Police Officer who regularly attends the Police Courts this is not news. But at a Court of Assize no defendant to a summons, no prisoner on bail, and of course no prisoner in custody, is allowed in Court until his case is called on; the only trial that he hears is his own. Why should there be this difference?

To suggest the sudden adoption in Police Courts of the Assize Court practice in this matter would be to acknowledge that a Summary Court is an imitation of an Assize Court; but what is more important, it would suggest that the principle of "public trial in Open Court" can be fulfilled only so long as you choose your public carefully. Both these suggestions happen to be generally true, but the second one contains the additional barb that if a defendant must not be allowed to hear any trials similar to the one about to be accorded to him, there must be something wrong with the trials. Exclusion cannot be begun merely on the grounds that defendants become artful when they are allowed to watch Justice struggling with her scales.

Police Review February 16, 1940.

Jeering at the Police

When two men were fined recently for being drunk and disorderly, their quite harmless drunkenness having been rendered disorderly by their conduct in jeering at a squad of Policemen marching to their beats, it was made plain that you cannot be prosecuted for jeering at the Police unless it happens that you were drunk at the time you jeered. Or at least, it became apparent that a prosecution for "using insulting behaviour whereby a breach of the peace might have been occasioned" would not have succeeded because the Police cannot be regarded as so susceptible to insult as to be likely to indulge in a breach of the peace. We have always thought that this was probably the case. But we are not sure that it is consistent with this view to hold that jeering at the Police is disorderly conduct. It it is, it seems strange that a sober man may behave offensively where a drunken man may not.

Most Policemen, we imagine, would feel impelled at least to take a sober jeerer to the Police Station, if only in order that he might bump his elbow on the way into the charge-room.

Police Review May 3, 1940.

The Removal of "Place Names"

The removal of rural sign-posts, which was at first left to the energies of local authorities and was carried out with widely differing degrees of thoroughness, merely touched the fringe of a defence precaution which was obviously destined to form the subject, sooner or later, of a Statutory Order. There are so many roadside signs, mostly of private ownership, which will help the lost stranger who can find no sign-posts. The only way to eliminate them was to prohibit them all, and then allow for exceptions. To specify these exceptions would be an impossible task; but there is the now classical method of leaving it to the Chief Officer of Police.

Hence, the Removal of Direction Signs Order, 1940, says first that "no person shall display or cause or permit to be displayed any sign which furnishes any indication of the name of, or the situation of, or the direction of, or the distance to, any place"; next that any such sign already being displayed must be removed or obliterated forthwith;. and then that a Chief Officer of Police may nevertheless allow any sign he thinks fit.

Queries that have reached us show that the Order may result in much confusion unless some pooling of ideas is contrived. The word "place," for example, must be given its obvious geographical meaning, i.e. (according to the Oxford Dictionary), "city, town, village, etc." So regarded, it can never mean a street, even if (to answer one rather naive correspondent) it occurs in such names as "St. James's Place."

A "place-name" is well recognised among topographers to mean the name of a town, village, or district; there is a Society for the Preservation of Place Names, whose concern it is to combat any tendency to divorce the geography of this country from its history by changing the names of "places." But the fact that it may include a "district" has led to a further complication. Should the campaign of obliteration be extended to urban districts in the central regions of large towns? If German troops reach Northenden, will they need the name-plate over the Northenden Bakery to convince them that they are in Manchester? Would a parachutist at Digbeth learn from the Digbeth Pet Stores that he was in Birmingham, assuming that he had not known it for some time? We think that all large towns could exempt at least their central districts from the ban on place-names. We heard the other day of a long-distance road transport driver whose lorry, a hundred miles from its base, was stopped because it bore the name of the town from which he came; he was told that the name must be painted out. He protested that a foreigner who assumed that he came from Edinburgh because of the name on his van might follow him to Plymouth in search of the Forth Bridge, and his employers, who own about 800 lorries, protested more strongly still. Surely their protest was justified? Only vehicles used locally can convey any useful information by their place-names. All these are matters for the chief Constables and the common sense of the Police. The latter has become a precious thing in these slightly hysterical times, though it is functioning under grave difficulties.

Police Review July 5, 1940.

Souvenir Hunting and "Derelict Articles"

The acquisition of "souvenirs"—pieces of German aircraft, spent tracer-bullets, incendiary bomb fins, etc.—seems pretty widespread. Women in the North-West district were recently reported to be making night-dresses from the silk-like fabric of German parachutes dropped to create an invasion scare. A War Reserve Constable has been fined for stealing instruments from a crashed German bomber. A Defence Regulation which is directed against this kind of thing seems to have been lost sight of. Regulation 79 (which bears the rather misleading marginal note "Derelict Articles") says that if a person "finds an article as to which he has reasonable cause to believe that it has been lost or abandoned, and that, immediately before being lost or 'abandoned' it was used or intended to be used for the purpose of an armed force . . . . the person finding the article shall forthwith report the nature and situation thereof, or, if the article is a document, cause it to be delivered, to a member of H.M. Forces on duty or to a Constable at a Police station, and save as aforesaid shall not remove or tamper with the article except with permission granted by or on behalf of a Secretary of State or the Admiralty." There is nothing in this Regulation which confines it to articles which have been lost or "abandoned" by the British armed forces—the phrase used is "an armed force"; the origin of the article may therefore have been Polish, French, Dutch, Czech, Norwegian—or German. A prosecution under this Regulation would therefore be appropriate in almost every case of war-souvenir hunting.

The position regarding leaflets is interesting. It is well enough known that Germans are forbidden to pick up British leaflets dropped by the R.A.F. Whether or not it was intended, Defence Regulation 79 appears to make it unlawful for the British to pick up German leaflets dropped here; the Regulation deals with articles which, in addition to being "used for the purposes of an armed force," have been abandoned (which is certainly true of propaganda leaflets), and then says that "if the article is a document," it shall be taken to a Police Station or the military authorities. Here, at least, is one sense in which the Defence Regulations will not be enforced. Those who wish to read the 39th edition of Hitler's sole speech will pick it up and keep it with impunity, whether or not it is legally (as it certainly is politically) a "derelict article."

Police Review September 20, 1940.

Bombed Houses—Removal of Own Goods

People whose homes have been destroyed or severely damaged by enemy action have been officially advised that any of their property salvaged by A.R.P. personnel will be taken care of for the time being by the local authority. They have also been told that money and jewellery, etc., will be handed to the Police for immediate safe custody, though even this will in due course be handed by the Police to the local authority. We understand that there was for a time an intention that money and small articles of high value should be retained by the Police and dealt with in the same way as other "found property," and that this proposal fell through when it encountered the question of the dividing line of comparative value. (We should have thought that administrative difficulties alone would have sufficed to kill it.)

Some grave problems are inherent in this business of property in bombed houses. We do not think that the conspicuous bravery of the Civil Defence Service, to which we pay respectful tribute, affords any reason for burking the fact that too much looting is going on, and that Civil Defence workers are doing a good deal of it. As this is, in fact, within the knowledge of every Policeman in the country, the mere mention of it should dispel any tendency to cavil at the arrangement whereby small and portable valuables are handed in the first instance to the Police. But what does seem to need public ventilation is the fact that property in bombed houses remains the property of the person to whom it belonged before the bombing; and that there is no encroachment whatever on that person's right to remove the property if it is safe to enter the house.

It is this question of access to the house that seems to us to afford full scope for a major racket. The final decision to exclude an occupier from a damaged building rests with an officer of Police whose rank is not below that of Inspector or with a nominated local government official (Defence Regulation 25); but the initial decision may appear to rest, where none of those officers is immediately on the scene, with the humblest and least responsible member of a Civil Defence section. Innumerable houses now stand empty at night while their usual occupants take shelter somewhere nearby. Returning in the morning to a bombed home, many householders are easily convinced by someone in a steel helmet that they are forbidden to go in; and (though this is less understandable) some of them appear to have been persuaded that, though they may go in their houses to "look round," they must not remove any property without permission from some higher source. Sometimes there occurs then a gap of a few hours while the householder seeks and obtains "permission" to remove his own property! Property has been stolen during these gaps, and members of the Civil Defence organisations have been charged with stealing it. We think the Government should make it clear to the simplest-minded that they lose no ownership of their property by the fact of its being bombed.

But we think, too, that it should be clear to the not-so-simple-minded that they have the property owner's duties as well as his rights, and that they must do their own share of looking after their goods. We have heard it suggested that the prospect of a State insurance against war damage to houses *and* contents has covered the whole of this business with the sickly disease of subsidised indifference, and that looters themselves are able to silence the voice of a quite reasonable conscience with the reflection that the "few little things" they steal will all go down in the inventory. This last is an illusion, and sometimes a wilful one. But a little official public advice would do a lot of good.

Police Review December 6, 1940.

Freethinkers in the Police

When we wrote, in our issue of January 3rd, that we fully believed some Benches of Magistrates would refuse to hear evidence from a Constable who declared himself, or was found, to be an atheist, we disturbed a correspondent who, as a freethinker, took up with us the question of "Rationalist" members of the Police Service and their status as witnesses. Has any Magistrate the power to refuse evidence for such a reason, he asks? "If not," he says, "I think it very perturbing that a paper with the long experience of the POLICE REVIEW can regard such a serious breach of the law as at all possible, particularly during a war for freedom of thought. The prospect opened up by your article will alarm many democrats, and I shall be grateful if you will clear up the position of myself and other Rationalist officers."

We propose to avoid being drawn into a Rationalist (though we should not shrink from a rational) discussion. We still think there are Justices who, on being confronted with a Rationalist Police witness, would be so shocked that they would not merely decline to hear his evidence but would want to know what he was doing in the Police Service of a Christian country. We have even seen their portraits in the evening newspapers, complete with bath-towel and large white moustache. Has our correspondent not read of Justices who will not hear the evidence of a man with an open shirt-collar, or of a woman with no hat? They do not rely for these inhibitions on any provision of the law; they are guided in the one case by the propriety of the stiff collar and in the other by the Epistles of St. Paul. The Rationalist view of the eternal verities is sometimes damaging to the sense of humour. We beg our correspondent not to be alarmed. Such an incident is certainly possible, but it would be sure of considerable publicity in a country where the freedom of the Press is so essential a counterpart of that freedom of thought for which, as he says, we believe we are fighting. The publicity would cause some outcry; the legal, religious, and political pundits would enter the field; and the wretched Magistrate would wish he had understood earlier that Police witnesses are not uniformed morons, delivering stereotyped evidence which is sanctified and acceptable only because it has been preceded by the mouthing of an oath. We happen to know that freethinkers in the Police Service are fairly numerous. One of their burdens is the fact that it should be they, more perhaps than their orthodox colleagues, who understand the nature of the oath. They go through the formality of taking it merely because they would sooner bear those ills they have than fly to others that they know not of.

Police Review January 17, 1941.

Queues

In 1893 the lessees of the Globe Theatre, London, were fined for obstructing the footway outside the theatre by causing a crowd to assemble. The crowd consisted of queues waiting, with the grim patience of British folk about to enjoy themselves, for the doors to open and admit them to a performance of "Charley's Aunt." It was pointed out at the time that, if the Police powers had been insufficient to deal with this obstruction, it could have been restrained by an injunction issued by the High Court. The case is reported as *Barber v. Penley* (1893), L.J.Ch. 623.

Theatre queues have defied the law and become an institution, supporting a whole community of tumblers, buskers, camp-stool proprietors and theatre messengers. The queue is the product of scarcity and the belief in fair play, and it is probably one of the best pictures of the civilised way of life, the veneer cracking only when someone tries to move up out of his turn. Now that shop queues are here the Police are faced with an extension of the problem set them years ago by the theatres—and never solved. The Chief Constable of Wolverhampton, it is reported, has determined to solve it by invoking the law of obstruction against shopkeepers who encourage queues. It is considered that they encourage queues by announcing the forthcoming sale of some commodity much in demand and keeping their doors closed until an advertised time. It seems to us that this encourages crowds rather than queues. Yet the patient shoppers, whose acquired self-discipline minimises the obstruction they cause and each of whom is, after all, entitled to use the highway, may also be prosecuted (according to a *Daily Mail* report) for aiding and abetting the shopkeeper. Apparently this will be done mainly in the case of "the professional queue-goer who makes a habit of shopping at as many places as possible and afterwards brags about it," for these offenders are to be the objects of special Police vigilance.

In some parts of the country various authorities have obtained by-laws *requiring* people to wait in queues—as in London, where the London Passenger Transport board can prosecute you if, when waiting at certain bus-stops with six or more people you do so "otherwise than in a line or queue," or try to start a third line alongside a two-abreast queue, or "take a place in a line or queue elsewhere than at the rear." The last two offences are usually dealt with promptly by the members of the queue, and even the first is an acknowledgement that the queue is a means of preserving the peace. If a queue is unnecessary it can, perhaps, be properly dispersed after a reasonable time by the Police; but someone has to decide upon its necessity or otherwise, and this requires imagination. People do not, as a rule, wait in queues for fun; the very existence of queues is evidence either of maldistribution of commodities or of an actual scarcity of commodities. The Ministry of Food are said, in the report from which we have quoted, to welcome the Chief Constable's decision. But if, as this suggests, the queues are formed at food shops, two considerations arise: first, if the problem is one of distribution the solution must be found and applied by the Ministry itself; secondly, if a genuine scarcity is the cause, queues can be abolished by rationing. Arbitrary Police action is, in our view, undesirable in the former event. In the latter it is distinctly dangerous.

Police Review July 4, 1941.

"V" Scribblers

A man whose house stands at a cross-roads and whose front garden has two very long and vulnerable fences has just told a Bench of Magistrates what he thinks of the "V for Victory" campaign. Having paid a man to wash the fence down and remove some scores of V's chalked on them (surely by children?), he found that two days later they had all been renewed. He knew who had done it, he said, and he wanted not only a summons against the chalkers, but also special Police protection for his property. The demand for Police protection was deflected to the proper address; but the Court were not satisfied as to the identity of the "V for Victory" enthusiasts and so he did not get his summons either. It is difficult not to feel a good deal of sympathy for him. Whatever the propaganda value of the "V" campaign in Germany and the occupied countries (and we believe it must be very great), the occupiers of chalked houses in those countries have two reasons for tolerance—first, that most of them want to annoy the authorities and do not mind if it is done for them, and secondly that the incitement to do it comes from abroad and not from a home Government which has always frowned on wall-scribbling of any other kind.

It seems but a very short time ago that people were being fined for chalking or painting on shop fronts and hoardings the words, "Defend Democracy—Anti-Fascist Rally at 7.30 p.m. To-morrow," and "Remember Spain," and "Stop Hitler Now" and "Back Mosley." The Police prosecuted these mutually repugnant parties with complete impartiality. They have been given no instructions not to prosecute the V-scribblers, but they may well conclude that prosecutions would not strike the right note, no matter how indignant the occupier of the V-scribbled premises. The deep desire in every childish heart to write upon every clean expanse of wall has suddenly been erected into a grown-up virtue, for it has not yet been officially pointed out that V's will not really do much good over here; and having its origin in the primitive artistry of cave-dwelling days it is sure of a greater response than any parody of the Fifth Symphony of Beethoven.

Police Review August 8, 1941.

War News, Alarm and Despondency

The long spell of bad news from some of the war fronts, and the apparent cogency of many of the parliamentary criticisms which Government spokesmen allow to go unanswered, have revived mention of the "alarm and despondency" clause in the Defence Regulations. Several M.P.s want it enforced more rigorously. It was born in the perilous days immediately following Dunkirk, when alarm was pretty rife among those who knew anything at all and despondency afflicted even those who knew nothing. If we had known then what we know now, alarm and despondency would have seemed inadequate words: but our Privy Councillors, who did know the facts, were stout hearted enough to pass the following Regulation:—

"Any person who publishes any report or statement relating to matters connected with the war which is likely to cause alarm or despondency shall be liable on summary conviction to imprisonment for a term not exceeding one month or to a fine not exceeding fifty pounds, or both such imprisonment and such fine." There follows a very necessary proviso absolving such a person if he proves "(a) that he had reasonable cause to believe that the report or statement was true; and (b) that the publication thereof was not malicious and ought fairly to be excused." This puts a heavy onus on the defendant; and when the Dunkirk mood began to lift a little, there was a sudden outcry for the repeal of the Regulation by champions of public liberty who drew on the Gestapo, the Star Chamber, and the witchcraft laws for their persuasive imagery. The Home Secretary undertook to instruct the Police (who, as a matter of fact, were debarred from bringing these prosecutions themselves) that the Director of Public Prosecutions wanted to hear of the most serious cases only. The Regulation has fallen into limbo.

But this is not because the offence of rumour-mongering is not fairly rife. Job's business is not quite so brisk as it was, partly because the South Pacific is a long way off, partly because the appetite for news, good or bad, tends to grow duller as a war drags on. It is the street newsvendors whose immunity from the "alarm and despondency" regulation is perhaps the most surprising. Their home-made placards and blackboards began to alarm the Newspaper Proprietors' Association when the Control of Paper Order abolished the printed placard, and they were told that unless they confined their chalked-up legends to the reproduction of actual headlines from the papers they had for sale, their supplies might be withheld. The proprietors were afraid of libel (among other things), for which they might possibly be held to bear some part of the responsibility. If this led to any kind of agreement between the proprietors and the newsvendors, the arrangement has since broken down. London newsvendors chalk up almost what they like, from facetious bits of "patriotic" doggerel to the most startling paraphrases of the news itself. Reporting them to the Director is a cumbersome business, unlikely except in an extreme case to result in a prosecution. Reporting them to the Newspaper Proprietors' Association is more likely to produce quick results.

Police Review March 20, 1942.

White Feathers

Mr. Bellenger, M.P., recently asked the Home Secretary whether he would introduce legislation to deal with people who send white feathers to ex-Service men discharged on medical grounds. The questioner seemed to think that, in view of the harm and suffering caused to the recipients of white feathers, the senders were guilty of creating "alarm and despondency." Perhaps the words "alarm and despondency" have acquired a special meaning since they were adopted in a Defence Regulation, but to the ordinary man they are still synonymous with putting the wind up you. Receiving a white feather does not put the wind up you; alarm and despondency would more likely be the portion of the sender, if you could find him. In any case Mr. Peake, the Home Office Under-Secretary, said that legislation of the kind proposed would be very difficult to frame and impossible to enforce.

There may be difficulties, though they are not apparent, in the way of enacting that no person shall send or give another a white feather in such circumstances as to imply that the recipient is lacking in patriotism. But how does the law stand at the moment? If the feather is sent by post and is accompanied by a letter or note accusing the recipient of being a shirker, of being unpatriotic, or of some other conduct deserving of public contempt and ridicule, a criminal libel has been committed, because the writing is likely to cause a breach of the peace. An envelope containing a white feather alone, though eloquent enough, would presumably not be a libel. If, on the other hand, the feather is handed to the recipient in the street, that is clearly an act of "insulting behaviour whereby a breach of the peace may be occasioned," and one justifying arrest without warrant under the Police Acts. It would seem more suitable, however, that the distributors of white feathers should be medically examined as to their mental age and balance. Mr. Peake thought that the remedy for this pernicious white feather mischief (which has already led to several suicides) is to be found in "an education of public opinion to a realisation of the fact that in this war, in which the whole energies of the nation are engaged, a man's patriotism and courage cannot be gauged by reference to the clothes which he wears." He added: "Civilians, whether ex-Service men or not, are required to perform the work for which they are best qualified and in which they can best serve their country, and I hope that the publicity which has been given to this matter will put a stop to this stupid and objectionable practice." Unfortunately, the publicity given to it, as to most Members' questions in these paper-controlled days, was practically nil. If any of these cases come under Police notice, we should recommend consideration of the legal powers already existing, as outlined above.

Police Review July 3, 1942.

The Vanishing Tramp

"Sleeping out" is a pretty rare habit nowadays—among civilians. The Vagrancy Act of 1935 did a lot to protect harmless people who genuinely preferred to sleep in the open, by removing the old phrase about "not have visible means of subsistence" and re-arranging the familiar words that remained, in such a way as to throw emphasis on the requirement that the sleeper should be unable to "give a good account of himself." What is a good account?

The Times of 30th March reported a Ministry of Health statement on the diminishing habit of "sleeping out," under the headline "The Vanishing Tramp." The occupants of casual wards on January 29th numbered 629, the lowest for a century; for comparison, the highest was 16,911 on May 27th, 1932. The reduction is attributed to (a) increased employment, (b) military service, and (c) a tendency for men who have drifted away from their families to seek them out again and settle down (query: is this because the wives are earning war wages, or because the general tragedy of the war wipes out all lesser differences?). No account seems to have been taken of people who still sleep in public air-raid shelters, though these number not a few. But to return to our question regarding the "good account," *The Times* report emphasises that gypsies and other self-supporting wayfarers are "technically not casuals." A tramp, according to the Oxford Dictionary, is "one who travels from place to place on foot, especially in search of employment." People like this (especially the "self-supporting wayfarers"—a new and apt phrase which might well be committed to memory by the Police) could surely give a good account of themselves when questioned by a Constable. It is still no offence—it is in fact less like an offence than ever it was—to sleep out if you are clean and orderly. What Anatole France called "the majestic equality of the law" still allows both the millionaire and the pauper to sleep under the sky.

Police Review April 9, 1943.

Bus Queue Offenders

The compulsory formation of queues at bus and tram stopping places now seems to be working smoothly enough, the queue habit being so deeply ingrained that any individualist guilty of anti-queue behaviour is quickly straightened up by the others. A few people still hate to find themselves at the wrong end of a queue, and when they join one they do so in a specially privileged position abreast of, instead of behind, the last couple. They get away with this unless (a) someone joins the queue behind them, in which event they must either hurriedly get into line or be crowded out, (b) a bus official or policeman comes along, or (c) the queue itself turns on them. If they manage to reach the bus step as one of a unit of three, they need watching.

The agile few who used to leap on to the buses before they got to their stopping places have found a new, and unlooked-for, outlet for their agility in leaping off again at the behest of the conductors. But until recently there was some doubt as to the attitude which might be taken by the Courts in cases where such a person boards a bus one stopping-place before the terminus of its journey in order to get priority over a large crowd waiting at the terminus. Refusing to leave the bus at the terminus is clearly an offence under Article 6 of the Regulation of Traffic (Formation of Queues) (No. 2) Order, 1942, which says that "if so requested by the driver or conductor every passenger shall forthwith leave the vehicle when it reaches the terminal point of the route." But there has been some discussion whether it it also punishable under Article 5 as "entering a vehicle when it is at or is approaching and about to stop at a stopping-place before any other person desiring to enter that vehicle who was waiting in a queue or line at that stopping-place." At Birmingham on 25th May two defendants were summoned for both these offences. The prosecution said that on 24th April there had been a football match at Aston. About 1,000 people were waiting in a queue at the tram terminus for cars to the city. The defendants, instead of joining the rear of the queue, had boarded a tramcar one stop before the terminus; and they refused to get off at the terminus when the conductress asked them to do so. The Stipendiary Magistrate, Lord Ilkeston, fined them both 20 shillings on each summons, with 4s. 6d. costs.

It seems likely that the conviction under Article 5 was based on the fact that the defendants' ride to the terminus was so short as to leave no doubt about their real purpose in boarding the tram. If they had boarded it a mile or more from the terminus this would not have been so obvious; and there is no provision requiring such passengers to prove an innocent intention.

As we remarked earlier there is no sign that the queue system is not working satisfactorily; and the occasions for Police action are accordingly rare. But in view of the quarrelsome and truculent behaviour which so often distinguishes people of the anti-queue sort, it may be worth while to repeat that, as the queueing Order was made under Defence Regulations, any offender may be arrested without warrant by virtue of Defence Regulation 88C, whether or not his name and address are known or ascertainable.

Police Review July 23, 1943.

Closed Doors at Public Houses

The "No Beer"signs in public house windows can usually be taken as meaning that the house is shut and will not be opened until there is beer. But apparently the sale of intoxicants is only one of the purposes for which a publican is granted a licence. The Cheltenham Licensing Justices, for instance, think that a licensee who regards his duty as nothing more than the retailing of alcoholic liquor takes too narrow a view of his place in society. "One of the most important functions of a public house is to provide opportunity for social intercourse and association in games and amusements," they say, "and even if supplies of exciseable beverages are sold out, there is no reason why these amenities should not continue."

So in Cheltenham the Police have been asked to report any licensee who ignores a request which has been issued by the Justices that they shall keep their houses open from 12.30 p.m. to 1.30 p.m. and from 8 p.m. to 10 p.m., and shall apportion supplies throughout the week. Some Cheltenham licensees have (according to the Justices) been taking advantage of the fact that demand greatly exceeds supply, disposing of their weekly allocations quickly, and then closing their houses, sometimes as much as three or four days a week; and this practice is said to show a complete disregard on the part of the licensees of the duty they owe to the public.

Presumably the Police will comply, but we must confess to some sympathy for the licensees, even for those who have been closing their beerless houses. A publican who provides incidental attractions for his customers seems to us to be in much the same position as a coffee-house keeper who does likewise. Few publicans would seek to be licensed, we imagine, if they were allowed to carry on business without; and but for the fact that they sell intoxicants, no opportunity would arise for official cognizance to be taken of the fact that they also provide dartboards and skittle alleys. True, they need a Justices' licence for public billiards and bagatelle, but so do people who are not publicans; and it is not suggested that "temperance" billiard halls should be ordered to keep open.The fact is that the "public service" conception of the licensee's business, which has its origin in the quite legitimate desire to allocate licences in the best public interest, can be so administered as to become almost a tyranny. Some confusion of thought may arise from an irrelevant regard to the Common Law liabilities of innkeepers, whose position is quite different; the public service provided by innkeepers is a matter of supplying food (which need not include intoxicants) and accommodation for travellers. Bed and breakfast is a far call from skittles, darts, pin-tables and the radio. We agree that, in itself, the absence of beer supplies is "no reason why the other amenities should not continue," but we think it is unconscionable to carry this simple truth to the point of threatening licensees who do not throw open their liquorless premises for the enjoyment of ancillary fun and games.

Police Review October 8, 1943.

Restoring the Signposts

When the first Removal of Direction Signs Order was made in 1940, "invasion" (that is, the word itself) seemed to mean exactly the opposite to what it does now; and when the Premier said "We shall fight on the beaches" he was not consciously describing what was to happen in Normandy four years later. The Order made its appearance in a somewhat feverish atmosphere, and in its first few weeks some fairly wild things were done by way of enforcing it. The London Estate Management Co., Ltd., painted out the word London, in order that a parachutist walking down Oxford Street might be unaware that he was not in Biggleswade, and many drivers of long-distance lorries were told that the names of their towns of origin must not be shown on the vehicles. A six-wheeler belonging to the Edinburgh Transport Company was stopped in the Midlands, for instance, and after its driver had held a short discussion with the Police it left bearing the legend "— Transport Company," to the utter confusion of the Nazis.

The new Removal of Direction Signs Order, 1940, makes it clear that what remains of "signpost control" does not apply to vehicles of any kind. The only sort of sign now restricted is "any sign which furnishes any indication of the name of, or the situation of, or the direction of, or the distance to, any place, and which can be seen and understood from a low-flying aircraft in the air." So presumably, in a prosecution, you would need the evidence of someone who had flown over the district and read the sign.

Police Review July 14, 1944.

Hoaxes and Public Mischief

The story was told recently of some forlorn wag in occupied Hungary whose pet dog had been killed by a German military lorry, and who, knowing the uselessness of any claim for compensation, managed to get an announcement inserted in a local newspaper stating that all dogs and cats belonging to *German* residents in the town were to be taken to the Police headquarters for registration. We hope he managed to conceal himself somewhere near the building during the next few days, so that he could overhear and relish the numberless conversations in low German between Police and animal-owners.

Hoaxes like this have been rare in this country lately, even before war removed the impulse to gaiety and found better work for hoaxers' hands to do.

We have a pretty bad record, however, both as hoaxers and hoaxed. The "public mischief" charge will tend to discourage this sort of thing now that the Common Law has been turned to such good account as it has in recent years, but the perpetrators of the most fantastic hoax on record went unpunished. It happened in 1809. Theodore Hook, one of the idle patricians of those elegant days, was strolling down Berners Street, London, with a kindred spirit, when the inconspicuous appearance of the house at No. 54 induced him to bet his companion that he would make it famous within a month. He wrote and posted about 1,000 letters purporting to come from No. 54 Berners Street, rented a room opposite, and invited his friend to sit with him on the appointed day to watch the fun. The first event on that eventful day was the arrival, at a very early hour, of twelve chimney sweeps from all parts of London to sweep the chimneys. Next came a large number of coal carts, each with a ton of coal for delivery. By this time the atmosphere was profane and vainly explanatory. Into it came a van-load of furniture, a dray laden with barrels of beer, a cart-load of potatoes, a hearse and three mourning coaches, eight men carrying a huge parlour organ, and shopkeepers and tradesmen of every imaginable kind with samples of their several wares—all converging on No. 54. When the whole street was choked with horses, carts, barrows and hysterical profanity, the Police arrived. At about the same time a number of doctors and dentists turned up to pay professional visits at No. 54, and a number of great men began to arrive. The Duke of York (who was then Commander-in-Chief of the Army) and the Lord Mayor of London both came in response to letters saying that a personal friend was lying ill at No. 54 and craved a last interview. They were followed by the Lord Chief Justice, the Archbishop of Canterbury, and the Governor of the Bank of England. The latter managed to efface themselves fairly soon, but the uproar in Berners Street went on for many hours among the smaller fry, who took an unreasonably poor view of each other despite their common adversity. As for the Lord Mayor, he went off to Marlborough Street Police Station to say the things that occurred to him.

Theodore Hook was neither prosecuted nor sued, because the evidence against him was thought to be insufficient. It's hard to believe that the required evidence would not be found if anyone acted similarly to-day; and even if he could not be indicted, he would probably be bound over before a Magistrate in "good behaviour" recognisances. Hook's prudently prolonged absence from London after this escapade is said by some people to have given rise to the expressions "Hook it,"and "Sling your hook."

It's a famous story.The last time it was told, we believe, was by Lieut.-Commander Gould in a broadcast on "Famous Hoaxes." But it belongs to history. The Common Law embers stirred up by *R. v. Manley* (1933) will have made most intending "jokers" of to-day think twice.

Police Review December 8, 1944.

Too Many Exhibits

The larceny of fifteen sheep presented a prosecuting Police officer with a familiar problem a few weeks ago: should he produce the sheep as "exhibits" at the Court hearing, or would one sheep be enough as a sample, or need any be produced at all? In the end he produced none at all and the justices made no request to see any.

This is what would so often happen if the justices were give a chance to show their common sense. Lately there have been a number of cases of child stealing, notably the removal of babies left in prams outside shops, and the babies have been produced in Court as exhibits. In one case the Magistrate was much amused at the idea of attaching a label ("Exhibit 4") to the infant and entering the particulars of it on the list of exhibits prescribed by the Criminal Appeal Rules; he asked whether all this wasn't rather absurd? And the label and the entry were forgotten.

It's very doubtful whether half the objects brought to Court as exhibits are of any assistance to the Court at all. The procedure is rich in anomalies. When a human being has been done to death with malice aforethought his body is never produced at the murder trial; but if someone kills a fowl with intent to steal it, the body of the fowl is often kept in cold storage so that it can be produced in Court, sometimes time after time. Generally the identity and the recent possession of goods which are the subject of a larceny charge are not in dispute, and yet it seems to be thought that the evidence of all the witnesses will be set aside as so much perjury unless the goods are to be seen on the solicitor's table, or in front of the witness box, or somewhere in the "well" of the Court. Why is it that, in a charge of housebreaking or arson or being found in a warehouse for an unlawful purpose, the Court, realising that the building cannot be placed before them, seldom require even a photograph of it? Like all customs for which there seems no adequate explanation to-day, this exhibit mania may have an ancient origin that everyone has forgotten. Is it perhaps a survival of the rule by which any chattel which had been instrumental in causing a death became a "deodand" and was forfeited to the Crown? Deodands began to die out when a Great Western Railway train caused the death of a passenger and the forfeiture of entire railway trains looked like becoming a regular event.

Police Review July 13, 1945.

Crowded buses

"There's a little 'bus that runs along the coast between St. Raphael and Cannes," said Lionel Hale on the radio the other day. "You don't hear, on this single-decker 'bus, the chilling words, 'I'll take one more.' No. The driver fills the seats first, and then every inch of standing room, and then fills the parcel racks with children, and after that you sit on the roof; and there are worse ways of travelling than dangling your legs over the roof as the 'bus goes along the Cannes road, round the hairpin bends, with the Mediterranean shining below you like a liquid sapphire."

One worse way of travelling is with your legs dangling among a tightly-wedged crowd in a London tube-train, with your elbows pinned to your sides and your neighbours' elbows resting on your throat. It is still unlawful for trains to carry more passengers than they can seat; but the railways have their own Police, and for them to start prosecuting their companies under the Railway Passenger Duty Act, 1842, would be like a dog eating its own tail.

In this country, the number of standing passengers actually carried in a 'bus does not finally depend either on the law or on the 'bus company's own staff regulations. It depends on the size of the 'bus and the relations between employer and employed. The larger the company is, the more remote and "touchy" the 'bus-crews are; the less urgent it becomes to make a profit quickly, the more impersonal and rigid becomes the process of earning what profit there is. It is in London and the large towns that you hear the words: "I'll take one more," "Only five standing please—six of you must get out," and "No standing at this time of day, ma'am," with all the crossness and argument and frequent unfairness that follow. In some of the quieter corners of England (Cornwall is one) people crowd into the 'buses like fishing-bait in a tin. The law is violated, in the person of the Public Service Vehicles (Equipment and Use) Regulations; but the law is far away on its bicycle, *en route* for a sheep-dipping, and the 'bus is one of a pair owned by a local man who knows and is known by everyone in a score of villages. In some parts of the North, 'bus conductors pack in as many standing people as they think reasonable, and then appeal for "fair play"—not for the sanctions of law. (Even so, two or three extra men have to be squeezed in at the next stop because they display little printed passes indicating that they are servants of the company.) It is in London, particularly, that the letter of the law is insisted on, where by paradox its relaxation would cause the most benefit. But it is not the Police (and we hope it is not likely to be) who insist on it. It is the conductors. The law is on their side and many of them are deeply conscientious.

Police Review October 8, 1946.

Tincture of Bookishness

A course of study at the proposed new Police College, says the report of the Expert Committee on Higher Training for the Police, must "avoid any tincture of bookishness." Admirable phrase—but how oddly used. A tincture, by dictionary definition, is either a "slight, super-added taste or quality" or "the finer and more volatile parts of a substance, separated by a solvent." It seems likely that the Committee meant nothing so nice as the latter, but had in mind the "super-added taste" —and found it unpalatable.

The Policeman who knows his job to-day, and even more the one who will know it tomorrow, carries more than tincture. With or without the College, he is a book-worm tinctured with Policemanly experience—when a particular experience falls into place in one of the pigeon-holes of his book-ridden brain, he beams his recognition that fact is shaking hands with theory. There is no escape: the most vital parts of a good Policeman's equipment are books and boots. Boots were supreme for many years; a man could get along with "fifty definitions," the pace of life made it possible to re-write a summons form six times, and the inquiring uneasiness of the intelligent Constable could be waved aside as "text-book." By the way, that last expression is almost a synonym for "tincture of bookishness."

Police Review April 4, 1947.

Double Snooks

The Ipswich Magistrates decided lately, in a case under Section 5 of the Public Order Act, 1936, that you are guilty of "insulting behaviour whereby a breach of the peace is likely to be occasioned" if you thumb your nose at a Policeman. They fined a man £2 for it, thus openly disavowing the doubt (which has assailed some of our readers in the past) whether a Policeman is legally capable of breaking the peace when insulted. The report does not say whether the man who cocked this intrepid snook went so far as to make it a double snook, but the fine of £2 suggests that he did. A pound a snook seems equitable, and conforms to the long-familiar Police Act maximum of forty shillings for insulting behaviour. The Public Order Act, it seems, has increased the hazards of life for the cocker of double snooks; he could get a fine of £25 and six weeks' imprisonment per snook. Partridge's *Dictionary of Slang* should be read in conjunction with Section 5 of the Act: "A gesture of derision," it says, "the thumb on the nose-tip and the fingers spread fanwise. Also called Queen Anne's Fan and Taking a Sight. A Double Snook is made by joining the tip of the little finger (already in position) to the thumb of the other hand, the fingers being similarly extended. Emphasis is given by moving the fingers of both hands as if playing a piano." The custom, it says, arose in the late seventeenth century; but how, no man knows. It is used for the easement of passion in every country in Europe. Already in England, perhaps, it was a tort. To Ipswich has fallen the stern duty of erecting it into a crime.

Police Review May 2, 1947.

Barking Dogs in the Night

A newspaper report says that, as a result of a complaint put up by Chesham Council, Buckinghamshire County Council have made a by-law "prohibiting the barking of dogs at night."

A news item like this can hardly fail to charm; and in a country where dogs have sometimes been cared for rather better than men and women, it will be greeted with indignation by those who champion the liberties of dogs and with gratification by those who will see in it a recognition of our dogs' ability to read public statutory notices. But it is hardly fair, in its brevity, to Buckinghamshire County Council, whose by-law almost certainly addresses itself to the owners of the dogs. In most localities dog-owners must not allow their pets to be a nuisance at any time; there is usually a by-law or a local Act against it. Buckinghamshire has taken particular measures about barking at a particular time. We know a dog, not in Buckinghamshire, whose night life could do with one of these by-laws. Our own night life would be the easier for it.

Police Review June 13, 1947.

Comic Police Uniforms

"Charity," wrote Paul to the Corinthians, "vaunteth not itself, is not puffed-up." And, he added significantly, it doth not behave itself unseemly.

In Dartford, Kent, its seemliness takes the form of a comic Policeman, wearing a brass door-knob on the top of his helmet and scores of buttons and stripes on his tunic, who goes round collecting for local charities. It is not clear from the report whether he collects in the street, or goes from house to house; but it seems more likely that he does the latter, with a Police certificate under Section 1 (4) of the House to House Collections Act, 1939. The Dartford Police recently decided, however, that he was at once vaunting, puffed-up and unseemly. They told him that an unfavourable view was taken of "the use of any uniform which burlesques Police uniform," and implied that if charity wanted any more permits it would have to get into plain clothes. The comic man went to his M.P. about this, and the M.P. told the Home Secretary, who, after consulting the Chief Constable of Kent, has decided that the Police ought not to object. "I shared your doubts," he wrote to the M.P., "whether any serious objection need be taken." So the local Police told the comic man that the objection was withdrawn, and within a few hours he was out again, with brass knob on, collecting for a local charity as if nothing had happened.

This is not the kind of charity, however, that has always been understood to begin at home. Two years ago, in another Police district, a man who wanted to scare some youths away from his chicken-house put on an ancient Police uniform that had been a family heirloom for two or three generations, and strode majestically down his garden towards them. He was prosecuted "for that he, not being at the time a Constable appointed under the Town Police Clauses Act or the Special Act, did put on the dress of a person appointed as such Constable," contrary to Section 12 of the Town Police Clauses Act, 1847. The Justices' Clerk pointed out that the summons should have gone on to say that he did it "for the purpose of thereby obtaining admission into a certain house (or of doing an act which he would not be entitled to do of his own authority, or for a certain unlawful purpose, namely . . .)." The Clerk did not add, as he might well have done, that this charge can only apply where the offender wears the uniform of a particular, named Constable. However, the Police substituted a charge under Section 10 of the Police Act, 1919, saying that the defendant, "not being a member of a Police Force, did wear without the permission of the Police authority the uniform of the Police Force." The Magistrates found him guilty of this, dismissed the charge under the Probation of Offenders Act, and made him hand the uniform to the Police (who, apparently, had not thought of charging him with "unlawful possession of accoutrements").

The Armed Forces won't have this sort of thing at all (Uniforms Act, 1894, Section 3), and the Merchant Service is the most touchy of the lot (British Mercantile Marine Uniform Act, 1919, Section 1 (2)). But surely there is a happy significance in this? They are the Armed Forces. Can you imagine a Polizei, a Gestapo, a Gendarmerie allowing itself to be publicly lampooned by people with door knobs on their hats? They are the State, national majesty itself in tight, bright clothing. The British bobby is a citizen, who may have to forswear his Sunday leaves, but not his sense of humour. Laughter is not the product of hate or fear, though when affectionate familiarity outruns discretion it may perforce be confined suddenly to the other side of the face. No Statute hampers the Dartford comedian. His is the uniform, not of any self-regarding Police Force, but of the bass-baritone beatsmen in the *Pirates of Penzance*, and there is no chance whatsoever of living down that universally-loved portrait. They keep on reviving it.

Police Review October 7, 1947.

Fun Factory

Whenever a new form of mass behaviour takes root among us, it seems that we must first attack it as men have always attacked the unfamiliar, and then, having failed to kill it, rationalise or try to ignore it. Sensitive anthropologists feel that they have done something positive and tidy about "holiday camps" by calling them a social phenomenon (and thus turning Dr. Fowler in his grave); much as the medical faculty feels itself halfway to vanquishing a new disease by giving it a name, a pigeon-hole and a column in the statistics. But if the holiday camps (or holiday villages as Mr. Butlin now calls his) are a social phenomenon, they are an old one in a concentrated form and a new guise; a guise of chromium, coloured plaster-work, loud-speakers and ordered gregariousness, instead of the aspidistras, fern-pots, marble-topped wash-standards, and careworn exile which they are replacing. The holiday camp is not, that is to say, any more "phenomenal" than Blackpool, Margate, Southend and some of their earnest imitators have been for fifty years. It enables its patrons to enjoy themselves more strenuously with less anxiety and bickering, and to do it in a kind of reserve where they can be furtively peeped at by the censorious passer-by. This is the main difference.

I have lately spent six breathless days at Butlin's Holiday Village, Pwllheli, among 5,400 other people in an enclosure covering about half a square mile. I never saw so much pop-eyed enjoyment going on anywhere in my life, nor, indeed, do I wish to see it again; it will always be enough for me to know that it goes on. Twelve hundred paid members of "Butlin's staff" (hand-picked for their charm and efficiency) look after this huge assembly, cooking and serving its meals, making its well-sprung beds, baking its bread and cakes, handing out its drinks; singing, acting, and playing to it; drilling it; teaching it to swim, play tennis, dance and ride; driving it around Snowdonia in motor-coaches, taking it up in aeroplances, minding its babies, and pulling its gigantic leg with roars of carefully scripted *bonhomie* from a hundred loud-speakers. Everything the holiday-making Briton saves up for is provided for an inclusive guinea-a-day—except rest and reading.

It is not the organisers' fault that you cannot get a night's rest. Indeed, one of the points they stress in their pamphlets (over the weighty signature of the B.B.C. Radio Doctor) is that a holiday does no good without adequate sleep. But if for sixteen hours you deliberately excite 5,000 people, predominantly young, by means of a breathless programme of entertainment in a place with all the skin-deep beauties of a million-dollar film set, they will not settle down at night when you think they should. You can wake them at 7.45 a.m. with an arch little ditty sung in "close harmony" over the loudspeakers, but you will find no scope for a lullaby. So until the small hours the flowering lanes between the chalets are filled at intervals by what I have always perplexedly understood to be happy song. Those who then roll over in bed and curse have no business to be at a holiday camp. Mr. Butlin will not have his clients' one annual playtime hedged around with restrictions; they can get into the camp (on the rare occasions when they go out of it) at any hour of the night, and there is no curfew. Anyway, practically all of them are there for one week only—Bolton week, Oldham week, Rochdale week, and so on; let them eat, drink and be tremendously merry. It's champion.

There is no library, and nobody seems to want one. There is a vast reading-room (the Campers' Quiet Lounge) with nothing to read in it except the words "Butlin's Holiday Camp, Pwllheli," on the mill-board covers that once, no doubt, contained periodicals—and may do so again. A smaller "quiet room," half a mile away, contains nothing to read except a printed card propped up on the immense table, announcing that the table once graced the German Embassy in London, and that over it Mr. Churchill warned Ribbentrop how dangerous it was to provoke the British people to war. (This, with some mammoth "period" furniture round the walls, is a monumental irrelevancy that puzzles even the campers; they look at it in absolute silence and go out quickly on tip-toe.) Among numerous shops there is the ubiquitous W. H. Smith and Son, where a highly efficient manager grapples amiably throughout a long day with a dense crowd buying (had you guessed?) picture-postcards of the camp. Occasionally you see someone emerging from here with a new book; never do you see him reading it. But I wish to record without comment that at noon on Friday all copies of *The Spectator* and *The New Statesman* had been sold. Outside the shop every morning there is a queue of five or six hundred people waiting for newspapers.

Throughout the day no camp official makes the slightest effort to cajole or beguile you—as an individual—to take part in the sports, the rambles, the holiday lovelies' competition, the dancing, the "keep fit" parades, the knobbly knees contest, or the Grand Rally (this last being a fatuous morning procession round the camp, headed by a group of comic-opera musicians on a trolley which is ecstatically manhandled along by campers). As an individual you can do precisely what you like, and go away from the camp into the mountains all day. (Hardly anyone does.) The persuasion is done by Radio Butlin and the "house captains," who loudly exhort the 1,200 campers in each of the four dining-halls, as they only less loudly clatter over their take-it-or-leave-it meals, to support their house in the various events by which one house may draw ahead of its booing rivals.

A social phenomenon? If anyone knows what that means it is perhaps the mothers with young babies, who get extra milk, orange-juice and cod-liver oil, attention and advice from trained nurses, and a daily service that washes napkins in an electrical washing machine, irons them, and sorts them into labelled heaps for collection by the mothers. Or those with older children, who can leave them in play-rooms all day with a trained nurse and such toys as they have previously seen only in the film shots of homes in Beverley Hills, Cal.

Much solemn nonsense is being propagated about the holiday camps by sad second-hand observers who see in them the *Kraft durch Freude* philosophy and the seeds of totalitarianism. This thing could have terrible consequences, they say; let these humble people get back to the aspidistras and the bamboo china-cabinets; let the mothers stay with their children and stop any bored howling with sticks of rock, as they used to do. Other aspects of brainless group-behaviour escape their strictures (unless they happen to live near a League football-ground). Many of these solid citizens joined with feather-witted vocal dexterity in the "scat-singing" led by the inimitable Danny Kaye at the London Palladium and elsewhere. There appeared to be nothing sinister in this; Mr. Kaye is not yet regarded as a menace to democracy.

There is always something occult about a crowd, because it seems to add up to something more than the total of its constituent members, the overplus being the embodiment of evil or the nucleus of good according to the preconceptions of the calculator. It must, of course, sadden any thoughtful person to see that, as administrative horizons widen, the individual matters less and less and the crowd becomes the unit. But where, outside the thin ranks of anarchy, is the Canute who will try to stop the process now, and force or entice the individual holiday-maker to turn his back on the ever-increasing possibilities of combination for enjoyment?

Holiday camps are a tremendous success, and they have come to stay. Then how could they be improved? How, without masquerading as summer schools, could they be made to serve (even though by stealth) the vital purposes of adult education? Somewhere in Mr. Butlin's advertising literature is the statement that he desires to "educate the people." It was presumably as an earnest of this intention that he brought to Pwllheli the London Symphony Orchestra and the Metropolitan Ballet. But they were only there for the opening week, and nothing like it has happened since. There is now a Butlin light Orchestra, which supplies stuff like "Blue Skies" and an orchestral arrangement of "I Hear You Calling Me" to audiences of 1,000 who listen attentively in a darkened hall and would certainly take Grieg, Tschaikowsky, Mozart, Verdi, Weber and early Beethoven. Music from a cinema organ pours in syrupy billows from the camp loudspeakers at intervals. And the dance-bands scream and thump with terrible efficiency in the neo-marzipan ball-rooms all the afternoon and evening. The décor of the ball-rooms, restaurants and bars is not, I should say, in the least educative, and it has been carried out with a stupefying lavishness that roars its own failure. Here, in short, is an opportunity to construct really beautiful places in which glimpses of the fuller cultural life may steal upon an unaccustomed community unawares. The people have been "conditioned" for forty years to the Hollywood standard of gingerbread and tinfoil architecture, and this is the cinema-goers' Nirvana. What about some English holiday camps with a discreet emphasis on the things that last and matter?

The Spectator August 27, 1948.

The Wishing Well and the Villagers

"On my beat," says a correspondent, "there is a wishing well which is situated on property around which there is a wall with a padlocked gate. This property is rented by the owner to a man who charges a fee of 6d. to people visiting the well. In addition to water being drunk from the well, money is also thrown by visitors into the well. This money is considerable, and the tenant, when opportunity permits, recovers a large quantity by means of a scoop. Casual visitors probably don't realise that the well is only about three feet deep, and when they throw their money in they don't intend it to be recovered. Local people are also known to be engaged in taking money from the well in the absence of the tenant (the place being a lock-up tea shop). Is there any offence of larceny?"

This comes fairly close to fortune-telling as a means of exploiting the credulous, and might even sustain such a charge—"using a subtle device to deceive and impose on His Majesty's subjects." One difficulty is suggested by the word "subtle": any "device" more unsubtle and generally half-witted would be difficult to imagine. Another is that few people, as potential witnesses, would admit that they had been "deceived or imposed upon"; they would more probably say that they knew the whole thing was nonsense anyway, and threw their money down the well for fun.

We think it possible that the lessee of the well, by lending even his dubious authority to the idea that you may qualify for good luck by throwing money in it, is "by conduct" causing money to be paid or delivered by false pretences—even if he is not thus "obtaining" it himself. But he is certainly, as occupier of the premises, acquiring a technical "property" in the coins that are put down his well; and the members of the guerrilla movement who sneak in while he's away to help themselves to the coins are all guilty, therefore, of larceny. The original owners may have "abandoned" the money, but the lessee hasn't—he regularly gets out there himself, with a scoop, to assert his shifty proprietorship. We are able to assure readers that this story is true. Only Balzac could have made it up.

Police Review September 3, 1948.

St. Jim's and Greyfriars

It was Samuel Johnson's belief that what we read with inclination makes the strongest impression. "If we read without inclination," he said, "half the mind is employed in fixing the attention, so there is but one half to be employed on what we read." This, I think, explains (without excusing) the fact that *The Pilgrim's Progress*, which so many better people have enjoyed, has never been more to me than a bulky volume with heavily-tooled covers and shiny paper, which wouldn't stay open on the table; whereas after thirty years I can still name every character at Greyfriars and St. Jim's.

A reasonably well-read and discriminating parent, no doubt, can open magic casements for his offspring, stealthily besetting their path with the "right" books, urging nothing, censoring nothing. It's undoubtedly the quickest way to literary maturity and the self-sought enjoyment of poetry, the crowning reward of readership. My own father, who sternly discountenanced the *Magnet*, the *Gem*, the *Union Jack, Pluck* and the *Nelson Lee Library*, was a vigorous advocate (at, I suspect, one or even two removes) of Sir John Lubbock's "Hundred Best Books." I recently found I had read nine of these, including *Zadig, Pickwick* and the one which Sir John compendiously called *Shakespeare*. But I remember that in his less guarded moments my father often spoke with affection of *The Adventures of Jack Harkaway*, genuinely regretting that those wonderful stories, serialised throughout his own boyhood, were not available for my brothers and me to read. I never heard anyone else speak of them.

Now there comes, as the product of dogged industry that it is humbling to contemplate, this remarkable book of Mr. Turner's*—"The Story of Sweency Todd, Deadwood Dick, Sexton Blake, Billy Bunter, Dick Barton, *et al.*" And in it Jack Harkaway has an entire chapter to himself. His creator was Bracebridge Hemyng, barrister of the Middle Temple, "who found that turning out fiction was vastly more profitable than sitting around waiting for briefs." Jack's escapades ran in *Boys of England* from 1871 until the end of the century; and, to judge from the excerpts Mr. Turner treats us to, they maintained a steady rhythm of torture, decapitation, all-in wrestling, graphic cannibalism and the competing stenches of blood and burning flesh. Kraft-Ebbing and the Comte de Sade had not then made their niches in our native vernacular; but the fate of Nuratella, the native girl who had betrayed Jack into captivity, would be classified as sadism in any newspaper report today. Even at school Jack was on terms with the headmaster's wife which pre-dated *Young Woodley* by sixty years. So this was the healthy literature of those who were young in the 'eighties and 'nineties! This was what Mr.George Sampson, of the *Concise Cambridge History of Literature*, devoured in his youth along with *Sweeney Todd* and *Spring-Heeled Jack*, to record in later years that he "found no harm in any of them."

Maybe there was no more "harm" in them than in the atrocities of Hans Anderson. On the question of harm, G. K. Chesterton once voiced a noble impatience with the thesis that a boy who couldn't read stole an apple because he liked the taste, while a boy who could read stole one because his mind was aflame with Dick Turpin. But how

***Boys Will Be Boys*. By E. S. Turner. (Michael Joseph. 10s. 6d.)

gentle, by comparison, were the *Magnet* and *Gem*, the furtive reading of every boy I knew, and of nearly every girl; furtive because parents condemned them unheard as trash and nonsense, and because their small bulk fitted them for bed-time contraband.

They were morally impeccable, these stories of Harry Wharton and Co. of the Remove, of Tom Merry and Co. of the Shell. For hundreds of thousands of lower middle-class products of the Education Act they portrayed (we thought) the romance of a public-school life that had been going on for centuries, and brought it within the ambit of our dawning literacy. Such an opinion can never be put to any test, but I would be ready to swear that, because they were about boys of our own age whose lives fulfilled our dreams of well-to-do elegance and *savoir-faire*, the *Magnet* and *Gem* had more influence, lasting influence, on people of my generation than all the other boys' weeklies together. The very appearance of these young gentlemen, as indicated in pendrawings which I now see to be pretty poor work, set standards for us that intensified the difficulties of our parents in the boys' outfitters's shops. No trousers could ever be too tight and straight, no turn-ups deep enough or angular enough, no Eton collar was ever just right. Nor could any barber produce that wayward shock of front hair, so carefully drawn, so carelessly English.

If we were less apt in adopting the moral code, this is because it was so consistently high and its observance so difficult at busy, rough-and-tumble day-schools; though Mr. Charles Hamilton (bless him!), who wrote these stories weekly for thirty years as Frank Richards and Martin Clifford (1,500,000 words a year), knew about our needs and difficulties; and, as our unofficial mentor, he was never "pi" or flat-footed. I think it is a matter of common consent that the character of Billy Bunter, the "owl" of the Remove at Greyfriars, was his most vital creation. I thought at one time that he owed something to the fat boy in *Pickwick*, but I see now that this was only because he was fat and rather unpleasant. Mr. Turner paints him thus:

> "The owner of the tightest trousers in Greyfriars (for some reason they were striped horizontally and vertically, instead of just vertically) was the perfect butt. He had few praiseworthy qualities, other than the power to incite mirth. He would borrow money with no intention of paying it back, he would pirate another man's tuck without a qualm. . . . He was never really unpopular—a fat boy never can be. His machinations were so barefaced and his *bomhomie* so suspect that it was a fellow's own fault if he was taken in by them."

This omits, of course, the astounding and incongruous fact that he was a clever ventriloquist, but perhaps Mr. Hamilton never really made adequate use of this priceless adjunct to the ideal school story.

Of all the Greyfriars characters, Bunter was perhaps the one most eligible for survival; and it is good to know that he still appears from time to time in unrelated (and much more expensive) publications—and that his adventures are available in Braille.

How old is popular literacy? Many of the "bloods" and "dreadfuls" examined by Mr. Turner were well established before the Education Act of 1870, and must, therefore, have been designed for the adult near-gentry. This is a sobering thought; for these publications, on the whole, were a pestilential lot, ill written and generally prurient. Some of the more modern are written in the language of newspaper "reportage" (still following the Northcliffe prescription of a two-line maximum for paragraphs), which is at least grammatical and is terse enough not to waste the time of the modern boy beset by so many counter-attractions. Before and during World War I they were better written, on the whole, than the works of, say, George Manville Fenn; to open one of his hundred-odd books today is to be shocked at the extreme poverty of the writing. Some of the most competent, I thought (and still think), were the *Jack, Sam and Pete* stories of S. Clarke Hook, which get a very cursory mention in Mr. Turner's book. He notes that Pete was a ventriloquist (which he failed to notice about Billy Bunter), but makes no mention of the glorious fact that this gigantic negro, perpetually showing a complete set of gold teeth as he roared with laughter ("Yah, yah, yah!") was a multi-millionaire. It was the essence of these stories that if Pete wanted to go somewhere at a time when there was no train to take him, he bought the railway and had one put on. He was magnificent, lovable, invincible in the ring—and admitted by many fathers as unexceptionable in order that they might read his preposterous adventures themselves.

Those who attribute juvenile crime to the effect of the "weeklies" may be partially right; it is my belief that behaviour of many kinds, good and bad, and at all ages, is a delayed consequence of early reading, so that the worst books are the ones that most merit the sociologists' attention. But there can be nothing to be said for the complaint that the current *increase* of juvenile crime is due to the weeklies. They are morality tracts by comparison with their forbears, and even the much-maligned Dick Barton is a pillar of respectability beside any comparable figure in the penny dreadfuls of the past.

Mr. Turner's researches must have been prodigious. From the innumerable references and comparisons in his book, a work of scholarship, humour, granite-like common sense and a great deal of tenderness, one concludes that he must now have read more bloods than any man living. I believe he enjoyed doing it at first, but I should doubt if he will ever look at another. I do not understand why he got Captain C. B. Fry to write an introduction. Captain Fry knows absolutely nothing about bloods. He cheerfully says so. During his six years as a boy at Repton and two more as a master at Charterhouse he "never saw or heard of such publications." There must, therefore, be something bad about them; but he does not know what it is. All things considered, it is a relief to know that Repton and Charterhouse did not see *Magnets* and *Gems*. They were not written for Repton and Charterhouse; they were written for the back-street boys, who bought them with the pennies they got by taking bundles of newspapers to the butcher's.

The Spectator October 22, 1948.

Treasure Trove

Some years ago a woman who had bought a second-hand pram found hidden in the lining of it a large amount of money in banknotes. She reported her find to the Police, and the original owner of the pram got to hear of it. A local "sea-lawyer" told both the women that they would be wasting their time if they quarrelled about it, because the money would be treated as "treasure trove" and forfeited to the Crown: and this quite erroneous information had at least the good effect of keeping them quiet while the matter was under investigation. In the event, no one ever discovered how the money got into the pram (which had had several owners, the earlier ones being untraceable), and the two women surprised all local observers by sharing the money.

This was not a case of "treasure trove," because that phrase applies only to *gold and silver*, in money, bullion, or plate. Not even precious stones can be treasure trove, as the Common Law stands at present—though the Judges might develop the Common Law a little if there were any sensational finds of such treasure anciently buried. In Saxon and Norman times there was always a good chance of finding buried treasure, and being hanged for saying nothing about it. After the Romans had been driven out by the invaders from the North, much of their money and plate lay concealed underground where they had hastily buried it during their many retreats. They doubtless intended to come back with fresh legions, reconquer the country, and dig up their wealth again; but they never got back. The Danes, Norsemen, and Saxons, having a good idea that these hidden hoards were in existence, imposed the death penalty on anyone finding one and concealing his good fortune; and the present-day misdemeanour of concealing the finding of treasure trove is a direct descendant of the crime thus created.

The President of the Royal Numismatic Society (numismatic = pertaining to coins or medals) has now raised a point that may lead to some reconsideration of the law about treasure trove. On December 18th a coroner held an inquest at Hunstanton on the finding of a hoard of metal articles at Snettisham. The find included some tin coins as well as gold, and the whole collection came from three different sites.

The Curator of the Castle Museum, Norwich, asked the Coroner to treat the three groups as one single hoard, on the ground that their archaeological value depended on their being kept together. As the law stands, the Coroner was unable to do this, and he directed the jury accordingly. The tin coins, it appears, are the most valuable from the archaeological point of view; and, says the President of the R.N.S., the division of the hoard into base and precious metals will mutilate its historical value by allowing the base metals to be dispersed as comparatively worthless. It must be obvious that, since the Coroner's interest in treasure trove is now purely historical and no longer inspired by a hunger for Roman gold, the law relating to treasure trove ought to be restated in accordance with modern requirements. The way to do this is to introduce a short Bill into Parliament; and such a Bill would serve a valuable purpose if it also cleared up finally the tangled mess into which the law about lost property generally has fallen.

Police Review January 7, 1949.

Noise

We all live in a mounting volume of din. It is measured in "phons" at the National Physical Laboratory, where the scientists decide how much of it we ought to be able to stand. Every now and then a new law appears, declaring this noise or that to be unlawful in stated circumstances, and is applauded. But it is seldom enforced; it seems to get drowned in the very noise it was designed to still.

When Sir Oswald Mosley's street-corner meetings in East London were providing the magistrates with "insulting behaviour" cases and the home-going business public with special evening reading, there was a widespread demand that the use of loud-speakers in the street should be prohibited. Some supporters of this proposal thought the ban should apply only to political meetings, because open-air religious meetings were resorting more and more to the use of loud-speaker vans and should not be penalised for the sins of the Fascists. Some M.P.s thought, on the other hand, that political meetings should be precisely the ones to be exempted, since the advent of the loud-speaker had made open-air oratory properly audible (and had vanquished the heckler) for the first time; it should not, they said, be banned merely because a negligible extra-Parliamentary party had misused it as a means of attacking the Jews. One also heard the view that the ban would amount to a rejection of the means of progress, the behaviour of the Luddites brought up to date.

No one seemed to remember that ten years before, the County Councils of London, Middlesex, Hertford and Surrey (to name only a few) had armed themselves with the following by-law:

> "No person shall sound or play upon any musical or noisy instrument or sing in any street or public place within 100 yards of any shop, dwelling house, or office to the annoyance or disturbance of any inmate or occupier thereof, after being requested to desist by any constable, or by any inmate or occupier so annoyed or disturbed."

It even went on to meet one of the objections: "This by-law shall not apply to properly-conducted religious services, except where the request to desist is made on the ground of the serious illness of any inmate of the house." Strictly regarded, the exception might involve some liturgical bias in the interpretation of "properly-conducted," but the intention may have been to outlaw the meeting that opens with a decorous hymn and proceeds to a provocative political harangue.

Now what is a bellowing loud-speaker if it is not someone "sounding upon a noisy instrument"? Most lawyers, briefed to defend the first microphone orator to be charged under this by-law, would no doubt try to establish that "noisy" was *ejusdem generis* with "musical," and must therefore mean barrel-organs, cornets, banjoes and other para-musical engines—not, at any rate, cavernous reproductions of the human voice talking. But the presence of the word "sound" as a verb should defeat them, and the pronouncement of a conviction and fine would reaffirm the King's peace. Won't somebody try it , please? You need only be the annoyed or disturbed occupant or "inmate" of a shop, dwelling-house or office within 100 yards of the infernal thing and ask the man using it to stop. As there is no likelihood whatsoever that he will take any notice, you will need a policeman handy to get his name and address by seeing his identity card. Thereafter, if the police seem reluctant to take action, you can yourself get a summons issued by a magistrate. You will have started a great libertarian movement, and laurels will be tenderly deposited round your statue on anniversaries of the House of Lords' final judgement in the case.

Thus should we rid our street-corners of the political stentor. We could now turn our attention to the zealots who drive about in loud-speaker vans and fill the reverberating streets with hoarse roars of invitation to public meetings. Even the borough councils do this in London, though by what process their town clerks dispose of the L.C.C. by-law I do not know. They began it during the war when they organised "savings weeks," but then they broke the by-law beyond all doubt by sandwiching their sermons on thrift between bursts of martial music. The thing has gone on at intervals ever since, one borough regularly resorting to it as a means of announcing "holidays-at-home" attractions in the neighbourhood to people who are trying desperately to work. The town-crier's bell is being supplanted by the municipal crooner.

A few years ago a motorist staged a practical adaptation of one of

Sir Alan Herbert's *Misleading Cases in the Common Law*. He drove about the centre of London with a powerful loud-speaker attached to the radiator of his car, a small microphone beside his driving mirror, and an amplifier below the dash-board, howling to other drivers such directions as he thought necessary to ensure their safety and his own unobstructed passage. He told the police that he first thought of it when he was forced to follow a horse-driven dray for about two miles at midnight—when by virtue of another benevolent regulation the use of his motor-horn was unlawful. "I know of no law to prevent one man speaking to another after 11 p.m.," he said. "You can't say I'm doing more than giving audible warning of approach, and that's always been an obligation, not a crime." The police scratched their heads; and, as commonly happens when the police have scratched their heads, they prosecuted him for "insulting behaviour." The by-law about noisy instruments escaped notice again—a great pity, for this was the kind of man who, once he had studied it, would have prosecuted the next policeman he found marshalling pedestrian traffic by loudspeaker.

There is already a provision in many local Police Acts that penalises the use of any "noisy instrument" for the purpose of "calling persons together, or announcing any show or entertainment, or hawking, selling, distributing, or collecting any article whatsoever, or obtaining money or alms." This enactment survives from the eighteen-thirties, when the competitive sale of muffins, "sweet lavender" and winkles called for adventitious mechanical aids. It may perhaps not apply to the orator whose gathering of admirers amounts to a "meeting" before he actually begins to bawl, and there is certainly an official reluctance to use it. Meanwhile, the volume of noise mounts steadily—and a general election approaches.

Recently I forced my way, head down, into an electrical shop to buy some lamp-globes. The entrance was guarded by a massive radio cabinet emitting rather more noise than the Brass Band Festival at the Albert Hall; and to make himself audible to me the shop assistant used his practised hands as a trumpet. When we had shrieked unintelligibly into each other's ears for a time, he went and toned down the noise a little. The manager saw him do it, and rather crossly turned it up again. I came away defeated. Now in some localities (but not, I found, in this one) borough councils have made a by-law saying that

> "no person shall in or in connection with any shop, business premises, or other place which adjoins any street operate any wireless loud-speaker, gramophone, or other musical instrument worked by mechanical means, in such a manner as to cause annoyance to occupants of any premises, or to passengers."

If there are other municipalities which have not thought fit to adopt such a by-law, I respectfully commend it to their notice; they can invoke section 16 of the Local Government Act, 1888, as their authority. To put it no higher, they would be doing something to ensure that their own loud-speakers got a fair hearing in the streets.

There are laws to control factory whistles, noisy animals, street shouting, whistling for cabs, steam organs at fairs, squeaky brakes on carts, rattling loads on lorries, defective exhaust-silencers and motor-horns at night. (It is an odd fact, by the way, that the one about motor-horns was re-enacted in 1941, when the blitz was thundering nightly at its worst.) These, it seems to me, deal with the *minutiae* of metropolitan din, and I don't mind so much if they are enforced no more frequently than the law against shaking doormats. But I do not understand why it should be so widely assumed that nothing can be done about the loud-speaker until M.P.s can be induced to jeopardise their own electoral prospects. The local authorities can cope with this.

Spectator January 14, 1949.

The Blue Lamp

The arrest of a missing girl for not producing an identity card is one of the crucial moments in Ealing Studios' new film "The Blue Lamp," first shown in London last week. The fact that the arrest was unlawful affords an excuse for this column's first excursion into film criticism; and the excuse is as welcome as the film, because this is the first time the Police of this country have been adequately presented on the screen. It is a murder story; the victim is Jack Warner as an entirely convincing Metropolitan Policeman who was just finishing his "twenty-five" when he was persuaded to stay on—and get shot; and the murderer is ideally arrested, after a car-chase that puts most of its predecessors (American or British) in the shade, by Jimmy Hanley as the young probationer-Constable who was Mr. Warner's protégé.

It may be captious to complain that you can't lawfully arrest an over-seventeen girl who is missing from home merely because she fails to produce an identity card. One knows that it is in fact done every day, and that it will go on being done until someone invites the views of the High Court on the matter—and even thereafter. Concede also that Jimmy Hanley, who arrests her, lets her walk in front of him to Paddington Green Police Station, so that it doesn't look like an arrest: and that when she says she doesn't want to go home again she is released. But this film bears the impress of Scotland Yard, by whose officers it was "vetted" so thoroughly that it is otherwise authentic in *almost* every tiny detail; and the fact sharpens criticism.

To the Police, the "almost" will be noticeable. Police uniforms have never before been so naturally worn by professional actors; helmets are well forward, armlets right, chinstraps "on the point." The only man with his trousers braced an inch and half from his boots is (unfortunately) a Chief Inspector. But the Sergeant who takes the "drunk and disorderly" charge, although the charge he actually reads out is immaculately right, goes "stagey" at the end: when the prisoner drunkenly replies "stewed rhubarb," the Sergeant lapses into the old, familiar stupidity by saying gloomily and loudly (but to no one in particular), "When charged, prisoner made no reply." And Jack Warner should have been told not to patrol the beat with his fingers dangling limply, like those of the American G.I.s we used to see marching in their undulating platoons (though he makes a magnificent old sweat and is perfectly cast). Life behind the scenes in this Police Station is rather jollier than some Policemen will have found it to be, and the benevolence of the Sergeants is reflected in that free use of "Sarge" and "Skip" by Constables that keeps so many departed disciplinarians revolving in their graves.

The main emphasis in this striking film is upon the defencelessness of the unarmed British Policeman in contract with the gunman. Jack Warner advances slowly and stolidly upon a cornered, screaming spiv who is obviously of the neurotic kind that shoots; and the murder is horrifying in the extreme. When the murderer is again cornered, at a dog-racing stadium after a terrifying car-chase plotted and controlled by the faithful "regulars" at Information Room, ten Police officers (still, presumably—and in this instance unbelievably—unarmed) advance upon him with equal stolidity and even more slowly. They (or some of them) are saved from death only because the crowd at the dog-track suddenly breaks after the last race and overwhelms the gunman in its homeward rush.

This emphasis may or may not serve as a stimulus to recruiting, and the film as a whole may or may not glamorise the gunman. One reflection it prompts is that while there may be some in the cinema audiences who will be tempted to join the Police for endless excitement under genial quasi-discipline, others may well be incited to emulation by the sneering, confident lawlessness of the power-drunk little gunman. One effect it is bound to have on most people: once you have seen it you look at all Policemen with a new respect and affection, and are buoyed up by the illusion that, though very occasionally they may get killed, nothing else can ever conceivably go wrong with them.

Police Review 27 January, 1950.

Insulting Behaviour

An injury, Lord Chesterfield told his son, is much sooner forgotten than an insult. But despite its profound social importance, this revelation was not to find expression in the laws of England until 1839, when counties and cities all over the country were busily establishing police forces on the new London model and promoting Parliamentary Bills to clothe them with authority. The legislators then attached a forty-shilling penalty to the use, in streets and public places, of "insulting words or behaviour with intent to provoke a breach of the peace, or whereby a breach of the peace may be occasioned." And having once admitted the principle that criticism must be restrained by the Police Acts, they emphasised their new sense of relative gravities by giving the police more arbitrary powers of arrest for insult than for aggravated assault. Lord Chesterfield, starting as a Polonius, had become a legal oracle.

They could hardly have realised what they were doing. Theirs was a less touchy age than this, their magistracy less imaginative, their newly-created police more cautious. Little could they have foreseen that the "insulting behaviour" clause would become a universal measure of deportment, an instrument of censorship, and a pigeon-hole into which a police service increasingly sensitive to public feeling could shove every public peccadillo not specially condemned elsewhere. No Eros stood then in Piccadilly, Fascist and Communist were unknown at the street corner, neighbours said fearlessly what they though of each other in strident Anglo-Saxon derivatives, and snooks (which, if Mr. Eric Partridge is right, had been used in controversy since 1702) were cocked with impunity.

"Did anyone seem insulted?" a police witness was asked by a London magistrate the other day when two students were charged with "insulting behaviour by climbing the statue of Eros." The policeman said that bystanders were angrily directing the climbers to come down, so angrily as to arouse in his mind statutory fears of a breach of the peace. It was enough. Forty shillings, please; and, remember, that statue was not put there for young asses like you to climb.

Eros now rivals the Oxford "Martyrs Memorial" as a challenge to the bibulous young, though it has yet to be crowned in the small hours with any article of homely earthenware. It leapt into fame among statue-scalers in January last year, when a clumsy climber was sentenced at Bow Street to three months' imprisonment because he had damaged Eros to the tune of £48, and then, afraid to come down, had held the police at bay for hours while a packed Piccadilly Circus watched entranced. But this case also provided reinforcement for those who, in legal circles, regard the "insulting behaviour" charge as the peace-officer's *vade mecum*. The Home Secretary ordered the man's release from prison because the "malicious damage" charge used by the police was not one which magistrates can try; it is a matter for juries. The climber got away scot-free because the police, deciding for once to take up a weapon more formidable and dignified than "insulting behaviour," had taken up the wrong one.

The insulting-behaviour charge, because it usually springs from circumstances which the defendant finds it humiliating to recollect, does not provoke appeals "on a point of law" to the High Court. So we are denied the views of His Majesty's judges on the propriety of its use in the many cases where the insult may have been trifling and the likelihood of a "breach of the peace" conjectural. One of its more cynical uses concerns a gap in the law relating to prostitution. A charge of "soliciting for the purpose of prostitution" depends for its success (in law if not in practice) upon proof that someone was annoyed. Prostitution is not a punishable offence, nor is soliciting. No offence is established even when the two together can be proved to have caused annoyance, unless the woman charged is already a "common prostitute." Here is a dialectical quandary that looks completely circular; how are you to get a woman convicted *for the first time* as a prostitute if she must already be a prostitute to qualify for trial? The police, without whose verbal ingenuity much of the law would remain academic, took up the challenge. On her first arrest they charged her with "insulting behaviour whereby a breach of the peace might have been occasioned," and said (by way of satisfying the rest of the clause) that the gentleman accosted "appeared annoyed." The next time she appeared in court that conviction was accepted as proof that she was already a common prostitute. Since no woman has ever challenged this procedure on appeal to the King's Bench Division, it is now hallowed by years of unquestioned practice.

If, as some reformers demand, we were so logical as to appoint a public defender as well as a public prosecutor, these and similar points might reach the High Court. As it is, they await the determined litigant who will take up the challenge alone. Such a warrior seemed to have been found recently in the person of a man who was called upon to answer the charge of "using insulting behaviour" as the result of a dispute over a cab-fare. He demanded to be told, in English, what he was charged with. You couldn't "use" behaviour, he said: that didn't make sense. (It did in 1839, when in another context you could be charged with "using loitering"; but this man belonged to the powerful school who deride a statute that is a hundred years old—unless it happens to be the Habeas Corpus Act, the Bill of Rights or some other bulwark of liberty that acquires strength rather than attracts ridicule as it gets old.) It was explained to him that the statutory phrase was "using insulting words or behaviour," and that the "words" had been dropped out for the occasion because what was alleged to have been insulting was not his language but the way he shouted it. He muttered angrily as he paid his fine, but no more was heard of him.

To the best of my belief, no one has ever compiled a list of the unsociable acts which have led to "insulting-behaviour" charges. Here is a beginning, though in some cases the magistrates have bridled their credulity and refused to convict:

(1) Over-impassioned heckling.
(2) Carrying placards contrasting the diet of the unemployed with the Lord Mayor's banquet.

(3) Arranging (with similar purpose) two rolls, a sausage, and a tin of dried egg on the red carpet outside a Piccadilly hotel.
(4) Demonstrators chaining themselves to railings. ("How can it be suggested," said a magistrate not long ago, "that that might not cause a breach of the peace?")
(5) Giving "peace" handbills to members of H.M. Brigade of Guards.
(6) Various kinds of traditional mayhem on Boat-race night.
(7) Dozing in a stranger's car on a parking-place.
(8) Letting the air out of his tyres.
(9) Throwing a municipally-owned lifebelt into the river for fun. (This got so "insulting" in London that the L.C.C. had it made a special offence; and thereafter there was no need to prove that it might lead to a breach of the peace.)
(10) Caricaturing the Minister of Transport, in charcoal, on a Belisha beacon.
(11) Peering into people's windows (though this is more popularly charged as "eavesdropping" under a statute of 1360, which is so old that no one has the heart to challenge it).
(12) Climbing public statues, the barbarity of the insult increasing with the height of the climb.
(13) Fighting in the street (The reasoning behind this is that you can hardly have clearer proof that "a breach of the peace might be occasioned" than the fact that it is actually going on.)
(14) Excessive vehemence in public discussion with the neighbours.
(15) Too-obvious chicanery in a bus-queue.
(16) Cocking a snook at a policeman.

This final instance raises a special question. Its latest occurrence was at Ipswich in 1947, when a man of great daring, stung by a resentment whose origin is unrecorded, thumbed his nose with great emphasis as a constable rode by on a bicycle. (A report in one of the less restrained newspapers said that he used both hands and twiddled his fingers.) He was fined £2 under the Public Order Act, 1936, for "insulting behaviour whereby a breach of the peace was likely to be occasioned." The 1936 Act had extended this convenient charge, formerly available only in certain Police Acts, to the whole country as a means of dealing with the Blackshirts; but because it carries heavier penalties than the Police Acts, it may gradually supersede them as its original purpose is forgotten. The Ipswich snook could have involved its cocker in a fine of £50 *and* three months' imprisonment. The point it raised was this: Since it is the duty of the policeman to preserve the peace, can an insult directed at him be held likely to cause a breach of it? Lacking high guidance, the magistrates at present take the view that a policeman has the same feelings as anyone else, and might forget his cloth. But the gravity with which the law now regards "insulting behaviour" may be gauged from the fact that the people who "use" it, unlike perjurors, dog-thieves and fraudulent company promoters, can lawfully be arrested by a constable without any warrant from a magistrate. You have been warned.

The Spectactor August 18, 1950.

Rival Psyches

At the moment anyone can set up in practice as a "psychologist," put his name and the word psychologist on a frosted glass panelled door, and comfort, frighten, mollify, flatter or mentally invigorate his patients (if any) for whatever fees he can get them to pay. This state of affairs is of great concern to the British Psychological Society, which hopes to establish for practising psychologists a status of known professional integrity, and thus make things difficult for the charlatan.

For the psychologist is not a charlatan. As a rule he has taken a degree or diploma in psychology or social science at a university, is expert in the application of intelligence tests, and knows about the springs of human behaviour. But he is not, except by rare coincidence, a doctor; and it is this which distinguishes him from a psychiatrist. The difference may have registered itself in the minds of a good many Magistrates, especially at Juvenile Courts, where they have a way of calling on a psychological report or a psychiatric report in circumstances which suggest that they do know the difference; but it has not yet got accepted by H.M. Judges, whose aloofness from current expressions really reflects a concern for the instruction of juries. So when a Judge said to a witness the other day, "You are a psychologist?" and was told that he was a psychiatrist, he no doubt did so in order that the witness could explain, for the benefit of the jury, that a psychiatrist is a qualified medical practitioner who is trained in the diagnosis and treatment of mental diseases.

It is a difference which ought to be known to the up-to-date Police officer. And once he knows, he can enjoy a little harmless prestige at the expense of those multitudes of people who don't. Try asking a few friends.

Police Review September 22, 1950.

Sunday Law at the Seaside

Many of our Sunday observance laws are examples of devices which, having accomplished a purpose and outlived their usefulness into a new age, are now irksome to many of those who wanted them. In the early nineteenth century and before, the Trade Unions and similar workmen's organisations were in favour of many Sunday restrictions on trade because they offered a prospect of Sunday leave, and had the powerful sanction of religious feeling, which could be adopted for the occasion whether it was truly felt or not. This year, M.P.s for seaside resorts are to be asked to press for the amendment of the Shops Acts, so as to allow children to buy buckets and spades on any Sunday of their summer holidays instead of merely on eighteen "high season" Sundays. At present, if a child's parents take him to the seaside early or late in the year, and arrive as usual on Saturday evening, he must wait until Monday for the bucket and spade with which to make his annual attack on our crumbling coast. He therefore watches with some bewilderment, often highly vocal, as his parents on the first Sunday of the holiday buy their cigarettes and sweets in shops festooned with buckets and spades, while he must accept a legal prohibition apparently aimed at him alone. The British Federation of Hotel and Boarding House Associations, which is sponsoring the new approach to Parliament, modestly asks for twenty-six bucket-and-spade Sundays instead of the present eighteen. Even this will leave twenty-six Sundays to irk those parents who are unlucky in the draw for annual leave.

Police Review January 19, 1951.

Spikes on Walls

A plain clothes Police officer searching premises at night during the investigation of one of those phenomena known as "noise heard and unusual lights seen," found himself confronted by a six-foot wall surmounted by two rows of iron spikes. There was no available way of continuing the search but by scaling the wall; and it happened that, in a stable at the back of a yard where he was standing, there lay an old leather saddle with stirrup-straps attached to it. He adjusted the saddle on the top of the wall, got himself on to it and dropped down on the other side, only to find that he had caught his left leg on a spike as he swung it over and torn his trousers badly.

When these searches result in the capture of an intruder, all goes well: the trousers are repaired at no cost to their owner and he is commended for his resource. In this case, no one was caught because no one had been in: the lights were those of a turning car in a street on the other side of the building and the noise was one of the noises that a man can hear when he has been too long on night duty. It was only when the occupants of the building, on arrival for business next morning, were told the story of the torn trousers that they had a look at their leather saddle, to discover that it, too, was extensively damaged by its impalement on the spikes. The discovery overcame their gratitude for the Police attention in the night, and was adopted as a neat answer to the complaint about the trousers. The matter was therefore dropped, with no particular good feeling on either side.

But what is the legal position about these horribly ingenious devices for discouraging intruders? There must be a limit to what you can do to keep people out. "Man traps" are not allowed, a row of Mills bombs along the wall would be thought excessive. There is authority in *Deane v. Clayton* (1817) and *Stewart v. Wright* (1893) for the proposition that householders must not resort to "unreasonable means of protection," but there is little guidance on what is deemed unreasonable. Broken glass set in cement could easily inflict fatal injury, for example by way of a severed femoral artery; and although barbed wire is not put up as a means of tearing out eyes, its purpose is to educate passers-by towards a habit of minding their own business in order that eyes shall not be torn out. Iron spikes were held to be a nuisance on the highway in *Fenna v. Clare* (1895), but they were on a window sill. The law about uncomfortable walls might be clarified.

Police Review September 28, 1951.

The Virtue of Registered Letters

A registered letter has an impressive appearance, involves the sender in reassuring formalities, and arrives at its destination in a special atmosphere of ceremony. Its sole value to the Police and to others sending legal notifications by post is that it affords proof of posting and (if it gets delivered) also of delivery. If it does not get delivered, being lost or stolen in transit, then apart from legal questions of "due notice" under numerous Statutes the system is of little value to either sender or non-receiver unless the contents of the envelope are of intrinsic value up to a certain maximum. A thing which, though unique and irreplaceable, is of sentimental value only might as well—or even better—be sent by ordinary post. And it seems that the same can be true of a notification.

As an example, the lawyer who had unsuccessfully defended a man charged with murder in the State of California entered an appeal against the conviction and sent a registered letter to the prison formally postponing the date of the execution. The letter was signed for, stamped "Received—Warden's Office," and then, perhaps because there was no one immediately present with authority to open it, was put by until later in the day. In the meantime the man concerned was executed. This story, with a reference to the investigation that followed the tragedy, is told by the former Warden of the prison in *San Quentin—The Story of a Prison (by Clinton T. Duffy, Peter Davies, 12s. 6d.).*

Another example came before a King's Bench Divisional Court on 8th November. A writ claiming £33 as the price of some goods was sent by registered post to the registered office of a company. (Section 437(1) of the Companies Act, 1948, says that "a document may be served on a company by leaving it at or sending it by post to the registered office of the company." Note that it does not stipulate "registered" post.) The letter was redirected to the company's "city office," and there received by a saleswoman during a staff holiday. She refused to accept the letter. She thought, because it was registered, that its contents were probably too important for her to attend to. So the defendant company never appeared at the hearing of the action, which went against them "in default of appearance." It was not until a sheriff's officer entered the defendant company's premises that they learned anything of what had been going on. In a further action which followed it was held that the writ was "not properly served" and that the judgement for the £33 must be set aside.

This was said to be in accordance with "the practice adopted since 1883 that service by registered post in such circumstances was bad." But when the case came before Mr. Justice Devlin in the Divisional Court, he held that the word "post" was wide enough to cover both registered and ordinary post. So the writ had been properly served.

The main reason why people shrink from opening registered letters not addressed to them is that they so often contain money. But whatever the reason in particular cases, the reluctance is a serious flaw in the legal process of "service by post."

Police Review November 23, 1951.

Exeunt Identity Cards

There may be few tears in the Police Service about the disappearance of identity cards, and perhaps one popular view will be that there is one less document to be scanned and paraphrased in the course of certain duties, one less register to be kept in Police Stations, and one less among the bundles of little forms to be carried in crammed uniform pockets. It is true that hospital cases and sudden death inquiries may be longer before identity is established, while deserters from the armed forces may be a little (though not much) harder to detect. But although it seems likely that the huge and generally silent majority of the people are quite indifferent about them, identity cards have for some years now attracted so much spleen from an angry minority, and stood out so prominently among the Aunt Sallies endangering the liberty of a freedom-loving people, that we may get along better without them. It is only when you stop to think how small a difference (if any) will be apparent in our lives, now that this great victory is won, that you realise the victory's mainly symbolical nature.

Police Review February 29, 1952.

£70,000 a day spent on clipping rail tickets

When I go through the barrier at a railway station I want my ticket clipped. It is something I've grown up with. I dislike being waved on by a clipper who momentarily feels disinclined to clip.

For if I get to my destination with an unclipped ticket I am burdened with some nameless guilt. When I hand it over, blushing, at Waterloo, I wait for the collectors to close in round me with their shoulders hunched.

They never do. Why? Doesn't an unclipped ticket matter? And, if not, why clip at all? I asked British Rail.

The question is worth asking if only for the staggering cost of the ticket-clipping system. Did you know that it costs the railways something like **£70,000 A DAY?**

"British Rail," they said (they've even clipped their own name), "leaves it to regional discretion. There may be some special local reason for clipping tickets on a certain day." But even then, went on British Rail, "it would be difficult to clip everyone's. Just imagine what it would mean in the rush hour."

If they had the time they would look at both sides of every ticket because the date is on one side and the destination on the other. But the most they can do, they say, is sample a few—and if you turn your ticket over as you proffer it the inspector will normally turn it back to see if you are trying to get away with something.

And another thing — the clipper at your local station knows you by sight, whether you think he does or not, even if you aren't a season ticket holder and even though you've never passed the time of day with him.

So he thinks you're unlikely to be using an out-of-date ticket, and the main reason for clipping tickets is thus absent.

Ever since tickets were first issued in the 1830s, clipping of some kind has been a rough-and-ready way of spotting the used ticket.

At my home station there's a back entrance with a booking office but no other barrier. The booking clerk clips every ticket as he sells it; his desk is covered with triangular confetti. Why?

"Probably because he's got the time," said British Rail. "We like the tickets clipped if possible, as a safeguard against re-use. But you shouldn't worry if your ticket is unclipped. Thousands are every day — probably a majority some days."

Reassuring, but there remains another anxiety. You go on to a platform with a respectably clipped ticket, looking the world in the face. You then remember you have left something in your car. You explain your way through the OUT barrier, you come back among a group of other people, and in the hurry the clipper seizes your ticket and clips it again.

This, surely, is something to worry about? If one clip is an official sign that the ticket's been used once, aren't two clips a sign that it's been used twice?

"Not at all," say B.R. "It doesn't matter if the tickets are clipped all round the edge. All the better in fact, because we'd examine them more closely."

And, by the way, the various shapes of the clippings identify the line or terminus where the clipping was done.

For instance, Waterloo clippers bite a W into your ticket. M is Marylebone, X for Charing Cross, V for Victoria and an inverted V for Paddington and the West Region. Inspectors on long-distance trains use coded clippers and Tube tickets are clipped in figures and letters.

Why not drop the whole thing and spend the money on improved travelling amenities?

They would like to. They want travelling inspectors to do all the clipping on the trains. They've been working towards this for years. They realise they couldn't do it in a jam packed commuter train, with people standing on each other's feet along the corridor, but what they lost there they would recover through the general economy.

Sometimes on one line they close one or two stations and set up an all-day ticket check at the others. Numbers of people hand in tickets which they say they bought at the closed stations and then they are up to the neck in it.

London Transport are specially fond of doing this on the Underground. But clipping plays no part in it. I asked a "clippie" at a Tube station why she had clipped my ticket and ignored the chap in front of me.

"Because you offered it for clipping," was all she said. But it was an illuminating remark, confirming (don't you think?) all that I've been saying.

News Chronicle 7 June, 1952.

The Danger of Identification Parades

Mr. Ernest Hardingham, a lorry-driver, of Colne, Lancashire, hitch-hiked to London to answer a charge, at West London Magistrates' Court on 25th January, of stealing ten tons of flour by means of a trick. It had previously been alleged that he called with his lorry at the premises of Chelsea Food Products Ltd., in London, and said he had come for ten tons of flour for the British Doughnut Company. A woman clerk accepted what he said, the flour was loaded on to his lorry, and off he went. When the British Doughnut Company received the invoice by post, they denied having either ordered or received the flour. On descriptions given then to the Police, Mr.

Hardingham was arrested and "put-up for identification." *Two witnesses picked him out as the thief,* and he was charged and remanded on bail. Before the business of the Court was over for that day, information was received from Chelsea Food Products that their ten tons of flour had arrived, after all, at the premises of a firm in Newport. The British Doughnut Company, it turned out, employed transport contractors, who employed subcontractors. And it was a sub-contractor's driver, not Mr. Hardingham, who had driven away the ten tons of flour. Accordingly the Police offered no evidence, and Mr. Hardingham was discharged. "This case," said the Magistrate, "underlines the terrible dangers of identity parades; it is not surprising that juries and Magistrates are very chary of convicting on them."

They are more than chary. They *will not* convict where there is no supporting evidence of a quite different kind: and in this we think they are right. Witnesses brought in front of an identification parade know already that somewhere, among the "eight or more," there stands the man the Police suspect. A passing likeness can, under such circumsances, become a positive identity. There is no "terrible danger" to the eight or more others, but this case shows that there is danger to an innocent suspect.

Police Review February 6, 1953.

The Pig and Whistle

The "interests of the public" may be jeopardised, it seems, by calling a new pub *The Pig and Whistle*, and they have to be considered by the Licensing Justices when a new on-licence is granted. So when Messrs H. & G. Symonds, the brewers, recently asked the High Wycombe bench to grant a licence for a Micklefield pub to be called *The Pig and Whistle,* their worships said no. You can call it *The Micklefield Arms* if you like, they said, but not *The Pig and Whistle.* But it was a fine old name, *The Pig and Whistle,* grumbled the brewers. Still, how about *The Coronation?* That was a bright and topical alternative? No, said the Bench firmly: *Micklefield Arms.* And that's how the licence was made out.

The Justices must have been basing themselves, and doing it very firmly, on Section 14(1) of the Licensing (Consolidation) Act, 1910, which enables them to attach any conditions to a new licence which they "think proper", provided they are "in the interest of the public." If the licensing beaks in Bucks, where conventions are subject to flux, think a whistling pig is so much *infra dig,* they should logically ban Dogs and Ducks.

Police Review April 17, 1953.

Literary Beggar

There was a young man of Japan
Who wrote verses that never would scan.
When asked why this was,
He replied "It's because
I've always made it a purely literary convention of my own to get as many syllables into the last line of a poem as I conveniently can."

He now has a counterpart, or disciple, who goes the rounds of the shops offering his little verses for sale; and a correspondent thinks this one merits a begging charge under the Vagrancy Act, 1824. "One of the places he entered," writes our correspondent, "was a Post Office. On inquiry it was found that on entering the shops he would produce to the person behind the counter an ordinary postcard, upon which were written the following words: 'Could you please find the producer of this card employment? If not could you help him by buying the card?' This was followed by the following verse" (our correspondent calls it a verse and that is how we know):—

"As your eyes these lines they scan,
You will see that it is offered by a genuine ex-service man."

They gave him threepence at the Post Office, but he kept the card. "In his possession," says our correspondent, "were found a number of these cards already written out and bearing the same words. Is this a case of begging? Is the public part of a Post Office a 'public place'? Or is this a case of a pedlar without a certificate?"

If we were a Magistrate we should not convict him of begging: we should stretch artistic credulity to the point where he became indeed a threepenny poet, on the ground that, equally with the man who sings "Loch Lomond" every time we stand in a theatre queue, he gives value for money. And we would let him off if he were charged as an uncertificated pedlar, ostensibly because he "offers for sale his own skill in handicraft" but really because we rather like the sound of him. Nevertheless a Post Office must, we think, be regarded as a public place.

Police Review August 21, 1953.

"Literary Beggar" Again

Two weeks ago we wrote about a "literary beggar", a man who composed wretched little bits of infantile doggerel and "sold" them in shops by virtually refusing to get out until someone, in exasperation, gave him the threepence he asked for his poem. It was a sunny day, birds were singing, Mr. Vishinsky had been seen with his arm round the French Foreign Secretary, and we had a birthday coming. So we wrote light-heartedly, and said we would not have convicted the man of begging, having in mind that wandering mendicants have been selling thoroughly inferior verses for about sixteen hundred years (probably longer?). We had only just drawn back on the verge of telling the story of Swinburne, who once told a solicitous friend that he was able to write just enough poems to keep the wolf from the door. "I suppose", said the friend, "you just hang out of the window and read them aloud to it"?

It wouldn't have done. We had already gone far enough to draw a very angry letter from a Metropolitan officer who, before he choked over an abusive *coda,* told us about another wandering poet who added to the enormity of his verse by wearing war medals he wasn't entitled to and throwing away a loaf of bread and some cakes that someone had offered him instead of money. "His sentence of three months appeared lenient", says this frightening correspondent. "If vagrants could depend on you", he continues (meaning us), "to dismiss these charges because you 'rather like the sound of them', they would be in their glory, the public would be in misery, and the Police would have a lot less to do. I hope", he concludes, "you receive a few similar letters".

We haven't, but we see what he means, and must write more solemnly. These men selling their poems are a menace. If they are bad poems they are begging. If they are good poems they are either demanding money with menaces or obtaining money, within the meaning of Section 1(2)(i)(b) of the Larceny Act, 1916, "by intimidation", and since that is a form of "taking" for which no special punishment is provided by the Act unless it amounts to robbery, they should be charged with simple larceny contrary to Section 2. The poems should be read to the Magistrate with the convictions—but there we go again.

Police Review September 4, 1953.

Drive on Right

If there were no other ideologies to divide mankind into two camps, there would perhaps be a state of cold war between those who drive on the left of the road and those who drive on the right.

The "Rule of the Road" in Great Britain, by which we keep to the left, is sometimes said to be a Common Law rule. But that is said by lawyers who regard any statute as a rather offensive upstart, and cling to the crumbling Common Law like shipwrecked mariners hanging on to a cork raft that keeps breaking off in their fingers; and it only means that we have kept to the left for a very long time. Actually we are now statutorily ordered to keep to the "left or near side of the road" by Section 78 of the Highway Act, 1835, and when we meet another vehicle we are required by Section 28 of the Town Police Clauses Act,

1847, to "keep to the left except in a case of actual necessity or sufficient reason for deviation". In the City of London, where these two Acts do not apply and you might think you could lawfully drive all over the road, the Police have such a strong Common Law sentiment that they would probably charge you with dangerous driving if you did it.

One of the few other countries in Europe that drives on the left is Sweden. But it is announced in Stockholm that the Swedish Parliament is to consider changing over to "keep to the right": a committee of Swedish M.P.s, just back from a tour of Europe's traffic centres, recommends the change because of increasing traffic between other countries and Sweden. Sweden wanted to change before the war—Norway and Finland, with which it has land frontiers, drive on the right, and the fact has long been a source of minor irritation. Most countries that have changed have hesitated—as Sweden has done—on the score that accidents would increase enormously until everyone got used to the new rule.

The London *Times* motoring correspondent points out that all the other European left-driving countries (except Gibraltar) are islands: the United Kingdom, Ireland, Iceland, Malta and Cyprus. Insularity will long nourish opposition to the kind of change that Sweden is about to make, although the change in Great Britain and the Commonwealth countries would enormously simplify the problems of our motor manufacturers, who at present must make cars of both kinds. But not only the Commonwealth still drives on the left: the rule survives in China, Japan, Java, Sumatra, Burma, Thailand, Afghanistan, Arabia and the Sudan. And in splendid isolation on the American continent, Paraguay drives on the left. We said that the rule "survives" in these countries: it looks more like a survival, a digging-in of heels, every time some other country changes over. Italy was once a mass of contradictions—you drove on the right in country districts and (on the whole) on the left in towns; and one of the better deeds of Benito Mussolini was to straighten it all out. If Sweden now goes over to the right, the diehards will close their ranks. We prophesy that the race to be last will be won by Great Britain, with that dynamic country, Eire, as runner-up.

Police Review December 4, 1953.

Street Exhibitions

Richard Carlile was a publisher and a freethinker; and the two characteristics combined, in the oppressive atmosphere of the first half of the 19th century, to keep him in prison for more than nine years of his short life.

He earned three of these years by causing an obstruction in Fleet Street. He had a passionate objection to paying the Church Rate in respect of his Fleet Street shop, and when the Church sent bailiffs to distrain on his furniture and books he was at some pains to find suitable means of retaliation. He was quite used to going to prison for his opinions, and had expected to go there for refusing to pay tithe; "but they took my goods instead of me," he told a friend; "I rate less than four chairs and a table." So he got someone to make him three large effigies, one representing a Bishop of the Established Church of England, one a Broker's man and one the Devil. "Bishop, Broker and Beelzebub" were then placed arm-in-arm with each other, in a kind of grotto Carlile made by removing the whole of his first floor window. Under the Bishop was a placard saying "Spiritual Broker", and under the Broker's man another saying "Temporal Broker". And the footways on both sides of Fleet Street were blocked for weeks by people who had nothing better to do than gaze up at Carlile's little tableau and pick one another's pockets. It was all rather laboured and childish, perhaps, by modern standards, but very few people could read and the simplest form of propaganda or public protest was the effigy and the caricature.

Carlile was indicted for causing a public nuisance, and tried by three judges and a jury in the King's Bench Division of the High Court. Many of his neighbours gave evidence of their annoyance. Mr. Gray, who kept the booking-office for stage coach seats at the Bolt-in-Tun, Fleet Street, said the crowds got in his way. Mr. Chandler, who kept the Portugal Hotel opposite Carlile's shop, said the Police had to clear a way for customers to get into and out of the hotel: the crowd, he added, stood over his area gratings and made it so dark in his kitchen that the staff had to burn candles all day.

Carlile, defending himself, cross-examined all the witnesses vigorously, not so much to establish his innocence as to ensure the utmost possible publicity for his beliefs and complaints. The law was operated unfairly, he said when he made his speech to the jury. There was a confectioner in Regent Street, a certain Mr. Very, who had a beautiful daughter serving in his shop. Her beauty was such that three or four hundred people used to assemble daily simply to gaze at her. The Police had to be on duty constantly to regulate the crowds. But was Mr. Very prosecuted in the King's Bench? He was not. The Police merely persuaded him to send his daughter out of town.

All to no avail. The jury said Carlile was guilty. The Court fined him forty shillings and required recognisances that he would behave himself for three years—his own of £200 and two sureties of £50 each. Carlile laughed at the suggestion; and off he went to prison for three years.

Police Review June 4, 1954.

Do it Yourself

A subject that ought to be beckoning the social anthropologist is the fluctuating proportion of citizens (male and female, with the male today, I think, slightly predominating) unable to knock a nail in straight or change a tap washer. The fluctuations almost certainly follow the curves of industrial change and the redistributions of wealth and leisure; but at the moment there is clamant evidence of a resurgent desire to "be your own craftsman," a powerful reaction against the mass-production of household commodities. It is fostered by and reflected in such agencies as "Inventors' Club" on television, the great and deserved success of the English Universities' Press "Teach Yourself" books (more than 5,000,000 copies in sixteen years), the tortuous ingenuity of the people who have now for many months contributed "Bright Ideas" on household convenience and improvisation to the correspondence pages of the *Star*, and the Second International Handicrafts, Homecrafts, and Hobbies Exhibition which was recently staged at Olympia.

It is an aspect of shorter working hours. With more time on their hands, people are either too short of money to "get a man in" whenever a sash-cord breaks or too concerned with what the money could do to brighten their longer leisure. But "Do it yourself," now becoming one of the great slogans of economic history, has a creative rather than a mercenary origin; the cushioned and gadgeted householder has got up from his chair to look for rougher and longer-lasting work than the pressing of switches.

And the mass-producers have been watching him. This creative urge is all very well so long as it is not allowed to affect the regular market. Any considerable making of chairs and tables at home might become a disturbing factor. As soon as any slack began to appear, therefore, the manufacturers began to take it up by the simple expedient of eliminating, in respect of a carefully judged proportion of their products, the last two or three touches on the assembly line and selling the goods technically unfinished. The stark simplicity of modern furniture made this a simple matter. You could buy your table top and screw the legs into it at home ("All you need is a screwdriver"), assemble your own bookcase by blueprint, paper a ceiling in a dance frock, paint your own bright pictures by numbers ("Training? Needless. Be your own artist today"), and plug in your own potter's kiln to a fifteen-amp point in the kitchen. By your own industry at home when you might have been resting, you perhaps released other workers who might have been toiling for you. And what would occupy their new leisure? Home industry.

The Chief Registrar of Friendly Societies has just reported that more and more people are forming "self-build" housing societies, established to enable members to build for their own occupation.

There are now 137, with 2,778 members, and their buildings are worth £653,000. (The twenty members of the Brighton Ex-Service Men's Housing Society, Ltd., for example, started to build their own homes in August, 1949, and finished them in just under the budgeted two years.) Every member of a self-build housing society has to fulfil his working obligations as a condition of getting a house, but this is merely the logical extension of a rule that is inexorable in every do-it-yourself undertaking.

Among the more interesting secondary consequences of this householders' revolution is a great increase in the production of labour-saving tools for home use, many of them displaying an inventiveness that borders on the ludicrous. The do-it-yourself market is the trying-out ground for many of these, though they take about ten years—the ratchet screwdriver is an example—to find favour with the "professionals." Many of them are patented and remain expensive, while the unprotected and more obvious ones set out for a big sale before the "inferior imitations" (which are sometimes superior) bring the price sharply down. They have little sale among master-men in the dourly conservative building, decorating and furnishing trades, but it is interesting to find that many professional painters and decorators, when they renovate their own homes in their leisure hours, discard the brush because they can do the work in a quarter of the time with the new sheepskin rollers.

The sale of small electric drills, capable of bench use to drive lathes or miniature circular saws, has greatly increased in the last five years, and a new one comes on to the market almost monthly. The manager of a service garage told me recently that there has been a steady fall in the number of people resorting to public garages for small drilling or brazing jobs—"and most of my clients," he said, "seem to have fixed these new rear reflectors they've got to have on their cars." I know two men who provided themselves with the funds for a family car holiday abroad by doing the whole of their own house decorations last year. At the Handicrafts Exhibition recently, a man showed how he built his own refrigerator in seven hours, four minutes, thirteen seconds, with an occasional glance at a stop-watch. He exhorted an audience to do the same.

As for the people who are still unable to ease a tight drawer or unstop a drain, a fluctuating aristocracy as I have said, these seem to fall naturally into two classes. One class, though decently ashamed of an ineptitude for which there is usually not much excuse, never quite gives up trying and is surrounded in its homes by pitiful examples of elementary disrepair or botched postponement. The other, butter-fingered by natural selection, is not above recognising a crude poetry in the horny-handedness of others, but makes a patrician virtue of necessity by keeping its own hands soft. The two classes have one thing in common. In the most elementary emergencies of household maintenance, they mutter, "I must get a man in." And they are a dwindling race of men.

New Statesman October 23, 1954.

The Solomon Case

Members of the jury: it is now my duty, on behalf of the Director of Public Prosecutions, to call your attention to certain aspects of this unpleasant case. I shall endeavour to be very brief.

You have all had an opportunity—or should I perhaps say a belatedly renewed opportunity?—to read this book as a whole. I'm sure that you have done so, and that you were careful to consider this so-called *Song of Songs* as a part of the whole—er—work. I offer no opinion, members of the jury, as to the relevance of these eight chapters to what may or may not be the purpose of the entire book; but you will no doubt give due weight, in your deliberations, to the fact that the book as a whole has for some considerable time been widely known as the Holy Bible, and that there has hitherto been no complaint of any kind against its publishers (the British and Foreign Bible Society), or its printers (the Cambridge University Press).

Having said that, I turn at once to my learned friend's insistence, in his speech to you, that the defendants, in publishing the *Song of Solomon,* were actuated only by the highest motives. It matters not, members of the jury, if their concern was to reform and elevate the whole of humanity. That is not the test. Let me remind you, subject to what my Lord will say when he sums up this case to you, of the only test that you are to apply in considering whether this so-called *Song of Songs* is or is not an obscene publication. "The test is whether the tendency of the matter charged as obscenity is to deprave and corrupt those whose minds are open to such immoral influences and into whose hands a publication of this sort may fall." Nothing there about intention, members of the jury. No considerations of literary merit or sociological zeal need trouble your minds. Is that stuff fit for an adolescent boy or girl to read? That is all you have to consider. Nor need you be influenced by any plea that this kind of writing is allegorical, and that the boy or girl might be getting the wrong end of the stick. Allegory, members of the jury? I hope you took careful note, as you read, of the chapter-headings to this self-styled *Song of Solomon.* You each have the book before you; perhaps you will bear with me as I indicate to you certain passages where the undeniably amatory nature of the text is, in the submission of the prosecution, obscene to an extent that can in no way be mitigated by any trumped-up or misleading chapter-headings.

In Chapter 1, members of the jury, you will have noticed Verse Thirteen: "A bundle of myrrh is my wellbeloved unto me: he shall lie all night betwixt my breasts." And you will have observed that the chapter-heading suggests how in that passage the Church and the Almighty are "congratulating one another." Was that the way it struck you, members of the jury? Whatever the casuistry of bygone theologians, did you think that was in fact a piece of thoroughly reprehensible erotica? Not very obscene, perhaps, but did it afford you an indication as to the plausibility of the chapter-headings? Look at the beginning of Chapter 7, where the Shulamite is apostrophised in terms which, you may think, a reputable publisher and a university printer might well hesitate to disseminate among our Sunday schools. "How beautiful are thy feet with shoes, O prince's daughter! The joints of the thighs are like jewels, the work of the hands of a cunning workman. Thy navel is like a round goblet which wanteth not liquor; thy belly is like an heap of wheat set about with lilies. Thy two breasts are like two young roes that are twins."

And what is the chapter-heading to that, members of the jury? "A further description of the Church's graces." And that, indeed, is what the defence has been asking you to believe it to be. Well, of course, it's a matter for you. You're men and women of the world. You will know about these things. And look a little further down, Verse Six: "How fair and how pleasant art thou, O love, for delights!" Even if you believed, members of the jury, that that had reference to "the Church's graces," how many young girls do you think would so regard it? My learned friend sought to call before you a long procession of eminent literary and ecclesiastical gentlemen, to say no doubt that this thing is really an allegorical poem of great power and beauty. No doubt you would have been able to hear a great deal of learned exegesis, parading before you, for example, Hengstenberg's identification of the Shulamite's navel with the chalice of the Church. Members of the jury, their opinion matters not in this case. I could have called expert opinion, too—opinion that this outburst is no longer considered by scholars to have been thework of King Solomon, that it belongs to post-Exilic times, or that it is a marriage liturgy of the cult of Adonis. We could have had a most interesting and learned debate.

But it would all be beside the point, members of the jury: all irrelevant and all, in my submission to you, disingenuous in intention. My Lord rightly refused, if I may most respectfully say so, to allow any of this evidence; and it would also have been wrong to encumber your minds with the views of the twelve superintendents of Sunday schools, who, unless I misunderstood my learned friend's skilful essay in the art of paraphrasing witnesses he is not allowed to call, were here to say that the *Song of Solomon* is not read by Sunday School children. Members of the jury, how do they know by whom it is read? Do you know what even your own children read? You do not. You perhaps try to protect them. You feel that the Bible should be in your homes, but you buy small block-covered ones and put them in inconspicuous corners of your book-shelves. And if in fact this farrago of sensuousness is written with "power and beauty," is it not obvious that the gravity of the offence charged is to that extent aggravated? If ill-written pornography can have harmfully telling effects, what is to be said about pornography that is beautifully written?

My Lord has told you, and I have ventured to repeat, that you must consider this book as a whole. My learned friend for the defence stressed the same necessity with such vehemence as to suggest to my own mind that he does not know what the rest of the book is like. I refrain, members of the jury, from directing your attention to certain passages in the Books of *Leviticus, Kings, Chronicles* and others, because those instructing me consider it undesirable that public attention should be drawn to them. But you will have read them. I ask you to say, with all those matters in your minds, that these eight Chapters of the Authorised Version of the Bible, whether they be an allegorical poem, a heathen fertility chant, a sensuous love lyric or a parable of the Church's devotion to its work, constitute an obscene libel under the Common Law of England.

New Statesman & Nation October 30, 1954.

"Unlawful Possession" and Beards

Section 66 of the Metropolitan Police Act, 1839, comes into the news again at the instance of Mr. David Hamshere, of Holland Road, London, who was "stopped and detained" by a Constable on the suspicion that he was carrying stolen property at 7.30 a.m. on Sunday, 11th October, 1953. The incident, said Mr. Hamshere in the High Court on 9th February, had resulted in grave injury to his reputation; and he wanted £5,000 damages, for which modest sum he sued Sir John Nott-Bower, the Commissioner of Police of the Metropolis, and the Constable (see *The Times,* 10th February, 1955).

The Constable said in evidence that Mr. Hamshere, who was wearing a rather dirty raincoat and carrying a blue rucksack, and who had an unkempt beard, was not the sort of person you saw in Kensington at 7.30 on a Sunday morning. He first saw Mr. Hamshere on a street corner, and thought he disappeared rather hurriedly at the sight of a Policeman. So he stopped him and expressed an interest in the contents of the blue rucksack. When these proved to be innocuous—Mr. Hamshere was in fact on his way to a day's work as a jobbing gardener for a lady living in Harley Gardens, Brompton—the Constable asked him for his name and address. "Why did you do that" asked Mr. Hamshere, conducting his own case in the High Court. Because, said the Constable, that was what one was taught in the training school. "If we stop someone and the explanation is satisfactory, then we ask for the name and address." (Convenient as this may be for the purposes of Police records, it is the one aspect of the case that may suggest a need for further thought: why should a blameless citizen, even with a beard and a rucksack, give his name to the Police if he doesn't want to? And how is he to know, in view of the unexpected display of Police power that he had just been treated to, that he need not then give any particulars of himself at all?) But then Mr. Hamshere produced a notebook of his own and began asking the Constable a few questions. Was there much crime in the neighbourhood, he asked? And, in view of the High Court decision in *Ludlow v. Shelton and Another* (1938), it was an extremely pertinent question. The Constable realised that Mr. Hamshere was going to be different from the usual "stop", and apologised to him for the inconvenience. "I was courteous and polite throughout," he said, in Court, "and did not at any time threaten to restrain Mr. Hamshere's liberty." Mr. Hamshere is in fact an unusual man. The Judge said of him: "He is obviously a well-educated and well-spoken man, he has a Master of Arts degree, he is a portrait painter of ability, an author, a public speaker, and he carries on religious activities of, no doubt, a most admirable nature. In addition, it appears he does gardening work for residents of Kensington, where he lives."

And he was dressed for gardening when the Constable saw him. "He is a gentleman of somewhat striking appearance," went on the Judge. "He wears a luxuriance of beard which, without offence to him, is not trimmed neatly into a point, but is a somewhat bushy growth all round his face." But his Lordship thought the Constable was doing "nothing less than his duty in the circumstances". The circumstances of course included the time, the day, the rucksack, and the beard. "I sympathise with Mr. Hamshere, but it is a great pity he didn't leave the matter alone after officers had explained the position to him at Kensington Police Station, when he called there to complain." Mr. Hamshere must be thinking this, too. His action was dismissed, with costs against him, and they must be heavy.

Police Review February 18, 1955.

Commercial TV and Fortune Tellers

It is announced that commercial television will not advertise matrimonial agencies, undertakers, cures for smoking or alcoholism, "systems of bust development not approved by the British Standards Institution", or fortune tellers. We found the last two interesting. We had not realised that there is now a B.S.I. bust standard, and accept it with some resentment as another step on the long downward slope to uniformity. But the reference to fortune tellers brings one up sharply against the realisation that broadcasting, under the I.T.A., will be slightly more likely to break the law than it has been under B.B.C. monopoly. Fortune tellers on TV? Rogues and vagabonds at your own fireside? We have grown accustomed to the zodiacal claptrap in the astrology sections of the Sunday papers, which has subsisted for years now on the very tolerant decision in *Barbanell v. Naylor* (1936), 101 J.P. 13, that to constitute the offence the fortune told must relate to an individual person. But we must watch for fortune tellers on TV, where they could do a lot more harm. The I.T.A.'s case for banning them is in fact slightly stronger than for banning marriage agencies and undertakers. Of the two latter, one concerns risk and the other certainty, but both are lawful enough. So is bust-development, but even that (though we seldom make use of a pun) is getting near to necromancy.

Police Review May 20, 1955.

The Unpunishables

The Third International Congress on Criminology, held at Bedford College, Regent's Park, last week, was an undoubted success. What makes a Congress a success? This one carefully abstained from passing any resolutions; it will be able to offer no spectacular solutions to the problem that was its main concern— the problem of the "unpunishables"; it talked and agreed and disagreed interminably. But now that men have been locking each other up in prisons of various kinds for some thousands of generations, it is probably time to consider whether "punishment", as traditionally understood, is not an outmoded way of dealing with the characterless morons who to-day are called psychopaths—the non-sane, non-insane offenders who do not respond to punishment of any kind. In Holland and Denmark they are dealt with in special experimental institutions, where there is a plan of remedial education and a system of rewards rather than punishments to develop the sense of character and self-esteem. And at last week's congress the criminologists from 42 countries, concerned as they all are with the prevention, and hardly at all with the detection, of crime, most valuably exchanged ideas that may lead to a reassessment of the value of mere punishment. The great numbers of learned papers that were read and discussed varied from the most surprising statistical inferences to the starkest of "human stories". The starkest, however, was not the subject of any learned paper or debate: it was merely that, when the people in charge of the Congress's book exhibition came to check their stock on the last day, six of the nicest books were missing. Criminology is not all theory.

Police Review September 23, 1955.

Drunk Arrests Drunk

A case reported last week in the London *Evening Standard* (29th December) illustrated the varieties of meaning that can be carried by the word "incapable", in its application to a drunken person. They begin where one Policeman sees helplessness in a single stumbling step, and end where another says, "Look! He's not drunk—he moved!"

A man was arrested at Ealing Broadway on Christmas Eve for "being drunk and incapable"—which, as every good Policeman knows, means that his offence was "being drunk in a public place", while his arrest for that offence was possible only because he was "incapable". But on the way to the Police Station, he and the Constable encountered another drunk, this time a "drunk and disorderly"; and while the Constable was trying to arrest the second man, and getting knocked about, the first man went to his assistance—to such good effect that the second drunk, the disorderly, was (at least in part) arrested by the first, the "incapable". At Court after the Christmas holiday, the disorderly was fined £2 and the "incapable" 10s. "We commend you," said the Chairman of the Bench to the latter offender, "for the assistance you gave to the Police officer."

Prima facie, this may look like fairly rough justice. If a man is capable of taking care of a Policeman, how can you say that he is incapable of taking care of himself? But being incapable is not what he was punished for. The fine of 10s. was for being drunk. The disorderly man was said to be "fighing drunk"; and because this is a highly infectious condition among drunks, the sight of it could very well transmute incapability into a kind of staggering aggression; dog eating dog, drunk apprehending drunk, and Peace on Earth overhanging the whole thing.

Police Review January 6, 1956.

The Detective and the Dodo

As long ago as 1900, the literary critics (they had them even then) were prophesying the end of the detective novel. "The detective in literature is hardly more than fifty years old," said an article in the *London Academy* on 30th December, 1905, "but already he is passing into decay. . . . From henceforth he retires to limbo with the dodo and the District Railway's trains. . . ."

The District Railway is still with us, and as for the dodo—well they *did* say the coelacanth was extinct. But if in Britain we abolish the death penalty for murder, what about the detective story then? It's a literary form almost confined to the three great death penalty countries—Britain, France and the U.S.A. Would the who-dun-it really flourish without the shadow of the gallows?

Police Review March 22, 1956.

Crime as a Pleasure

At Walsall on 11th May a man was charged with taking and driving away a motor cycle without consent, and his solicitor based his defence on the wording of the defendant's own insurance policy, which said (according to the *Manchester Guardian* for 12th May) that he could drive any vehicle for "social, domestic, or pleasure purposes". The defendant's action this time came under the "pleasure" heading, said his solicitor, and therefore the policy was in full operation; and a representative of the insurance company made the interesting admission that his company would be liable "even if a policy-holder committed a criminal offence in using a machine other than his own". Notwithstanding a Police submission that the policy would only cover the *legal* use of another person's motor cycle, the Magistrates upheld the defence.

If this decision stands, and receives High Court authority, does crime acquire the status of a pleasure? Is it no longer a compulsive urge, a psycho-neurotic backfire, or even a business? Most policy conditions allow the policyholder to drive any vehicle "not belonging to him", and say nothing about the consent of that vehicle's owner: the only apparent restriction on the car-thief is that he can't use the car for business—only for social, domestic and pleasure purposes. Well, we know now that "joy-riding" is one of these. Who first called it that? Let us all blame him.

Police Review May 18, 1956.

Punctuating the Law Reports

The niceties of "indirect speech", as illustrated in the Law Report columns of *The Times*, produce many charming inversions. There was recently a beguiling story about an angry Dutch sea-captain who assaulted an immigration officer as his ship was entering the Royal Dock at Grimsby. The immigration officer had climbed on to the bridge to ask the Captain some routine questions, at a tricky moment in the process of navigation. The Captain ordered him off, and, when he refused to go, tried to throw him off. The Justices said that was not an assault, but the High Court held that it was. The Lord Chief Justice, however, remarked that the immigration officer had added fuel to the fire by saying that he would get off the bridge if he were asked properly. "Well! My goodness gracious," said Lord Goddard: "I don't wonder the Captain lost his temper." But *The Times*, in reporting this, was not trusting itself to inverted commas. It said: Well! His (his Lordship's) goodness gracious. He did not wonder that the Captain lost his (the Captain's) temper.

And if there is any more convoluted way than that of getting rid of inverted commas, we will eat our (the POLICE REVIEW's) hat.

Police Review July 27, 1956.

Insulting the Police

There is as yet no reliable answer to the old problem about the legal susceptibility of a Constable to what the law, in its local manifestations, calls "insulting words and behaviour." If you insult a Constable, can that be regarded as "likely to provoke a breach of the peace"? Some Magistrates have held that the very status of a Constable as one who guards the peace makes it juridically impossible that he, of all men, should ever be provoked into breaking it. We ourselves are waiting for the day when someone is charged with using insulting words or behaviour towards the Lord Chancellor or the Attorney-General, and the same Magistrates are faced with the job of telling those exalted guardians of the peace that they cannot be insulted.

There are, at least, no such inhibitions in Rome. One day last July Miss Elsa Martinelli, who (though this is one of the things you should know) is Italy's leading actress, was trying to park her car in a "no-waiting" area. Three Policemen told her to take it away, and she thereupon addressed to them a stream of insulting profanities that set the law of Italy into rapid motion. After a mere eight months' preparation, the charge of insulting the Policemen came before the Magistrate on 9th April this year. The prosecution had been working out the surprisingly generous proposition that insulting three Policemen at once is only one offence. But the Magistrate held that it was three offences, and sentenced her to six months' imprisonment on each. Eighteen months for insulting three Policemen is a sentence that may prove discouraging to any Roman who thought of upbraiding the entire Constabulary at its next ceremonial parade. Still, Signora Martinelli is to appeal, and we will report further in 1958.

Police Review April 19, 1957.

The Law of Gravity

A reader asks (hot from the theatre) whether it is lawful to make fun of the Police Force on the stage. Alas, yes: even the Police Act, 1919, which might have stopped all this laughing, says in Section 10 that non-Policemen can wear Police uniform "in the course of a stage play." And then, in case this might be thought to authorise no more than the utmost propriety and verisimilitude, it adds "or music-hall or circus performance." Circus! There might be a shred or two of pathetic dignity about some music-hall Policemen, but everyone knows what they want with Police uniforms at a circus. And yet it was recorded of Mr. Robb Wilton, who died a few weeks ago, that the best audience he ever had for a burlesque of a Policeman was one composed of Policemen. We had better not be too grave; though Sydney Smith did say once that he had sunk by his levity while other men, contrary to the usual laws of nature, had risen by their gravity.

Police Review May 31, 1957.

Killing a Man Twice

Last month Dr. Glanville Williams, broadcasting on "Homicide and Medical Negligence," ran true to his usual form as a prodder of the legal imagination when he posed the question whether a man, in the eyes of the law, can be killed twice. Among the impressive fish that rose to this bait was Professor A. L. Goodhart, of Oxford University. "A similar, though not identical, problem was set some years ago," wrote Professor Goodhart in a letter to the *Listener* on 11th July, "in an examination paper at an American law school. Jones, who is preparing to explore a desert, fills a reserve keg with water and straps it on his pack-mule. His enemy, White, secretly introduces a deadly poison into the water. Two days later Black, a second enemy, overtakes Jones in the desert and shoots a hole in the keg, so that all the water is drained out. Jones dies of thirst. Both White and Black are probably guilty at least of attempted murder" (concludes Dr. Goodhart) "but are either or both guilty of the murder of Jones?"

Let battle commence. Our view is that White committed no murder, because his *modus operandi* never came to fruition: Jones drank none of his poison; for Black saved his life from one peril by an act that brought about his death from another. But neither do we think Black committed murder. Dying of thirst in the desert is not an inevitable consequence of losing all the water that you began the journey with; and if this was an American desert (as suggested by the pack-mule), the chances of being spotted by the frequent aircraft are fairly good and growing better day by day. Moreover, the question says nothing about Black's state of mind. He may have been a "second enemy" but may also have relented because he learned that Jones's water-keg contained only poison, and ridden out fast to get rid of the poison in a way that would still protect him from having to be openly friendly. (Hollywood has taught us how "crazy and mixed-up" these people are.)

Attempted murder? White is in a worse position here than Black: it is a position rather similar to that in *R. v. Dale* (1852), 6 Cox 14, where the prisoner put poison in a sugar-basin intending that it should be taken, and it was not. The fact that Jones died had nothing to do with the way in which White rather wanted him to die; the latter's intent is clear from the start. Black has a number of pleas open to him, apart from the unconvincing change of heart suggested above. We would rather be in Black's shoes than White's.

Police Review July 26, 1957.

Exploiting the Blind

If you want to make a house-to-house collection in aid of your own summer holiday, your application for a licence to do so, under the House-to-House Collections Act, 1939, will probably be refused, though the right of the local authority, or the Police, or the Home Secretary, to refuse you the licence is far from clear. When one of these licensing authorities is faced with some specially impudent proposition, it seems that the lawful course is to grant the licence for one year and refuse it for the next on one of the grounds set out in Section 2 of the Act, all of which depend on the way you have carried out at least one collection, except the clause that would reject you as a man with a conviction for rape. The object of your collection must not be "begging," it is true; but it can be any kind of charitable purpose, "whether or not the purpose is charitable within the meaning of any rule of law." And you may be encouraged by the decision in *Pointon v. Hill*, 48 J.P. 342, that you are not begging if you are "seeking assistance under exceptional circumstances for a lawful object in an orderly manner."

These considerations may give some encouragement to the growing number of firms who are now marketing domestic articles at excessive prices by representing that the goods are made by blind people, or wrapped and packed by blind people. Mr. Collins, M.P. for Shoreditch and Finsbury, asked the Minister of Labour on 27th November whether,

> to protect the blind and prevent fraudulent trading on the sympathy of the public, he would introduce a regulation requiring that firms claiming to promote the interests of the blind, who were not already registered as charities or under the National Assistance Act, should be compelled to register, and that authority should be taken to grant or refuse registration.

It was a scandalous practice, said Mr. Collins, and was on the increase. "It is no longer confined to firms with registered trade names such as 'blind employment,' who masquerade as the real thing, but includes firms who, by trading on the natural sympathy of the public, charge 2s 6d. for an article that is not worth 2d. by printing on the envelope 'Packed by the blind.'"

The Registration of Business Names Act is one of the means by which the Minister of Labour can be kept informed about new firms with names that suggest the employment of disabled people, whether blind or sighted. The Parliamentary Secretary to the Ministry of Labour, Mr. Carr, agreed with the questioner that some of these activities harm the interests of *bona fide* organisations and of the blind themselves, and he thought it "most undesirable that by means of misleading representations public sympathy for the blind should be exploited." He was considering the problem, he said, and meanwhile much could be done by suitable publicity.

At the moment there is nothing criminal in what is being done. A firm with 1,000 employees, two of whom are blind, can lawfully say that if you buy its merchandise you are giving employment to blind persons. How much, on the strength of this, could it put up the price before it was actually obtaining some of the money by false pretences? It is the impossibility of deciding this that suggests the parallel with the pre-1939 racket in house-to-house collections, especially with those that collected "waste materials" from door to door and then sold them "in aid of the hospitals." It was found that the hospitals were in some cases getting about 2 per cent. of the proceeds.

Police Review December 13, 1957.

The Twenty-five Books of M. Girodias

In fulfilment of the British Government's obligations under a United Nations convention, the Home Office periodically notifies other governments about books in the English language which are considered to be obscene. There is a special urgency about this information in the case of obscene books which are printed abroad in English and obviously destined for export to England, usually in the suitcases of returning English tourists. Some such books are done up in effective disguises, *Lady Chatterley's Lover*, for example, sometimes having the covers of a cookery book or a catalogue of foreign stamps. Customs Preventive Officers accordingly look with special interest at cookery books and the like, and the smugglers' resources are nearing exhaustion. A recent development suggests that they may now be encouraged to seek new methods.

One French publisher who goes in for some "daring" and experimental literature, and prints it in English for the delectation of Britons either living in or visiting France, is M. Girodias, proprietor of the Olympia Press. His firm has produced some fine and notable books, and it would be wrong to say that its main business is in erotica or pornography, in whatever language. But thirteen months ago the Ministry of the Interior (i.e., the French Home Office) placed a ban on twenty-five books on the Olympia Press list, acting under a law of 1881 that forbids the sale or importation of "literature likely to harm the State and public welfare."

Now in France they have a special branch of law called the *Droit Administratif*. It enables a French citizen to challenge the actions of officialdom and often to get them over-ruled. M. Girodias availed himself of this. He took the matter of his twenty-five books before the Administrative Court in Paris on 16th January, and there argued that in the past the Police had actually brought prosecutions in respect of some of the twenty-five books—and had failed. Some of them were on sale in Britain and America, he said, and "English-language pornography is hardly likely to do much harm to public welfare in France." The Administrative Court agreed with him, and over-ruled the Ministry of the Interior. So if our Home Office is still unfavourably disposed to the twenty-five books of M. Girodias, there may now be an era of special vigilance in the cold, draughty, and curiously non-erotic barns that in this country we call Customs sheds.

There has been a similar setback for official opinion in America, where the obscenity laws vary from State to State and it is only when the Customs or Postal authorities are involved that you get a Federal view of the matter. This has happened in the case of a large collection of erotica that had been impounded by the U.S.A. Customs at New York docks. It is now on its way to the Sex Research Institute of Indiana University, which was founded by that famous investigator of human frailty, Dr. Alfred Kinsey. It was a collection that had been accumulating for seven years, as the U.S.A. Customs officials rummaged, unearthed, whistled, and confiscated. In this country it would have been burned, but perhaps in America there are a lot more people who must examine it and approve its confiscation, and much more protracted lawsuits about it.

The social science students of Indiana University asked the Government if they could have it for research purposes. No, said the Government, it's too bad even for that; and anyway we know in advance what you would purport to find out by research—that people buy pornographic stuff because they like it. When at last the Government were about to destroy it all, the University opposed their intention in Court, and the Judge held that the Sex Research Institute had "a genuine scientific purpose" in wanting it. A recent decision of the U.S. Supreme Court says that obscenity means anything whose "dominant theme appeals to the prurient interest of the average person, applying contemporary community standards"; which got rid of the idea that adult literature must be judged on what it might do to children. In the present case the Judge could not doubt that all the material seized was thoroughly obscene even by that definition, "but it is not going to be seen,' he said, "by the average person." So the students are to have it. May they make far-reaching discoveries about contemporary standards of prurient interest. But will the U.S. Customs authorities burn this new Kinsey Report, or will it be allowed to go to some other University, so that the students of the second can tabulate the prurient reactions of the first?

Police Review January 24, 1958.

The Law of the Sabbath

To say that a thing is too easy is really to say that the doing of it does no one any good. It is too easy to make fun of the Lord's Day Observance Society.

We have in this country many laws that are outmoded, obsolete, anachronistic, and infuriating. Most of these are left to lie fallow and do no harm; not a good principle, because some ass can always resuscitate one when he discovers it and start a prosecution in order to be different. But this is the way in which obsolete laws get repealed—a sudden new series of prosecutions calls attention to their existence and Parliament administers the *coup de grâce*. Now it might be thought, to judge from the indignation commonly expressed about the absurdity of the Sunday Observance Acts, that these would be repealed almost any day and the stage set for the kind of Sunday we all want. They are always in the news, mainly through the activities of the Lord's Day Observance Society; and amongst the latest news about them is the enforced decision of the Coventry Cathedral authorities to abandon their proposed Sunday ballet performance in the ruins of the building. They could have done it lawfully enough if they had gone on with their amended decision to make no charge for admittance, and rely on people sending donations afterwards; the Sadler's Wells Ballet Company were giving their services free. But they found that there was an unexpected volume of objections to Sunday performance of *Les Sylphides* in a cathedral, whether it was contrived to be done lawfully or not. So the project was dropped. Fun for the kill-joys, said many people.

But the Sunday Observance Acts go on and on. It is obviously because a significant number of people want them to do so. If Mr. Harold Legerton, the tireless and likeable general secretary of the Lord's Day Observance Society, were secretary of an anti-swearing league and went around reporting offenders under the Profane Oaths Act, 1745 (which belongs to the same legislative period), that Act would soon be repealed, because too many people swear and too few think it ought to be a criminal offence. The Home Secretary said in the House of Commons on 1st May that "Sunday observance is a matter of conscience on which public opinion appears deeply divided," and that he was not prepared at present to make any statement about Government policy in the matter. (Our guess is, however, that there will soon be an inquiry, possibly by a Royal Commission.)

Meanwhile two things must be said for the Lord's Day Observance Society. First, it is a highly efficient and active movement, doing its job fearlessly, cheerfully and well, whether or not you like it or its job. Secondly, it knows the kind of Sunday it wants; and this is more than can be said of its opponents, many of whom probably want Sunday to be in some way different from the rest of the week, and would create new anomalies in any Statute they could devise to establish the difference. For our part, we think that any new anomalies could hardly be worse than the old, and we should like to see Parliament trying.

Police Review May 9, 1958.

"Nude Theatre Clubs"

Paterson's Licensing Acts may not always be right (this statement is designed to shock people into reading on), but it has always been found to be safe enough on the law relating to clubs. It has a useful note on the probable meaning of the expressions "temporary member" and "honorary member" in Section 143 (2) (e) of the Licensing Act, 1953. But for that section, you might think that a person is either a member of a club or not a member. It requires the secretary of a club which wants to supply intoxicants (and therefore must be registered) to supply a return to the Clerk to the licensing Justices showing

> the rules of the club relating to the *election* of members, and the *admission* of temporary and honorary members and of guests.

The legislators must have seen some difference between "members," "temporary members," and "honorary members," and thought it necessary to know how they are elected (which is the full member's way of getting in) and admitted (which is the short-term way). But Section 144 (1) (g), which provides for the compulsory closing of clubs to which "persons are habitually admitted as members without an interval of at least forty-eight hours between nomination and admission," makes no such distinction. "This sub-section," says *Paterson* (1958 Edition, page 1033, note 1).

> uses the term "admission" and the word "members" without any qualifying description. It would seem, therefore, to apply to members of all kinds.

That is how it seems to us, too.

But this is not the way it is being interpreted by the growing number of "nude theatre clubs" in London. These are quite a new industry.

Nudes on the "legitimate" stage are required by London County Council regulations to stand quite still, no merciful exceptions being allowed for coping with flies or the sudden desire to sneeze. The nudes in the theatre clubs, because their employers feel that they have discovered the perfect formula of immunity, are said to hop around generously. The lawfulness of this beguiling mobility turns on the question whether the people who go to watch it are really "members" of the club.

Mr. Paul Raymond, who is the "owner" of a nude theatre club in Soho, was asked the other day by the *News Chronicle* what he thought of the news that the L.C.C. is to bring a test case against one of these clubs "on the ground that the practice of admitting persons to membership at the box-office is a breach of regulations." (Having explained that theatre clubs are "not subject to censorship," the *News Chronicle* added that members pay an annual subscription of ten shillings and an average of fifteen shillings for a seat.) Mr. Paul Raymond's view was this:

> My conscience is clear. I invested £125,000 in this club, so it's not likely that I'd risk breaking the law. It's true that we do admit patrons as *provisional members* on the payment of fifteen shillings at the box office. But forty-eight hours must elapse before they become full members.

Italics ours. "Provisional members" are yet another kind, not provided for anywhere. What are they? In our view they are "members," without modification; and if the "nude theatre club" to which they are admitted is a club that supplies intoxicants, they can't be members until forty-eight hours after someone already a member has nominated them. Can they be guests? No one seems to have thought, so far, of a way in which to prove that they are not "guests." But it is odd that the only way to stop "nude shows" should be to get them struck off under the Licensing Act. If this goes on, we may soon witness a fierce struggle between the shows and the drink, perhaps with a brief experimental period of "temperance nude shows." This would be brief because most people need the drink to sustain them during the show.

Police Review August 1, 1958.

"Whom, He Alleged . . ."

We had no intention of embarking on a grammar lesson this week (or any week, on this page), but it happens that the word "alleged," which is so popular in Police reports, and which ruins more English sentences than any other word except "who" and "whom," has come into the news by way of the Court of Appeal.

In *Cadam and Others v. Beaverbrook Newspapers Ltd.* (*The Times*, 30th January, 1959), a libel action which has not yet been tried, the point at issue is whether it is a libel to publish in a newspaper a report of the fact that someone has issued a writ against someone else alleging conspiracy. Lord Justice Hodson and Lord Justice Morris were asked to do no more, at this stage, than to say (and they did) that the *Daily Express* would be allowed to "plead justification," on the ground that the writ was in fact issued and the newspaper was merely reporting the truth when it said so. Whether that was a good defence would have to be decided, in due course, by the Judge who tried the case. The question was described by Counsel as "perhaps the best-known outstanding point of law in defamation that has never been decided—a point on which there is no real authority." Lord Justice Hodson asked Mr. Gerald Gardiner, Q.C., whether he thought that the word "alleged" carried any weight at all in a newspaper report. "I have always wondered why newspapers put it in," said his Lordship. To which Mr. Gardiner replied that "it might be thought to safeguard a newspaper from appearing to suggest that the charge was not contested."

This, indeed, seems its only purpose; but even then you have to use the word very carefully, and not resort to it in every case in which you have not inspected some actual proof. If you are writing of "Mr. Smith and his wife," for example, you do not, for lack of a chance to inspect their marriage certificate, refer to "Mr. Smith and his alleged wife." But you could do even this more safely in a Police report than in a newspaper report, for the one is so much more private and, in a sense, privileged than the other. The one Police context in which the word "alleged" has acquired a position from which no revolution will ever dislodge it is that in which

> Police Constable 123 David Jones reports that at 4 p.m., 5th February, 1959, he was requested by A. B. to obtain for him the name and address of C. D., *whom, he alleged*, had just assaulted him.

This grammatical howler is at least 120 years old in Police reports, as you can discover for yourself from old local records. It may be that, if we used the phrase "he said" instead of "he alleged," people would see that the preceding word should be who and not whom. Even the dullest "whomer" might jib at saying "whom, he said, had assaulted him."

All the phrases with "alleged" in them have long been Police clichés. There are many others. Frank Sullivan once listed a few:

> *Q*. What does an autopsy do? *A*. It reveals.
> *Q*. What do the Police suspect? *A*. Foul play.
> *Q*. What is there no sign of after crime? *A*. There is no sign of a weapon . . .

etc. But the Police are by no means alone in all this. There are some verbs in common use that are married to nouns beyond hope of separation. "Boggled" is one; its partner is "imagination." Nothing ever boggles now except the imagination, though horses used to do it a lot, and boggling was really invented by horses. There is, however, one cliché that we have seen often in Police reports, and the temptation to expose it has just won a sharp battle with the conscience that keeps on saying this is a Law Page. Why do so many people speak and write of going through documents "with a fine *tooth* comb"? Sometimes they even report that they have done it "with a tooth comb," as though there really were combs you could use on your teeth—dropping the pretence that the comb itself had the *fine* teeth that would miss nothing. The fine tooth comb is a daft metaphor. Out with it.

Police Review February 6, 1959.

Police Discretion

Not long ago a letter on the motoring page registered alarm at the way chief constables were using their "discretion" (i.e. picking and choosing victims) in the enforcement of the law. Its writer, without actually saying so, seemed to feel that every law in the good book should be either enforced or scrapped. He was concerned with what he called "the image of law enforcement in this country"; and it was "undemocratic and harmful" to this image that "a small group of high-ranking officials should have such wide powers to interpret, and in some cases to thwart completely, the wishes of Parliament."

It isn't consciously undemocratic. Often they don't know what the wishes of Parliament are.There are two views of this. The parliamentary draftsmen take one view as they lick into statutory shape the wishes haltingly expressed in private members' bills, or give effect to ministerial law-making intentions. The judges take another, even deciding sometimes that they know more about Parliament's intentions than Parliament does.

The truth is (luckily for us) that there's too much law to be enforced. On the day I read that letter I walked from Waterloo Station to Holborn, cocking a special (and once-practised) eye for violations of the Laws of England. I got the following bag:

A girl feeding the pigeons inside Waterloo Station.
Two cars with expired Excise licences.
Three cars with none at all.
Twenty-three cars parked wholly or partly on the footway.
One lorry with its lowered tailboard hiding the rear number plate while in motion.

A furniture van with its rear number chalked on the back.
One flag-day girl shaking a collecting box in people's faces.
One boy throwing a half-eaten egg sandwich into the roadway.
Three shop awnings that you had to duck under.
A cycling window cleaner carrying a ladder on his shoulders.
And a painter on a window-sill wearing no means of preventing a fall.

I would say it was a typical lot. And among the things too numerous to count were cars bearing advertising "stickers," vehicles waiting on double yellow lines, and disembarking bus passengers throwing their tickets away.

I've known policemen who would have hated to let any of these escape. They would all have been seen as personal affronts. But even a policeman like that couldn't have coped with more than one of them. If he chose the cycling man with the ladder, who was actually the most dangerous, all the rest would have got away. So perhaps he would have chosen the three shop blinds on the ground that they might have knocked his helmet off (they ought to be 8 feet from the ground).

But it has to be faced that the great majority of policemen would have chosen none of them. Which in itself would have been a choice. And the chief constable's "discretion" is merely the same choice writ large, with the difference that chief constables—who have no time to go around looking for car licences, number plates, flag-day offences, litter bugs, men on window-sills—don't exercise their choice until an offence is actually reported and the papers come before them.

Should they exercise any at all? That's a more practical question. We all know that they do. So does the Director of Public Prosecutions in the cases sent up to him. Letters of caution are sent, if the accusation seems well founded enough—you can't caution a man for not having committed an offence, or half committing it. Papers are marked "No action" or "Refer to DPP." Or sometimes the chief constable merely has to approve what a subordinate has already done in "refusing a charge": a station sergeant has a discretion about accepting or refusing charges that is sometimes called "quasi-magisterial." Where does that come from? What provision of the law or the Constitution gives it to him?

No one seems to know. Some legal authorities find that it has existed long enough (though it can't be more than 150 years) to have become part of the Common Law and the Constitution.

On this convenient basis, anyway, the police decided in April, 1966, that the 1963 Betting and Gaming Act was not going to be enforced against clubs unless there was cheating or a get-together of known criminals. This was a decision not to carry out the "wishes of Parliament," because—in this context—those wishes concerned unlawful games and had nothing to do with cheating. And the police decision was openly announced as being due to "the uncertainty of the law, and the expense and manpower involved in keeping gaming observations in the clubs."

The Gaming Act deadlock, of course, isn't confined to London or any one police district. It's different with Sunday dancing. At Torbay a new police superintendent has ordained, to the dismay of the locals, that there shall be no more "public dancing in clubs and hotels on Sundays, and no public drinking in clubs and hotels after 10.30 p.m. on Sundays." (He must have meant without special "supper hour certificates.") This debauchery had been going on for a long time, setting the law at naught. It still goes on in places like Bournemouth and Brighton, where the police exercise their discretion differently.

Torbay will have to grin and bear it until the police regime changes again, or Parliament changes the law for everyone, or the judges (given a chance somehow or other) find that the law has been wrongly interpreted.

They did this recently in a speeding case by invoking the magical formula *de minimis non curat lex.* Some roads are subject to a speed limit because they are "restricted roads," which means that they are lit by street lamps not more than 200 yards apart. (Dogs are not allowed to run loose on these roads, for reasons only tenuously related to the lamp posts.) One speeding defendant, finding that his lot of lamps were a few feet more than the 200 yards apart, appealed against his conviction. A year or two ago he would have been bound to win; and probably the AA would then have taken up the convictions of a lot of previous victims and got them "pardoned." Not any more. The High Court held, in effect, that when Parliament said 200 yards it meant 200 and a bit. "Discretion" was working, for once, against the individual and in favour of the law.

De minimis carries over into law the maid's extenuation of her illegitimate baby; but it doesn't always work. In the Court of Appeal the other day it failed a man who pleaded (a) that he didn't know there were any cannabis "scrapings" in his pocket, and (b) that they made up only a negligible quantity anyway. (A month earlier another appellant had succeeded on the grounds that the amount of heroin in a tube in his possession was "so small as to make the tube empty"; but the scrapings in this pocket could be measured in milligrammes.)

Parliament makes many laws on the tacit understanding that they will not on any account be enforced. This, when you come to think of it, must be a principle of the Constitution too. The House of Lords showed their eternal grasp of it when (to the joy of us all) they said Miss Stephanie Sweet had been wrongly convicted of "managing" a house in which, without her knowledge, her sub-tenants smoked pot. Their lordships said Parliament hadn't meant to do what it had done.

So we've come a long way since Junius. "In a State where discretion begins," he wrote, "law, liberty, and safety end." He wouldn't have said that today, when nearly everything not prohibited is compulsory —but for "police discretion."

New Statesman October 11, 1959.

Lolita

Never has there been such a *furore* about any book as the advance publicity for Vladimir Nabokov's novel *Lolita*, which accordingly sold 30,000 copies in its first week and may now be expected to outsell *Hall and Knight's Algebra*, though not for the same reasons. It has been reported widely, though no one knows on what authority, that when the publishers threw their publication-date party, which significantly took place at the Ritz, a message was received during the revelry that the Attorney-General had decided not to prosecute *Lolita*. (It had already been reported, a little less widely, that he had once sworn to prosecute if ever it appeared; and it may be remembered that it had already been successfully prosecuted twice, as an import, before it found a British publisher.) To prosecute it now would in fact be foolish. The new Obscene Publications Act would let in a flood of unimpeachable expert evidence that the book is a work of literary virtuosity (which, in our view, it is) to be set off against other evidence that it is a work of odious and cynical depravity (which, again, we think it is). There would probably be a slightly bewildered acquittal; and Britain would be laughed at wherever books are held to be important. Even if there were a conviction, no one would be a whit the better off, except the publishers, who, whatever the Court did to them, would be martyred beyond the dreams of avarice.

Police Review November 20, 1959.

Useless Jurors

"A case has just come to my notice," writes a correspondent, "in which an almost stone-deaf woman has just served on a jury for four days, and for two of those days she left her hearing-aid at home. On the day she left home without it, she stayed overnight with her sister-in-law and didn't go home again until the following evening. She was too shy to tell anyone at the Court that she was without her hearing-aid. Is this a matter that I ought to report to the Clerk of the Peace?"

It is better, probably, to report it to the Clerk than to be perpetually uncertain whether a duty has been discharged or neglected; but the removal of that uncertainty will be the only consequence, for there is absolutely nothing that the Clerk can do about it. Even if a defendant convicted by that jury got to know that one of his jurors had heard nothing of the trial, no appeal based on that discovery would, we think, be likely to succeed: the proviso in the Criminal Appeal Act, 1907, Section 4 (1), might well be thought sufficient to dispose of most such cases:

> Provided that the Court may, notwithstanding that they are of opinion that the point raised might be decided in favour of the appellant, dismiss the appeal if they consider that no substantial miscarriage of justice has actually occurred

and this may be coupled with the fact that Section 15 of the Criminal Justice Act, 1925, allows a jury to be reduced from twelve to ten "through illness *or for any other reason*," though it would be imperative, if this were to be specifically relied upon, that consent in writing should have been obtained from prosecution and defence.

The trend of judicial thinking about juries may be judged, too, from what Lord Justice Devlin said last month in a lecture at the University of Chicago. "There have been trials in Wales, and in the colonies," he said, "where jurors after the trial was over have deposed that they knew no English; yet they had been allowed to take the oath without objection." Presumably this must have happened in cases where the jury was sworn *en bloc*, so that the foreigner in its midst went undetected. But while it is fair to say that a person who will sit through a criminal trial without understanding a word and without, therefore, having any idea what his duties are supposed to be, must be sufficiently close to mental deficiency to make his non-participation vastly preferable to active membership, there must also be something wrong with everyone else on such a jury, to allow the farce to go on.

The truth is that we have absolutely no means of ensuring that any member of a jury is not a mental defective, a thief, a housebreaker, or a murderer. And whereas a Judge will usually excuse a juror in a capital murder trial if he gets up and says that he has a conscientious objection to the death penalty and that his judgement would be clouded thereby, a man who got up and said that he was a professional burglar would probably be told to sit down again. The jury, in fact, is so dear to us all as an imperishable heritage from the past that we must be careful not to think about it too much.

Police Review February 26, 1960.

National Scar

I had an uncle who had to be discouraged from showing reluctant acquaintances an operation scar across his abdomen. I believe people do this less now than they did, and that it is because the proportion of patients who do not have to be buried after their operations is now so large that a hospital scar confers little more status than an OBE. I remember appreciating that only a few people might want to see my uncle's scar, but in those days (and I knew this, too) it was almost unendurable to have one that you couldn't show. Every Edwardian novel had a character whose old wound was troubling him, though he usually got this in the Boer War or the Boxer Rebellion. I wanted one.

I've got it. The National Health Service have supplied it free, which is to say that I have paid hardly more than £400 for it in stamps over the past fourteen years. As wiser people would have known, now that it is here I take little real pride in it, but its acquisition has widened my experience, which was small, of nurses, surgeons, anaesthetists, hospital food, the things that can happen to the helpless, trusting, and simple, how very much the nursing sisters know and how much they have still to learn.

Take this last item first. There is a thing called pre-operation syncope. There is no treatment for it, no cure, not even diagnosis, and it was un-named until my own case occurred and I named it in order to be able to study it (no one can study a disease until it has a name: a less modest worker would have called it Rolph's Disease). One of its causes is being swung by two nurses, using a blanket as a hammock, from a bed on to a high trolley, dressed (I wonder why?) in someone else's pyjamas, thirty-five minutes before the surgeon arrives to do you. In that horizontal thirty-five minutes, bereft of a pillow and realising that corpses do not have pillows, screened from the vulgar and deserted by the nurses, I relived one life and laid some sketchy foundations for the next. Had I arranged everything? Would I be remembered? Beyond the grave, or urn, did one's atoms fuse with others to form unidentified flying objects, did one's mind take its seat somewhere among the eternal, universal consciousness, was there a long queue of the unborn, lengthening and muttering as the Family Planning Association tightened its grip? The current surgical stories passed through my mind ('That seems to be that, gentlemen, unless indeed there is some small thing I could do as an encore?'; 'Mr Anaesthetist, if the patient can manage to keep awake, it is surely not asking too much that you should do the same').

At last they came and wheeled me into a snow-white little power station occupied by the Ku Klux Klan in uniform. One gentle female voice which said 'Let me have your left arm, and just relax' was followed by another saying 'Your wife has been on the phone'. It was in the seven hours between those two remarks that I acquired the scar.

I had been told that a Health Service patient cannot hope to read or write in hospital. Readers and writers needed 'amenity beds'. But within a day I was sitting up and reading Frank O'Connor's study of the modern novel, *The Mirror in the Roadway*, and beginning to feel that this life, after all, was good enough for however long it might take to read whatever else this beguiling man has written. The next day I read Sir Stanley Unwin's unputdownable *Truth About a Publisher*, and as my comrades snored that night I lay reflecting on the many-sidedness of truth. The day after that I read Hugh Klare's remarkable *Anatomy of Prison* with an enjoyment sullied only by the jealous realisation that I couldn't have written it myself, and turned then to a treat long and deliberately deferred, Barbara Wootton's *Social Science and Social Pathology*, a monumental work (it should, I think, have come out in three separate volumes, for then it might have been tackled by some of the people whose education is such a desperate social necessity) which proves three things I earnestly wanted proved. First, that the concept of criminality as a 'thing in itself' is rooted in the righteousness of people ranging themselves on the side of the Establishment; secondly, that the 'maternal deprivation' hypothesis in criminology is due to a desire to see women 'back where they belong'; and thirdly, that the ordinary thief's attitude to the law is the same as the motorist's.

So a National Health patient in a general ward *can* read if he wants to badly enough. I admit that I was in a village hospital, that my ward contained only four beds, and that for most of the time my only companions were a schoolboy of thirteen and a retired coachman of 89 who has been bedridden for the past five years. The old man slept most of the time, and I kept the boy quiet at the material times by setting him sums, English, and 'general knowledge' papers on the basis that he got a penny for every point scored and paid me back a halfpenny for each error or omission. He got about 1s 6d a day, and I will concede that to this extent I did pay for an amenity ward.

Throughout an un-nursed life I've been sentimental about nurses, seeing them as angels of pity and comfort and always giving them my seat in trains. I think now that I have been right about most of them. But some are diminished by the enjoyment of bossy authority, some throw off a good deal of their kindness with their squeamishness, and some quarrel too openly and pettily in front of the patients, usually about infringements of territory. All of them have sycophantic convulsions when the doctors are around (which the doctors contemplate too placidly); and all of them are slaves to routine, which begins at 5.30 a.m. with a cup of tea. I can take a cup of tea at any hour of day or night, was always watching the door for its appearance at 5.30, and could have kissed the nurse who brought it (she got me a second cup sometimes); but why in God's name do they wake tired invalids at that hour to give it them, and keep on waking them up to drink it before it gets cold? Once the tea had come, you see, nothing further happened for an hour and a half. I think I shall try to bring to the forefront of my recollection, and keep it there, the extraordinary kindness of those nurses to me; for I know it was only solicitude that made one of them sit me up every time she rustled by, and that made another one lay me down, the first because of some post-anaesthesia state that could lead to pneumonia unless I sat up, the second because there was undue strain on the wound unless I lay down. Those two had me up and down like a jack-in-the-box while they were on duty together, but they are a pair of poppets and I would go on doing it now if I thought it would make them happy.

At 10.30 on the first Sunday there was a sobering event which, I suppose, happens only to National Health patients. The ward door opened and nine severely dressed, rather small people came in, the last two gravely carrying a harmonium. They arrange themselves in a semi-circle and sang a hymn I had never heard, going on for a long time. A homely, non-clerical man then prayed for our recovery, the government and the United Nations; there was more singing and a benediction; and then they all filed out, the harmonium going last. They were unannounced, and no-one said anything about them when they had gone. We were all a bit thoughful, I believe. The occurrence had a faintly prophetic flavour. 'Disease', wrote Samuel Johnson, 'generally begins that equality which death completes.' But we were all, at that stage, getting better, or thought we were. Now we felt a bit worse. They could hardly have been out of the building when I found myself reading a Great Thought attributed by one of the Sunday papers to Abraham Lincoln: 'Serving God is doing good to man, but praying is thought an easier service and therefore more generally chosen'.

Since I came out I have been reading that the Department of Nutrition of the London School of Hygiene, having done a pilot study of hospital meals in West Cornwall and found them seriously deficient in nutritive value, is starting a national survey on the same lines. The Cornish meals were unbalanced: a surfeit of poor quality food produced a 'calorific satiety' which had the result that half the meals were left on the plates. The meals described are remarkably similar to the ones I had: 'the customary three main meals – morning, midday, and evening – early morning tea, mid-morning drink, afternoon tea and bed-time drink'. The Report urges that 'hospital kitchens should be done away with and replaced by central kitchens, each of which could serve a large number of hospitals'. This kind of thing is well done nowadays, and the meals can be piping hot when you get them; but I am bound to record that all our plates in Ward II were spotless when they were taken from us, and that when I sent down to the chef an arrogant demand for Christmas pudding he came up himself, a very young man in a chef's hat and white coat, offered me a large piece (although it was mid-March), and wanted to know if he was to make brandy sauce.

I hope I have not conveyed the impression that I thoroughly enjoyed acquiring my scar, because (if the truth must be told) I did.

New Statesman May 14, 1960.

Fingerprints From All

I know a man who aggressively refuses to put either name or number on his cottage, because it was there centuries before its neighbours were built. It's thought that he accepts, in secret, the development that he is now No 8, but that he would go to prison in defiance of any law that made him say so.

It is such men we must think of if we are to plan a national fingerprint registry. We have a long tradition of tolerance for dissenters, and such men are its authors. Most of us obey the law's requirements that we send our children to school, license our dogs, put numbers on our motor cars, serve on juries. But most of us are sheep. Some people object, and because it would be a nuisance to compel them the law exempts them, usually in categories. When we had compulsory military service it exempted pacifists, and when we had compulsory vaccination against smallpox it exempted people like George Bernard Shaw. The pacifist had to declare and explain himself at a kind of mock trial, and the anti-vaccinationist had to go to a solicitor and say, with his finger on a little red wafer, that he was against having cow's blood squirted into him or his children.

The social advantages of a complete fingerprint registry are so obvious to me (I'll mention some in a moment) that I could easily forget the passionate resentment of those who would see it as an outrage on civil liberty. There are three good reasons why it wouldn't do for any legislation to forget this. First, taking fingerprints by force really would be an outrage, even if it were possible and legal. The only way to fingerprint a vigorous and determined man who keeps his fists clenched is to give him an injection and make him unconscious first. Neither the police nor the prison service would ever resort to this: the police because they have no power to do it, the prison service because, although they *do* have the power, they can afford, much better than the man with the clenched fists, to bide their time. Secondly, the prisons are already much too full with nonconformists of other kinds. Thirdly, the effect on the public of a few such incidents would probably sink the whole project. Physical compulsion is simply not on. Objectors would have to be exempted.

On what grounds? I suppose the objectors might find something in Magna Carta or the Bill of Rights that guards the sanctity of fingertips. They might claim, and even contrive to establish, a right to remain incognito that was somehow overlooked (for it certainly wasn't specifically suspended) when we were all made to carry identity cards. Crooks might object that a man is entitled to commit his crime *before* being fingerprinted. We are, in my view, lucky to have a National Council for Civil Liberties, ready to denounce the proposal as 'the first step towards a police state' although the first step seems to me to have been the Domesday Inquest of 1086. All these are relevant thoughts.

But first there would have to be a long programme of public instruction and preparation, designed to rescue fingerprinting from its exclusively criminal record and convince the objector that it would degrade him no more than the law that numbers his driving licence and compels him to sign it (have you signed yours?). Fingerprinting started innocently enough, as the means by which the native employees of the East India Company, not yet able to write their names, signed for their pay with thumbprints. This was better than putting a cross, because some of them liked drawing other men's pay as well as their own, and they did look rather alike to the sahib at the paytable. Soon enough the Indian Police Service was using the assembled prints as an aid to tracing offenders in villages where *everyone* looked alike and took trouble over it. And in 1901 Sir Edward Henry, appointed to Scotland Yard, brought the system with him.

If only it could have arrived under some such auspices as the Black Death, as a means of separating those who had had it from those who hadn't, it would have been accepted as tamely as the invaluable Births and Deaths Registration Act 1874. Then it would be easier to convince people that a national fingerprint registry would further the ends of social welfare.

Hundreds of 'missing persons' suffering from loss of memory would be quickly identified and restored to their families. Bodies found in the streets would no longer be buried, as they often are, in nameless graves which the relatives never hear of. Legatees, insurance and other beneficiaries, pensioners, long-lost claimants, bogus or otherwise, to disputed estates – all could be identified within hours. (The Tichborne case, the tragic story of Adolf Beck, the prolonged Druce-Portland farce could never have happened.) Every kind of fraud or deceit now effected by the forging of a signature, on cheques, receipts, promissory notes, post office savings bank books, agreements, disclaimers, manuscripts, paintings, would (or could) be almost eliminated: a thumb-print beside the signature, nearly impossible to fabricate, would often be more legible than the scrawled name itself. Checking and verifying would of course be computer-work, which is now in the course of development.

I have always felt that there would be opposition to such a proposal, but the feeling gains no support whatever from the people I ask personally. Most of them say they wouldn't mind, they would comply without fuss. Some of them say that only people under, say, 30 years of age should be done; old people ought to be exempted because the process might shock and distress them. This, again, is the criminality view, propitiating as it does the deeply held belief that fingerprinting should only be for wrongdoers and ignoring the value of fingerprints as a step forward in geriatrics. (On 17 November 1937, nearly 30 years ago, Mr Rupert de la Bère said in the House of Commons that there were 'over 9,000 such persons' – i.e. lost and aged people with their memories gone – 'in asylums, hospitals and other places in Britain.')

If it were proposed that the printing be done during childhood – the first week at school might be the best possible time – we should no doubt be invited by the less rational libertarians to see ourselves as a nation out-Heroding Herod. There is much propaganda work to be done, and it had better not be Scotland Yard propaganda – the immense gain to criminal investigation and the prevention of delinquency, self-evident to those paid to think about such things, would soon become evident to everyone in the reduced crime figures. Whoever organises the propaganda I hope that no one, while it is going on, will be heard to suggest a national paw-print register for lost dogs.

New Statesman May 20, 1960.

Rude Words

In his speech to the jury in the *Lady Chatterley* case. Mr. Gerald Gardiner, Q.C., assured them that, in acquitting the book on the grounds that its value to literature outweighed its use of improper words, they would *not* be extending any licence in the use of those words to "any scribbler who writes a novel." It was true enough. But it might be very difficult to persuade any jury, in the case of a book prosecuted *merely* for using those words, that their use would "tend to deprave and corrupt" anybody. Since they are all words that everyone has known from childhood, how can depravity and corruption follow from seeing them on paper?

This may be in the minds of Sir Charles Taylor, Mr. Stephen McAdden, and their Parliamentary colleagues in sponsoring the "Obscene and Profane Words Bill," which would clean up English literature (with a £100 penalty for each copy of each book containing a bad word) starting, it must be supposed, with the Bible and working its way through Chaucer, Defoe, Dryden, Swift, Donne, James Joyce and the chaps who keep on writing these great long novels about the war.

But if there is indeed too much swearing going on, and rude words have become a fresh menace to youth (or something), it can only be because the Police are neglecting the plain duty laid upon them by the Profane Oaths Act of 1745. This is a duty upon every Constable not only to *seize* and prosecute "any person who shall profanely curse or swear," but also to prosecute any other Constable he finds not seizing and prosecuting cursers and swearers: the whole Act was conceived in the dog-eating-dog tradition. The Constable who goes around not seizing these people is to forfeit forty shillings, "to be levied by distress." And, observes *Stone's Justices' Manual,* 1960 Edition, page

2399, if the Constable's worldly goods add up to less than the forty shillings, he is to get imprisonment regulated by the scale in the Magistrates' Courts Act, 1952.

This is a lot heavier than the fine for swearing itself, which is only five shillings for "every person of or above the degree of a gentleman." It is two shillings for people who are not gentlemen, except that in the case of a day labourer, or a common soldier or sailor (A.C.s had not then been invented), it is only a shilling.

Police Review December 9, 1960.

Hooligan Damage

The destructive urge seems a noxious form of insanity to anyone over the age of about 40, particularly when he is the owner of the thing destroyed and the damage is the work of that newly discovered sub-species of the human race, the teenagers. But most normal people have consciously wanted, in their youth if not later in life, to smash or rip things. The Malicious Damage Act is not a Mental Deficiency Act. The British Transport Commission will know how to deal with known "hooligan" passengers on its football trains: it has an efficient and resourceful Police department, including plainclothes men who can travel with the hooligans and watch for the next outburst (mail-bag thieves may even find this a simple way of diverting the detectives' interest). But the B.T.C. is in one respect worse off than a cinema proprietor whose furniture and fittings are wantonly damaged: the B.T.C. cannot lawfully exclude all teenage patrons, as the cinema owner can. It can say, as one of its representatives did last week, that anyone found damaging its property will be put off the train ("If they're not fit to ride they can walk") *and* prosecuted into the bargain. But it can't say, as the cinema can, "You shall not come in here if I don't like the look of you, i.e., if you have sideboards meeting under the chin, or pointed shoes, or if you are chewing slowly with your mouth open."

There was a time when the cinema could have hired a few off-duty Constables to sit among the teenagers and watch them, but this practice seems long to have been frowned upon. A letter in the *Daily Herald* of 6th April, having observed that "a few hooligans get swelled heads because they go unpunished," added that "any town bothered by them should recruit a volunteer force of commando Constables to haul them before the Magistrates—if they used their powers the problem would be solved." But the hooligan heads might be even bigger.

Police Review April 14, 1961.

The Guilty Traveller

A few weeks ago a man (who shall be nameless though there is no harm in saying that he lives at Guildford) went to Cambridge on business and stayed one night. He bought a first-class return ticket taking him through from Guildford to Cambridge. Being one of those men who cannot sleep in hotel bedrooms, he was a tired man on the return journey to King's Cross next day and he slumbered soundly in his corner seat. A ticket inspector gently woke him and asked him for his ticket. After some sleepy fumbling he produced it and then settled down again. At King's Cross there was an open platform and he was therefore under no necessity to find his return half ticket again. It was not until he reached Waterloo to entrain for Guildford that it occurred to him that the train "jumper" had kept the half ticket when he produced it on the Cambridge line. He held a season ticket from Waterloo to Guildford, but it was 12 days out of date. (He had not been using it.) Should he go to the Waterloo booking office and buy a single ticket to Guildford? He did not. Boldly he walked through the barrier, displayed his out-of-date "season," and settled down to sleep again in the waiting Guildford train, though this time the sleep was slightly fretful and troubled, "I've paid the fare, haven't I?" he muttered to himself. "They've got the money?" He slept.

At Woking another ticket inspector got on the train. Again the man had to be woken up. Sweating slightly, he got his coat down from the rack where it was buried under other people's luggage, found his season ticket, and boldly displayed it. "Thank you very much, sir," said the inspector, and passed on. Sleep being now out of the question, the quasicriminal braced himself for the final ordeal at Guildford. Putting on what he hoped was a nonchalant air, he hurried through the barrier overdoing the nonchalance to such effect that he dropped the season ticket as he was returning it to his coat pocket. The collector picked it up and handed it to the wrong man, who disowned it. This brought it under scrutiny. All was lost. "Could I have your name and address, sir please?" "No. You can have the money; here it is." "I'm sorry, sir, I must have your name and address." He got home and recounted the agonising story to his wife. "What am I to do? It will ruin me. Won't the newspapers lap it up?" "But why didn't you get another ticket at Waterloo and reclaim the money?" "Didn't want to miss this train." "Where do you put return half tickets while you're travelling?" "I've got a small ticket pocket in here," said the unhappy man, and pointed to the side pocket of his jacket. "They never get lost in there, or mixed up with anything else." He put his fingers into the ticket pocket, stopped talking, and slowly turned crimson. "Well?" said the wife. Incredulously he pulled out the return half ticket from Cambridge to Guildford. "They never took it from me after all," he whispered. "I was half asleep. I didn't know he gave it back to me."

What offence had he committed? No prizes are offered for the answer, though any reasonable prize would have been offered for a solution at Guildford station.

Police Review May 26, 1961.

See a Solicitor

People understand well enough when they should see a doctor, a dentist, or even perhaps a surveyor or an accountant or a bookmaker. But a solicitor is, to many people, a man to keep away from until things have gone almost irretrievably wrong: they subscribe to Coleridge's view of the lawyer—

He saw a lawyer killing a viper
On a dunghill near his own stable;
And the Devil smiled, for it put him in mind
Of Cain and his brother, Abel.

Not even Police officers are always properly aware of what a solicitor can do for a person in trouble; and although it is a very recent innovation it is already largely forgotten that free legal *advice*, as distinct from legal aid, is now available under the legal Aid and Advice Act—a person on National Assistance is entitled to an hour and thirty minutes' consultation, free of charge, with any solicitor on the Legal Advice Panel, and anyone else can have it for half a crown.

To bring home to ordinary people what a solicitor can do for them, the Law Society has authorised the publication of a Hodder & Stoughton half-crown paper-back called *The Services of a Solicitor* and written by Mr. H. J. B. Cockshutt. It is simply written, though in places it resorts to some rather pedestrian dialogue between imaginary characters (the clumsiest of these is between two solicitors talking shop over a meal); and it deals with house purchase, hire purchase, belonging to committees, letting your wife drive the car (or being allowed to drive hers), making your will, and a dozen other everyday problems. It even tells you how to *find* a solicitor, which an astonishing number of people don't know.

Police Review June 9, 1961.

TV Crime and Cops

The Home Secretary's proposal for an inquiry into the effects of television on the young has had a warm welcome, except among the young. The B.B.C.'s portrayal of Bill Sikes's murder of Nancy in *Oliver Twist,* described by the Postmaster-General as "brutal and inexcusable," was probably watched by millions of children who have seen death in all its forms on the small screen in the past few years—and, in our belief, are totally impervious to it. We know of three children who, after the murder of Nancy, were mainly concerned to establish (by fierce argument) whether the liquid on the floor was Nancy's blood or the water spilled from a jug by Bill Sikes in washing his hands after the job was finished. But people of our age (and even the Postmaster-General's) have forgotten the imperviousness of children to stories of blood and sudden death, even though we ourselves were brought up on Grimm and Andersen and the chances of being turned into frogs, statues, beetles or toads and of being roasted in a witch's oven or swallowed whole by a wolf wearing a night-cap, or of decapitation. Children are more adversely affected by stories of injustice than by stories of death: they remember the witch's death in *The Tinder Box* not because the old lady was slain by a soldier, but because that soldier owed her such an enormous debt of gratitude and ought to have been heaping on her the treasure she had shown him how to find. But are we, for that reason, to stop them seeing stories of ingratitude, banishing *King Lear* from television until 11.30 p.m., the hour at which modern tots seem to rise, stretch their arms, and indicate to their parents that it is time for bed?

There may be a stronger case for examining the effect of television crime plays on adults, because of the way in which (George Dixon apart) the Police are presented in the role of seekers after guilty truth. This is something that ought to be keeping senior Police officers, Home Office experts and the Royal Commission awake at night. As the captive millions sit and absorb their televised versions of reality, they see Policemen behaving as though Magna Carta, the Bill of Rights, Habeas Corpus, the Judges' Rules and the National Council for Civil Liberties had never been heard of. Are they gradually coming to *accept* an image of Police brashness and perfidy, to say nothing of Police powers, that is totally different from reality? Chief Inspr. Maigret can do many things, because he is an officer of the French *Police Judiciaire,* that English Policemen can't do—and that even the local French Police can't do. He can require a houseful of people to stay indoors, and he can order a woman's husband to leave the room while she is interrogated. At least he *could*: the French criminal procedure has lately been much revised; French detectives have less freedom of action—and French crime is said to be going up "accordingly." But Maigret can still, in France, get away with the procedural equivalent of murder. So can the resourceful, poker-faced Lancastrians in *Z Cars*. And the television Cop is unfortunately about the only kind of Cop now seen by the ordinary citizen.

Police Review April 6, 1962.

Complaints about the Police

I have seen both sides of the current controversy about 'police and public'. I think I have occupied fixed positions on one side and the other for long enough to be able to move about without losing the outline of the problem; and this involves a process of reassessing and rearranging beliefs and scepticisms.

This is another way of saying that it leaves one perched on a very high fence. I know to some extent how well- or ill-founded are some of the allegations currently being made against the police. I know how ready some citizens are to make these complaints; how apt some police are to provoke them; how bad a business it is for a policeman to have a complaint recorded against him, true or false. I do believe that the complaints are growing in number at the present time, because Chief Constables' reports say they are; and I do understand that the right to complain about the police is as inherent in our system of democracy as the right to compain about the milk or about the bus service. I have lately been assured by a French lawyer that this aspect of democracy in England is a pathetic instance of self-delusion: he believes we put up with far more at the hands of our police than the French do, because we work off our resentment by way of 'questions in the House' and committees of inquiry and royal commissions, all of which (he says) are used as whitewashing devices, restoring comparative quiet until the next storm—but none of which ever leads to anything. We never really get anything changed, he says, because we accept the illusion of change for the reality. In one sense, at least, this Frenchman seems to me to be right, even if he is wrong about all the rest: policemen seem to me to be little different from what they were forty years ago.

For in 1921, when I went into the police service as a youth of nineteen, there had been the same difficulty as there is today about attracting recruits. The rates of pay had recently risen in the same spectacular way as happened a year ago, when the newspapers were talking about 'thousand-a-year constables'. But it still was not a popular calling; it did not attract the right men. The men I found myself serving with jokingly referred to themselves as a Fred Karno's Army. They were all shapes and sizes—by police standards, that is—mostly demobbed soldiers and sailors from the first world war, and many were rather wild and disposed to kick over the traces. Accordingly the sergeants, the back-bone of any police force, were 'giving them socks'. The discipline, in other words, was tough; and whereas it was not unduly difficult to get into the police, it was noticeably easy to get thrown out. For the next ten or twelve years the worsening condition of the labour market outside was a powerful incentive to good behaviour inside—and in fact in any 'safe', pensioned job. That, indeed, was the main difference between then and now: the men who did not like it then stayed on because they saw no alternative: whenever a man threw his hand in voluntarily, the rest of us used to whisper excitedly about him to each other, as if he were Captain Oates going out into the snow; while the men who do not like it now can always get another job, nearly always at better pay.

Even so, this is a temporary difference, and one that has cropped up over and over again. In terms of popularity with the public, a more significant comparison might be drawn between the police at any time in the past forty years and the police at the time of Sir Robert Peel's men in the eighteen-thirties. In Peel's time they patrolled in pairs because they dared not go about alone; they often fought for their lives, they were hated and dreaded, and anointed from the windows of upper floors as they passed by below. In May 1833, when they tried to break up a meeting of the National Union of the Working Classes near Grays Inn Road in London, a policeman was stabbed to death. The coroner's jury insisted on calling this justifiable homicide—though the coroner had argued with them for two hours: and their verdict was greeted, by the working classes throughout the country, with passionate approval.

Almost certainly there was more serious crime in those days as compared with today, but there were relatively few minor lawbreakers. There was less than half the population, and a mere fraction of the number of laws waiting to be broken. But the interesting thing about a comparison between these nineteen-sixties and the 'hungry forties' of the last century is to be found in the reasons for the many idle hands for which the Devil has found work in both periods. Then, young men were idle because there was simply nothing for them to do, and no one seemed very much to care. Now, young men may be idle because they do a forty-hour week and have not solved the problem of leisure. But if young men are not nowadays driven into crime by the same urges, they may be eased into it by the same vacuity of mind. It is always important to recognize that only a tiny proportion do in fact resort to crime, but when a street-corner group is moved on by a policeman as a kind of precautionary measure, whether or not it is a lawful action, there are two ways of doing it; and one of them asks for trouble. And even though I be the millionth man to say it, the growing mass of statutory prohibitions and penalties, particularly about the use of road vehicles, makes potential delinquents of us all.

It is this as much as anything that makes it easy for anyone who has served in the police force and left it, to see both sides of the police-and-public question—and to see why it is that the very phrase 'police and public', instead of connoting a partnership, describes an antagonism. I would shrink from pretending to any olympian standard of judgment about anything, but I do find it astonishing that the critics of the police—I meet many of them nowadays—are reluctant to listen to one word in their favour, and equally astonishing that the police, the local authorities, and the government are so determined to make no admissions or as few admissions as possible against them.

Behind the scenes there is little evidence of this reluctance to believe complaints from the public. The Police Federation of England and Wales—the rank-and-file staff association—has told the Royal Commission recently that the present system of investigating complaints is 'satisfactory', and that the public too would be satisfied about it if it knew how thoroughly complaints are investigated. I wish the public *could* know this. The unhappiest memory I have of the police service is of the beaver-like industry with which, in many cases, a policeman's superior officers will compile a dossier against him when a complaint comes in. I have sometimes felt sick at heart to see it going on, though it never happened to me; and I have longed to be able to tear all the papers up, with their pompous minutes and sanctimonious condemnations, and tell everyone not to be such solemn fools. I believe it is better now than it was. But no policeman who has once had a compaint recorded against him, whether it was established or refuted, is ever in quite the same position again. So, unlike the Police Federation, I *would* like to see the more serious complaints (at least) investigated by some independent tribunal.

What are the complaints usually about? Officiousness (these usually come from motorists, some of them being justified and some over-hasty); violence; and misuse of authority. I suppose most of us recognize that government in a civilized state, although it rests upon the consent of the many, rests also, in extreme necessity, upon the infliction of violence on the few. Suppose that, experimentally, you decide to defy the law in some small matter, just to see what would be the outcome of resolute 'civil disobedience'. Suppose you decide to refuse payment of a threepenny bus-fare, and you stick it out, through all the to-ing and fro-ing at the court, until at long last—and it does take a considerable time—the police come to take you to prison for non-payment of your fare and your fine. Perhaps you barricade yourself in your house (after all, people sometimes do this, knowing all the time that they cannot really win). If you do, the police will let the matter drift for a day or two—perhaps even a week or a month or two—in the hope of meeting you out of doors when you get hungry. But eventually, if there is no other way, they will break down your door and take you to prison; and on the way there the harder you fight the less gentle will they be. Violence, that is to say, lies at the far end of every road on the criminal map, though some of the roads are far longer than others; and it is a tribute to the universal common sense that the violent end is so seldom reached.

Then, misuse of authority: that is the product of inadequate or inexact prescription. The Common Law was always precise enough about what a policeman could do in the way of arresting people and searching houses. But among the hundreds of acts of parliament that now fall to the police for enforcement, there is little mention of method or specific powers. The result is that the policeman, left to fill in the gaps in practice, extemporizes. And he gets so used to doing it, without ill-consequences to himself, that he loses sight of whatever restrictions there may be. It is very convenient for the authorities to leave the constable in the dark about the true extent of his powers, because whether he is resourceful, or persuasive, or just bull-necked, he will somehow or other get over the difficulty on his own; and if he thus runs into some troublesome and litigious character who gets damages against him for wrongful arrest, the taxpayer will pay the damages. Put rather baldly, that is the system. And although in general I am against written constitutions and over-careful rules and regulations, in this one instance the system seems to me unfair and rather cowardly. It is unfair to the citizen, because no man can possibly know how far the police can go, up to what point he can lawfully withstand them; unfair to the policeman, because it gives him the rather degrading status of a professional scapegoat.

I wonder sometimes whether it is thought that to prescribe police duties too exactly would be to inhibit valuable initiative among policemen? Is it supposed that a really complete manual of police instruction, if such a thing could be compiled, would have all the policemen working to rule? A glance at some of the local police instruction books, compiled in the cities and counties themselves, would dispel any such belief. Some of them are vast and flatulent works, approaching precision of language only about the things that do not matter; prescribing, for example, almost the geometrical angles at which a policeman shall put down his feet when walking. I ought to know: I wrote one of them, the closest approach to anything truly comic that I have ever done. Hardly any notice is ever taken of them. The policeman of today is not the product of written prescription: he is the product of slow centuries of experimental development, and thus he will go on. He ought to be supplied with a code of instruction about civil liberties and police powers; but first, a select committee or a royal commission would have to find out what kind of things he had been doing and whether they were desirable or not, and parliament would then have to enact accordingly.

Against that background, the proposition I began with falls into perspective: the proposition that the men and women we call the police are not much different from what they were forty years ago. If they were then more reliable in the sense that they stuck to their job for twenty-five years or more, that may well have been because there were no other jobs to stick to. Complaints against them are about as frequent now as they were then, tending to multiply under the influence of publicity and resulting in some kind of committee of inquiry about every five years, and a royal commission about every twenty or thirty. In this country there is no shortage of libertarian watch-dogs, but not many are bulldogs: they do not hang on for long; they bark for a while and then they go sulkily away, munching a White Paper. Life is so busy.

So long as this goes on, nothing much will change. I will go so far as to prophesy that in fifty years' time there will still be men in the police service who should not be there, still men in the priesthood who should not be there and still men in prison who should not be there. The best we can possibly do is to keep all these to an absolute minimum.

The Listener May 24, 1962.

The Tablets of the Law

Most people would suppose, if you asked them, that 'proceedings in the law courts' are all taken down in shorthand. It would only be when you began to particularize about 'proceedings' and 'law courts' that they would concede that there must be selection. There is unlikely, for instance, to be much demand for full details about Mr Jones's 67th horizontal drunkenness or the insulting words directed across the street (to the peril of the Queen's peace) by Mrs O'Grady to Miss Rafferty. But jury trials, at least, always seem to require the presence of a busy shorthand writer, and the judge himself does a fair amount of writing while the evidence is being taken, garrulous witnesses being directed by counsel to 'watch My Lord's pen'. It seems a reasonable supposition, therefore, that a full record exists of every trial of any importance. The supposition is quite wrong.

Take criminal trials first. 'Shorthand notes *shall* be taken,' says the Criminal Appeal Act, 1907, 'of the proceedings at the trial of any person on indictment who, if convicted, is entitled or may be authorized to appeal', nearly everyone is 'entitled, or may be authorized', to appeal on one ground or another. And when a statute says 'shall', there is usually a rocket for someone in the event of non-compliance. Here, however, there is no penal sanction. The appeal judges 'will proceed on the material available', including the barristers' speeches at the trial *(R.* v. *Rutter,* 1908), though there will be no record of the speeches unless someone has asked for them and agreed to pay. The absence of a shorthand note will not invalidate the trial. But the fact that the judges 'may be placed in a position of great difficulty through the absence of a transcript' is recorded in the law-books (*R.* v. *Moran,* 1910) more in sorrow than in anger. Similarly, said the Court of Criminal Appeal in *R.* v. *Rimes* (1912), it is of great importance that the utmost care be taken by shorthand-writers in order to ensure that the notes and transcripts shall be as perfect as possible'.

And although the utmost care is taken, perfection is still a long way off. The 'official' shorthand-writers are in fact employees of profit-making undertakings, no doubt because as civil servants they would be difficult to sack for negligence or inaccuracy. But they are a wonderfully efficient and unflappable body of men and women, a source of astonishment to anybody who knows what their duties entail. I know one at the Old Bailey whose shorthand, even at the end of the most hectic days, looks as though lithographed for learners. No counsel appearing there has ever spoken too quickly for him: The quickest in recent years, I suppose, was the late W. A. Fearnley-Whittingstall QC, but even when that explosive advocate's words were coming too fast for normal comprehension, this man would have time to look up and wink as you came in at the court door.

Now that I have been obliged, in the course of compiling books about recent prominent trials, to study some voluminous typewritten transcripts from these shorthand-writers' notes, my confidence in them is diminished. I realize that for more than 50 years, since, that is to say, the mandatory requirements of the Criminal Appeal Act, 1907, we have been asking these men to do what is quite impossible, treating them as infallible machines, accepting their shorthand as a recording method that cannot err. But some of the witnesses, for example, in *Regina* v. *Penguin Books* (1960) were distressed after the publication of *The Trial of Lady Chatterley* to find themselves represented as saying what they were quite certain they had never said. Those of them who looked up the 'official transcript' (typewritten from the shorthand note) agreed that it supported the published version but insisted that it was wrong. In other instances, having been present throughout the trial, I *knew* the transcript was wrong, obviously because of mishearing, and had altered it accordingly.

A man's freedom, possibly I suppose his life, might depend on this. There are reassuring indications that the Court of Criminal Appeal, faced with a conflict between an appellant's story and the official record of his trial, will give preference to the shorthand writer's version when it favours the appellant. Last year, for example, a man appealed against conviction on the ground that, although he had pleaded 'not guilty', he had had no trial. (The record said that he had pleaded guilty.) The Registrar of the Court of Criminal Appeal, thinking this rather odd, found out that everyone else in the case was satisfied that the man had pleaded guilty – trial judge, counsel on both sides, court officials, etc. The Lord Chief Justice sent for the original shorthand note. This said: '*Q*. How say you, are you guilty or not guilty? *A*. Not guilty'. (The shorthand sign for 'not' *could* be mistaken for a quotation mark.)

The doubt was enough, said the Lord Chief Justice: the man's appeal was allowed. This may be a chance in a thousand, but there could be no neater illustration of the importance attached to the shorthand note. As to completeness, the shorthand note even in a criminal case (other than murder) does not include counsels' speeches unless some specially interested party is paying for them. It includes all the evidence, submissions by counsel on points of law, the judge's rulings on them, the summing-up, the verdict, evidence of character, and sentence.

How do you set about getting a copy of a transcript? In a criminal case, the firm employing the shorthand writers will sell you (at a price fixed by the Treasury, which at present runs at 1s. 6d. per folio of 72 words) a copy of the transcript, but only if you are 'a party interested', a status now given a more elastic meaning than it had a few years ago, but still in each case requiring certification by a judge. In a civil case, by odd and inexplicable contrast, anyone can have a copy of any transcript (except of proceedings before a judge in chambers) and obtain it direct from the firm responsible, without the aid or approval of a judge or anyone else – if he can afford it. The full daily transcript of a High Court hearing might cost 50 guineas a day. When I wanted a full transcript of the ETU trial, which had lasted 40 days, the question whether I could afford a transcript thus presented a difficulty. But by a miracle of good luck I was able to borrow a copy from one of the lawyers in the case (it filled two suitcases).

This seems to me an odd system. Solicitors receive enormous bills for the transcripts of trials, passing them on, of course, to their clients. Even subsequent copies of a transcript, required, say, for an appeal, are little cheaper than the first one supplied, although they are presumably run off on a duplicating machine from a long-lasting stencil. I can appreciate that 'outsiders' ought to pay something for a copy, but why should the litigants have to pay? They don't have to pay the salaries of the judge or the court officials, or the expenses of the jury.

This quiet little corner of the shorthand-typing industry may or may not be a comfortable monopoly that wants looking into; but is shorthand-typing still the best method available, now that the tape-recording of speech has been brought to such perfection? If the evidence of witnesses were today being chipped out on stone with a mallet and chisel, the introduction of handwriting would now have to go through a long incubation period, fraught with suspicion and the fear of novelty: there's nothing like stone. At the beginning of this century the judges were saying that shorthand depositions (i.e. records of evidence given before magistrates) could not be allowed, but in 1949 a Departmental Committee on Depositions reported with approval on the practice of taking evidence in shorthand, transcribing it out of court and in due course reading the result back to the witnesses in open court. In 1960 the Clerk to the Nottingham Justices adopted a system of verbally transposing questions and answers into narrative form, speaking into a microphone so that everyone could hear him. His words are 'recorded on plastic belts, visible grooves being cut into the surface. The belts are then taken out of court, and the recording played back and typed'. This is then the deposition, and is read to the witness in open court.

Some frightening things can be done with the human voice on magnetic tape, by skilled manipulators intent on falsifying the record. It is not easy to see who would want to do this in court, but safeguards could be quite simply arranged. At least two machines would need to be running together, their tapes being changed at different moments. Tape recorders break down? So do shorthand writers, who also take afternoons off or decline to work through a late sitting. It is time for justice to drop the quill pen, take a look round and turn every modern resource to its own advantage.

New Statesman June 1, 1962.

No Room Anywhere

It was inevitable that the adventures of P.C. Thomas Rintoul, of the Stirling and Clackmannan Police, should attract widespread attention in the Press. It was intended that they should, in order to call attention to the frequently heartless treatment of the down-and-out in London. As an 18-year-old Police Cadet he played the part of a homeless wanderer in London—it was part of an "initiative test" in which he was allowed to participate by his Chief Constable. He visited hostels, "reception centres," and railway waiting rooms, he slept on park and embankment benches, and he well and truly encountered:

> the insolence of office, and the spurns that patient merit of the unworthy takes.

"Call me Sir," they snapped at him at the hostel inquiry pigeon-holes, and he was sharply informed that there was no need for him to speak in his native Glasgow accent. In a one-and-sixpenny (post free) pamphlet called *Room?* and published by the Voluntary Hostels Conference, The Tower Room, St. Botolph's Church, Aldgate, London, E.C.3, P.C. Rintoul presents a perfectly factual, dead-pan account of four weeks' misery in wonderful London—a Police report, pure and simple, with barely a subjective note from beginning to end. It's the most scarifying account to have been published for years about the treatment of the poor by the only-just-not-so-poor who happen to have a little authority. Four such weeks would be good initial training for every Policeman. Judges and Magistrates would be the better for it, too; and it might work a wondrous change in the attitude of pawnbroker's assistants, hostel attendants, and all those who have forgotten the meaning of "There, but for the grace of God. . . ."

Police Review December 28, 1962.

The Nazi Insult

The Bow Street Magistrate had taken a rather different view from that of Mr. R. E. Seaton at London Sessions about the degree of insult in Colin Jordan's Trafalgar Square speech. "Hitler was right," Jordan had told a partly Jewish audience. "This country's real enemy is the Jew." We had fought on the wrong side in the war, he said, because we were the tools of the Jews. However much Jordan, off the public platform, may protest that he would not be in favour of putting millions to death in gas ovens, his public words can only be taken to mean, at least, that it was all right for Hitler to do it. And there aren't many people in this country who would not be stung to anger and loathing by such a statement. The Bow Street Magistrate thought that the speech of John Tyndall, Jordan's henchman, on the same occasion was rather less insulting than Jordan's, which was "about as bad as anyone could possibly imagine." Tyndall hadn't appeared to advocate mass murder; he merely said poetically that in our democratic society a Jew was "like a poisonous maggot feeding on a body in an advanced state of decay." So Jordan got two months and Tyndall six weeks.

When they appealed to London Sessions, the Chairman said that Tyndall's words were "much the more vitriolic" and upheld his conviction (though he reduced the sentence). Jordan, for some reason, he let off altogether.

Small wonder that the Police appealed. It has often been said that the question whether particular words are sufficiently insulting to justify a conviction under Section 5 of the Public Order Act, 1936, is a question of fact, not a question of law. And only a question of law can be taken on appeal from Magistrates' Courts (in Petty or Quarter Sessions) to the High Court. There is a way round this. A question of fact can be regarded and treated as a matter of interpretation, and then it suffers a kind of sea-change into a question of law. Apparently this was how the Police got Colin Jordan before the Divisional Court last week (*Jordan v. Burgoyne, The Times,* 20th March), where it fell to him to satisfy the Lord Chief Justice, with Ashworth and Winn, JJ., that the people who took umbrage at his remarks in Trafalgar Square were not "ordinary reasonable British people" but "obvious deliberate troublemakers." To sustain a conviction, he argued (conducting his own case with skill and obvious relish), the words used had to be "not merely highly insulting but also insulting to the reasonable citizen, who was provoked to violence."

The Act says nothing about provocation to violence; only that "a breach of the peace was likely to be occasioned." The question for the High Court was whether these words could be properly construed to mean "likely to lead to a breach of the peace by the ordinary citizen in the circumstances of the case."

"Having read the speech," said Lord Parker, "I cannot imagine any reasonable citizen, certainly not one who is a Jew, not being provoked beyond endurance. This applies not only to Jews but to coloured men and to quite a number of people in this country who were told that they were the tools of the Jews and had fought on the wrong side. . . . Even if it be assumed that the body of young persons around the speaker's platform were hooligans and intended to prevent him speaking, yet the Police prevented *them* from obstructing the speakers and the defendant then addressed them as 'the red rabble present here.' These words were deliberately intended to be insulting to the people who were being restrained by the Police. It is a clear case for conviction under Section 5. . . . The appeal will be allowed and the case will go back to the Quarter Sessions."

It is a case of great importance. The Public Order Act of 1936 comes back into its own, after a London Sessions decision that would have made it a dead letter. The Police are spectacularly cleared of the absurd charge, much heard during the troubled thirties, that they are reluctant to act against fascists and Jew-baiters. And with this new curb on Sabbath-afternoon rhetoric, there may even be a few more Sunday leaves this spring and summer.

Police Review March 29, 1963.

Laughter and the Law

The maniacal deeds of vandalism and destruction committed by gangs of youths and by football crowds in trains have revived the proposal that the parents of juvenile offenders be more often made to pay for the damage done by their offspring. The statutory power to do this already exists, and as the Deputy Chairman of Nottingham's City Juvenile Court pointed out in a *Times* letter on 13th December, many of the families thus concerned are on National Assistance and/or unemployment pay, and in any case the family is unlikely to be rich. "To impose a large debt on such a family has one almost certain consequence: the mother will take employment, and her unruly son, now subject to still less supervision, appears before us next time with four or five cases of breaking and entering." This, says the Deputy Chairman, is why Juvenile Court penalties are often so absurdly small.

There is one aspect of the problem that seldom receives attention—and is rather beyond the reach of the criminal law. This is the fact that nearly all vandalism is group crime: only a lunatic smashes up public property by himself, unless he is a man trying to get arrested. The group does it for enjoyment and laughter. Cruel though this laughter may be, all laughter is in some degree cruel. How about making group behaviour as important a school subject as maths, history, or (to bring it right home) biology?

Police Review December 20, 1963.

Trespass by Police

Intention may often be sufficient to get a man into trouble with the law, but it seems less potent as a means of getting him out of it. A doctor at Preston had every intention of signing a medical recommendation to the effect that Sir John Townley, of Bilsborough Hall, ought to be taken to a mental hospital "for observation." (Lady Townley had already signed the emergency application, under Section 29 of the Mental Health Act, 1959; and one doctor's recommendation would therefore have been enough.) The doctor went to Sir John's house and took the necessary form with him, but naturally enough he forbore to complete it until he had actually seen the patient. With him were two Policemen and Lady Townley's brother.

The doctor went in first and was told by Sir John to get out. "You have no right in here," said Sir John, "you need two doctors"—the first statement being correct and the second not. "I'm going to my bedroom," he added, "and you can get out." The four intruders followed him to his bedroom, where the doctor explained that he would have to go to hospital for a little while whether he wished to or not, and that he (the doctor) held an "emergency application" in his hand. The whole thing, retorted Sir John, was a put-up job, a conspiracy to get him out of the way. Then the doctor said he would have to give Sir John a sedative injection, and left the bedroom to prepare it. At this point Sir John said he wanted to telephone the Chief Constable and tried to leave the bedroom. One Constable between him and the door tried to restrain him, and the other Constable came across to help. Sir John thought the latter was going to hit him, decided to hit first, and broke the second Constable's nose. Then the doctor came back, administered the injection, and called an ambulance. Then, and not before, he filled in the recommendation about removal for observation.

The Garstang Justices later convicted Sir John Townley of assaulting the Constable and causing him actual bodily harm; and he appealed to the High Court on the "point of law" that since the doctor had not, at the time of the assault, completed his medical certificate, he and the Policemen were trespassers, and it was lawful to assault any of them when they refused to go.

"It is unfortunate," said the Lord Chief Justice, "because I am sure the doctor refrained from filling up the recommendation because he honestly wanted to see whether it was a proper case in which to make a recommendation. . . . There were four trespassers in the house without any lawful authority, whom the appellant was not prepared to eject forcibly, because he retired. . . . He was told that, while the injection was being prepared, he was not at liberty even to leave his bedroom, and he was forcibly restrained. Unless it is to be said that a householder is to sit down and submit not only to his liberty being infringed in the house but also to assault by injection, and to his liberty being removed, I cannot say," went on Lord Parker, "that to hit out at a person in such circumstances is an unreasonable use of force." So Sir John's appeal was allowed with costs (*Townley v. Rushworth, The Times,* 5th December, 1963).

Police Review January 3, 1964.

Who Owns the Gas-meter Money?

"When an entry is made in our Crime Book of a gas-meter break." writes a puzzled reader, "the offence is always shown as being against the Gas Board. People I know of have been arrested for breaking into their own meters. Now, after a recent programme on TV, it appears that the householder is responsible for paying the money back to the Gas Board. As we are often asked by the householder whom the money belongs to, perhaps you could clear up the point."

One up to TV. If more people knew that the phrase "breaking into *their own* meters" sadly misrepresents the situation they would stop breaking into them and there would be more room in the Crime Book. In the Gas Act 1948 (Schedule III, paragraph 38), it is made clear that all apparatus, "let for hire and marked with a sufficient mark indicating the *ownership* of an Area Gas Board" is the property of the Gas Board. Taking money from a gas-meter is therefore stealing from the Board—except, presumably, in the case of a man whose belief to the contrary is so strong as to amount to what the larceny Act calls "a claim of right made in good faith." Ignorance of the law (even of the Gas Act) can never be an excuse; but if a householder believed *very* strongly that the money in the meter was his (so long as he paid up "on the day") and that he was entitled to take it out and use it—well, the Court *might* call it a claim of right to get itself out of an embarrassment.

What always seems to us a little hard is that when a burglar gets into the house and empties the gas-meter, then the loser of the money is not (as you might think) the Gas Board, but the occupier of the premises. So far as his gas bill is concerned, it is as though the bill is still unpaid. On the other hand, when the occupier helps himself, the money is miraculously transformed into the property of the Gas Board and it is he who is the thief. Some people see this as a perfect example of the way in which the "little man" in the modern State is pushed around, but you have to remind yourself that the "little man" can't be *quite* such a pitiful victim as he wants to be thought, if he is resourceful and ingenious and (dare we say it?) delinquent enough to go forcing open the gas-meter. The answer to the many people who want to know who owns the money in the meter is that it is the Gas Board—unless the money is stolen by a third party. Then it is the householder. You can't win.

Police Review March 3, 1964.

Placards

I am old enough to remember when placards for the evening papers were wholly printed. They looked more compelling and startling than the hand-scrawled ones of today. BALDWIN CONFESSES, they said; ENGLAND COLLAPSE, and COUNTESS IN THE BOX. But they never had misprints, and you can see now that life was the duller for it. Today if I did a spectacular murder and put bits of the body in a dozen different parcels offices, the placards for a while would have a machine-printed ROLPH at the top, as they had CHRISTINE until we had all finished with her, and the latest developments about me would be scrawled below in charcoal. This is fame. But think what can happen when the key word has not been printed and everything is charcoal. A couple of weeks ago the police were looking for a man who might be able to help them find out why four dead women had been found without clothes on, and suddenly a placard said NUDE POLICE SEE MAN. What devilish thing were they up to now? One had seen Barlow with his collar undone, but where was it to stop? A public inquiry having established to the general satisfaction that the police must not beat people while talking to them, were we now to have selected groups of these endlessly resourceful strategists bursting naked into the interview room, hunching themselves silently round the victim, and grimly watching as he broke down and told all with his face covered? The Judges' Rules, so recently and so carefully made more unintelligible than ever, must go back to their lordships for an addendum on what parts of the interrogator should be concealed during the interview, and a direction that a careful record be kept of the period for which the suspect was subjected to the other parts.

New Statesman (London Diary) May 15, 1964.

Furtive, Shameful, Pleasurable

Seneca (the younger), who knew so much, had some baffling blind spots. Until he was sentenced to suicide he was Nero's tutor, and you can tell that he was an observant man. And yet "Why," asked Seneca, "is there no man who confesses his vices? It is because he has not yet laid them aside. It is a waking man who can tell his dreams."

Wrong, of course. Though I suppose it depends on what you mean by vices and confessing. Vices have to be pleasurable, since otherwise no man would want to have one and, if he did have it, there would be no virtue in his giving it up. And about confessing, some men used to tell of their vices on the rack, many still disclose them to priests, but Seneca, I fancy, was speaking of those who trumpet their vices unracked and without grill, who cry them aloud in market places, write about them in *Punch*.

My news is that the virtue of giving up vice can, with great care, be converted into a vice as furtively and shamefully pleasurable as any of the hopelessly addictive ones. Of the vices which I trumpet below, all except one may be little more than idiosyncrasies, but the exception is epoch-making. It is non-smoking. I will start with it.

A heavy smoker until two years ago, I have made a vice of non-smoking. This is not merely the one way in which it can be endured, it is a means by which it can be sensuously enjoyed. If you were formerly a pipe-smoker, you must carry two pouches and a pipe. You start each day with one pouch full and the other empty. Whenever you feel the urge to smoke, you fill the pipe, stick it in your mouth, take it out again and, by means of a matchstick, dig out the tobacco into the other pouch. The sight and scent of the tobacco will have given you all the nasal and salivary enjoyment you once had as a smoker, without the discouraging features that all pipe-smokers and their wives put up with—airtight dottle in the bowl, burned tongue, juice running up the stem, holes in trousers, raincoats, tablecloths, breath reeking like very old heavy machinery.

If you formerly smoked cigarettes or cigars, you throw one into the fire or out of the window at exactly the intervals at which you used to be stubbing them out. If you were a chain-smoker you count thirty-five between throws.This will work out dearer than it does for pipe people, but a cheap vice is not worth having. Besides, I am addressing myself mainly to pipe non-smokers: cigarette non-smokers must work out their own routine of sin. Perhaps I could just mention that some people throw their cigarettes into wastepaper baskets, retrieve them at the end of the day and arrange them in the box for the next morning.

All this comprises merely the mechanics of enjoyably vicious non-smoking, the stage-managing side, enabling you to go about among people as one who has renounced smoking, raising the palm of the hand against seducers who have not, but wish they could. On this basis a man can erect a new secret, second personality. He experiences a vast accretion of self-esteem. He observes smokers with compassion, travelling in their railway compartments to study them and make notes and little sketches. He avoids all controversy about smoking and health. He took up his new position voluntarily, neither frightened into it by medical reearch reports nor goaded into it by the tobacco companies' elaborate TV reassurances.

The truly vicious and ecstatic non-smoker goes around muttering anti-smoking epigrams which parody famous advertising slogans. Accordingly it is a vice that comes easiest to the man who has always habitually talked to himself. This happens to be another of my vices, though I now keep it under stricter control than I did three years ago. That was when I met an American security man who told me a very sinister thing. His department had developed to a high point of efficiency (he said) the technique of planting little tape recorders ("bugs") in people's offices and private rooms. Their purpose was always to record conversations between pairs and groups, but he said it was amazing how many soliloquies were recorded by these bugs, how revealing they sometimes were, and how frequently it occurred that what a man said to others was less important—even to the police—than what he said to himself.

Well, this is bound to have a constricting effect on the remarks that a man will now address to himself. Even where, having mislaid something essential, one would have said no more than "You ass! Why can't you be a bit more methodical?", one is scared now into silence by the implications this could have if it were taken to have been hissed at someone else.

Seneca would have said that those who talk audibly to themselves are the insane, who believe themselves to be continually accompanied, and the deaf, who cannot hear themselves and believe they are merely thinking. He would have been wrong again. The deaf are caught addressing themselves audibly because they can't hear people approaching. As you get older, this is something you have to watch. Special reasons for this are now given.

The auto-conversationalist reaches his peaks of eloquence when angry, the anger being usually directed against inanimate things. The brand image is the rather deaf elderly retired man, with a hammer. The older he grows, the more likely it becomes that he will hit his thumb and the more strident, abandoned and profane will be his observations. I know a retired banker of seventy who always begins mowing from the same corner of his lawn, and this corner is close to a tall hedge concealing him from the highway. When you hear him getting out his motor mower it is time to hurry round to the hedge and compose yourself to listen, for it is a kick-start mower which never starts up in less than fifteen minutes. Each successively futile kick is followed by a louder oath than the one before. You have to listen with a straight face, for if you start grinning you get a little crowd in no time, their crude laughter will bring his angry white head over the hedge, and the show will be over too early. I mention him because I too am a curser of inanimate things.

Unlike him, I am not content with crisp monosyllables. I apostrophise these things in actionable language and at some length. But only when alone: I am ashamed of it and wish not to be overheard. The shame, however, is detached and objective: I do not wish to give up the habit, because it is a solace and therefore enjoyable. It is, that is to say, a secret vice and it is among my favourites.

If I have so far had your indulgence, this is the moment at which I lose it. For my next favourite is the stealthy pinching of the top of the milk. I like "topper" on porridge and in coffee. I carefully conceal from the rest of the family the fact that I secretly misappropriate this uppermost inch of richer milk from the bottle; and they all know that I do it. The fact that it has gone is never visually obvious, for the milk below isn't all that different in colour. My wife often says she simply cannot understand why there are always two or three milk bottles in the fridge with an inch of milk gone, but she does understand really and so do the children. No one ever lets on. Every now and then I amalgamate the contents of bottles so that, although the metal-foil tops are missing, the milk comes right up to the rim. This way, I tell myself, the tits get the blame. Our local tits barely wait for the milkman to walk away before they are down on the bottles, burrowing through into our topper. The family are very good about this and the collective anger is turned generously upon the tits.

Our thoughtful milkman has lately been putting an anti-tit sheet of cardboard across the tops of the newly delivered bottles. This I have had to throw away.

You meet people who say that their favourite vice is reading in bed. Vice? Bishops do it. The only vice to which it gives rise, however, is one of mine—the ecstatically self-deceptive ten minutes, after the cat has been put out and the bolts are shot, spent in collecting the armful of books and papers which the collector knows will never be looked at because he will go straight to sleep. It is better, and it is also more depraved and self-indulgent, to mount the stairs with half a library than it is to read even the shortest chapter in bed. The pleasure of reading in bed is as nothing to the preparation for it. This is why I prolong the preparation to the exclusion of the event; and it is how not reading in bed can become an art as well as a vice.

Other vices of mine, though lesser, are more damaging to disclose with so many psychiatrists about; but I am emboldened by my own loquacity to reveal just one more. Buying coathangers by the dozen, at fairly regular intervals. Where do all the coathangers go? Manufacturers (they tell me) turn out hundreds of thousands a week. Shops sell them all. Householders use them while they are on their way to wherever it is they go. But there are never enough, some coats and dresses are always having to share. Why? All my life I have been buying them by the dozen, I have watched a thousand shop assistants trying to make neat parcels of them. When I see them on racks in Woolworths, it is only if I am on my way to the most solemn appointments that I can refrain from getting another dozen. Even if the leak is ever traced and plugged, so that coathangers at last pile up in the houses, there will remain the problem, my problem, of addiction.

All the preceding problems are vices of abstention. An abstainer, according to Ambrose Bierce, is a weak person who yields to the temptation of denying himself a pleasure. That is true vice, and jolly enjoyable it is.

Punch June 1, 1964.

Fitting Punishments

Long and dirty-looking hair may yet lead to a revival of interest in the "Bill of Rights." Is it one of the sacred rights of the Englishman to go around looking like a Rolling Stone? We confess to a belief that most people, taking on a new employee, would choose the one with the short hair cut rather than the one who looked like an engine-room Robinson Crusoe, but recent cases of discrimination against the unbarbered by Headmasters, trade unions, factory managers and (latterly) an Employment Exchange have culminated in a requirement that a Rolling Stone type must have his hair cut during a conditional binding-over. Will this become a condition of probation orders, along with undertakings not to smoke, drink, go with girls, watch football, frequent pubs or cinemas, play billiards or stay in England? A Scottish Court recently allowed a litter-bug to sweep the streets instead of paying a £10 fine for smashing a bottle of stout and leaving the glass where it lay. This may be a special Scottish custom, but there is much to commend it and we may be moving into an imaginative era of fitting punishments carefully to offenders.

Police Review September 18, 1964.

Obscenity defined

Lady Chatterley was not the first victim under the Obscene Publications Act, 1959. She was about the fifteenth, but the others had been girlie paperbacks that Lawrence himself would probably have burned. Some of them had attracted monstrous prison sentences for which the Court of Criminal Appeal had substituted fines.

No doubt the Chatterley case was a misfortune and gave the book millions of readers who will never see "Sons and Lovers," the poems, or the matchless short stories. But let us be fair to the Director of Public Prosecutions.

Here was a book that for 30 years had been a challenge to authority. Little booksellers had gone to prison for selling it, Customs men had impounded it, French shops had done it up in cookery-book jackets for home-going Anglo-Saxon tourists; and it was a set book in English universities. Now came an Act which allowed its defence on the grounds of literary merit, even sociological and ethical merit. And now came Penguins saying "We are going to publish this book on September 1." What would you have done, as DPP?

"Right," you would have said, "they've got their new Act, they've flung down the challenge, let them have their jamboree. No court has ever yet been able to hear what kind of book it was meant to be. I don't know. Now we'll get a decision, and it doesn't have to be mine."

The acquittal, which outdid in social impact the Seven Bishops and Somersett the Slave, induced a short-lived euphoria.

Under the law as it stands (as under the law which it replaced) two courses are now open to the police when someone complains about a book. (Contrary to the general belief, they spend little time *voluntarily* reading books and disapproving of them.) They can prosecute an author, publisher, printer, and bookseller for publishing, which means in any way making public a book which they think would, *taken as a whole,* "tend to corrupt" a reader "having regard to all relevant circumstances." This gives the defendants the right to be tried by jury, but exposes them to the risk of three years' imprisonment or whatever fine the Judge works out.

Or the police can go to a magistrate, as they did about "Fanny Hill," and get a warrant to seize all available copies of the book that worries them, together with copies of any other such book they then discover, so long as all of them are "being kept for publication for gain."

If they don't use this warrant within 14 days it will lapse. Before the 1959 Act they could take their time, and did. (They have taken as long as nine months.) And the warrant will admit them to the premises only once; they can't (as they used) make a series of raids. They therefore tend to turn up with a big van.

Now comes the first defect in the new Act. Having driven away with the books, they can go into purdah, and the Act has failed to say for how long. Again, this used to be months. The Society of Authors' original Bill, as drafted by Mr Norman St John Stevas, required the police to take the books to a magistrate "forthwith," the magistrate to report the facts to the Attorney-General "forthwith," and the Court to issue a summons within seven days of the Attorney-General's consent. It didn't similarly tie down the Attorney-General, because he can be called to account in Parliament.

The second snag appeared in the "Ladies' Directory" case. Only too well aware of what the Director of Public Prosecutions can do by means of common law "conspiracy" charges, the Society of Authors committee had got a clause into the Bill prohibiting prosecutions under the common law (the only previous machinery). Here now was the DPP prosecuting the "Ladies' Directory" man not only for publishing an obscene book but also for conspiring with his prostitute advertisers to "corrupt public morals." And the convictions were upheld by the House of Lords, with the eloquent and solitary dissent of Lord Reid.

The third snag could not raise its ugly head in the "Fanny Hill" case because this was merely an action against the book, not a prosecution against a person. It was an application to have Fanny adjudged obscene and ordered to be burned. Expert evidence was admissible to save her from the flames—and would have been equally admissible if the case had been a prosecution against publisher and author.

Also admissible, however, was the intervention of any publisher, printer, bookseller or distributor who felt that the imminent destruction order threatened his business interests. This could not happen if there were a prosecution.

If the DPP goes for my publisher while I am abroad, it is no one's job to write to tell me that my book is in trouble. Many an author has learned of his book's condemnation only when he has read it in the newspapers. If I did get to hear of it, and wrote to the DPP or the Court claiming the right to be heard in defence of my book, I should be told that as a nondefendant I had no such right.

When the Society of Authors tried to get such a right written into the Bill they were told by the Home Office and the law officers that it would be totally improper. You could not invite, or even allow, authors and others to put their heads into nooses like that. Our tradition against self-incrimination forbade it. Why, their interference might land them in prison. It was much better that their books should be condemned and their publishers fined or imprisoned in their absence.

In this sense, authors are better dead, but while they are alive their safest course is to be expensive and well known. When Tana de Gamez's novel "Like a River of Lions" was banned by some of the public libraries, her protest was brushed aside with the explanation that "Tropic of Cancer" and "Peyton Place" were allowed on the shelves because Henry Miller and Grace Metalious were renowned. Your novel, she was told, will be allowed some day if you become famous and successful.

This would be of little use to John Cleland, but it may be of interest to Hank Janson, which is where we came in.

The law can never fail to look ridiculous when it is chasing erotica. But I have tried to indicate one or two ways in which, by amending the 1959 Act, it could regain a semblance of dignity. Unless we are to scrap the obscenity laws altogether (a course which I, personally, would now reluctantly reject), we ought to go on working towards the perfection that we can never attain.

Guardian December 2, 1964.

On "Having a Go"

"Public Relations" took a long time to achieve respectable status in Police administration, and critics of the Police have usually said that it is in this field that the administration is most feeble. The critics have seldom been people with first-hand experience of telling the public what they ought to know—and withholding what *some* members of the public ought not to know; but surely the most vehement of them ought to have been mollified by the Press conference held at Scotland Yard last week. Mr. Ranulph Bacon, Assistant Commissioner, Metropolitan Police, used the occasion to tell the public that the Yard wanted to know about "groups of men, apparently nervous men, in stationary cars—don't wait for the donning of stocking masks or the picking up of pick helves. If they look suspicious, dial 999." Mr. Bacon was also reported as having urged the public to "have a go" at arresting or restraining gunmen carrying out raids, and the newspapers and TV newsmen reported the determination of selected members of the public to do nothing of the kind. But Mr. Bacon actually said something much more rational, which many papers did not report fully. He had been *asked* what advice he would give to members of the public who saw a gunman carrying out a raid. What, we wonder, did the questioner expect him to say? "Have nothing to do with it—you might get shot"? He said what any responsible citizen would say: "It depends entirely on how you are placed in the situation, but if you can have a go, then have a go." That might include slamming an open door, nipping for cover where you could telephone, driving a car across the path that the gunman's car must take, or a hundred other unforeseeable actions, including the dialling of 999. Nowhere in Mr. Bacon's remarks, so far as we can see, can you find an exhortation to the private citizen to join battle with an armed man, but that was how he was interpreted by officials of the British Safety Council. They said his advice was "utterly irresponsible" and "suicidal." One of them told *The Times* that "You are not being a coward if you keep out of this and let the Police deal with it." If that isn't irresponsible it is difficult to conceive what is.

But where the British Safety Council could help would be by throwing all its weight into the support of Mr. Bernard Braine, M.P., who wants "maximum co-operation from the public and the authorities to reduce the number of firearms held illegally." He believes that "both Parliament and the public could do more to help the Police in their efforts to counter the crime wave." Parliament can do even more than the public. For our part, though we deprecate the term "crime wave," we hope Mr. Braine and his supporters will press for the *total* prohibition of pistols and revolvers for private use and a tightening of the law about smoothbore shot guns, rifles, and firearms of every kind. This is where Parliament could help; and one of the first law reforms to be expected from this avowedly law-reforming Government is surely a new Firearms Act on these lines.

Police Review January 8, 1965.

Ignorantia Juris . . .

There was a rather odd outburst of indignation recently when the National Council for Civil Liberties published a new edition of its *Handbook of Citizens' Rights* (2s. 6d., if you want one, from 4 Camden High Street, N.W.1). At the first opportunity we settled down to read a copy.

Was this the subversive screed that Lord Shawcross (quoted in *The People*) described as "a useful guide to the inexperienced criminal"? Is this what *The People* says will "hamper the Police in their work"? A correspondent has angrily called our attention to the following passage on page 43, in a chapter on "Arrest, Bail, and Police Questioning":

> If you are arrested and not told the ground for the arrest, you should ask on what ground, and the Policeman is under duty to tell you. If he merely asks you to go with him to the Station, and does not state that he is arresting you, you are not bound to go, though he may then arrest you. It is, however, advisable not to resist if he says he is arresting you, because you may thereby commit further offences, and he will in any case be called to account later if the arrest turns out have been wrongful.

This seems to us to be an unexceptionable statement which might (with a change of personal pronouns) be a direct quotation from *Moriarty's Police Law* or from a Home Office Circular to Chief Constables. But we are told that it has caused indignation among our correspondent's colleagues, who feel, it seems, that a kind of resistance Police Force is being organised.

Publications of this kind are plentiful in America, where civil liberty can suffer sudden set-backs despite all the safeguards in the American Constitution. But there is very little in the *Handbook of Citizens' Rights* that cannot be found in any legal text-book on the subjects concerned; and that little is confined to unimportant errors like the description of "aggravated assault" (on page 43) as a felony.

A rather soberer publication is the Central Office of Information's "Reference Pamphlet" No. 49, which is entitled *The English Legal System* and which you can get for 3s. from Her Majesty's Stationery Office. This gives a clear and rather dull account, accurate (so far as we can see) to the last comma, of the judicial system of England and Wales. "Individuals," it says in an Introduction, "obey the law out of a sense of private conviction or public duty—or in the last resort, because they know that if they fail to do so they will be penalised by the authority of the State." You could arrange the law-abiding citizens you know under these three headings—those who are law-abiding because they think it morally right, those who will do their "duty" right or wrong, and those who do it because of the Policeman on the corner. At the moment those in the first category are the ones to be most encouraged; the second can be rather a menace; and the third are having the time of their lives.

Police Review January 15, 1965.

Judges' Perks

Among the lesser known facts that have emerged into the cruel glare of publicity since the start of the controversy about the Judges' Remuneration Bill, there are some odd "fringe benefits" attached to being a High Court Judge. A Judge, for example, can take his own cook with him when he goes on circuit, in case the locals try to poison him. He can also take his own butler, so that no local wine-waiter can drop anything into the port. These two functionaries cost the taxpayer £8 10s. a day. Every High Court Judge can also have a clerk—a nice little job, this, with very little work, a seat on the end of the Bench, and a salary from public funds. Public funds also pay for the Judge's Marshal if he wants one, and this official's job is to fight off the highwaymen and cut-throats lurking in every Judge's path. The Attorney-General told the House of Commons last month that, since cooks became so hard to get, there has been a "central pool" of Judges' cooks. Butlers, too, buttle less eagerly than they did. So there is a central pool of butlers. If all these functionaries were scrapped, and the Judges had to content themselves, as Magistrates and even Recorders do, with three-star hotels and ordinary Police protection, quite a lot could be transferred to their pay packets.

Police Review August 13, 1965.

How Do You Plead?

Twelve years ago we hanged Timothy Evans for killing his baby. Someone, probably Christie, had killed its mother as well, but one death was enough for a hanging and the killer of Mrs Evans went officially unidentified; the implication being that it was Evans, the moral certainty being that it was Christie. Suppose that Mr Justice Brabin's inquiry now comes up with the finding that Evans was wrongly convicted of killing the baby and could never have been rightly convicted of killing its mother: what do we expect the Home Secretary to do?

The Timothy Evans Committee, and the Evans family, are demanding a posthumous 'free pardon'. It is sometimes said that the announcement of a 'pardon' is the Crown's way of maintaining the fiction that, although the convicted person was really innocent, the

Crown can do no wrong. But this can't always be so, because these pardons are of two kinds: free and conditional. The free one has no strings attached and is sometimes even accompanied by a little money as a solatium. The conditional one, now obsolete, requires you to 'abjure the realm' or accept transportation to the Colonies, and it means 'We still believe you did it, but we won't punish you if you go and die in Botany Bay.' So a free one really means 'We don't now even think you did it, but of course we can't say so; however, you are formally forgiven for what you didn't do.'

Murder, in fact, shows the 'pardon' fiction at its most poignant, but the trouble really starts at the other end of the scale of gravity. Take the case of Mr Henry King of Kilburn, summoned before the Watford magistrates for not having a test certificate for his lorry. He pleaded guilty, but before the case went any further the magistrates discovered (probably in the process of looking up the penalty) that the lorry didn't need a test certificate because its weight was over 35 cwt. Never mind, the chairman said: Mr King had pleaded guilty and he would be fined £5. Mr King seems to have been dissatisfied; and three months later he was granted a free pardon. The Queen, apprised that he didn't need a test certificate, had forgiven him for not having one.

I have felt for years that until the superior courts, at least, reject all pleas of guilty, all admissions and all confessions we shall sustain a double standard of justice—careful trial for the crook who knows his way through the courts, and slap-happy, rubber-stamp methods (working against the clock) for the 'technical' delinquent and the man who offends without guilty intention. There was little enough evidence against Timothy Evans apart from his confession, which he repudiated as soon as he had the right audience. Of course they always do, since that is the only way of recovering their right to a trial—it isn't much use pleading 'not guilty' and then saying 'Yes, sir, that's my confession'. But why give the confession any credence in the first place, why thus encourage its preparation and use? It is not generally known that many police officers, who value confessions more as signposts to further inquiries than as probative evidence, would gladly forgo the necessity to 'put them in'.

If you plead guilty you have usually, but not inevitably, thrown away all chance of appealing against conviction. You may find, for example, that you were mistaken: what you thought you were admitting was something quite different from what the judge sentenced you for—many a man has not really known what he was supposed to have done until he heard the judge or magistrate denouncing his wickedness in down-to-earth terms. But the Court of Criminal Appeal will not listen to you unless it is satisfied that you really didn't understand the charge against you, or had no intention of admitting it, or could not legally, on the facts, have been convicted of it. Failure to understand a charge, and inadvertently admitting a charge, are both more frequent, even among intelligent persons, than is widely supposed, though the Court of Criminal Appeal has always found it difficult to believe that either of them can really happen. But that is not the worst of it.

Too many are persuaded, sometimes by policemen, but mostly by lawyers, that it will be 'better for them' to plead guilty. The court, it is urged, will be more lenient. This would be shocking enough even if it were true, but what is equally shocking is the pretence that it's true. The only defendant who can ever earn leniency by pleading guilty is the one who then, by grisly agreement with the prosecution, goes on to give evidence against his confederates. Sometimes a man is told: 'There will be no publicity'. No? Quite often the very impact of the guilty plea, as in the case of an eminent man accused of a sex offence, or of a policeman-turned-thief, will ensure more shocked publicity than any strenous denial and 'my client has a perfect answer to this ridiculous accusation'.

The general supposition seems to be that today everyone who needs a lawyer will have one, either privately or through legal aid, and that therefore everyone will be fully advised as to how he should plead. In 1963 legal aid in criminal cases was being granted to only 19 per cent of those tried by juries and only 0.9 per cent of those tried by magistrates. Among the rest, anyone who mistakenly pleaded guilty when he should have contested the case would have found, if he troubled to appeal, that the judges do not regard the lack of a lawyer as a ground for interfering with a conviction or sentence. A case that illustrates this came before a Queen's Bench Divisional Court on 20 November 1963.

Miss Margaret Fysh, then 28, had been a mental patient all her life. One day in the kitchen at her home, in the course of an argument with her brother, she poured boiling water over him from a kettle. She was charged before the King's Lynn magistrates with causing him grievous bodily harm. She had no legal adviser, she was not offered legal aid, and she pleaded guilty. The magistrates sent her to Rampton, the special hospital for criminal defectives. Then a solicitor took her case to the Queen's Bench Division on an application to have the conviction quashed and the Rampton order rescinded. It was argued on her behalf that the scalding was an accident, her brother having 'jogged her arm', and that it was 'contrary to natural justice' that a court should accept a plea of guilty from someone it knew to have been in a mental hospital for years and to be without legal advice. 'We think it a great pity,' said the Lord Chief Justice, 'that she was not granted legal aid and represented, but this is no ground for quashing the conviction.'

There are many magistrates' courts in which it is considered to be extravagant to grant legal aid to anyone pleading guilty, though these people are often the most likely, at least in indictable cases, to need it.

The Lord Chief Justice has done his utmost to expose and condemn this wretched parsimony. A better way would be to enact that at least every charge of indictable crime should be properly heard and tried, regardless of any wish expressed by the defendant at the time.

New Statesman October 1, 1965.

"Too Many Young People . . ."

Much fun has been made of the "judicial homily," the not-always-measured remarks addressed by Judge or Magistrate to the man he is about to sentence. No doubt this often goes on too long—Hatry had to listen to his Judge for seven minutes before he learned that he had got fourteen years—and the process can be needlessly cruel. The famous instances, of course, that have kept the comic tradition alive are these three:

1. Whether you may be forgiven in the hereafter for this dreadful crime will be a matter for another and, if I may respectfully say so, a Better Judge.
2. Here are you, a young man with all the advantages of a secondary school education, instead of which you go about the country stealing ducks.
3. If ever there was a worse case of a man robbing his master, that case is this case.

The speakers must all, presumably, have known what they meant. But their failure to find the right formula should not be taken as an indication that the homily is never justified at all. Judge Aarvold, the Recorder of London, told the Magistrates' Association last week that they *should* give reasons for their decisions and sentences. "The convicted person," he said, "is entitled to know what he has done and why he is being punished; and the Magistrate, if he gives reasons, will be dealing with the offender and the offence he has committed instead of dealing with the offence in general terms," "Dealing with the offence in general terms" would include, one supposes, the Judge who said "Too many young people in this country are stabbing their uncles in the back with flick-knives." But the Recorder is right. Some prisoners don't really know what they are charged with until the Judge is expressing his disgust.

Police Review October 22, 1965.

The Paddock

You know what house agents are, but they did call it a paddock. Paddock? A field for horses near a stable, said the dictionary. Well, there was actually a three-sided shed in this one, smelling slightly of one-time horse. The paddock is too big for scything (by me) and too small to merit the cost of one of those roto things, at least this is the way I have talked to myself. So the grass grew shoulder-high around the clumps of giant thistle, and we averted our eyes from it, shamefaced and useless land-owners.

You need animals, people said. Sheep? Too many foxes. Geese? You heard. A cow or cows? They moo in the small hours. A horse? A pony!—the children would ride it, this would make it hungry, it would keep the grass short and turn it into manure for the garden, the perfect economic cycle.

We turned to one of those societies for rescuing worn-out horses from being worn out. We had to put our name down and wait many months to get one before the winter. The winter won, but at last a rather stern-looking animal arrived, we paid his horse-box fare, and he settled down, if settling down is standing in the middle of a paddock with your lips drawn back. He was broken-winded, had summer itch, and mustn't be saddled or shod even in winter, but he was rather fat. He would begin eating grass as he got thinner? Not on your life. He ate the bark from the trees, and the blackthorn hedges, and became more and more unapproachable as the thinness set in.

So we bought great bags of oats, and for oats he would come at a call. We would keep him alive on those until the short spring grasses came once again. The grass he wouldn't eat was now lying dank, long, matted and flat.

We overdid the oats, and revealed to him that he could take the fence to the main road with the greatest ease, especially in pouring rain and at dead of night. Angry neighbours rang up and we had to go out and catch him. One kindly farmer put him in a loose box to wait for us, and he kicked it to pieces. Worn out, we sent him back to the society for worn-out horses and resignedly, and rather expensively, arranged to have the paddock cut twice a year.

Three years and £40 later the children, through neighbourly associations, envy, and that powerful girl-horse relationship crying in vain for the research that will one day explain it, had become pony addicts. Pressure built up, and this time we bought one. It was second-hand but not antique. It would pay for itself, we told each other again, by eating the grass and manuring the garden and making the children happy.

Some dilettante nibbling began. After some months the grass had grown as much as it ever did and the new pony, which had looked all right on arrival, looked dejected. It needed company, people said. A second pony? Come off it. Donkey? Some ponies won't speak to them. Goat? My wife went to market and came back with a nannygoat standing in the back of the car. Tethered in the paddock with a mobile shelter for cold or rainy days, this eats more grass before breakfast than the ponies have done in a month. The pony has become so attached to it that, whenever free to roam, it stands very close to the goat, not eating but (we hope) learning. The grass defeats them both, and is now being expensively cut again.

Nor is that all.

These lessons had been duly registered and absorbed when the pony suddenly realised what he was there for, and began eating grass ravenously, tearing it out in great tufts with sideways swings of the head. Horrified, the children promptly locked him in the stable. Why? Why, oh why? Did you say why?

He must not eat grass in the daytime, they said, reading from pony books. (Or something.) They have also been mixing with some pony and horse people, who abound in these parts and who know far more about horses and ponies than horses and ponies do, and even look more like them. A horse that eats too much grass, it now appears, will succumb to one or other of two deadly complaints: inflamed hooves (laminitis), or grass-tummy. The latter, to me, is just like saying that a child eating too much jelly will get jelly-belly; but I know when, and when not, to say these things. A horse that eats too much hay will get red eyes and a cough. A horse that eats too many oats will jump fences and run away, always at night and in the rain. I am just passing on my experiences.

But can you not see what has happened? Pet ponies, including those innocently bought as lawn mowers, are being sacrificed to a short-sighted and self-indulgent Puritanism. Originally constructed to enjoy grass, they are being schooled to recognise the sin of enjoying what is enjoyable. Horse owners place them on grass and then watch narrowly to see that they fully understand their duty of not eating what they are standing on. At the first mouthful they are caught and shoved into their stables, there to poke their heads wistfully out until nightfall. A superstition having grown up that it is safe for them to eat grass at night, they are liberated after dark. This is the time when in fact they eat nothing, and if you go out with a lamp to see whether they are eating you wake them up, and they crossly turn their haunches on you, nor can you blame them.

I think there can be few people as ignorant of all these evolutionary changes as we were. I do not know. But let me tell any such that the horse, which still thinks of itself as a grass-eating animal, is not in sympathy with these changes and is not to be blamed for them. He is a victim of this paddock business. Though, as Josh Billings said, if animals had reason they might act just as ridiculous as we menfolk do.

Punch December 15, 1965.

Crime Prevention goes Crazy

Another event of the week had the effect of showing once again (and it seems to be growing more necessary to have these illustrations) that crime prevention can sometimes go too far. At Lambeth Magistrates'

Court two men were committed to Quarter Sessions for sentence on charges of stealing ancient manuscripts from County Hall, the headquarters of the Greater London Council. They had been allowed access to the Council's archives "to get background information for a model of the Crystal Palace." One of the men was building this as a hobby. The archives were looked after by one elderly lady. Anyone inside when she went to lunch was locked in. The two men used this locked-in period to sack the books and documents ready for removal. When she came back, and walked down a corridor to hang up her coat, they slipped out with their booty. And what do you suppose the Greater London Council's solution is? "In future," they told *The Times* (15th January), "the only people to be allowed access to the book store will be members of the libraries staff." Simplicity itself. By analogy, a good way to prevent road accidents would be to forbid the use of the roads; you could stop bigamy by abolishing the ceremony of marriage.

Police Review January 21, 1966.

Dealing with Shoplifters

A few months ago a well-known self-service store found, to its dismay, that its shoplifters were beginning to ply their trade elsewhere. The larceny figures had taken a disturbing dive. The sales manager said there must be something wrong with the way the goods were set out, the display manager ordered a complete shift-round—everything to be within the smallest customer's reach—and the security manager took on two extra floor detectives. The latest news (I learn) is that the pilferage figures are now climbing again to the level at which a modern self-service store can hold up its head.

To see that story in its proper setting, you need to consider next the case of the widow said to be suffering from severe depression who, on 29 March this year at Brighton Quarter Sessions, was fined £500 for stealing a packet of raisins and a further £500 for stealing four pairs of shoes from Marks and Spencer's. In another Brighton shop she had stolen a towel and two pairs of stockings, and for this she got 12 months' probation, with a condition that she attend hospital throughout that period. She had pleaded guilty on all counts and asked for eight other offences, all committed within the previous two years, to be taken into consideration in sentencing her. She had private means of £20,000. Her house was stacked with goods she had stolen and hoarded. And she had five previous convictions. 'I understand you are ill,' the Deputy Recorder told her, 'and you will receive treatment for that in hospital. But you have been a very wicked woman and you are to be punished for it.'

Whether or not this was what she needed as a very wicked woman, it was quite likely what she wanted as a disturbed, irrational and bewildered one. Shoplifting seems to have reached a stage where even the punishments could now be displayed on self-service lines. There are magistrates who (though there is little enough that they can do about it) see in these acts of seemingly compulsive and largely non-mercenary stealing a genuine cry for help. The Deputy Recorder at Brighton of course responded to this cry with conspicuous generosity, but there are magistrates' courts in famous shopping districts—Great Marlborough Street is one—where as a general practice the shoplifting fines are enormous by comparison with those elsewhere. They make no difference except to the feelings of the righteous, but the penal philosophy behind them is as old as hanging. Where the theft is easy to commit and hard to bring home to anyone, like the theft of a mountain-side sheep, you hang the few people caught because that is cheaper than employing a lot of shepherds—and others get to hear about it. Even now the theft of a horse, sheep or pig is an 'aggravated larceny' carrying a 14-year penalty, while stealing a jet airliner, the House of Commons mace or the Crown jewels is only 'simple larceny' with a mere five years (10 years the second time you do it) because the greater difficulty of the undertaking limits the number likely to go in for it.

It is known, in fact, that fines are as effective as imprisonment. But even if imprisonment could ever have been a practical solution, it is out of the question today. The prisons could never accommodate the offenders nor, since so many of them are mothers, could the child-care authorities cope with their disrupted families. Fines, probation and conditional discharge are the only other available sanctions. A fine is seldom really appropriate, seldom adds anything to the very salutary finding of guilt, and seldom seems proportioned (as it should be) to the defendant's condition. The £1,000 fine on the Brighton widow must have seemed appropriate to her judge; but if she needed the kind of hospital treatment that you get as a condition of a probation order, the accompanying fine was futile—except as a warning to others that kleptomania is best on a small income.

Probation is hardly more suitable. Something like 80 per cent of the offenders are women, whereas the proportion of women probation officers to men is only 30 per cent. In any event probation officers don't want shoplifting cases, which are usually impossible to supervise (they are quite often *au pair* girls due to go home long before a probation period could expire; at one Paris employment exchange a constant topic of conversation is said to be the stores in London which don't prosecute). A conditional discharge for 12 months is probably the most effective sanction, though its public impact is wrong—people tend to see it as a complete let-off. It should, I believe, include a requirement to report at least four times to the police, or better still to the manager of the shop, as a means of keeping the thing alive. And it should finish, instead of being allowed to peter out as at present, with a cautionary letter from the court, by way of a reminder that the whole affair, whose lesson gets a little dimmed by time, had better be seen as a pointer for the future.

But in view of the public interest in it, the offence itself is strangely neglected by criminological research. The report compiled for the Institute for the Study and Treatment of Delinquency in 1959 by Dr Trevor Gibbens is the most recent survey, and he tells me that all its figures would be much higher today. Shoplifting is believed to have been keeping pace with other kinds of crime, but the recent proliferation of self-service stores has given their display counters the special quality, the impersonal vulnerability, of British Railways, the nationalised industries and the customs service. When Gibbens was at work on them seven years ago, the shoplifters most often convicted—i.e. most often caught—were children between eight and 13. It would have to be 10 to 13 now, for the under-tens can no longer steal. But most of the rest are women stealing clothes and food, youths stealing clothes, and men (almost exclusively) stealing books. Nearly a third of Gibbens's whole sample turned out to be immigrants—white ones from Europe and Eire; only 4 per cent were coloured ones from the Commonwealth and not one of them was from the West Indies.

Most of Gibbens's findings, indeed, could serve as fascinating hypotheses today. Is it still true that the great majority of shoplifters are first offenders (i.e. first time caught committing *any* crime)? Is it true that among the men there is the greater proportion of previous convictions? Are the women mainly over 40? Do the relatively few professionals still go over, after a time, to the more profitable larceny of shoppers' handbags and wallets? Is it still the commonest of all offences, including even motoring, among men over 60?

Other opinions expressed to Dr Gibbens might hardly merit further attention. Some store detectives thought there was 'a high correlation between homosexuality and shoplifting in men': they may have learned since that homosexual men are likely to do their own shopping. Dr Gibbens himself, looking into the theory that women stole umbrellas as compensatory phallic symbols, found that they did it when it was raining. And he failed altogether to find the supposed connection between shoplifting and menstruation, change of life or pregnancy.

What I should expect to find from a fresh inquiry is that if, when stopped by the detective and questioned by the manager, you deny your guilt *too* strenuously you are much more likely to be handed over to the police because all shops are now afraid of expensive civil actions for wrongful arrest. In Gibbens's sample the four commonest motives seemed to have been depression, resentment, keeping up appearances, and meanness. To these I think we would now have to add adventure (we've become very juvenile in the self-service stores) and escapism. But I believe too, not to be too nice about it, that we are nearly all potential thieves, much as we are all active liars. And since shoplifting is by far the easiest form of theft, requiring no planning or effort (the display managers do the planning for us), the liar's impunity will in due time become the thief's unless new preventive means are found. Of these, the best I have heard of is the ticket clipped on to all private belongings as the shopper goes in, so that he pays on the way out for everything not ticketed. *But* unless all the stores did this simultaneously, the ones that did might as well go into liquidation in the ordinary way.

New Statesman July 1, 1966.

Term of Art

"I submit, my Lord, that this is a term of art." Do you know what that means? You will hear counsel saying it in some Court or other every day of the week. Term of art? They say it about obstruction, danger, bodily harm, fear—all kinds of things are said to be "terms of art," and others (for the purposes of legal argument) are declared not to be.

Well, if you can find a definition of this much-used phrase in any work of reference you will be lucky. We refer to it this week for two reasons. First, a correspondent recently asked us what on earth it meant (and we tried to tell him); and secondly, the Court of Appeal (Civil Division) has been having a field day with it in *Syndall v. Castings Ltd.* (*Times,* 11th October).

This was the case in which a widow wanted her late husband's illegitimate child excluded from benefit under a life assurance policy. The policy named as beneficiaries any "dependants or relations" of the deceased man, and the widow said this did *not* include an illegitimate child by some other woman. Lord Justice Diplock and Lord Justice Russell agreed with her, and Lord Denning (the Master of the Rolls) emphatically did not. The illegitimate child, a little girl of four, was clearly a "relation" of her father, said Lord Denning. "An illegitimate person has a father and mother, brothers and sisters, all of whom are connected with him by blood though not by marriage. All are his relations."

Lord Denning's dissenting judgment is, as nearly all dissenting judgments are, the most persuasive and human, not to say the most eloquent. "We have been pressed by counsel to give the words an extraordinary meaning. 'Relations,' it is said, include only legitimate relations; 'descendant' means only a legitimate descendant. . . . I have no doubt that that argument would have been acceptable in the nineteenth century. The Judges in those days used to think that if they allowed illegitimate children to take a benefit they were encouraging immorality. . . . We should not be compelled against our will to shut out this little girl because she is illegitimate. That would be so unfair that I would not agree to it."

But the other two Judges could and did, so the little girl was excluded. The words, *dependants, relations* and *descendants,* they said, were "terms of art." Lawyers, said Lord Justice Diplock, had been compelled to evolve an English language in which words and phrases were more precise in meaning than in ordinary language. "Those words and phrases are called by lawyers 'terms of art.'. . ." The lexicon of terms of art is to be found in the decided cases and in the text-books. For lawyers they do not mean, that is to say, what they mean to you. An illegitimate child is not merely a bastard child: he is a bastard child with all sorts of legal disabilities.

The "term of art" most frequently coming up for Police interpretation is "annoyance." It is not enough, in an "annoyance" offence, that someone didn't like what was going on. Doing an act "to the annoyance" of residents means a lot more than making them frown. They may be annoyed, but not enough to fulfil "annoyance" as a term of art, a lawyer's word.

Police Review October 21, 1966.

Fraudulent Spectatorship

David Linehan, a 20-year-old labourer from Hammersmith, went to the Motor Show at Olympia last month and appointed himself lift attendant in one of those lifts that the passengers can operate for themselves. He "admitted" people to the lift, charged them half a crown a time, and got the money because it was in fact a clandestine way in to see the Show. Mr. Eric Reid, a security officer to the motor trade, got to know what was going on. With another officer he followed four people into the lift, saw Linehan hold out his hand and heard him say that it cost 2s. 6d. each to get in. One of the passengers gave him 10s. Mr. Reid then gave him 5s. for himself and his colleague because (he said later) he "thought it was necessary to establish that he had given the man money to admit him to the building."

In due course Linehan appeared before the West London Magistrate on a charge of "attempting to obtain 2s. 6d. from Mr. Reid by false pretences." The Magistrate dismissed the charge without calling on the defendant to say a word, "On the face of it," said the Magistrate, "he was dishonest in making money for himself, but what false pretence did he make?"

We should have thought the false pretence was that Linehan was doing something for the 2s. 6d. that the sneak-in patrons couldn't have done for themselves. "There was a fiddle going on," said the Magistrate. "Mr. Reid wasn't taken in by it. Everybody will try to get into an exhibition through the back door if they can get in without paying the proper amount. I can't see the slightest difference between this type of case and the gentlemen with the big top, where the canvas of the tent has not been properly laced and a little boy lets people in at 6d. a time. He is not pretending to be Mr. Smart. He is just a little boy working a racket."

The difference seems to us more perceptible. No one would suppose that a little boy, keeping cavey and holding open a tent flap while someone crept in, was a bona fide circus employee; and everyone paying him 6d. would be rewarding his enterprise and recognizing his help in a nefarious little swindle. It is rather more likely that the man working the lift will seem to be in *some* kind of authority. But the security officer who saw the four lift passengers pay their money to the bogus lift attendant could have nobbled them all for conspiring to defraud, and no Magistrate could have cavilled at that. Of course he couldn't lawfully have arrrested them, but it looks as though he arrested the lift man for false pretences?

Perhaps one day soon we shall have a new Theft Act—it is already in draft and is soon to come before the House of Commons—declaring that it is "criminal deception" when a person "dishonestly, with a view to gain for himself or another, by any deception induces a person to do or refrain from doing any act." Then the man in the Olympia lift could be charged with having, with a view to gain, induced people to sneak in by way of his improvised entrance.

Police Review November 18, 1966.

The Great Escape Hysteria

Innumerable propagandists, by way of calling attention to their desires, have gone as publicly as possible to prison. The modern method, brought to its latest perfection by Alfred Hinds and less adroitly taken up by Frank Mitchell, is as publicly as possible to get out. And thanks to the daft scale of values by which our news items rank for precedence, no Pankhurst, no Gandhi, no Lansbury ever earned himself as many column inches by laying down demands as a condition of coming out as Hinds or Mitchell by laying down demands as a condition of going back.

Three aspects of this new problem have combined to give Lord Mountbatten's report the special urgency that got it into print inside two months. First, the new talk about life imprisonment *meaning* life 'or at any rate not less than 30 years' (to say nothing of Blake's 42). Second, the enormous sums of money with which the business world today so patiently sustains its parasites and enables them to rescue their captured mates. Third, the frenetic press stories about Frank Mitchell, 'the Dartmoor axe-man', and the flood of exhortations ranging from 'Lock up your daughters' to 'Sack the Home Secretary'.

At any given moment during a working day there are in England and Wales about 2,000 prisoners employed outside the prisons. To be exact, in 1965 there were 1,337 working on farms and 521 on 'other outside work', which would include Frank Mitchell's quarry party and his fence-erecting job near the military firing range at Bagga Tor. (In this party's eight years of existence Mitchell is the only man ever to have absconded from it; and nothing that even he has done since he absconded has justified the 'axe-man' hysteria or thrown the smallest doubt on the wisdom of starting him on an outside working party.) Every one of these 2,000 men represents what Roy Jenkins has called a 'calculated risk'. Hundreds of them go into pubs—they are working for civilian employers, they don't have to be back in the prison hostel until 10 p.m. And because we never hear about them we leave our doors unlocked at night, send our wives out alone and think Roy Jenkins is doing rather well.

But the effect on us is less important, because it's more ephemeral, than the effect in the prisons. Since the Blake affair (and 'the prison system', says Lord Mountbatten, 'had no plans for a prisoner like Blake') the regime at Wormwood Scrubs and many other prisons has become a deeply discouraging one for the custodial and teaching staff. The resumed locking and unlocking and head-counting and escorting has put the clock back 50 years. Mitchell has succeeded in putting a stop to the fencing job at Dartmoor, and the mates he walked away from are all back inside. But Hinds and Mitchell and the others have precipitated something that none of them presumably wanted—the Mountbatten Report on prison security.

This has had a good enough reception to make room, after the lapse of a week, for a more critical appraisal. It finishes with 52 numbered recommendations which will probably become collectively known as the Mountbatten Plan, and Mr Jenkins has said that he hopes to implement them all. I've been doing some homework on the origins of these 52 suggestions. I find that 46 of them have been made before—and no Home Secretary has ever taken much notice of them. Prominent among Mountbatten's predecessors was the seventh report of the House of Commons Select Committee on Estimates in 1952. But ironically, the most fruitful source has been the annual reports of the Prison Commission. It is commonly said that when this became the Prison Department of the Home Office it lost its identity and therewith much of its effectiveness. My own belief is that the change made little difference and that the Prison Commission was a disheartened body anyway.

The six new suggestions among the 52 include the 'staggering' of exercise periods for prisoners on the escape list, the sample searching of 'hostel men' (the prisoners who go out daily to civil employment) on their return at night, the supply of dangerous prisoners' photographs to the local police, and the use of microphones in the 'visiting booths' at closed prisons. This last one is linked with the surprising statement, in paragraph 310, that 'the rules about visits to prisoners on remand are less stringent than those affecting convicted prisoners'. They are less stringent for visiting lawyers, and Lord Mountbatten has shocked the Law Society by suggesting, accordingly, that lawyer-and-client interviews in the prisons ought to be bugged (we shall hear a lot more about this); but did the Mountbatten party go to a remand prison—Brixton for example—at visiting time and see the unconvicted men (who *might* be innocent) talking cosily to their wives, standing up and shouting through a three-inch strip of close-meshed iron grille? Even at Dartmoor the convicted men sit at tea-tables with their families. Lord Mountbatten speaks of 'the unsentenced prisoner's . . . general right to receive as many visits as is desired, subject only to any general or particular directives by the Home Secretary.' To find out what those directives have achieved, Lord Mountbatten ought to have tried visiting someone at Brixton, without disclosing who he was.

But among the recommendations that are *not* new, an especially welcome one is No. 47—that 'a liberal prison regime and reasonable living conditions, including improved hygiene, can reduce the pressures to attempt escape'. And in paragraph 323 Lord Mountbatten condemns (as so many of us have) the degrading and insanitary 'slopping out' arrangements perpetuated in the new prisons at Blundeston and Gartree and even the newest and yet unopened one at Albany in the Isle of Wight. He has condemned this because he saw his terms of reference—'to make recommendations for the improvement of prison security'—as an invitation to criticise anything that intensified the natural desire to escape.

The only way to make it certain that your prisoners will never escape is to kill them. By comparison, not one of the ingenious devices recommended by Lord Mountbatten can be effective. (There is one that would turn every cell into a weighing machine by mounting it on 'pressure transducers' and fitting it with an alarm that goes off if the occupant's not there when he should be.) Every prison must have a way in, and even if you abolish all gates and use helicopters, the helicopter is also the way out while there are prison staff to be impersonated. The unusual value of this new report, and of the emotional impetus that threw it up, is that the daily fuss about normal escape figures may go on long enough for it to catch hold of something. All its predecessors have sunk without trace.

New Statesman December 30, 1966.

Reorganising the Police

I can remember when Police Federation representatives were marked men. To the senior officers they were crypto-commies, agitators, mikers. To the rank and file they were harmless asses, elected as

Federation representatives unopposed because everyone thought the whole thing a farce anyway.

Today the Police Federation is, in effect, a well-organised, efficient and highly articulate trade union; and, *mirabile dictu,* Arthur Evans, its extremely able secretary, has just got a CBE. (No one has had more to do with its emergence from ineffectual yesmanship than James Callaghan, who was its parliamentary spokesman and adviser until he assumed responsibility for its pay.) So it is not surprising, though it is little known, that it was a Federation initiative that led the Home Office to commission, through its new Police Advisory Board, the three 1966 working parties on *Police Manpower, Equipment and Efficiency*. And while their joint report* comprises the most informed and down-to-earth analysis of police problems ever published in this country, it sets out, as a plan of reorganisation, the absolute minimum that must be accepted by the police, by the local government services and by the taxpayer if law and order are to become again synonymous.

The Police Federation itself stopped the thing from getting too revolutionary, especially on recruiting training and promotion matters. Its working party members opposed the Home Office and local authority view that the height standard (now 5 ft 8 ins) should be abolished altogether. The chief constables oppose this too; they can disregard the standard if they get Home Office approval, but they never try. My guess is that the 5 ft 8 ins standard will have to go. Merely reducing it by one inch would add another 400,000 men to the pool of eligible manpower.

The Federation also had to oppose (but only, I believe, because it cannot yet command majority opinion) the recruitment of university graduates under conditions made specially attractive for them. But that, too, will come. So will the working party's recommendation that graduates and people with two A-levels be exempted from education exams for promotion. But given some standard of literacy and intelligence among recruits, the subsequent promotion exams in 'educational subjects' might as well be dropped altogether. At present their fatuity reveals no more than the criss-cross-quiz minds of the chaps who set the questions, and many a don would fail in them.

It has long been known that recruiting, at present going fairly well, is a less urgent problem than 'wastage', or premature resignations. Using the phrase 'annual voluntary premature wastage', the Report calls it AVPW and predicts that 1966 will prove to have produced its worst figure for very many years. After all we have been told about this in chief constables' annual reports, it came as a shock to the Police Federation and, I suspect, will jolt the chief constables too, to learn from a firm of management consultants that the wastage rate in the police service is not so bad as in industry—and that, even of those who

* **Cmd 84527** *HMSO* 10s 6d

do 'chuck the job' untimely, 10 per cent come back to rejoin. In the fire service throughout the country the wastage rate is nearly double that of the police, but we don't hear much about that either. What we do know is (a) that there are more policemen per population now than ever before, and (b) what it is that provokes the early departures and sustains the quick change-over. The report names a good many reasons and brings them together in a chapter on 'Man Management', which seems to mean treating men as if they had grown up and thus making it possible to recognise among them the people fitted for higher rank. Examinations don't really do this and the police service has always pretended that they did. It is true, as Mr Crosland has said, that the country is examination mad, but its police service is the maddest of all.

The working party must have heard some illuminating stories about mismanaging men, but it keeps quiet about them. Here, for the deprived reader, are four typical ones. (a) An off-duty constable looked up from weeding his rose-bed and saw the ginger cat from next door scratching up his seedlings. A well-aimed clod having induced the cat to move along, a cat-lover wrote to the chief constable to denounce the method. Thus began a minor Odyssey of report-writing which ended, at long last, in a reproof for the gardener. After so much, it was more than he could take. The AVPW figure increased by one. (b) A constable was called back to his station after a night's duty and then told he must get into uniform before he could be dealt with. Back home (four miles) to get into uniform, back again to the station—to be told that when he went off duty he forgot to put his lamp away. (I know a lamp story even dafter than that, but it ended in tragedy.) (c) A sergeant got a hot water bottle for his wife in bed because she was in pain. The bottle burst and scalded them both, and the sergeant had to report sick. His chief constable demanded a special report to explain why the wife needed a hot water bottle in July. (d) A constable who put in an application for annual leave was made to rewrite it four times to get the punctuation right. The fifth one he wrote was his resignation.

True stories all, indicating that a disciplined organisation without 'man management' training puts too much power into the hands of small people. Unless such petty tyrants are totally eliminated, 'discipline' can always be a malicious pastime and real communication between the senior and lower ranks an impossibility. Without such communication the police service is almost comically inadequate and its relations with the public will always be difficult.

> We think that there has been in the past (says the Report on page 124) a tendency for the senior ranks to overlook the need to pass on information. Rumours tend to circulate unchecked, and members of a force may learn about new items of equipment from the newspapers before they have authoritative information from their

own officers. Such a lack of communication reacts badly on morale and hampers efficiency and personal initiative.

I should be very surprised if they got that profound truth from any senior officer. But it has enabled them to put their finger on the one real weakness in the whole system—itself, maybe, the outcome of recruiting bodies, rather than minds. It prepares the way for a forthcoming periodical bulletin which, published by the new Police Research and Planning Board and reaching all levels of the service, should allow the rank and file to see for the first time what police duty is really about, and should have two or three generations of taciturn brass-hats revolving in their graves.

For the rest, the 'unit beat policing' method which is to replace Mr Plod will do much to take the monotony out of beat life, and a little, though I believe less than is hoped, to lessen the friction between unform and CID. And the centralised dictating system, enabling a beatsman to telephone reports to a bank of tape-recorders in a central typing pool, will eliminate the maddening lectures in English composition hitherto given by mentors who seldom knew what they were talking about.The one thing that startles me is the proposal that a 'probationer constable' on duty should never be alone, and never able to take on the simplest of jobs, for *his first 30 weeks.* Has something awful happened to make this waste of manpower really necessary? If so, it will be a long time before the undermanning problem yields even to the admirable proposals here 'commended' (nice word) to the police authorities by the Home Secretary.

New Statesman January 27, 1967.

Souvenir Thefts

Crime prevention officers must have been watching with interest the recent advertising campaign mounted by Trust Houses Ltd., who have decided that the excellence of a hotel can be judged by the extent to which its patrons pinch the spoons. We make no apology for "pinch," for the context necessitates some such euphemism for larceny. Trust Houses Ltd. like you to take their spoons, and the theme of their advertisements is "come and take all the spoons you want." Taking their spoons angers them no more than if they were the owners of public swimming pools and you came away with some of their water in your hair. Last year they lost 9,752 spoons by larceny, or by what would have been larceny if the spoons had been taken "without the consent of the owner." They loved it; or, if it disturbed them at the time, they have decided to love it now, and use it a a slogan. Last year, too, they lost glasses (which all hotels and pubs do), toilet rolls, ashtrays, light bulbs, thousands of coat hangers and a chair. All these, apparently, they now treat as "souvenir thefts" and indications of prestige.

Other hotels seem a little detached and unimpressed, rather taking the line that *their* clients are not of the spoon-pinching class, and that of course, if that's the kind of people you like lunching with, a Trust House might be the place for you. (Incidentally, it's the place for us.) But a comparison that unavoidably suggests itself is that of the supermarket management which called for a report from one of its stores because the shoplifting losses had gone down. There must, said the management, be something wrong with the display. The figures were disturbing. Attention and report, please.

It may all amount to a coming change in the law of property. But whether it does or not, there is no longer any ground for excitement when an arrested suspect is found to have Trust House spoons in his pockets. They are his property, with the compliments of the management.

Police Review February 10, 1967.

The Queen's Uniform

It is unlawful for anyone not in the Forces to wear without permission (and whether in public or not) "any dress having the appearance or bearing any of the regimental or other distinctive marks" of any of Her Majesty's Forces. There is an exemption (in the Uniforms Act 1894) in favour of stage performances, circuses and music halls—though not, oddly enough, for theatre clubs, since the exemption for plays applies only in licensed theatres. It is also an offence, and quite a separate one, to wear any such uniform in such a manner as to bring contempt upon it. The penalty for merely wearing it is five pounds, and the penalty for bringing contempt upon it is ten.There is no exception in favour of beatniks, weirdies, junkies, or any of that contemporary fringe of prematurely worn-out philosophers who have grown tired of the earth and want to get off before they are 18.

At the annual conference of the British Legion on 28th May, a delegate complained that "these young people are making a mockery of uniforms that you and I were proud to wear." Another speaker had seen "two long-haired trogs, one with a ribbon in his hair, wearing the red frock-coats of the Chelsea Pensioners." (Government surplus stores sell the uniforms and pawn-shops sell the medals.) The Police were urged by the conference to "enforce the law"—presumably the Uniforms Act—and we rather hope they will, so long as they select only the more blatant and most publicly flaunted instances. It doesn't much matter if a Royal Marines pith helmet is being worn by somebody in bed. Surplus Police uniforms (we should reflect) find their way to some remote parts of Africa and are put to some very odd uses, but no one knows or, therefore, worries.

Police Review June 9, 1967.

Agent Provocateur

Bertrand Russell has said that few people can be happy unless they hate some other person, nation or creed. In organised societies of course we appoint people who can be hated when one feels like it – tax collectors, traffic wardens, travelling ticket inspectors, deck-chair attendants, policemen. But in England we hate none of these enough to abolish them, and indeed we keep on inventing more. After a hate lasting 500 years we did almost abolish the 'common informer' in 1951 (his spirit lives on here and there) because we had invented the policeman for hating in his stead and found we could punish him more easily when he abused his authority. By 1589, when Elizabeth I passed an Act designed to limit his scope, the common informer was well established as a kind of ecclesiastical nark exposing Popish recusants. But under an Act passed 40 years earlier the informer could already earn quite a living by rounding up vagrants, suing the city authorities that had failed to cope with them and pocketing half the penalty (the other half went to the Crown). The vagrant thus informed upon was to be branded, given to the informer as his slave for two years, fed on bread and water and caused to do 'all such work, how vile soever it be, as he shall put him unto, by beating, chaining or otherwise'; and if he escaped before the two years were up he was branded on both cheeks and adjudged a slave for life, liable to the death penalty for any further running away. The professional informers, who didn't want all these slaves, sold them to people who did. And the varous unofficial ways in which a pauper could be tricked or enticed into becoming a vagrant seem to constitute the earliest known instances, in England, of the *agent provocateur* at work.

Throughout the 17th and 18th centuries all the statutes about public order, safety and 'morals' depended absolutely for their enforcement upon the common informer; and the *agent provocateur* came inevitably and firmly into his own. It is odd that, although the French had christened him in the 18th century during Fouché's counter espionage campaign, the term was not used here until 1896, when William le Queux imported it for the purposes of his book, *The Secret Service*. In fact for a very long time it applied only to 'fifth columnists' employed to stir up compromising political action – and has always remained, significantly, untranslated. The Czarist governments used such agents to foment risings which could be used as a reason for dispatching ringleaders to Siberia. In the 19th century, American industrialists used them to induce strikers to commit unlawful acts and provoke armed clashes in which a selection of inconvenient people could be shot. And at about the same time in England, industrial strife produced the classic *agent provocateur* in the person of Sergeant Popay of the Metropolitan Police, who in 1842 joined (incognito) the National Political Union, addressed revolutionary speeches to its meetings, got its wilder members to commit acts of violence and damage, and then denounced them to his superiors. He was then himself denounced in the House of Commons as an *agent provocateur*, and the idea was born that this was what the police might turn into if you paid them (or even promoted them) by results. Popay was sacked, but his spirit lingers on; and the police 'image', in the ancestral memory, is still tarnished by him.

This summer the Judges decided (*Sneddon v. Stevenson, The Times*, 7 June) that 'there is nothing wrong in a police officer encouraging anyone to commit an offence provided he is acting on the orders of a superior officer who genuinely thinks that the nature of the offence, or the circumstances in the locality, make such behaviour necessary'. Mary Sneddon was convicted at Nottingham of soliciting for the purposes of prostitution. Just before midnight on 18 August 1966 she was talking to a man when a police car drove by. It turned round and stopped, and beyond dispute this was done to attract her attention. She walked over, opened the car door and asked the police driver if he 'wanted business'. 'How much?' he said. She got in. And at once she was driven to the police station and charged.

She appealed against her conviction on the ground that the policeman had aided and abetted her act of soliciting, that he was therefore an accomplice, and that accordingly (under the rule of evidence relating to accomplices) his story should have been corroborated. The Queen's Bench Judges said the policeman was 'no party to the offence'. The girl was loitering and soliciting already. (On what evidence?) Even if he *was* a party to it, they ploughed on, he wasn't an accomplice within the meaning of the law about corroboration. 'This court frowns upon the practice of a police officer being employed to commit offences or to encourage others to do so,' said Lord Parker, the Lord Chief Justice. 'In this case he did not commit an offence, and there was nothing wrong in him encouraging her, *because he was acting upon the orders of those in authority*.'

No one seems to have liked this much. The Lord Chief's predecessor, Lord Goddard, would certainly have disliked it, for in *Brannan v. Peek* (1948) he said:

> It cannot be too strongly emphasised that, unless an Act of Parliament provides for such a course of conduct (and I don't think any Act does so provide), it is wholly wrong for a police officer, or any other person, to be sent to commit an offence in order that an offence by another person may be detected.

'Sent to commit an offence', which Lord Goddard thus condemned, is in this context hard to distinguish from 'acting on the orders of those in authority', which Lord Parker has now approved. But Lord Goddard was always consistent about this. In 1948 he was asked by Oxford County Council to say that a Henley publican ought to have been convicted for watering down his whisky. An inspector of weights and measures had ordered half a pint of whisky (!) from a particular bottle on the shelf behind the bar. 'It's not for sale,' said the publican. 'I keep it for myself.' (Like most licensees he was always being asked to drink with his customers, and – like many of them – he kept a watered whisky for the purpose.) Three times the official demanded that he be served from that particular bottle, and at last the publican gave in because he thought he might be obstructing the man in the execution of his duty. The inspector then prosecuted him for selling adulterated whisky. The Henley Magistrates threw the case out.

They were manifestly right, said Lord Goddard, who dismissed the Council's appeal, made them pay the costs of it and had some robust things to say about *agents provocateurs* as a species. But if we thought we could get rid of them instead of just hating them, we ought to do it more effectively than we did in the case of common informers, who come from the same stable, emit much the same odour and yet survive in isolated pockets like the Inland Revenue Regulation Act of 1890, which pays blood money to people informing on each other about tax evasion. (The blood money itself is taxable, but because of its source the recipients are denied the pleasure of informing on each other.) Possibly the *agent provocateur* has his nasty little place in any society unable otherwise to control its crime, and he will be tolerated wherever he is considered a lesser evil than the ones he provokes for punishment. For my part I would simply dispense with him and take the consequences.

New Statesman September 8, 1967.

Dixon's Homilies

Poor old Dixon, the homespun philosopher who can drink a cup of tea without moving his chinstrap, is losing his Police Station. Dock Green, otherwise Leman Street, is closing. Can George himself survive? It's significant that when the Police are debated in the House of Lords, George's defenders are usually the octogenarians who, before their Chamber was wired for sound, brought along their ear trumpets. The younger ones prefer *Z Cars* and *Softly, Softly* (including, it is rumoured, Lord Willis, who "created" George but no longer writes the scripts).

Now George himself is in the dock. On Saturday evening, 2nd December, he was involved with some take-and-drive adolescents, and he wanted the names and addresses of some of their known playmates. So a Detective Sergeant approached a Probation Officer. This moved the West London Probation Officer to horror. He wrote to the *Guardian* on 8th December (his facts were challenged by Mr. Paul Fox, the B.B.C.-1 Controller, in a subsequent letter) to say that "no attempt was made to gloss over this glaring breach of the confidentiality of the Probation Officer's relationship with his client. If as a result of this programme one delinquent or near delinquent youth, or one parent of any adolescent, says to himself that this is the way Probation Officers behave, the damage will be incalculable."

Still, it's worth while to try calculating it. If the missing or "wanted" boys are subject to probation orders, the fact will be known to others besides the Probation Officer. The Police (including the omniscient George) ought to know anyway, and the Court will know. If the boys are not subject to probation orders because they have not themselves been in trouble, but are known to the Probation Officer as friends (perhaps good and steady ones) of boys who have, then it would indeed be improper for the Probation Officer to disclose them to the Police. There exists in some areas an unofficial system of supervision called "voluntary probation." This occurs when the parents are worried about their child's habits or associates and get the long-suffering Probation Officer to "take him on" for a time as a kind of protégé, without any word to the Court or to the Police. We mention this last, not because it is the least important but because it is so perfectly illustrative of the confidence with which many parents regard the Probation Service, and which could be irretrievably damaged if they thought their son's or daughter's name might be passed on to the Police.

Dixon of Dock Green, writes the West London Probation Officer in his *Guardian* letter, "is a programme which apparently seeks to influence as well as to entertain, if we are to believe the evidence of Dixon's little homilies which close each programme." For our part, we could do without those little homilies.

Police Review December 15, 1967.

Queueing Up

In a NEW STATESMAN competition for invented proverbs in 1943 Mr Gerald Challis won a prize with 'Don't join a queue unless you know what's at the end of it.' I remember doubting its wisdom. It was a time when any sizeable queue would have a smaller one facing its head. The smaller one was to find out what the bigger one was for; it didn't want to be a queue but the police, by that time thoroughly queue-conscious, made it into one because formless groups, or knots, had become intolerable to them. In the bigger one there were always people who had no idea what they would be able to buy when they got to the door (my mother once waited 40 minutes for oranges and found she had qualified for rubber goloshes). The length of the queue satisfied them that it must be something worthwhile. Everyone wanted everything. I'm told that this still goes on in countries where they are not yet having it so good. The slaves of ancient Egypt queued for their rice and there were breadlines in Tolstoy's Russia. The OED says the British started queueing in 1837, but we ran true to form by giving a French name to a verb expressing such docility in a tough island race with a murderous history of civil war. Which was odd, since the country in which you fought, and fight, hardest for a bus seat is France.

And now I see that a man has written to the Consumer Association's magazine, *Which?*, complaining about the rail-less parallel queues in places like banks, post offices and Gas Board showrooms (where people queue, the *dernier cri* in docility, to pay their bills). These, he implies, defeat the whole patience-wins concept of the queue. 'Post office clerks should put up a notice about the time of closing their windows. At my local post office,' he says, and he could be at work on my own biography, 'after waiting behind a dozen people I at last reached the window: the clerk shut it and I had to join the *end* of another queue.' The editor of *Which?* is accordingly suggesting to the Post Office User's Council that counter-clerks give some advance notice that they are going to coffee. I notice that in most of the banks a counter-cashier, when he is disappearing for the coffee-break, not only waits until his place is momentarily queueless but grabs a small piece of paper to hurry off with. There may be nothing on the paper but I see it as gesture to the proprieties and to the notion of natural justice, the parents of the queueing system.

Queues have had a long love-hate relationship with the law of England. The 19th-century theatre managers were sometimes prosecuted for obstruction when they allowed their patrons to line up for the chance of a seat or a ticket. The Highway Act of 1835, under a provision re-enacted in 1959, used to punish those who 'wilfully obstructed the free passage of a highway', and the courts cared not whether the theatre-goers had been fighting or waiting in a line. Then, as more and more people went to the theatre, especially to the Edwardian music halls, the queues got more numerous, the courts grew more tolerant, the police came to like queues better than struggling crowds, and two new customs were born: the substitution of folding camp-stools for the people who used to stand and wait, and the busking industry.

In 1940 the High Court decided that a shopkeeper who caused a queue to form outside his shop could not be punished if he was 'carrying on business in the usual way'; but in the three subsequent years it held that an 'unusual way' would include serving customers through the window, showing bikinis on live models and advertising counterpanes by displaying a popular beauty queen in bed. In the two latter cases there had been scrums rather than queues; and so there had in other instances where shopkeepers were fined for window displays of ladies' hairdressing, all-in wrestling and dog-clipping. In recent years radio and TV shops have been fined because of the crowds outside on Grand National, boat-race and election days. But during the Second World War the queue had gradually won its way into the law's formal approval, and in 1942, roughly a century after its admission to the language, it achieved statutory recognition in a Regulation of Traffic (Formation of Queues) Order.

This not merely allowed people waiting for buses to stand in queues and obstruct other people: it ordered them to. It told them to form up two deep on the indicated side of the bus-stop signpost. It added that they were all to face the same way and that this, logically enough, must be the direction from which the bus was expected. For it recognised that getting them into line was only half the battle, useless if they were going to erupt into a struggling mob as soon as the bus arrived. Accordingly:

> No person shall take or endeavour to take any position in a queue otherwise than behind the persons already forming the queue; or enter or endeavour to enter a vehicle before any other person desiring to enter that vehicle who stood in front of him in the queue.

This is why we all have to face the same way. If the law allowed us to flop about as we liked, it would be unable to prove that a queue-jumper was 'behind' anyone else. But it has never really worked. For instance, the people in my queue always seem interested in several other bus stops offering them a second choice, and they rotate in a way that is hard to bear. When several buses come along at once, every queue dissolves into a heaving mass of skilled elbows; and a number of losers must either try to merge themselves with the people still at the head of the reformed queue or wretchedly go to the back and start again.

The 1942 Order enabled Regional Transport Commissioners to issue directions for 'giving priority to any class or classes of passengers' waiting in queues. Can you believe that? In the provinces they did it for season-ticket holders (they never dared try this in London), and it says much for British queuemindedness that lines of patient people would watch without violence as a season-ticket holder usurped one of the bus seats for which they had all waited in the rain. This, in turn, was the formal recognition of an *ad hoc* priority system that began with expectant mothers. Queuemindedness is of the same stuff and origin as Western man's solicitude for the pregnant. During the war the ration book of an expectant mother carried a distinguishing mark entitling her to preferential treatment. The Ministry of Food started an experimental and semi-official scheme for giving her priority in the shopping queues. When it was found that mums-to-be were collecting the ration books of their favourite neighbours and doing their shopping as well, queuemindedness showed another of its varied qualities in the strident boos going up from the ranks of the non-pregnant. The scheme was abortive. It was Rabelais who said, and he must have known, that 'everything comes if a man will only wait', but women know much more about queues than he did. 'Queueing up' – even dictionaries allow this now – is true waiting. And true waiting means waiting without anxiety.

New Statesman March 8, 1968.

Insulting Footballers

It can only be a matter of months before someone introduces, in the House of Commons, a Referees (Protection) Bill. It will be "talked out," since nothing compares with football as a topic for excited and prolonged eloquence; and we shall hear no more of it. This will be a pity, for such an addition to the law of England could prescribe necessary limits to the fabled authority of referees at League soccer matches. Much comment has been provoked by Press reports about what referee Tommy Dawes of Norwich is alleged to have said to a Constable who went on to the pitch to improve the players' language. "I wasn't having Policemen coming on to my pitch."

There has even been Press comment to the effect that the referee is "in sole charge of the playing area" and can order a Policeman off when he comes on it in the course of his duty. A football pitch, said one report, "is the holy of holies—and the man in the middle is the law."

The man in the middle is "the law" about the rules of the game, and no more. Like all the players and all the spectators, he is a man in a public place and must behave himself according to the law of the land, of which this is a relevant example:

> Any person who in any public place . . . uses threatening, abusive or insulting words or behaviour . . . whereby a breach of the peace is likely to be occasioned, shall be guilty of an offence.

It's Section 5 of the Public Order Act 1936. Can it apply in a football ground, and on the actual pitch? Under the same Act a "public place" includes

> any open space to which, for the time being, the public have or are permitted to have access, whether on payment or otherwise.

And the public, whether they have paid or climbed over the fence, have access to the pitch whether they are permitted or not. They regularly prove this by swarming over it under the stress of excitement, sometimes during the match but normally driven by triumph or despair when it is over.

Referee Dawes's observation was prompted by an episode now well-known enough to be eligible for burial, but here's the story briefly for beginners, P.C. Green, on "special duty" at Fratton Park ground, Portsmouth, received complaints about the language being used by one of the players. This was John Talbut, centre half for West Bromwich Albion who were playing Portsmouth in the fifth round of the F.A. Cup. Talbut had received a sharp kick on the ankle, which is always an effective aid to articulation. "You dirty . . ." he shouted, addressing himself to the Portsmouth man who had kicked him. The Constable came on to the pitch and remonstrated with him. "I told him it had nothing to do with him," said Mr. Talbut to the Press later. "After all, the crowd were doing their share." The referee had come over and said his piece. And some of the Press reports seem to have concluded, because the Constable didn't spend the rest of the afternoon on the pitch, that the referee had "ordered him off."

So it might be as well to record, in case such an issue is ever *really* forced to a bitter-end conclusion (which Heaven forbid), that when it comes to breaches of the peace, and the insulting language that is always on the point of causing them, the referee is *not* the man in charge. He's in the same position as anyone else in a public place. So is a player with an ankle which, accidentally or not, gets kicked. So is the man who kicks it. But the idea that any word, or combination of words, uttered by a man with a painful ankle could cause a breach of the peace at a soccer match is one that we are taking time to think over.

Police Review March 22, 1968.

The Passport Puzzle

Three and a half years ago we used this title for an article that got us into trouble with a number of readers (it was on 27th November, 1964). This is what it said:

> There is no statute authorising the issue of passports. There is no right of appeal. There is not even any "right to a passport." It is true, of course, that no one needs a passport to leave the country. When the Police impound someone's passport to ensure that he stays in Great Britain they are doing something for which they have no authority and which need have no effect, though they have been doing it for so long that it feels statutory and well-founded.

And it's a bluff that works. Readers were incredulous that it could be merely bluff. Some said it was a Common Law power (which it is not). Others said they were looking into the matter and would let us know chapter and verse for the lawful validity of passports (and we never heard from them again). And now the Home Secretary has had to tell the House of Commons, as a result of a *Daily Telegraph* test case, that "there is no question of denying British subjects their right to leave this country without passports. But in order to be able to exercise proper control over the movement of aliens the immigration service must ascertain which passengers are aliens and which are not. So they want to see passports."

The *Daily Telegraph* had had what it thought was a good idea. It sent Mr. Ian Colvin, one of its editorial staff, to try and get abroad from Heathrow Airport without a passport. He took his birth certificate and his driving licence and other guarantees of British respectability; but the immigration officer brushed them aside, applying "a strict test of proof of British nationality under the Aliens Order 1953." (That's Mr. Callaghan's phrase; and in case it was meant to be artful we pause here to point out that what came under the Aliens Order was not the test of proof but the British nationality.) Mr. Ian Colvin was turned back. "Of course he is a well-known journalist," Mr. Callaghan told the House, "but none of the documents he produced technically satisfied the immigration officer that he was a British subject *or a person to whom leave to embark under the Aliens Order 1953 should be granted.* So in the spirit of a test case leave was refused."

Fair enough. Well-known journalists sometimes commit crime and even treason, and you can't keep them in the country by impounding their birth certificates or driving licences. And "the immigration officer" (said Mr. Callaghan) "had to make a quick decision. . . . In the circumstances he thought it right to require stricter proof than would probably have been asked of a passenger who had inadvertently left his passport behind." So would we. A test case establishing that you do not, after all, need a passport to leave the country might fill the customs sheds with people who had lightheartedly thrown theirs away.

The whole thing began with the impounding of Sir Frederick Crawford's passport on his arrival from Rhodesia—he has sympathies with Mr. Ian Smith; and the Home Office didn't think it was "in the interests of Britain that this gentleman should travel about in Europe." Not having a passport doesn't keep him at home, but it would make life in Europe as awkward for him as the Berlin Wall. At the time of writing this the question is still on the boil. Sir Frederick Bennett, Tory M.P. for Torquay (he's got Sir Frederick Crawford staying in his constituency) is planning a trip abroad without a passport to see how *he* gets on: he has told the Home Secretary that "in the absence of your being able to point to any specific legislation, I am prepared personally to put this matter to the test." He thinks it will be impossible for the officers at London Airport "to suppose that he, a member of Parliament, might be an alien."

But they might suppose he was bunking because he had committed some crime, and not even British subjects can do that—not even M.P.s. The whole controversy, however, will probably blow over, and it will be a pity. Immigration officers, no less than the Police, ought to know where they stand.

Police Review May 31, 1968.

A Five-Tone Horn

Except in the case of fire brigade vehicles, ambulances, Police vehicles, Forestry Commission vehicles used for fire-fighting, and rescue operations in relation to wrecks or coal-mine disasters, no one may use a two-tone horn on a motor vehicle. Would anyone want to?

One tone seems enough for most people, but some drivers obtain release for their exuberance by means of a horn using three or more tones. In the House of Lords last week Lord Leatherland asked the Government if there were any regulations to prohibit "multi-tone horns," and if so why the Police were not enforcing them? There were none, he was told. So the car he was complaining about in particular, which played the first line of "Colonel Bogey," is immune from the Motor Vehicles (Construction and Use) Regulations because that famous line uses five tones.

The men who drafted the Regulation had never given "Colonel Bogey" a thought. But the Mechanical-Copyright Protection Society have. They have never given their consent on behalf of Lieut.-Colonel Ricketts, the man who wrote "Colonel Bogey," or of his heirs and successors, for the reproduction of the famous tune on motor horns; and they have written to Lord Leatherland and the Government telling them so. If the Construction and Use Regulations had prohibited the use of horns playing "two tones or more," "Colonel Bogey" would have been safe but the Ricketts family would have been done out of any royalties that may now accrue. The episode, however, should encourage the Mechanical-Copyright Protection Society to see if there are any living relatives of Mendelssohn. These might be entitled to a small rake-off every time a Police car or an ambulance brays its path through the crowded streets, on the ground that it is reproducing the ass's complaint from the Overture to *A Midsummer Night's Dream*.

Police Review June 7, 1968.

Baffled!

Speaking as one morphologist to another, do you know what it is that we do? We study form. You may well have been doing it for a lifetime, and none the richer. You are the wrong kind of morphologist. The better kind studies the ultramicroscopic structure of your molecules; and mine. And marine eggs. He also studies the great graptolite populations of the early fossiliferous rocks.

Not that the language comes easily to me either, and not for the want of trying. I gave up biology (because that's what this is about) at an earlier age than most people; and so long ago that I forget whether there was, at the time, any to give up. And now the rhythm of nature brings me face to face with it again, in the shape of a fifth-form daughter who comes home with what she calls Bilge Prep and can't do.

I have pored over this Prep until hypochondria has set in, pain developing in the inter-ventricular septum. I had known before that I had too much chyle. Chyle? Fluid formed by action of pancreatic juice and bile on chyme (*OED*). Chyme? Food converted by gastric secretion into acid pulp. Yes, I know, but this is biology; you can always turn over. We faced it together. We had a theory, mine actually, that the biology textbooks are written in a kind of code so that the facts of life can be wrapped up a bit decently. If you looked up the words in dictionaries and encyclopedias you could decipher this code.

The theory was wrong. In my home there are more dictionaries and encyclopedias than in any four-bedroom house in Northern Europe. It is the outcome of prolonged weakness at the front door, which is reflected also in a vast collection of lavatory brushes, two fire extinguishers, and (outside) a heap of stable manure that has stood neglected and mourned, dry as chips, for three years. Do you know, there are words in this biology business that no dictionary knows, no encyclopedia admits? Naturally enough there is no explanation of them in the text books that make them up. Clarity and communication are none of their business. The dictionaries disagree even about pronunciation. Beio.lodzi, says the *OED*, but *Nuttall's* says biolje. I went around saying biolje for some time, but people, ordinary people, are too ignorant.

Have you got any enterokinase? No? Well, that just shows you don't know what it is. You go away and look it up. Don't ask me where—you won't find it in the books of reference. My daughter told me that the pancreatic juice, containing trypsin enzyme, combines with the enterokinase of the intestinal juice to carry on protein digestion. We both felt glad that it did and hoped our confidence was not misplaced; but it's taking a lot on trust, since men are clearly able to compile dictionaries without having any, or at least knowing they have any. They don't even know that their intestinal juice contains any erepsin, which, my daughter asserts in one of her rough-books, "completes digestion because the polypeptides are broken down to amino acids." The lexicographers acknowledge and define their amino acids, but they are callously unaware that these are broken-down polypeptides and in fact probably think they wrote their dictionaries without having any polypeptides at all. I find that sickening.

Have you got a pyloric sphincter? Want to borrow one? You would if you knew what it did and found that you were without it. The pylorus, I now know from my daughter, who got it from her rough-book, wherein she copied it from someone else's rough-book, watches over the gate. (Gr. *pyle*, a gate, *ouros*, a watcher.) What gate? Well, I don't mind telling you now we've embarked on it all, though it coarsens the thing a bit. It's the lower orifice of the stomach, leading into the intestines; and biologists discovered in 1615 that it was called the pylorus. They had known since 1578 that a kind of contracting ring round it was called a sphincter. So for three hundred and fifty years any adequate person has had to have a pyloric sphincter.

Why? I don't mean why have one, but why call it that? It's not as if it were international and you could work your way round the world on it, like *bellis perennis* for daisy. Foreign people call theirs something quite different. Even when an English biologist sees one of those plants that live on decaying vegetable matter he calls it, according to my daughter's rough-book, a saprophyte. It may be all right learning these words when you are fifteen, because after all you don't know any better. But when you've been learning words for half a century (longer, really), newcomers like entelechy are ridiculous.

Newcomers, my daughter says? A person's entelechy (explains one of her school books) is his soul. The man who found that out was Aristotle, and that was in 335 BC, though we didn't find out that he had found out until 1605, and by 1905 we had got him into one of those smaller bookshops along the Charing Cross Road. *The Works of Aristotle* was a little fat green not-in-front-of-the-children book. It cost me, as a child, 8*s*. 6*d*. in pocket-money and hours of frustrated pruriency. What had I bought? What could I not have bought with eight shillings and sixpence? I still don't understand why you could only get it at those little shops, which you never see anyone entering or leaving and whose furtive patrons must come along underground passages.

Without biology, of course, or without what fifth-form people and encylopedists call biology, we would all be carbon copies of each other. But do you know what the *OED* calls it? "The study of human life and character." You might have thought that was biography, but the *OED* says a biography is "a written record of an animal or plant." So where are we getting? As you plunge on, you find that they both mean each other, and you remember in vain that according to Edmund Clerihew Bentley:

The art of Biography
Is different from Geography.
Geography is about maps,
But Biography is about chaps.

So biology, too, must be about chaps; but kept fit for publishing by resort to polysyllabic euphemisms and the pretence that gender and the old seven-year-itch are not the same thing. The books, even my daughter's rough-book, all talk of "the" endothelium of tessellated squamus, not his or hers. This must be why, when we have done this homework together, we have always got it wrong. "Describe how you would demonstrate plasmolysis in the living cells of a filamentous alga." How delicate can you get? I never knew that you could have just one alga. Algae had always seemed to me an irreducible minimum, helping each other along in pairs, obviously having children though you could never see them and had to take their biological mutuality on trust.

I only know that you could never teach yourself biology with the aid of the available text-books, somebody's lecture notes in a rough-book, fifth form drawings of the oesophagus, and a row of dictionaries. Anything else you can teach yourself. I know a man who decided to read for the Bar while he was a prisoner of war in Germany. Some parts of his studies, without a tutor, he found totally unintelligible and therefore learned them by heart. When the exam papers came through the Red Cross he insisted, because he knew his answers would be word-perfect, that he be invigilated while he wrote them. (A German camp guard did it.) They were in fact a complete reproduction of the relevant chapters in the book he had learned, but he didn't know what it was all about, and says he still doesn't, though he was duly "called." I suppose you could do this with biology. There are books called *Teach Yourself Biology* and I know the author of one. He is a complete man, but I believe he regards his readers as incomplete; he sees them as vertically bisected tadpoles whom he sends off on lifelong journeys in search of their other halves, which they will never find. Biology is not for me. It is too late.

Punch August 14, 1968.

Deprave, Corrupt or Enrage

Without saying that *Last Exit to Brooklyn* is not an obscene book, or even that its publication was justified by its message, the Court of Appeal has made the prosecution of obscene books both easier and less probable. This is always a likely consequence of clarification, and few recent statutes have stood in greater need of clarification than section 4 of the Obscene Publications Act 1959:

> that publication of the article in question is justified as being for the public good on the ground that it is in the interests of science, literature, art or learning, or of other objects of general concern.

At least a dozen countries were operating such a clause years before we decided to try it – some with jury systems, others without. In most of those countries Lord Justice Salmon's words will be read with great interest and, I believe, some surprise. What he did was to offer a kind of model summing-up for use by trial judges in future cases. 'Members of the jury,' they will now have to say, 'you will consider the number of readers you believe would tend to be corrupted by this book.'

This, for a start, sent up some legal eyebrows. Where did this new idea about numbers come from? Not from any term used in the Act itself. Yet it's no more than a commonsense inference. The psychiatric evidence called by the Crown against *Last Exit* was that it was particularly likely to have an adverse effect on latent homosexuals, sometimes estimated as about 20 per cent of the male population. You might have expected to hear this account of the book from someone who had yielded to the temptation to throw it away half-read; but anyone who stuck it out must surely accept Mr John Mortimer's contention, made on behalf of the publishers and totally overlooked by Judge Rogers when he summed up to his jury, that the graphic description of Brooklyn depravity and degradation was both compassionate and condemnatory; and that its only effect would be to make the horrified reader want to do something missionary about it. 'In short,' said Lord Justice Salmon, paraphrasing the defence that Judge Rogers had left out, 'instead of tending to encourage homosexuality, drug-taking or senseless, brutal violence, it would have precisely the reverse effect.'

So to return to the model summing-up: 'You must consider then the strength of the tendency to corrupt and deprave, and the nature of the corruption and depravity. You should assess the strength of the literary, sociological or ethical merit which you consider the book to possess.' (Sociological and ethical influence must come under the compendious term 'other objects of general concern'. In the *Chatterley* case this was deemed wide enough to let in some marriage guidance.) 'You should then weigh up all these factors and decide whether on balance this publication is proved to be justified as being for the public good.'

And, lacking this kind of guidance, the *Last Exit* jury had been 'thrown in at the deep end of section 4 and left to sink or swim in its dark waters'. Future juries will be thrown in with rule books, but the paradox still facing them will defy objective solution. They can but guess whether the corruption of some readers is to be justified by the dynamic anger or compassion of others, basing their conjecture on how many readers they think they can see in each category. The Court of Appeal's judgment introduces this problem specifically for the first time, necessarily leaving it unanswered. 'This court does not propose to express an opinion whether books like this are obscene; still less whether their publication is justified as being for the public good. These questions are not for this court to decide; they are wholly within the province of the jury.' The jury had not been told how they must be approached because Judge Rogers, like everyone else, simply didn't know.

No one, in fact, knows whether *Last Exit to Brooklyn* is a criminally obscene book in the eyes of the law or whether its obscenity serves an acceptable social purpose, because the book has never been properly tried by a jury. In this country it will never be thus tried now, for the Court of Appeal's decision has the same effect as acquittal by a jury. Suppose the resourceful and fearless Mr Calder now said: 'You have all been fooled. I am guilty of publishing an obscene book. It is intentionally depraving and corrupting, it has no literary merit, its social commentary is humbug, its ethical tone nihilistic. I published and fought for it merely to expose the fatuity of the law. Actually it will probably do a lot of harm, so now I want to change my plea to guilty, and see whether my sentence will reflect all the disgust I've been hearing about.' The law cannot listen to him. In respect of *Last Exit*, he cannot again be prosecuted, even if some future publisher could.

But this is because, as defendant, its present publisher is now *autrefois acquit;* a man must not be twice placed in peril before a jury on the same facts. What about another summons like Sir Cyril Black's, asking a magistrate to make a local destruction order? This is not a criminal proceeding; and the magistrate could now have the guidance of the Court of Appeal's interpretation. He might well decide, with that interpretation in mind, that the book was irredeemably corrupting and order its destruction. If this were arranged in different localities at suitable intervals, *Last Exit* could be kept in the public eye for many years. But only the Director of Public Prosecutions can do this now; and he won't.

How are other books affected? The most you can say about any other books that may come before the courts is that they will be tried more carefully and judged according to rules that the legislators never thought of; that now, even more than hitherto, they will stand a better chance of acquittal if they condemn bestiality than if they make it seem enjoyable; and that the jury (or the magistrate) may have to listen to expert evidence from sociologists and professors of social ethics as well as all the other professors they have been getting used to. Above all, the trial judge will now know what section 4 means (i.e. what three much respected judges in the Court of Appeal think it means); and what he says to his jury will be more important than it was, for example, seven years ago in the case of *R. v. Clifford* (1961). For in that case a man sentenced at Surrey Quarter Sessions to nine months' imprisonment appealed on the ground that the judge who tried him hadn't told the jury they must be satisfied the book was 'something more than shocking and vulgar'. The Lord Chief Justice said: 'You only have to pick the thing up to feel quite certain that no jury could conceivably have failed to convict.'

It is indeed worrying that since 1959, when depravity or corruption for some was recognised as cathartic or ennobling for others, a lot of juries must have said 'Guilty' without knowing how to do the sum. Perhaps some of the publishers of books they have thus convicted may now decide to have another go. But John Calder's service to publishers and to literature is that he has enabled the judges to spell out, as never before, the true absurdity of the law as it stands.

New Statesman August 9, 1968.

Stop, Search and Explain

Mrs. Gillian Hughes, a London teacher, has started off this season's furore about "searchers in the street." Or rather, it was begun by the three plain clothes men and a uniformed Policewoman who "jumped out of a car" in Hereford Road, Westbourne Gardens, as she was walking by with her son and his friend, and asked if they could look through her handbag. They turned it out, made the boys turn out their pockets, and frisked them. She doesn't say that they searched her in person. But she wrote to *The Times* on 14th August, described the episode, and asked whether no one was immune from this kind of affront? (The Police had been looking for "drugs.")

Then the correspondence started. *Times* readers were appalled, amused, sympathetic with the lady or with the Police, inclined to think the incident justified by the drugs menace, disposed to believe that the drugs menace has been over-emphasised and that everyone has gone crazy. A lawyer wrote to say that the Police were empowered to search for drugs by the Metropolitan Police Act 1839 (which they aren't), but never empowered to search anyone's person (which they are). This last one (in *The Times* of 16th August) was almost funny:

> First and foremost (its writer said) it is not generally realised by the general public that the Police have absolutely no power whatever to search their person. Whilst it is true to say that they do have the power to search one's property with a search warrant (and sometimes without), there is no legal authority at all which gives them this power when applied to the person. If the Police do contend that they have this power I, for one, would be most interested to know what this authority is and, I strongly suspect, so would many criminal lawyers.

He really ought to have left all those criminal lawyers to speak for themselves. Or perhaps if he had consulted one, his attention might have been directed just in time to the terms of Section 6(1) of the Dangerous Drugs Act 1967:

> If a Constable has reasonable grounds to suspect that any person is in possession of a drug in contravention of the principal Act [Dangerous Drugs Act 1965] or regulations thereunder or in contravention of the Drugs (Prevention of Misuse) Act 1964, the Constable may—
>
> (a) *search that person,* and detain him for the purpose of searching him.

Most unusually, this provision omits the familiar clause about the searching of a woman not being done by a male officer, probably because long practice has rendered it needless; but the presence of that modification in so many former statutes shows clearly enough that when an Act says "search that person" it means search *him* and not merely his bag.

The debate continues, but up to the time of writing no one has said anything about the vital word in Section 6(1), namely the word "reasonable." If there are not reasonable grounds to suspect that the person to be searched is in possession *either* of stolen property or a drug, the search will be unlawful. And if the Judges interpreting Section 6(1) follow the "stop, search and detain" cases under the Metropolitan Police Act, the question whether the alleged grounds for suspicion were reasonable will be treated as a question of law, not a question of fact. This is another way of saying that the way to the High Court is unusually wide open for outraged citizens.

Police Review August 23, 1968.

Easy Money

Had I got the camera? I thought *she* had it. I went back to make sure it wasn't still on the hall table, the agreed pool for the last-minute things we forget. Binoculars, Thermos, passports, maps, cam—Not there.

"Did you ever put it there?"

"Of course I put it there. I——"

"I didn't see it."

So she didn't see it. Anything to put me in the wrong. We began a frenzied search, starting with the bags already in the car and ending on the second shelf in the larder . . . Let it go. We mustn't keep the Browns waiting again this year.

I always hate coming without it. No need to drive like a madman. "Where did you see it last?"

"Must we go through that again? On the hall table, with the binoculars and the Thermos and the pass—Oh, God!"

"Well?"

I hadn't, in the stress, brought any of them. The Manual of the Institute of Advanced Motorists, Limited, would be less limited and more advanced if it had a chapter on Preserving an Impassive Profile with a Scornful Wife (or Woman) Looking Fixedly at It. Still, we were able to make a renewed and fruitless search for the camera.

The Browns were waiting: it was the first time, we learned, that they had ever completed *The Times* crossword.

* * * *

I have one of those insurance policies under which you can get a little cash if you lose so much as a pocket comb. Back from holiday I wrote to the company. Had I, they wrote back, told the police? I phoned them and said of course not.

"This is just a loss. Not a burglary or anything. I'm not saying it was stolen."

It didn't matter. I must tell the police. It *might* have been stolen. Where had I seen it last?

I went to the police and was told someone would have to come and look at the "scene." A young detective called on us. Where had we seen the camera last? He looked at all the doors and windows. I think he measured two of them. He questioned us both closely. He asked about the neighbours, their children, the tradesmen, the daily woman, the paperboy, the gasman. He wrote down a minute description of the camera. He silently read all this through and then tapped his pencil on it. If the camera turned up we would let him know?

Turned up? We looked at each other. If it turned up, one of us said stiffly, it would be him letting us know.

But in the end the insurance people sent me a cheque for £18 10*s*. 0*d*. and I bought a second-hand Japanese camera for £4.

I don't call that wrong. Well, all right, I was £14 10*s*. 0*d*. better off in cash, plus all the money I would have spent having the colour snaps developed and printed at Boots. But look what I'd had to put up with, and anyway you can spend the money how you like. I don't call that Easy Money. But read on.

* * * *

Next to the hall stand is a kind of tub thing that you stand umbrellas in. Or we do. I think it was originally a butter-tub and an antique shop had stained it, knocked it around and sold it as something else. About once a year our daily woman empties out the umbrellas, turns it upside down and sweeps up anything else that comes out.

It *may* have fallen off the hall table and into this thing, I don't know. It seemed none the worse. the shutter and lens were undamaged. It was dusty and a year's toffee-papers were sticking to it. We were too taken aback for the necessary recrimination, we simply held hands and faced the new moral problem: What should "A" do?

A, said my wife firmly, should write to the insurance company at once and make a clean breast of it. I took this badly. What exactly did she mean, clean breast? Whose? My conscience was clear. I went over it all carefully with her, the way you go over things with these people, knowing in advance (I mean) that they won't listen.

"You must write and tell them what's happened"—you could hear it through the fingers in your ears. I would telephone, I said firmly. People neglected the telephone. Two businessmen, I said, would spend a month's correspondence and a three-hour lunch over some simple proposition that could be settled on the phone in two minutes. It was fortunate, I added, that I played golf with the agent who had handled the episode so well.

He was aghast. Not, now, old man. Leave it, leave it. Saturday perhaps?

But listen——

Leave it, old man. This is something you don't know how to handle.

My wife was going to her mother's for a week. I would say no more to her, and tell him all about it on Saturday, well away from the clubhouse.

Saturday came. He left it to me to raise the matter. I'd been paid, hadn't I? An insured camera was lost, genuinely lost?

And found again.

Oh, but look, it *was* lost, wasn't it? There was no trickery? Well, then.

But perhaps we had been careless. We should have——

The police were informed? They came and checked up? Asked all their questions?

They didn't look in the butter-tub.

Why the hell should they? Did I want them turning my house upside down? "Listen, old man. That little matter is closed. Ruled off. Claim settled. I've left the department. People have died. The auditors have been in. Come on."

* * * *

On the Monday at the office I raffled it, ten bob each. Eight pounds! So during the week I bought her a little welcome-home present (a used transistor radio, actually, for listening to the cricket without disturbing her). I never look for prostrate gratitude or bowing or anything, but I welcome something warmer than her response to that transistor.

"You will have to pay them all back," she said.

What!

"And get the camera back. Mother and I agreed that the insurance office *must* be told. So we told them. They were very grateful. You owe them £18 10*s.* 0*d.* or the camera."

I shall not go on. One hateful cheque counterfoil tells the rest, and can be seen by appointment. In the train I have jerkily covered the backs of many envelopes and the margins of many newspapers with repeated calculations. I still want to know just how easy that money was, whether it was easier for someone else than for me, and what lesson, if any, is to be drawn from it. I think the lesson has to do with keeping one's big mouth shut.

Punch November 29, 1968.

Criminology

It only means the study of crime, or, better still, the study of crimes. A good many people take it to mean looking for fingerprints or fragments of cloth or hair, or writing up old murder stories for the evening papers, preferably the tales with women in them. At any lecture on criminology to a Police audience there will always be one listener who will want to know, at question time, whether criminology has ever resulted, anywhere in the world, in a reduction of the amount of crime going on. Every now and again one of the newspapers will remind its readers of the existence of the Institute of Criminology at Cambridge, and observe that the crime figures have doubled since it came into being.

Some crime figures have more than doubled since then; and, in a perverse way, you could lay the blame at the door of the Cambridge Institute of Criminology, for it has done a good deal to clarify the figures and the methods of recording reported crime. One thing criminology does is help towards giving you the measure of your problem. England is widely regarded as crueller to its children than any other nation in Europe, and this is because it has an N.S.P.C.C. which finds out what is going on and publishes annual reports. Where ignorance is bliss, tis folly to pay criminologists.

But criminology also involves the Policeman in the whole range of social services affected by crime. The day has gone when he could see his job in isolation, care nothing for what was done by the probation service, the prison service, the mental health services or the children's officers—and have any hope of being a good Policeman. This is what refutes the frequent criticisms of the "juvenile liaison" schemes. This process of intercepting delinquency at an early stage, often without recourse to any Court of law, has had to go through the inevitable period—in the twenty or more Police areas that have adopted it—of suspicion, ridicule, distrust, and accusations about empire-building, self-seeking and job-making. "Some senior Police officers." said the *Guardian* on 13th December, "say flatly that it will not work; others say it is impracticable when Forces are under strength." And they certainly do. So do a lot of Magistrates, who add that the Police should stick to their own job. "Some social workers" (The *Guardian* again) "say that any form of work with children and families should be operated or closely supervised by local authority welfare departments." And they do. Co-ordination has a long way to go, and there are still people in the social welfare services who (not without some reason) hate the sound of the word: co-ordination might make life a bit easier for the problem families, but it does so by making life rather more complicated and documentary for those looking after them. Police attitudes to these schemes are discussed by Miss Maureen Cain in the October issue of the *British Journal of Criminology* and in a report published last week by the School of Social Study at Glasgow University (10s. post free).

Police Review December 27, 1968.

Guilty by Numbers

It only seemed a matter of time before someone refused to wear one of those big numbered labels round his neck in the dock of a criminal Court. The trial of the Kray twins, Ronald and Reginald, their elder brother Charles, and seven other men at the Old Bailey last week was held up for over an hour because they defied the order of Mr. Justice Melford Stevenson to wear their placards so that the jury could identify them. Four of the men tore their placards in half.

There is absolutely no sanction against such a refusal, and absolutely no power to require that such placards be worn. There is not even a power to require that a man stand up or sit down: in the dock a man usually does one or the other and is allowed to please himself, and we have seen a man lie on the floor throughout his trial because no one though it was worth a fight to make him sit up. And since a man on trial is presumed innocent until the jury says otherwise, he can please himself about wearing a humiliating placard in the dock. The Old Bailey Judge last week, bowing to the inevitable, had the numbers placed on the outside of the dock. But a far better method is to give the jury (as is done in some American Courts) photocopies of a drawing showing the position of the men seated in the dock, with "outline" faces occupied solely by the numbers that indicate their positions. Of course the prisoners can refuse to sit in the positions indicated; but if the prison officers find themselves unable to look after that the case can always—and justifiably—be put back until the prisoners are ready to co-operate.

Police Review January 17, 1969.

The Right to be Let Alone

A good many Police officers, especially in the senior ranks, tend to look askance at the activities of the National Council for Civil Liberties—until the man in need of that Council's services or championship happens to be a Police officer or one of his closer relatives or friends. The truth is, none of us can do without some such organisation, and the countries in which they are not allowed to exist are countries that most people want to get out of but are prevented by twenty-foot walls or military observation posts. So the Council's newest compaign (put over, incidentally, in a highly professional way) for the protection of privacy, the "Right to be Let Alone," concerns all of us. Its publicity hand-out quotes Professor Harry Street as saying that, whereas the present law does not adequately protect the Englishman in his private life, "there is little hope that the Courts will remedy this defect without Parliament's help." And this, of course, is because no one has enough money to give them the chance. The Common Law Judges might well find a remedy for breach of privacy if some wealthy litigant got his case as far as the House of Lords. "In this age," says the N.C.C.L., "information is power and it is also profitable. The invaders have new weapons which include the computer and a wide range of electronic and photographic devices." The fact that the invaders may one day themselves be invaded has never been enough to stop this kind of thing. It may be worth commenting that there is one kind of invasion that it might be disastrous to stop: in an increasingly individualistic world, where (for instance) old people shut themselves away with teapot and television and never see a neighbour, a person can die in solitude and lie dead for weeks, or longer, because no one—including the Police—feels justified in "invading." And there have been cases in which a tragic crime has gone un-prevented because some Constable has taken too literally his orders never to go into private premises except with a warrant or as an invitee.

Police Review February 28, 1969.

William Burroughs on the Police

Do you know what hepatitis is? It's inflammation of the liver, and the virus that causes it was once a healthy liver cell. This reminds Mr. William Burroughs of the Police, who, he says, were once a healthy social cell. Mr Burroughs is the author of *The Naked Lunch* and for 15 years he was a junkie ("I was bored, I met addicts, that's all"). And he thinks that the healthy social cell known as the Police has suffered "a steady deterioration and especially since Hiroshima . . . possibly because of the radiations." That, believe it or not, is what he told the *Guardian* on 5 July; and his point was that the Police "exist only in so far as they can demonstrate their authority. They say they're here to preserve order, but in fact they'd go absolutely mad if all the criminals in the world went on strike for a month. They'd be on their knees begging for a crime; that's the only existence they have."

Well, is it? And would we? Rousseau used to say that crime could be abolished by a stroke of the pen, that is to say by repealing the whole of the criminal law. That sounds a little more feasible than Mr. Burroughs's theory, and rather closer to the British belief that you can abolish something by calling it something else (crime would have to be called *something*). But a one-month strike would hardly be long enough to empty all the C.I.D. in-trays. If there could be a five-year strike among the crooks Mr. Burroughs would have something to write about, for the effect on the national economy would be profound and might, for a time, be devastating. He's in a better position than most of us to work out what would happen to insurance, safe manufacturers, burglar alarms, the legal profession and the famous adding machines and computers. But while all this was going on he would still need Policemen to look out for some of the natural phenomena that have nothing to do with crime and a lot to do with the quiet life: floods and fire, deaths in the street, missing persons, lost children, collapsed buildings and collapsed morale. Morale owes a lot more to some symbolical street presence of law and order than it does even to a literary awareness of hepatitis and Hiroshima.

Police Review July 11, 1969.

"An Englishman's Home . . ."

It seems that Sir Edward Coke never really said: "An Englishman's home is his castle," though nothing will now change the folk-belief that he did. What he said appears twice in his works: in Part III of the *Institutes* he said: "A *man's* house is his castle," and in *Seymayne's Case* (1605) he said: "The house of *everyone* is to him as his castle and fortress, as well for his defence against injury and violence, as for his repose." So he seems not to have been making any special reference to Englishmen or, perhaps, to what English law thinks about them, and he may have been merely quoting, as judges sometimes will, from an earlier writer—Sir William Staunforde, who wrote a book called *Pleas of the Crown* in 1567 in which he said: "My house is to me as my castle, from which the law does not compel me to flee." (Incidentally, Lord Jowitt's *Dictionary of English Law* says this was written in the reign of William and Mary, namely late 17th century, but Lord Jowitt must have been having one of his off days. Even Sir William Blackstone says in his *Commentaries*: "My edition is dated 1607 but I do not think it can be the first.")

None of them, anyway, seems to have been specially concerned with Englishmen's houses, and they wrote about houses rather than homes. And these reflections are prompted by a news item that seems to be having a somewhat protracted life, starting with an all-night party in Holland Villas Road, Kensington, on 4 July. It was a party given by a prince and attended by a princess, and the house where it was held seems to have emitted an unprincely row to the annoyance of some neighbours. When the Police were informed (as they so often are) and said they couldn't interfere (as they usually have to say) there was much local indignation; and a Policeman was reported to have said: "An Englishman's home is his castle."

Then on 11 July there was a letter in the *Daily Telegraph* from Sir Frank Medlicott, solicitor and former Liberal M.P., who said: "It is doubtful if this was ever a precise statement of the law on this particular point, but in any case it was formulated long before sound amplification was invented." There was recently a dance in the S.W.1 district of London, writes Sir Frank, "at which the sound was amplified to an utterly unreasonable level, despite the fact that there is a children's hospital within earshot, a large hostel where nurses were trying to sleep, and the homes of hundreds of people who had to be at work next morning. In this instance, also, the police said they had no power to do anything; and notwithstanding every protest and every plea, the deafening din went on." Sir Frank wants the Home Secretary "to consider what is needed to be done to bring the law into line with the changed conditions in which we live," by which he means partly that no one seems to care a damn about anyone else, and partly that their unconcern can be electrically magnified into an earsplitting din in the small hours.

Sometimes, of course, the police *do* contrive to do something about nocturnal din from parties, and it is done by threats or persuasion according to the level of intelligence and cooperation that marks the behaviour of the revellers. But, as so often where the Police are called to do something for which the law has never made provision, it is a bluff. There is a feeling in the air that something will sooner or later be done about this by Parliament, if only because of the danger that exasperated citizens will "take the law into their own hands." This process lately took the form of tipping a punt-load of stentorian pop-songsters into a normally quiet reach of the River Thames at two o'clock in the morning—people in neighbouring punts and launches were trying to sleep. A more effective form might be to stage noisy all-night parties in the houses next door to selected Ministers of the Crown, but perhaps we had better move along to the next subject.

Police Review July 25, 1969.

Law and Order

This is a phrase that is hardly ever out of the news. Do you know who started it? Until quite lately the usual phrase was the "Queen's Peace" (or the King's), but the expression Law and Order has superseded it, though everyone now pronounces it Lore and Order (which could be quite a different thing?). Its inventor seems to have been Aristotle, who said in Book VII of his *Politics* that "Law is a form of order, and good law must necessarily mean good order." He had possibly been reading Cicero, who had said 300 years earlier that "the safety of the people shall be the supreme law" (*salus populi suprema lex esto*). That wouldn't be a bad Police motto? Come to that, it might fittingly be adopted by the Football Association, British Railways, the Anti-Apartheid movement and Keep Britain White. To have even-tempered football, unslashed railway seats, racially-liberal rugger teams and the rest of it without having physical safety would be a meaningless luxury, anyway.The trouble is that order has always been something that lawyers expect of other people. The average lawyer's office is like Mark Twain's: "Have a place for everything and keep everything somewhere else—this is not advice, it is merely custom." Or more like the Lore and Order we started with.

Police Review December 19, 1969.

The Whispering Act

It looks as though there will now be a prolonged row over the drafting and meaning of the Official Secrets Acts, and especially Section 2 of the 1911 Act, which says (with the more familiar bits left out but without damage to the context):

> If any person having in his possession or control any . . . information . . . to which he has had access owing to his position as a person who holds or has held office under Her Majesty, communicates the . . . information to any person other than a person to whom he is authorised to communicate it,

he is liable to two years' imprisonment. This becomes suddenly and loudly topical just now because of the summonses served on the *Sunday Telegraph* and its editor and one of its writers in respect of the publication of a "leaked" report on Nigeria. But as Sir Lionel Heald, a former Attorney-General, has said in a letter to *The Times* (20 March) "the Act makes it a crime, without any possibility of a defence, to report the number of cups of tea consumed per week in a government department, or the details of a new carpet in a minister's room." This, as Sir Lionel points out, is because the offence is "absolute." The Act says nothing about the importance or triviality of the information—"it simply uses the clear and unambiguous words 'any information.' "

So here we have a complaint, not about obscurity or ambiguity or double negatives, but about clarity. Successive governments have always resisted any amendment of the Act on the ground that questions of public interest are unsuitable for decision by the courts—you have to lay it all down in the statute. So, presumably, you shove everything in. And I can remember an occasion when a senior Police officer was authorised by his Chief Constable to receive pressmen and tell them "anything within reason" that they wanted to know about a newly opened Police headquarters, and got a subsequent telephone call from one of the news-hawks who had forgotten whether the new H.Q. had sash windows or casements. The worried officer (he was always worried) simply refused to say. "When in doubt, say nowt," he told me afterwards.

Police Review March 27, 1970.

"Craving Leave" in Affidavits

An old colleague writes to ask me whether the law doesn't "cover itself with ridicule" among ordinary chaps by the language used in affidavits. He recently had to swear a statement in which he was required to "crave leave to refer to paragraph so-and-so" of an earlier affidavit by someone in the same case. He didn't feel craven about any of it, he said. The affidavit also required him to say not only that he had been informed about certain facts but also that he "verily believed" them. You either believe a thing or not, he says, and you don't need adverbs like "verily" if you do.

I agree about the first criticism but not the second. Craving leave to say things you are entitled to say is ridiculous and abject, and suggests that you are still living under some monarch who can send you to the Tower of London for speaking your mind in defence of your legal rights. An affidavit is supposed to be confined to "such facts as the witness is able of his own knowledge to prove" (according to *Rules of the Supreme Court,* Ord. 38, r. 25), except on interlocutory motions, "on which statements as to his belief, with the ground thereof, may be admitted." So if you want your beliefs to be admitted, you have to do a bit of decent craving. But a belief, in the language of plain men, can mean half-a-mind, an inclination to believe; it might be wrong, so you must at least declare that you "verily" think it is right. You can believe impossible things, as the Queen said to Alice. "When I was your age," she explained, "I always did it for half an hour a day. Why, sometimes I've believed as many as six impossible things before breakfast."

Police Review June 26, 1970.

Haircut, Smith

A Police Cadet reader has asked me whether he has any redress against a Superintendent who has required him to get his long hair cut or else. I know of no human hair charter that could be invoked against the Discipline Code or any local Standing Orders. If a fully-attested Police officer were told to get his hair cut in the interests of smartness, he would have to do so or find another job where long hair was welcomed or tolerated; and I suppose a Cadet is in the same position. I read the other day about a New York Policeman whose hair falls below his collar and who, instead of being told to get it cut, was transferred from his Harlem beat to the fountain in Central Park, where the hippies would appreciate him. And they did. He held political meetings for them, and then he called a press conference to ventilate his grievance about the hair. The result was a disciplinary hearing, the outcome of which is not yet known. But I would expect it to show that in a dispute with the Chief Constable about the length of your hair, he would be likely to win. Just lately I've seen some cases that are so eligible as to make it a miracle that a helmet stays balanced on top.

Police Review July 10, 1970.

Coprology?

Last week at the fourth National Conference on Research and Teaching in Criminology there was much discussion about "Police Discretion," which has lately come under observation almost as though it were a new development. The Cambridge corridors and smoke-rooms were crammed with distinguished people who knew each other so well that they went around without their lapel badges, and in conversation you had to trap them into revealing identities you were ashamed of not knowing. (It's the clumsiest one that always works: "By the way, how do you actually *spell* your name?" Even if his name is Jones you can always say you'd heard there was an "a" in it.) But the kind of discretion under consideration was the discretion not to prosecute offenders (or suspects), and this sub-divides into cautioning, overlooking, not noticing, losing the papers, or dropping an inquiry because other duties simply crowd it out. The discussion was franker (and more stentorian) in the bars and smokerooms than during the formal sessions, but it was fairly plain that while we have 47 different Police Forces in England and Wales we shall have 47 different concepts of Police discretion. It's obviously a thing of immense importance to the criminal statistics, whose compilers are at the mercy of the 47 discretionaries, and it would be surprising if it were allowed to go on much longer without some attempt to assess its effects. A Home Office research committee is accordingly looking into it officially at long last; and although we may never hear much about its discoveries, or at any rate the public won't, there will inevitably be recommendations from the Home Office in due course that should lead to rather more uniformity of practice.

In the last decade the Policeman has been seen as an instrument of social control who is himself controlled and moulded by what the public think of him. Such influences interact in a way that the criminal law is unlikely to acknowledge, and there has developed a school of thought among criminologists which is known as the "interactionist" school. A dialogue is going on that becomes more and more involved (not to say incomprehensible) year by year, though the disputants show every sign of knowing what their own words mean even if they misinterpret their opponents'. You can be sure of one thing: the Policeman is going to be studied, assessed, logged, researched as never before, and a long name will soon be invented and applied to a department of criminology which will devote itself to Copper-study. If it is called Coprology there will be trouble as soon as the Police have looked it up.

Police Review July 17, 1970.

Carry on "Calcutta"

I hear that some of the playgoers who went to see Mr. Kenneth Tynan's simply-dressed production at the Round House are not convinced that the Attorney-General's decision has to be the final word. They were as outraged by the spectacle as many of the people who haven't even seen it yet, and of course there are several threatened interests from whom nothing has yet been heard—for example the theatrical costumiers. The Attorney can kill any hopes under the Theatres Act 1968, but he has no power to stop any private prosecutor from having a go under the Obscene Publications Act 1959. It's surprising how many people believe that the Director of Public Prosecutions must undertake all proceedings under the 1959 Act: he is concerned only with "destruction order proceedings" under Section 3, and he was brought into those by a last-minute amendment to the Criminal Justice Act 1967 as a result of the *Last Exit to Brooklyn* case. Sir Cyril Black was the last man to use that section as a private complainant, but he or anyone else could still risk his money on a private prosecution under Section 2 for "publishing an obscene article." The script of *Oh Calcutta*! is an "article" for the purposes of the 1959 Act—"any description of article containing or embodying matter to be read or looked at or both." Publishing it ("whether for gain or not") must include showing it to the shivering cast, the stage manager, the lighting men, the Police officers and Sir Peter Rawlinson. Of all those, which would it tend to deprave and corrupt, "having regard [as the Act says] to all relevant circumstances"? All the theatre critics, having now pronounced upon it, could be called by the defence to say that they felt all right after it, though it wasn't funny enough.

But if anyone was so foolish now as to take out a private summons, some friend concerned to protect him ought to persuade the D.P.P. to step in, take the case over, and offer no evidence. He would be getting off lightly. If the case went on, and especially if it got before a jury, Mr. Tynan might be tempted to subpoena the Attorney-General or someone from the Law Officers' Department to say why there had been no Theatres Act prosecution. It would be a very expensive prosecution, doomed to failure and left with at least its own costs to pay. The real prosecution will probably drag on for "duration" in the only court that can really adjudicate in these matters, the court of public taste—where the only rule that runs is the most immoral and merciless law of all, the law of supply and demand.

Police Review August 7, 1970.

A Taste of Prison

You don't often see the Magistrates Association publicly at odds with the Howard League for Penal Reform, and when you do it's interesting to have a ringside seat. Mine is fairly close to the ropes because behind those impersonal titles are the names of some people who are good friends of mine; moreover, I believe from the start that the Magistrates Association is answering a charge that hasn't actually been made. The Howard League said (in a memorandum about remand centres which it submitted to the Home Office and then published) that "the courts still appear to use remand centres as places of punishment" and that "one reason why youngsters are remanded in custody is for medical reports." Those two statements are widely separated in the memorandum, and they do *not* mean that "magistrates send young offenders to prison on remand to await medical reports as a form of punishment." But, according to the *Guardian,* 22 August, this is what the magistrates have taken it to mean; and an official of their association has publicly denied it.

I wonder why? Remands for unnecessary and irrelevant medical reports have been commonplace for years, and at Bow Street in the days before the Street Offences Act (to take one example) they were a well-established way of getting a young prostitute off the streets. Their justification was that they jolted a good many kids back into decent circulation. Everyone knew the medical excuse was little more than an excuse, though in rare cases you might find that the girl had V.D. and get her to do something about it. But I thought everyone knew, also, that even now some magistrates will occasionally use the "remand for medical report" as a way of teaching a sharp lesson to an offender they have no intention of sentencing to imprisonment. As Mr. Clive Davies put it in an article on "The Punitive Remand" in the *Justice of the Peace* for 10 January.

> The most convenient formula for use in making punitive remands is to "remand for reports," the request for reports being merely a sham if in reality the intent is to punish. Now, one unfortunate consequence of this is that the scarce and valuable time and skills of psychiatrists, medical officers, probation officers and others are being deliberately wasted. . . . The prison medical service meets growing numbers of requests for reports each year and, even so, considers that it is not adequately discharging its duty to the courts. In these circumstances, to send what are in effect bogus cases seems highly irresponsible.

To me, that makes sense and accords with experience. The Howard League didn't actually make the allegation that the magistrates deny, but I don't mind making it for them: if I am asked whether I can really suppose that a bench of magistrates will deliberately remand someone in custody "for medical report" when their sole object is to teach him a lesson, I can only reply that I jolly well know they will.

Police Review September 4, 1970.

Marriage Guidance

By long tradition the Police do not interfere in disputes between husband and wife except where the dispute takes a course likely to end in grievous bodily harm, or unless it is conducted in a street or public place in language (if there is any left) that shocks the passers-by. Or unless the husband, or perhaps the wife, happens to be a member of a Police Force, in which event the interfering is usually prolonged, nosey, and painstaking. But there are many true stories of young Constables who have gallantly stepped in to modify a matrimonial dispute on a Saturday night and have found themselves suddenly adopted as the family enemy, uniting the angry spouses as effectively as an invasion from Mars would revive the United Nations.

Scottish cities have a city prosecutor to take up such cases when they have gone far enough. Last week at Edinburgh William Dowie was charged with striking his wife in the face in an endeavour to settle which television programme they should watch. They had been out for the evening and were home just in time to see *This Week*. It happened to be the edition in which Mr. Edward Heath was telling what should have been a united nation just what the Tories were going to do. Mrs. Dowie switched him on and Mr. Dowie switched him off. She protested that she should be allowed to watch her Prime Minister if she chose, and her husband, in the course of dislodging this revolutionary notion, committed the assault. "There would seem to be some political overtones in this case," said the Deputy City Prosecutor when the case came to court; so it may have been that Mr. Dowie had wanted to watch *Up Pompeii*. But the manner in which he had asserted this none-too-clear legal entitlement cost him a night in the cells; and next morning Bailie Russell Fox, admonishing him, said it was unusual for a political argument in the home to end up in that way. No doubt Mrs. Dowie, for that one night, slept safer, but it seems a complicated and elephantine form of marriage guidance.

Police Review October 9, 1970.

Hamlyn Piper

Miss Emma Hamlyn of Torquay, who died in 1941 at the age of 80, was the daughter of a local solicitor and she inherited a taste for law. She left a bequest for the furtherance "by lectures or otherwise among the Common People of the United Kingdom of the knowledge of the Comparative Jurisprudence and Ethnology" (that's the study of race) "of the chief European countries." Her idea was that the Common People should come to know "the privileges which in law and custom they enjoy in comparison with other European peoples." So the trustees organise an annual course of Hamlyn Lectures by some "person of eminence" and then the lectures are published in book form by Stevens & Sons.

This year the person of eminence was Mr. Henry Cecil, whom you and I think of as the author of *Brothers in Law* and many similar books (though none better), and whom the legal profession knows as his Honour Judge Leon, the recently retired judge of Willesden County Court. His subject was "The English Judge." He managed, as few men could, to combine a well-merited tribute to their lordships with an equally merited knuckle-rapping that makes rather exciting reading. I warmly commend it to you. It costs 35 bob (or £1.75) and it's not a big book, but at the least it ought to be in the Police libraries. Henry Cecil, long may he live and write, never for a moment forgets that a Hamlyn Lecture is a lecture for the Common People. Nevertheless, at his first lecture, at any rate, his audience consisted mainly of distinguished lawyers and judges. The 93-year-old Lord Goddard was there, and slept peacefully on the platform. Sir Jocelyn Simon was there (the president of the Divorce Division), a day or two before his elevation to the peerage in the New Year Honours. Lord Denning, chairing the meeting, warmed all hearts with his tribute to "Harry Leon" and Henry Cecil. And none of these leading jurists visibly batted an eyelid when Mr. Cecil said that "it has long been traditional that judges should take no part in political matters." He allowed that "there was a time very long ago when judges could in fact be Members of Parliament," but told us it was now long established that they took no part whatever in politics. What about people like Mr. Sam Silkin, Mr. W. T. Williams, Mr. Frederick Crowder, Sir David Lockhart Muir, Mr. W. T. Wells, and many others—all of whom are Q.C.s, all recorders (i.e. judges of quarter sessions), and all Members of Parliament? And what about people like Lord Goddard, up there on the platform, and numerous other judges (including Lord Denning) who have played a considerable part in the framing and parliamentary discussion of Bills like those dealing with abortion, the death penalty, Commonwealth immigrants, and the rest? Anyone who tries to discern a pattern in the English judicial system and its supposed aloofness from politics and parliamentary legislation is attempting the impossible; but no one has made the attempt as entertaining as Mr. Henry Cecil, and literally no one has ever told the story in such scrupulously simple and everyday language.

Police Review January 22, 1971.

Patience and permissiveness

The patience of the public is just about exhausted, said Mr. Norman St. John-Stevas, M.P., in the House of Commons on 20 January. He was speaking about the "moral pollution" of the book trade, and he had asked the Home Secretary to introduce early legislation "to amend the law relating to obscenity." Mr. Mark Carlisle, the Under-Secretary at the Home Office, said the answer was No. He had a great deal of sympathy with Mr. St. John-Stevas's feelings about "the increase in the number of pornographic titles produced recently." (Titles? Mr. St. John-Stevas had felt it necessary to add, as an afterthought, that he was not talking about any titles chosen by newly created peers—only about book titles.) But, said Mr. Carlisle, he of all people must know the difficulty of finding a proper definition to take the place of that which exists in the Obscene Publications Acts of 1959 and 1964.

Mr. St. John-Stevas, in fact, was part-author of the Act of 1959 and his book *Obscenity and the Law,* published in 1956, concluded with a draft Bill that would have done far more, I believe, to rationalise the obscenity laws than the existing statutes have done. It is significant that he has now joined Sir Alan Herbert among those members of the "Herbert Committee" who have declared that the Act which crowned their efforts should now be tightened up. I think the trouble is the misunderstanding of the definition that speaks of publications which "*tend* to deprave and corrupt"; too many people, including lawyers, treat this as meaning that someone must be shown to have been depraved or corrupted. But a tendency is not a happening. The Leaning Tower of Pisa has been tending for 620 years to fall down. No one would require a description of its collapse, with photographs of the rubble, before believing that it had been suffering from this tendency all this time. I don't myself believe that a better definition than the 1959 one is likely to be found.

Police Review February 12, 1971.

How do you pronounce?

How much does it matter if you don't bother about mispronouncing your words? This is a constant source of discussion (or argument, really) between my wife and myself. Her view, and she knows more about English than I shall ever have time to learn, is that pronunciation is a matter of choice and is always changing with the times. I accept the idea of change but ask her if you don't distort a word like desiccated if you pronounce it *dess*icated—nowadays everyone does. Then I show her the dictionary which says "de-*sicc*-ated." She sweeps it aside and asks me if I remember Edwards' Desiccated Soup, and I say yes I do and the people who made it called it de*sicc*ated soup (I knew a chap in the business). Then I run slap into trouble. To siccate is to make dry. Siccation is the process of drying. So what's *de*siccation? Making something damp again? It's like denigration: to nigrate is to make black, so to denigrate ought to be to make white again. But the dictionaries now tell you to say *denn*igrate. We never finish the argument.

But shortly it will open up again, with me strongly fortified. At Hampshire Assizes three South African business men were sent to prison last week after a nine-day trial for smuggling cannabis. They had packed about 100 lb. of cannabis in tins with yellow labels bearing the words DESSICATED COCONUT. A Southampton customs man noticed the spelling, and thought that anyone genuinely desiccating coconut for a living would probably have learned to spell what he was doing. And at the same time (said the *Daily Telegraph* report on 27 March) the port health inspectors were anxious to test the contents of the tins because they hadn't seen desiccated coconut arrive in tins before. There were 430 tins, and 358 of them contained cannabis: the others contained coconut which seems to have been desiccated all right, whatever the spelling. The three men had bought the cannabis in Durban for £50, and its value in Britain was said to be £30,000. Why don't we call it siccated coconut? Then no one would get into trouble.

Police Review April 2, 1971.

Bingo and the People

"Do you not agree," writes a reader of this page and friend of mine (which must sometimes be a difficult double role to sustain), "that the time has come to call a halt to this tremendous bingo business? Millions of people wasting their money and time on a daft game that we used to call housey-housey? New bingo halls are opening by the hundred, they must be raking in millions—someone is going short and it's probably the children."

Well, no. "Calling a halt" to this kind of thing means making it criminal—there's no other way. That means shoving a few more people into the crowded prisons because we think (or someone thinks) that bingo ought to be prohibited. Or, as George Orwell might have said, "Baccarat good, bingo bad." About half a million people play bingo every day, and last year they won £150,000,000 in prize money—not much at a time, enough to buy the Sunday joint or a bottle of Scotch. And they did it in about 1,400 bingo clubs, all licensed by magistrates after getting a certificate from the Gaming Board for Great Britain. And why "call a halt" to that? A lot of good neighbourliness flourishes in the social atmosphere of the bingo club, and a great number of lonely people make their only contacts there. If they win a few bob, there is someone to congratulate them, which is more than you can say about the much less likely event of a secret win on premium bonds. Recent relaxations of the gaming laws have led to a lot of trouble, but not because of what happens in bingo clubs. Moral disapproval of bingo is too much like the shocked dismay that once greeted dog-racing: it was bringing the excitement of the racecourse to the millions and it would ruin them. We had no Adolf Hitler to warn us that "the goal and the road must be determined by concern for the preservation of the health of our people in body and soul—the right of personal freedom recedes before the duty to preserve the race." It was Hitler who receded. I should say that bingo enthusiasts do less harm than football fans, and we've got too many laws already; especially with promotion exams looming up.

Police Review June 18, 1971.

Bill of Wrongs

Most people, when they talk of the need for a Bill of Rights, are really asking for a Bill of Wrongs. They want the law to lay down what it can't do to them; and there's a pathetic belief that, from then on, such a law would remain forever unchanged. I said just now that we have too many laws already, and I was delighted last week to read (in the *Daily Telegraph*, 12 June) that Sir Geoffrey Howe, the Solicitor-General, is anxious about "the mountains of unintelligible law now existing" which ought to be either improved or removed. And Sir Geoffrey was announcing, in a speech to the Society for Individual Freedom, that this government has no intention of introducing any Bill of Rights. The difficulty about a Bill of Rights, he said, was that under our political system no Parliament can bind its successors. When you sit quietly for a few minutes and think of some of the Parliaments we have had, this turns out to be rather a good thing; but whatever a perpetually binding Parliament might think it was doing for posterity, however skilfully it devised a "this is for ever" form of words, if the people didn't like it that would be the end of Parliament. A daft House of Commons, with a premier like Hitler or Caligula, could enact that all babies born with blue eyes were to be drowned at once; and the House of Lords would be powerless to stop it. But not a baby would be drowned. Possibly some troops and Police would be killed and a few houses blown up, but within 48 hours the Palace of Westminster would be occupied by parents of blue-eyed babies, supported by the altruistic parents of some brown-eyed ones, looking for absentee legislators who realised they had gone foo far. "The only way" (Sir Geoffrey Howe again) "in which to enshrine a Bill of Rights in our law is to do so after a revolution, in which we overrule our constitution and write some new document to install in its place." And the only way to get rid of that would be another revolution. There's a lot to be said against the law of England, but at least you can say it. No need to scream and kill people.

Police Review June 18, 1971.

"New Yorker" v. L.C.J.

Lord Widgery has come in for an all-out attack in a leading article in the *New Yorker*. The American Bar Association, an organisation which in America is august and dignified but unpopular, holds a big meeting every few years and this time chose to hold it in England, booking the hotel accommodation a couple of years ago. The *New Yorker* seemed to disapprove of this, to begin with. The meeting was held in London, it said, not because England was the home of Magna Carta but because more members would attend if they could combine a holiday abroad with a "business trip" and deduct some of the expenses from next year's income tax. Fair enough, but just as any stick is said to be good enough to beat a dog with, any kind of tomato seems good enough to throw at a judge—"the whole convention was an outing at the taxpayer's expense." But I bet that if the judges had made some resounding statements in defence of civil liberty, you wouldn't have heard a word about the public expense or next year's income tax. Lord Widgery's crime was to say that "any rule requiring the attendance of a suspect's lawyer during Police interrogation is unacceptable," and he deplored the recent ruling of the U.S. Supreme Court that the interrogation must not go beyond the point at which the proceedings become "accusatory" unless the suspect is told of his right to remain silent and to have a lawyer. And the *New Yorker* laments: "Although the Lord Chief Justice of England may be little more than a figurehead at home, without much power beyond getting a decent table at Claridge's" (now who on earth, or even in New York, told them that?), "American lawyers and American newspaper readers are likely to be more impressed by this bewigged and stately creature than by their own Chief Justice. In that sense, then, Lord Widgery lent the weight of a thousand years of British law to one side of what has become both a legal and a political battle in the United States." And this was unmannerly and injudicious, made all the worse by being bewigged and stately. Ah well, the controversy will go on at least until English law says what Lord Widgery declares "unacceptable." Then it will become a War of Independence.

Police Review August 6, 1971.

Mind and Mischief

Psychiatrists, when you meet and talk to them, usually seem the humblest of men. They don't really know much, they seem to say, they are still inquiring; and they receive the most dogmatic statements of laymen (there have been a lot of these lately) with almost exaggerated respect. This aspect of their humility always reminds me of an occasion when Professor Einstein, visiting Princeton University, was asked to sign the visitors' book. He wrote his name, saw the word "qualification" at the top of the next column, and after a moment's hesitation wrote "student." Well, all right, not *all* psychiatrists are like this and every now and again you will meet one who clearly believes himself to be God. But their position of mysterious authority has been largely made for them by laymen, especially in the criminal courts, and they really have much in common with King Canute, who did *not* tell his toadying courtiers he could stop the tide coming in but arranged a demonstration to show that the tide took no notice of kings and that he had got the royal feet wet.

Nevertheless I do not go along with a correspondent who wants me to join him in a campaign to get forensic psychiatry "exposed" as a fraud and the evidence of psychiatrists made inadmissible in criminal cases. They are usually very intelligent chaps and what they have to say about a defendant may be very illuminating, even if it has little to do with medical knowledge or practice. They are the victims of a general belief that they understand the springs of human conduct and will one day discover the "cause" of crime; but I wouldn't exclude their evidence any more than that of a village priest (who often does the same sort of job for much less money) or even a lady who has once told the prisoner's fortune from tea leaves. I merely think we should join them in their own belief that too much shouldn't be expected of them.

Unless we do, there may one day come a danger that we shall get something like Russia's Serbsky Psychiatric Institute, which gets rid of political undesirables by certifying them insane, an old Russian custom greatly developed by Stalin. It was recently exposed by a long-respected party member, Mr. S. P. Pisarev, in a letter to the Academy of Medical Sciences, which got smuggled out of Russia and published in the *New York Times*. It protested against the "unending and frequent mistakes" in diagnosis made by the time-serving psychiatrists in the Serbsky. There was a fearful row, and no one seems to know where Mr. Pisarev could now be found. I've got nothing against our own psychiatrists so far, except the way they spell the word. But the whole thing needs watching. My own confidence in forensic psychiatry took a further knock when the editors of *Oz* were remanded to prison for medical reports; not because of what the unfortunate Prison Medical Service would be expected to do, or because the editors got their hair cut, but because that kind of thing helps to expose the D.P.M. as a diploma in promoting mystery.

Police Review September 3, 1971.

Left-handed perjury

One day somebody will write a Study of Falsehood, with some such title as *The Place of the Liar in Social and Political History*. Its readers will feel as though they are looking in a mirror. Lying is the foundation of social decency and good will and one of the principal instruments of government, whether by dictators or by cabinets or elected committees. If you were to say from the platform at a public meeting: "Hands up anyone who has never told a lie?" there would be no movement; but if, exceptionally, one hand *did* go up, it would be somebody adding one more to his record.

It wasn't until the sixteenth century that Parliament in this country decided that telling lies in the witness box must be put in a different category from telling lies in a royal proclamation or an election manifesto. There had certainly been perjury, and penalties for it, in Anglo-Saxon times; but those were concerned with "judicial oaths" sworn by jurors and "compurgators." Lying witnesses were left alone. Anyway, there was some uneasiness about punishing any form of perjury, since that might be interfering with the business of the Gods. By the time of King Cnut the law had grown a little more confident of its status, and a man who swore a false oath had his hand cut off—the hand by which he did the swearing.

I was reminded of all this the other day by the experience of a woman I saw giving evidence in a forgery case. "Take the book in your right hand," the usher said to her as she arrived in the witness box. She hesitated. "I'm left handed," she whispered. Sensation. (The procedure of the courts makes no provision for left-handedness.) The usher looked round rather anxiously for guidance, and none came. He picked up the book and firmly put it in the lady's right hand. Then he found that she was wearing gloves. "Please remove your glove," he said, and she did. But why? Suppose her right hand was an artificial one, habitually covered with a glove? What oracle has ever said that no glove must come between the witness's fingers and the Good Book? I would bet my last bit of decimal currency that these little refinements in the oath-taking ceremony have been evolved by superstitious, time-serving functionaries anxious to ensure that everything is "done right." There must be an ancestral feeling in the courts that if a left-handed man takes the oath with his right hand he is not "properly sworn" and can get away with whatever lies he fancies. I remember seeing the late Mr. Justice Charles glower at a Jewish witness who, having no hat with him, held a sheet of paper on his head as he took the oath. "Are you a Jew?" asked his lordshop angrily. The witness said he was. "Then take the oath properly," said his lordship with what seemed like studied offensiveness. Was it because the Jew, on a subsequent perjury charge, would have been able to plead successfully that he was bare-headed when he took the oath?

Perjury has a long history, and there was even a short time when the breach of a "promissory" oath (like a Policeman's oath of allegiance and good intention as a Constable) would have been regarded as a perjury. Pollock and Maitland, in their *History of English Law,* quote ancient legal authorities as making "every kind of official misdeed a perjury, as being a breach of the offender's oath of fealty": the learned authors call this "ridiculous but instructive," but it wasn't ridiculous in the days when petty officials (as well as princes and earls) were beheaded or burned for breaches of public duty which happened to offend the Church.

Hasn't the time come to abolish oath taking in the courts, merely telling witnesses they may be prosecuted if they tell lies, and not trying to frighten a predominantly heathen population with words about Almighty God? People have been having fun with it for a long time now. George Arliss, for example, once described himself in the witness box as "the greatest living actor," and when the judge intervened to make sure he had heard right, Arliss explained, "You see, my Lord, I am on oath."

Police Review October 22, 1971.

Coroners ought not to be gagged

That is not my heading—I've copied it from *The Times* of 11 November just to show how wrong *The Times* can be. Of course coroners should be gagged. They talk far too much and they inflict immense and acute suffering in the process. *The Times* leader was of course on the Brodrick report "Death Certification and Coroners" (Cmnd. 4810, H.M.S.O., £2.35 and worth it). The report, in disapproving of "coroners' animadversions," or what you and I might call line-shooting, says that if a coroner thinks action should be taken to prevent recurrence of some kind of accident he should refer the matter "to the appropriate expert body or public authority"—and announce that he is doing so. Of course *The Times* doesn't like this, and I suppose less responsible papers would like it even less. Coroners' denunciations are usually good copy. "It is the publicity in these cases," says *The Times*, "that provides the assurance that some action will in fact be taken. It is the coroner's critical remarks that attract the publicity. He should not be gagged." Logically this should mean that every time you submit a report recommending action on some matter affecting public safety you should send a copy to the press.

But it would be very unfair to judge the 229 coroners in England and Wales by the behaviour of their relatively few public moralists and orators; most of them probably deplore that behaviour as much as the bereaved relatives who are its most immediate victims. Anyway the Coroners Society of England and Wales has welcomed the Brodrick Report as "extremely good." I suppose the most important of its recommendations is that we should abolish the power of a coroner to name some person as guilty of homicide and to commit him for trial. I remember a very experienced Detective Sergeant coming in to me when I was on duty as a station officer (and was young enough to be his son), and saying: "I've got this chap committed for trial on a coroner's inquisition. What the devil do I do with him?" I hadn't the smallest idea. "Take him to Brixton Prison," I said in the voice I used when I was trying to sound confident and well-informed. So off he went. Brixton Prison took the man in with unruffled hospitality. Two days later a solicitor got him bail, and three weeks later the D.P.P told an Old Bailey judge there was no evidence and the man was discharged.

Still, the Brodrick Committee has come up with a good recommendation about treasure trove. This is, in effect, that the law should be changed so as to take care of historically valuable antiquities, and not merely of "gold and silver found hidden, the owner being unknown." The original intention of the law of treasure trove was that the king should get all the loot buried by the Romans when they were clearing out of Britain in the fourth century A.D. (They hoped to come back and dig it up for themselves.) Archaeologists have long been aggrieved that only gold and silver are protected, and they are excited by the possibility that, at long last, the law may protect antiquities of all kinds.

Police Review November 26, 1971.

Litter Vigilantes

Last week, using the heading *The Law in Whose Hands?,* I was holding forth about the oft-repeated admonition "You mustn't take the law into your own hands." I've always had a sneaking sympathy for the man who, with one eye closing up and blood streaming from his nose as a result of an unprovoked assault, is expected to go in search of a Policeman while his assailant walks away. Now I have been taken to task by a reader who thinks me "irresponsible." (Actually he's a bit more than a reader; more like a scrutineer who gets a pound every time he can prove me wrong. If only that were possible he could be living in affluence; but he would have to be better at it.) There is a growing apprehension about volunteer law-enforcement, and it seems to find some of its scope for ill-feeling in attacks on the private "security" firms like Securicor. I cannot understand why these organisations, which do a job of immense social value, should engender so much anger, or why anyone should be surprised in the present state of law-enforcement that they exist. They always have and, unless the law prohibits them as the Public Order Act of 1963 prohibited "para-military organisations," they always will. And any government that prohibited them without at the same time trebling the strength of the Police Forces would have a very short life. It doesn't look as though any foreseeable government will either prohibit security guards or effectively add to Police strength.

But there is much scope for the volunteer law-man (or "vigilante") in the enforcement of the Litter Act 1958. This I suppose is about the most neglected statute since the repeal of the Profane Oaths Act 1745, under which every cuss-word was supposed to cost you a shilling if you were a labourer or a common soldier and five bob if you were a gentleman. (Incidentally there was encouragement for the vigilante even in this instance, because a Policeman who heard someone swearing and did nothing about it could be ordered to forfeit 40 shillings; if he couldn't pay the 40 shillings, which was a lot of money in those days, the bailiffs would come and take away his settee.) However, in Staffordshire there is a man who has assumed the mantle of litter warden, without anyone's asking him to. He is Mr. Ray Seaton of Wombourne, near Wolverhampton, which won fame as one of Britain's best-kept villages during the Festival of Britain in 1951. Since then, like many nice villages, it has grown into a "dormitory area" and has a population of 12,000. So it has litter-bins to go with them; which, of course, most people ignore as they do in my village. The message of the litter-bin to most people seems to be: "Throw your rubbish on the ground just here: you will thus make it easier for someone to put it in the bin for you"; which I suppose is a minor improvement on having it thrown all over the village.

Well, Mr. Seaton of Wombourne collects sacks of litter every week and takes them to the local authority's dumping ground. He has been doing it for two years, and the clerk to the parish council has been helping him—the council itself have actually given him some kind of badge as their voluntary litter warden. He told *The Times* on Christmas Eve that he had "cleared debris from the village stream and hauled away old prams, bedsteads, oil drums, bicycles, tyres and a discarded gate from the village playing field. I sweat and strain," he said, "but everywhere is just as bad a week later. . . . It's a lost cause, but one can't give in to litter louts."A crank? Mr. Seaton, I would say, is no crank. He is doing a job that the local authority should do and I wish there were a million like him. Of course this would enable the local authorities to shirk the job more happily, but no one would really mind their being happy so long as the streets were clean. The worst outcome would be that the nation would be divided into two great classes, the chuckers-down and the pickers-up; at the moment the division is as between Mr. Seaton and the rest of us, and the latest news about him is that he has reported someone to the Police, with whom the case is "under consideration."

Police Review January 14,1972.

Whiskers

The Police authorities are fighting what seems a losing battle against whiskers. I thought the Police Service would be only less conservative than the Brigade of Guards in its firmness about hairy Policemen, but I suppose you have got to keep recruits somehow and one of the Chief Constable's current problems is how to specify hair-lengths. To judge by some of the young Bobbies I have seen lately it defies solution; I saw one the other day who looked like Wilkie Collins, and his helmet, the size of which was obviously irrelevant, was as if perched anywhere among the foliage where it could find lodgement. A correspondent who *has* been told to get his hair cut or get out has written to me inquiring about his legal rights. I can't see that he has any. It's all a bit like Queen Victoria's reaction to the idea that the Navy should allow beards. Well, all right, she said, "but on no account must moustaches be allowed without beards. That must be clearly understood." Time marches on.

Police Review January 21, 1972.

The Scope of Obscenity

The judges in the Queen's Bench Division have had to decide whether "passengers" in a street would be likely to be annoyed by an obscene monosyllable of great antiquity. Mr. Herbert Garrett of Cricklewood was driving through Willesden when he was directed by a Constable on duty to pull into the kerb. There then ensued a conversation in which an angry Mr. Garrett used (six times) a word which is permissible only among self-selected Anglo Saxons. (Now I come think of it I once heard a Pakistani using it in Bradford, but he was smiling all the time and he may have been putting it forward as a hallmark of British citizenship.) In Mr. Garrett's case, there was evidence that two women were shocked at his language, perhaps because it was being addressed to a Policeman, perhaps because it was being used at all. They told the Policeman that Mr. Garrett should not be allowed to get away with it, and he was prosecuted.

The Willesden magistrates decided that you could not be sure, "in this day and age" (a phrase for which they ought to be prosecuted themselves), that anyone would be annoyed by this much-used word. So they dismissed the case, and the Police decided to appeal (I wonder why they thought it mattered?). And Lord Widgery said the magistrates' decision was "not open to them"—there was actually evidence that two women thought Mr. Garrett's outburst was "shocking." The magistrates had "found the word obscene but contradicted themselves by remaining unconvinced that it would annoy passers-by," said the Lord Chief Justice. Their lordships were not impressed by the contention of Mr. Garrett's counsel that "it was the sort of language that might be used by two workmen walking down Wandsworth High Street." (Wandsworth? Why bring Wandsworth, or even workmen, into this low story? It's the sort of language that you can sometimes hear when you are walking through Middle Temple Lane, or even coming out of the Atheneum, though it should be admitted that, in all likelihood, someone would be telling a story.) Anyway, on the evidence of the two shocked ladies, the case was sent back to the Willesden magistrates with a direction that Mr. Garrett be convicted. The report I've seen doesn't reveal whether he, too, had to pay for the Police appeal. But what the press reports (notably not *The Times*) *did* say was that the High Court had ruled that this word was "still obscene." The High Court said nothing of the sort. It said that two women in a street had been annoyed by it; not, in effect, depraved or corrupted, but just shocked by it. The judges might have been saying that the word was profane, which I suppose it is likely to remain, or indecent, which it is in the process of ceasing to be but, as for the word itself, it started life innocently enough in Chaucer's time; then it became obscene, probably because of the way you could say it; and now it's a bit less obscene than it was because, with great patience, you can sometimes find it in the newspapers. But you can't help wondering whether the women would still have been shocked if they had heard the Policeman being abused in words which had all been taken from the Book of Common Prayer.

Police Review February 11, 1972.

Forgotten Bye-laws

No one can blame the Greater London Council, but when it was called the London County Council it passed a bye-law (actually it was as long ago as 1900) saying that

> no person shall exhibit any flash light so as to be visible from any street and to cause danger to the traffic therein, nor shall any owner or occupier of premises permit or suffer any flash light to be so exhibited on such premises.

And a flash light is "any light used for the purpose of illuminating, lighting, or exhibiting any word, letter, model, sign, device or representation in the nature of an advertisement, announcement or direction, which alters suddenly either in intensity, colour or direction."

Did you ever hear of that? There's a multitude of places in Greater London where it seems to be totally unknown, though I suppose all these red and green commendations of toothpaste, booze and eye-shadow have been duly considered and approved by little gatherings of permissive experts. A friend of mine driving along a suburban high road late one night had to take a skidding turn into a side road because another driver had mistaken a green shop-sign for a traffic green. Actually, he said, no one could have mistaken it for a traffic light if he had looked at it properly; but "when you are approaching an intersection which appears to have no traffic lights, you are watching the cross-road with extra care, and if something just above your head suddenly turns green you think there must be traffic lights after all." Personally I thought this might be a better excuse about a red light than a green one, but I don't see how it could be denied that there was a danger to traffic. I know some London cross-roads where you approach a veritable blaze of reds and greens. I can never understand why it's tolerated.

Police Review March 9, 1972.

Barking Dogs

Dogs play a larger part in the lives of the Police than in the lives of almost anyone except bookmakers, but there is no one who suffers more than the Police from their incessant barking. The Police view of barking dogs is formulated largely on night duty. I knew a Sergeant who was driven so close to insanity by the downstairs dog that he got into the habit, arriving home from night duty before anyone in the house was astir, of giving the dog a careful mixture of chopped meat, aniseed, and laudanum. The dog couldn't resist the aniseed, gobbled up the meat, imbibed the laudanum, and slept the clock round. The whole thing was exposed when the downstairs people took him to the vet, who said someone was doping him. It could only be the previously sleepless Police Sergeant upstairs. There was a fearful row, and the dog—as dogs nearly always do—emerged the victor. And yet, such is the spirit of man, whenever the Sergeant was on night duty as acting station officer, which was frequent, any dogs down in the kennels were always sleeping peacefully. I draw no inferences. I also remember that when I myself was a station officer (and I was known to be specially allergic to the barking of dogs) more than one of them got away during the night. I never knew how, but the man who probably did know is a man I shall always think of with affection.

They've been having this problem at Hampstead Police Station, which has a compound for stray dogs and a local population of inveterate dog-losers. In Downshire Hill lives Mr. Gerald Paterson, a barrister, and his windows not only look down on the dog-compound, they allow its noise to invade the house, despite double-glazing and internal shutters. I suppose the Police must have explained to him the provisions of Section 3 of the Dogs Act 1906, which says that if a Police officer has reason to believe that a dog found in a highway or place of public resort (by anyone) is a stray dog he may seize it and detain it until its owner has turned up and paid all the expenses of keeping it. Anyway Mr. Paterson at last applied to the High Court for an injunction requiring the Police to stop the noise. It was granted, and suspended for four weeks so that the Commissioner of Police can have some sound-proofing work done at Hampstead Police Station. Mr. Paterson's counsel, Mr. Christopher Slade, Q.C., said that his client's complaints to the Police "had been met with only a polite brush-off," which presumably meant that he had been told politely there was nothing much the Police could do. Well, probably there wasn't, since all the known ways of stopping a forsaken dog from barking would be angrily condemned if officially resorted to by the Police. Mr. Paterson may have started something, and this may be a social change which is long overdue. When the 1906 Act was passed you didn't get many Police stations whose found dogs had to be accommodated under barristers' windows. The people who had to put up with the barking were the poor—and the Police. I don't myself believe that any soundproofing will be very effective: when Mr. Paterson's judicially imposed four weeks of further suffering are over, we shall hear more from him. The solution required is a nation-wide one, and Mr. Paterson may be the instrument of it. My own suggestion would be that all dogs at Police stations should be collected by the dogs' home officials not later than 8 p.m. *daily*, the added cost being met from the Police rate; and that anyone bringing a stray dog to a Police station after 8 p.m. should be charged with insulting behaviour likely to cause a breach of the peace, the dog itself being told to report back next day unless it preferred to go home.

Police Review April 7, 1972.

Ruling to Work

I've always rather wanted to live in New Zealand, but have funked the upheaval and the parting with friends and family; and it's a bit late now. But if any possible development in this country could, even now, get me on to a V.C.10 for Wellington it would be a decision on the part of the Police here to fall into line with everyone else and (since they cannot strike) "work to rule." Consider what it would mean: no offence would be overlooked, from pitch-and-toss to homicide. Probably 10 million cars at any one time would be off the road, waiting for garages to put them right according to the law. (That would be nice in its way, but mine would be among them; and when you are saying "all these cars ought to be banned from this area," you are never thinking of your own vehicle.) In the small hours, every burglar alarm would mean turning the occupier of the premises out of bed. Every dropped bus-ticket and ice-cream carton observed by a Policeman (on his way to or from the courts) would occasion a summons. Please go on adding to the lists, it's inexhaustible: I want to tell you about a letter I've had from a lawyer in New Zealand.

Barristers and solicitors out there work in partnerships. You see on office doors "Smith & Jones, Barristers and Solicitors"; or even

"William Smith, Barrister and Solicitor." They tend to do a different kind of job, but they needn't. But, says a letter in the February *Newsletter* of the Auckland Law Society, the number of them who are practising solely as barristers is increasing, and it looks as though these will soon want to run their own show, as the Bar Council does here; and even to "elevate themselves to a status superior to their own partners in a firm." We don't want any United Kingdom practices over here, says the writer. "I refer in particular," he goes on, "to the rules which prevent barristers from going into solicitors' offices, entering into correspondence either with each other or with solicitors, or speaking directly with witnesses within the precincts of a court; and which demand the appearance of instructing solicitors with counsel at hearings, introduce the barrister's clerk as the fee-fixing agent of the barrister, and involve the formality of marking briefs."

Did you know that our barristers are forbidden to do all those things? Looking at them carefully, I realise that I've seen every single one of them transgressed. I've been at a conference in a solicitor's office which was attended by the barrister (his own chambers had the decorators in); it's well known that barristers and solicitors write to each other—what else are they supposed to do, leave messages in hollow oaks or milk bottles? I've seen many a Police officer instructing counsel in court because the solicitor couldn't be there: sometimes the judge will grouse and sometimes pretend not to notice; I've known more than one barrister to fix the fee himself and say "Tell my clerk, will you?" And many a brief goes "unmarked" because no one remembers to mark it.

Well, none of all this matters very much. But I've also been a party to long conversations, in the "court precincts," between wigged-and-gowned barristers and the witnesses in the cases they were concerned in. No doubt it was all very wrong (though I couldn't tell you why); but no harm ever seemed to come of it. The Bar Council and the Law Society have always kept up their sleeves, if they will pardon the expression, the notion of working to rule. I hope the Police will do the same, at least so long as I'm around.

Police Review April 21, 1972.

Justice Awake

Mr Justice Crichton was *not* asleep at Lewes Assizes last November when he was trying Alan and Keith Langham for murder (*The Times*, 25 April). They both appealed against their conviction on what the Lord Chief Justice called "the somewhat unusual ground that the judge, at material times, either was asleep or appeared to be asleep; and each contended that, on that ground, justice was not seen to be done and that the proper course was to order a new trial on the fresh evidence about the judge's conduct." The Court of Appeal had before it an affidavit from a solicitor, which said that "when the evidence was coming to an end and the counsel's speeches were beginning, the judge was sitting with his head resting on his hands, his eyes shut, and his head nodding"; and "for approximately the next quarter of an hour the judge was manifestly asleep from time to time."

The Court of Appeal decided that the judge couldn't have been *really* asleep because his notes and his summing-up showed that he had missed nothing. What about the complaint that he *appeared* to be asleep? "While that, if true, is a matter which the court would certainly deplore," said Lord Widgery, "it is not sufficient ground for the submission made that justice was not seen to be done." In 1961 there had been a court martial appeal (*R. v. Edworthy*) in which, though it was said that the president had had to wake up the judge advocate during the trial, Lord Parker said that was "not enough to defeat the verdict if it had not led to some deficiency in the judge advocate's summing-up." Then Lord Widgery observed that, although there had been three experienced counsel in court when the judge was supposed to have been asleep, none of them found it necessary to wake him up, or to "acquaint him with the fact that his appearance from the court seemed to be less alert than it should have been."

To me, it's one of the miracles of our judicial system that the judges can keep awake. It's the decorum which induces the sleepiness. You can keep awake more easily at a Salvation Army meeting than in the uneventful course of a village church service, while there is something about the proceedings before a Middle Western court in America that makes sleep impossible. Mr. Justice Finlay, when his court resumed after lunch, used to walk slowly up and down the bench behind his chair because he was afraid of going to sleep; and he sometimes had to tell inexperienced counsel, who might have found this distracting, to take no notice of him and pretend he wasn't there. I was told, though I can't vouch for it, that Sir Percival Clark, appearing for the defence in a case though he was in fact senior Treasury counsel at the Old Bailey, had once stopped in mid-speech and accused him of being asleep. "You are quite right," said his lordship to everyone's surprise, "and I am very sorry. Perhaps I can ask you, Sir Percival, to repeat your observations from the point at which you noticed it?" Sir Percival bowed and said it didn't matter. But it was from that day that the walking up and down began.

Police Review May 5, 1972.

So you won't talk

Some year ago the Ministry of Transport (or it may have been the Home Office, whose research unit is always hungry for detail) decided that it would be useful to know the ages of motorists involved in traffic offences. At that time Women's Lib was no more frightening than a third-rate TV performance of *The Lysistrata*, so no trouble was expected in the way of obstruction from women asked to declare their ages. But the women were most unhelpful. "Just what on earth has that to do with you?" they used to say when the Constable asked for the date of birth, even though that always sounds *slightly* less nosy than "How old are you?" And since it wasn't statutory and there was no penalty for refusing, the whole scheme collapsed. Now, by virtue of Section 225 (1) of the amended Road Traffic Act 1960 (Section 161 (1) of the 1972 Act), the failure to disclose this private sadness can be punished with a fine, which a number of determined women have paid.

It is obvious that if women got themselves really organised about this, the scheme would collapse again, for the courts could never contain nor the Police Service cope with the volume of ageless offenders. But women are not really so fierce and resolute as they sometimes seem, and will mutter their dates of birth, when asked, because life is too busy for that kind of fussing. The truth is that the growing insistence of "the State" that it must know the intimate details of its members' lives is a result of the growing power of anonymity. In the forest clearings where the ancient Britons lived, worked, slept and scratched, everyone knew everyone else and there was no need to give someone the power to go round asking other people's ages. There is a tribal community in, I think, Greenland, where there are no Police or magistrates, no prisons and no scales of punishment. Everyone knows not merely everyone else, but what property he possesses, and even the sledge-dogs are known to everyone by name (it would be useless for a man to steal another man's dog and pretend it was his). If someone *does* steal or commit an assault or violate the moral code, the elders meet to make sure who it was and then publish his name on a board. And that's all, except that there is probably some voluntary official who sees to it, when he passes the board from time to time, that the offender's name hasn't got covered with snow. Where a criminal can't take refuge in the vast anonymity of some place like London or Manchester, life is more difficult for him, and the difficulty grows as the places of possible refuge get smaller. And when everyone knows he is a criminal, the stigma is more powerful than prison can be for a man whom nobody knows.

Police Review June 16, 1972.

Ghoul-control Duty

If you knew that an air-liner had crashed within a mile of your house, or you heard about it on your car radio less than a mile distant, what would you do? (Let's assume you are not a Police officer or a doctor.)

Whatever your motive in hurrying to the scene you would, in the seemingly official view, be conducting yourself like a ghoul; which means that you would be like an evil spirit which, in Moslem countries, is believed to prey on human corpses. The right thing to do is to stay at home and do your preying by proxy, contemplating the corpses on your television and letting the cameramen get on with their vital work of photographing your nightly dose of tragedy. "It was ironic," wrote two doctors in *The Times* on 21 June, "that only yards from the scene of Sunday's air disaster, with B.B.C. cameras dwelling upon the wreckage, a B.B.C. reporter could—with no sense of the bizarre—condemn the 'ghouls' who flocked to see."

There isn't really much to be said for cursing this perfectly natural human appetite. The sensible thing to do is to recognise its existence (instead of condemning it in angry astonishment whenever it appears) and control it. Recognising it means adopting the attitude suggested by Logan Pearsall Smith:

> There are men and women born into the word to do its work and win its prizes. Others, simply to look on and see what happens. These two kinds of people feel ashamed when they meet each other.

Our situation ought to be a bit easier now that we have television newsmen to feel ashamed for us, while getting on with their ghoulish business of photographing the dead for us. But the Police responsibility for providing access to scenes of disaster, which is concerned with essential services, is not concerned with sightseers or even with the normal users of the highway, and the latter ought to be diverted as soon as possible on to other routes. Here the broadcast news services could help by keeping quiet for a reasonable time, instead of interrupting comedy or pop programmes with a "news flash" giving careful indications about the exact location.

But at some time or other it must have been decided that flying over towns was no longer dangerous. The Air Navigation Orders used to require that no aircraft should fly over a town at such a height that, "if the means of propulsion failed," it was unable to land outside the town. Today the law says, and has said it since 1920, that the offence is flying "in such a manner as to be the cause of unnecessary danger," with no mention of means of propulsion. And the penalty is still £200 or six months. Compare that with the penalty on motorists.

Police Review June 30, 1972.

Blue Publications

This phrase has at last got itself enshrined in *The Times* law reports. "In arriving at the value of blue publications for the purpose of determining a fine for evading the prohibition on their importation," said *The Times* in reporting *Byrne* v. *Low* on 15 July, "the court is not restricted by distinctions between the so-called black market and white market." A man had imported 1,000 magazines and 650 films which contravened the provisions of the Customs Act 1952 about indecent articles. Section 304 prescribes a penalty of "three times the value of the goods or £100, whichever is the greater," and by Section 305 the value of the goods is to be "taken as the price which those goods might reasonably be expected to have fetched in the open market." The Harwich justices had fined the man £3,000, and when he appealed to Essex Quarter Sessions the fine was reduced to £100, though the sessions added a suspended sentence of 12 months' imprisonment. The chairman at quarter sessions took the view that, since the import of this kind of thing was prohibited, there couldn't be any recognised "open market" for it in England; therefore the only way of computing the penalty was to adopt the £100 alternative. The Lord Chief Justice thought this was wrong. What had to be looked for was the price which a willing seller would accept from a willing buyer at the port of landing. That was the "open market" for the goods for this purpose, and the penalty could go up to three times *that* figure. The goods came from Denmark and the Danish invoice was for £2,335. The magistrates had taken that as the open market value, and decided that they could go up to three times £2,355 if they thought fit. "They were entirely right," said Lord Widgery. And the case was sent back to what has since become the Crown Court with a direction "that the penalty be reassessed in the light of the High Court's opinion."

Why "blue" publications and films? No one seems to be sure how this adjective arrived. Even Mr. Eric Partridge, in his *Dictionary of Slang and Unconventional English*, which seems to have traced most of these things with a thoroughness that has taken all the gratification out of swearing, can only guess. He thinks it arrived in 1830 (which is unfortunate, perhaps, because that's about the time when the Police arrived with their blue uniform). He harks back to a vast seven-volume work called *Slang and Its Analogues*, by two even more industrious chaps called Farmer and Henley who took from 1890 to 1904 to complete their job; and they said it came from "the blue dress of harlots." In 1859 there was a smaller work called *The Slang Dictionary*, whose author, J. C. Hotten, traced it to a series of French books called The Blue Library. The *Oxford English Dictionary* doesn't pretend to know where it came from and just says it means obscene, and then confuses everyone by recalling that the Blue Laws were "severe Puritanical laws said to have been enacted in the 18th century at New Haven, Connecticut." Bluebooks (it adds) are "official reports of Parliament issued in a blue paper cover." Well, the annual report of the Commissioner of Police of the Metropolis comes out in a blue paper cover and it's a Government publication. If anyone buys that in the hope that it's blue we may yet see the Commissioner prosecuted under the Trade Descriptions Act.

Police Review July 11, 1972.

Non-insulting Behaviour

The men on duty outside No. 10 Downing Street are now entitled to claim that they've seen everything, and Bow Street to claim that the scope of the insult has been explored to the uttermost. Last Saturday five naked girls and a man (who seems to have had some kind of covering) were arrested outside No. 10. They were performing a publicity stunt for a Rock Festival, and proposed (they said) to hand a petition to Mr. Heath, who wasn't there. If he had seen the petition he would have found that it asked him to play the piano at their forthcoming festival. It also protested about the amount of rock 'n' roll music on radio and TV, though the press report (*Observer*, 30 July) doesn't say whether they thought there was too much or too little, or whether they wanted it diluted by Mr. Heath playing the organ.

Now the law doesn't really cope with Downing Street nudity except by admitting the possibility that it's insulting. Beyond question it is a method of calling attention to oneself, and seems likely to remain so for a few more years; after which it may be insulting to go around with clothes on. Meanwhile it still causes indignation, and the *Oxford English Dictionary* (thinking perhaps of Mr. Heath) says that to insult is "to offer indignity to; to affront, outrage." There was a different problem in *Brutus v. Cozens* [1972], where the accused had gone on to one of the Wimbledon tennis courts while a championship game was in progress to protest against the South African government's apartheid policy. He blew a whistle, threw leaflets around, sat down on the court and had to be removed by the long-suffering Police. The Wimbledon crowd were infuriated, shook their fists at him and, in some cases, tried to hit him. He was charged with insulting behaviour under the Public Order Act 1936. The magistrates dismissed the charge because they thought all this was not insulting, the Queen's Bench Division said they were wrong and it was, and the House of Lords held *unanimously* on 19 July (Reid, Morris, Dilhorne, Diplock and Kilbrandon) that the magistrates had been right after all. The word "insulting," said their lordships, had to be given its ordinary meaning. It was not a question of law (which means that there was not really any right of appeal on it). "The spectators might have been very angry and justly so. The accused's conduct was deplorable but it could not be said that his behaviour had insulted them." The House of Lords could not accept the Queen's Bench view that the word "insulting," for the purpose of Section 5 of the Public Order Act, could mean "behaviour which affronts other people, and evidences a disrespect or contempt for their rights, and which reasonable persons would foresee was likely to cause resentment or protest."

So what on earth can insulting really mean? I intend no "disrespect or contempt" for the House of Lords; and if I did, well, there's always the Official Solicitor. If "giving a word its ordinary meaning" is the same thing as giving it the meaning that the dictionaries give it, what more is needed than the *Oxford English Dictionary*'s "to affront, to outrage," which dates from 1620? *Nuttall's Dictionary* says the same. *Webster* (if you like an American version) says "to treat with insolence, affront wantonly." And all the lesser dictionaries take it from there. I've seen a man charged with insulting behaviour because he carried a placard exhorting passers-by to "Prepare to meet thy God." I've seen a man actually convicted because his placard said "This war is the Devil's business—Do not fight." And many a man has been convicted of insulting behaviour (*not* sedition) for putting stickers in telephone booths saying one should refuse to join the Army. My own view is that all these convictions were crazy, but what is the right word for a House of Lords decision like *Brutus v. Cozens*?

Police Review August 4, 1972.

Wigs and the Rule of Law

Members of Parliament have been revealing (according to *The Times Diary* on 14 August) that trade-union leaders don't accept the Industrial Relations Court as "part of the High Court" because it is "minus the wigs and gowns and the fusty atmosphere of the older courts in the Strand." Trade-union conservatism, says the *Times Diary* man sagely, is something that has to be reckoned with.

I believe, in fact, that the majority of people suppose a man is cleverer because he has a wig on. When stipendiary magistrates first began to be appointed, the barristers who were getting the jobs wanted to be allowed to wear their wigs and look the part. The idea was rejected because they would have looked more important than lay justices, which they are not supposed to be, or cleverer, which they have been known to be. So to this day a magistrate seems to many people of a lower order of authority, and even intelligence, than a wigged judge. It would come as a surprise to most people to find that in the Downing Street courtroom which houses the Judicial Committee of the Privy Council, the highest court of appeal in the British Commonwealth, their lordships sit without wigs or gowns and look just like people. Wigs and gowns are inseparably associated in the popular mind with the "rule of law."

Have you had enough of that phrase, "rule of law"? It has never had such an airing in this country, surely, since James II was got rid of and

William of Orange was brought from Holland, long to reign over us happy and glorious. To most people, though, the rule of law simply means sending people to prison for disobedience: it was much used when the three dockers (who do *not* now look like becoming martyrs) were sent to prison for contempt in defying a court order about their methods of picketing. Yet it is supposed to guarantee all kinds of "rights" to the citizens, for which there is no firmer authority than the opinions of great writers on constitutional law, such as Dicey in the past and Friedmann today. Professor Friedmann, in fact, says in his *Law in a Changing Society* (which you can now get in a Penguin edition, not for recommended holiday reading but to keep as a priceless reference book) that the rule of law "means no more than organised public power—any system of norms based on a hierarchy of orders, even the organised mass murders of the Nazi regime, qualifies as law." And Friedmann points out that to one man the rule of law means the safety of private property, to another the protection of private enterprise without State interference, and to another the "right to work" when a trade union says not.

The alleged confidence in wigs and gowns may seem a little comic, but it seems to me something worth pandering to. Behind all the cynicism about lawyers (some of it justified) the great mass of the people have a necessary confidence in the courts, and anything that helps to sustain it is good. Trade union orators may defy the courts through their microphones, but where do they turn when they feel wronged and see no other way out of their troubles? When the Electrical Trades Union realised, at long last, that its branch elections were being "rigged" by communists, it invoked "the rule of law": it went to the High Court and asked a wigged and gowned judge to rule that all the crooked election results were invalid. There was no law about it, and the judge had to make it. It's the same idea that brings worried people to Police stations, often with complaints that lie far outside the scope of Police redress. The public don't see this on television, because there is no brutality in it, or bribery or cooked-up confessions. But somehow or other they all know it's available and they like to hear it called the rule of law.

Police Review August 25, 1972.

Murder Made Easy

What is the difference between a terrorist, a guerrilla, and a resistance fighter? There's no more subjective choice in the world today. "No one has ever thought of referring to the French Resistance as the French terrorists," wrote Professor A. L. Goodhart in *The Times* on 13 September. "They never attacked peaceful travellers gathered at an airport nor did they kill a group of unarmed athletes waiting to take part in the Olympic Games." Professor Goodhart's statement of the Geneva Convention about the recognition of guerrillas as "legitimate combatants," which then follows, falls rather below this standard of clarity when it says that "stated shortly, guerrillas must fight a war against their armed enemies as regular soliders do—they must not attack non-combatants." Attacking non-combatants is precisely what all civilised war leaders do nowadays, as when we roasted 135,000 people in our firebomb attack on Dresden in World War II. (During nearly six years of war the total of civilians killed in Great Britain was 60,000: see A. J. P. Taylor's *English History, 1914–1945*, page 411.) But terrorists, guerrillas, and resistance fighters are alike in believing they are *always* at war, the declarations and treaties of statesmen being irrelevant. So when our Defence Regulations allowed the "presumption of death by enemy action" when civilians disappeared during World War II, they established a ghastly (if unintentional) precedent for unexplained deaths in guerrilla or terrorist conditions. This is the problem faced by the Police of Northern Ireland and, to a lesser extent, the Republic of Ireland, when men are found dead with hoods over their faces and placards on their chests. They may be the victims of private murder having no connection whatsoever with the current political troubles. Private and public murder have between them suspended the law of homicide.

Police Review September 22, 1972.

Television Gets it Wrong

I don't want to increase the acreage, which will run into square miles by the time this is in print, of paper devoted to the Longford report on pornography; but there is a sparkling chapter by Malcolm Muggeridge which, like everything he writes, will make him hated by many, loved by some, and read by all. It's about television. "To the ordinary, non-sociological person it cannot but seem clear," says Mr. Muggeridge, "that if elevating television programmes elevate, then degrading ones degrade." And "it seems fair to say that the programmes shown are, for the most part, vulgar rather than vicious, smutty rather than specifically pornographic, infantile rather than pernicious. It would be difficult to think of any form of human entertainment more intrinsically fatuous and demeaning than give-away programmes like *Double Your Money*, an ostensible "religious" programme like *The Stars on Sunday*, or that weary old biographical number, *This Is Your Life*," but "they have to be seen as on a par with the offerings of any popular newspaper, magazine or theatrical entertainment. Short of demolishing the whole structure of our present way of life, there would seem to be little that can be done to make them better or, for that matter, worse." Let me pause for a moment to say that I don't find it difficult to think of programmes that would be more fatuous and demeaning than the ones he names, but I refrain from suggesting them for fear that some lynx-eyed producer, exhausted by scraping the barrel, will decide to put them on.

The thing is, television will not merely survive this kind of exposure, it thrives on it. And there will always be plenty to nourish it. What is in short supply is technical criticism about programmes presenting developed social techniques like Police work. No doubt the companies go to a lot of trouble, and pay out good money to the "advisers" whose names roll up on the credit-list at the end of a crime story, but is it not astonishing how often they get things wrong, with never a word from anyone? You do get an occasional query from some eminent lawyer: Mr. Justice Megarry, for instance, delivering the Riddell Lecture this year to the Institute of Legal Executives (who used to be called solicitors' managing clerks), had a go at a series called *Justice* in which Margaret Lockwood appeared as counsel for the defence. Before one case came on, prosecuting counsel told her he wasn't going to put in a certain letter because (he said) it was damning to the defence and would "therefore" be inadmissible! She looked up and told him it would be all right. "So far as I know," said Mr. Justice Megarry, "the duty never to mislead the court has not been extended into a duty to give advice on evidence to the other side." In one of the "Misleading Cases" still associated with the name of A. P. Herbert (who must often twist in his grave), Alastair Sim as the judge actually tells his jury that they must return a verdict of *Guilty*—they just have to take it from him. That verdict would have been on its way to the Court of Appeal before the ink was dry. In last week's *Softly, Softly: Task Force*, whose Chief Constable had unlimited time for standing about in full uniform while rival Police departments searched for a missing girl, the charge against her had been reduced from "homicide" to manslaughter on grounds of diminished responsibility. (What she got, nevertheless, was a life sentence, at the age of 16.) There must be *somebody* who could advise about all this. But perhaps the experts have all been made redundant.

Police Review September 29, 1972.

House Numbers

Do you know the law about the numbering of houses? There's a provision in the Towns Improvement Clauses Act 1847, Section 64, which declares that every occupier who fails *within one week after notice* from the local authority to put on his house a number "approved by the authority," or to renew it when obliterated, can be fined £20 and may in addition have to pay the local authority for doing the job he has neglected to do. I have no means of knowing how many local authorities have availed themselves of this power and got their streets properly numbered; but the same Act *requires* them to cause all the houses and buildings in their districts to be marked with numbers "as they think fit," and the number who don't think fit must far exceed those who do. Seemingly if the town hall doesn't think fit to do anything about it at all, the numbering never gets done and the roads are given over to Chez Nouse, Dunroamin, Ersanmine and The Elms.

There has lately been a correspondence about this problem in the newspapers, both national and local, the central concern of it being the inconvenience and danger to important and national services. The problem for doctors, Police, the postal service and the fire service is obvious enough: emergencies have plenty of time to turn fatal while drivers of official vehicles are crawling along at night looking for non-existent house numbers. What is less obvious is the danger to traffic; obvious enough, of course, if you happen to be behind a driver who is thus engaged (and maybe merely going to a party or to look at a house he hopes to buy), slightly less obvious to that man himself, but forgotten by everyone as soon as he has found his target and everyone is on the move again. Nothing is ever done about it.

So far as my own limited travels suggest, this is about the only civilised country where it happens. Every house in New York has a number, and the street *names* (which are often numbers too) are displayed on street-corner posts, which show not only the name of the side street on one arm of a signpost but the name of the main street on another. In London, a stranger can walk the entire length of Oxford Street (to take only one example from thousands) without knowing where he is, and on the way he will pass side turnings (some of them famous streets) which are destitute of nameplates. There is much to be said for the American corner-post, which is still there to tell you the street name when the corner house (which in England carries the name if anything does) has been demolished.

It's surprising that, among our countless societies for the suppression of this and the encouragement of that, there is no society for the naming of streets, with representatives going round putting up nameplates where they are needed. If they got themselves prosecuted for "defacing" or marking buildings without the consent of the occupiers (which is unlikely but not inconceivable), their fines could be paid out of subscribed funds and the resulting publicity would be sure to result, sooner or later, in a great awakening of local authorities from their comfortable sleep.

I was once talking to a London Police Sergeant when a man came up and asked him how on earth he could find number 97? "All streets in London," said the Sergeant with impressive self-assurance, "start numbering from the G.P.O. And if you don't know where that is, think of St. Paul's Cathedral, which is close to it." The man went off filled with new hope, and I went off enriched (I thought) with a new piece of useful knowledge. It was years before I discovered he was wrong, though he was very nearly right; and even so, his belief was based (it seems) on a tradition which had no legal basis. It all seems very odd to me, especially now that town planning has an opportunity to mean something that can be useful as well as aesthetic or infuriating. No doubt the local authorities could be forced to do their job by someone like Mr. Raymond Blackburn with an urge to apply for *mandamus* orders against authorities which seem to him to be falling down on their jobs.

Police Review November 24, 1972.

Boo

When political feelings are running high, the Police at open-air meetings—or, for that matter, at indoor ones to which they have been called—are likely to feel that one man booing in the crowd is more dangerous to the peace than 50,000 booing at Leeds United. "Boo" is a criticism, the shortest one, I suppose, in the critic's vocabulary (which, on the whole, is a bit longwinded). There have been convictions for shouting Boo, following arguments as to whether it was insulting behaviour or an insulting word. (The *Shorter Oxford Dictionary* says it's a word, "an expression of contempt or aversion", and that it dates from 1801.) But it is also international. They boo in Denmark, Gemany, Austria and Italy at least. On 4 February, to my horror, three men in the audience at the Vienna Opera House who didn't like our beloved Gwyneth Jones as Aïda (and what's the matter with them?) started booing her while she sang. *Aïda* runs for four hours, and after two hours the Police moved in and arrested the three booers. Then it turned out that the rest of the audience supported the booers; they began chanting "Where's the manager?" The guest producer was Nathaniel Merrill, of the Metropolitan Opera at New York, and he had been trying to put over a new interpretation of Verdi, which may have been what got poor Gwyneth Jones into trouble; and he got some boos also. Then it all finished with cheers and a "standing ovation" for the leading tenor, smiles all round, and the release of the three booers.

Which seems to show that booing may be less wicked than it sometimes seems to the Police. At the end of one of Bernard Shaw's plays, the thunderous applause was followed by one strident boo. "I totally agree," said G.B.S. from the stage, "but what are we two among so many?"

Police Review February 16, 1973.

Diabolical Liberty

I wish I could find out who first used that phrase. It's been current at least since my own childhood, which is longer than I propose to reveal; and someone must have invented it. When the Marlborough Street magistrate, Mr. John Hooper, had a three-card-trick man before him on 16 February he fined him £40 and was then confronted with the inevitable request for "time to pay". Mr. Hooper told him to get a message on the grape vine. "You find-the-lady people are among the most prosperous people in town," he said. A *Daily Telegraph* man discussed this with an eight-man card team waiting for its clients outside Bond Street Underground station. "It's a diabolical liberty," said one of them, meaning Mr. Hooper's assessment of their income. It also meant that he was angry. It was not merely a liberty that Mr. Hooper had committed, it was a diabolical one. It was of the same nature as would be committed by the Devil himself; and yet card tricksters can't really believe in the Devil. "It is the Devil's master-stroke," said George Meredith, "to get us to accuse him."

Police Review March 2, 1973.

Inventive Prevention

I know a nurseryman who makes a regular practice, when sowing or renovating lawns, of putting a small pile of cheap grass seed at each corner for the birds. He replenishes each pile when it has got too small to distract the birds' attention from the posher and more important seed in the ground. It seems to work, too. He says it costs much less than bird-scaring devices, and is less trouble than tying lengths of cotton from meat skewers. So I find it hard not to sympathise just a little with the Wolverhampton crime prevention officer who has been suggesting that householders leave a couple of £1 notes on their mantelpieces, in the hope that burglars may be induced to pocket the money and leave. The Townswomen's Guild said it was "flabbergasted at the idea", and saw it as putting temptation in people's way. ("After all, would it stop at just a couple of pounds?") The officer's idea was that many break-ins are done by men who have been out on the beer and are housebreaking for kicks. But he has been told to delete this advice from future lectures to householders, on the ground, I suppose, that it could result in what everyone nowadays calls escalation.

Police Review March 30, 1973.

Who Closed Downing Street?

All my life until three or four months ago (certainly for more than 50 years) Downing Street has been a public thoroughfare—i.e. a street—and anyone might enter it at either end, pass along it and proceed on his way. One night recently I wished to pass that way, but found the Whitehall end barred by a heavy fence with a small gap in the middle guarded by two Police officers. I asked if I might pass along this thoroughfare and was refused. "We have to prevent access to No. 10." I told them I did not wish to have access to No. 10 but only to walk along Downing Street and out at the other end. "We cannot allow you to do that, sir."

Now let me disclose that all this is copied from a letter in *The Times* of 24 April from a Mr. Neil Fisk, of Pinner. Up to that point Mr. Fisk and I have had a common adventure. Henceforth his story is more exciting than mine, reflecting a braver spirit in a way that shows why I've never become a village Hampden. Mr. Fisk wanted to know "what statute authorised them to refuse him a passage". Neither of them, he said, knew. He asked them how he could find out and they directed him to "the Police station in Derby Gate, only 100 yards away". He went there and asked the duty officer. The following dialogue, he says, took place:

> "I don't know, sir." "How can I find out?" "It's not a statute, it's a regulation, sir." "What is the number of the regulation, please?" "I don't know, sir." "How can I find out?" "Will you wait a minute, sir?" So I waited.

In "less than a minute" a Sergeant was telling him that the closing of Downing Street had been done by the Prime Minister's direction. "Then the basis of the Police refusal of right of way to me is the Prime Minister's personal fiat, is it?" "Yes." So Mr. Fisk went home and wrote to *The Times,* hoping to find out whether any of its readers—"or perhaps the Police Commissioner"—could tell him whether *any* public right of way in England could be arbitrarily closed by the Prime Minister's personal fiat, or was its operation restricted to the one in which he happened to be residing?

Mr. Fisk mustn't take it amiss, and may accept it as some sort of tribute, if I recall that there's one born every minute. I mean a Mr. Fisk, not a Policeman who can be manoeuvred into inventing rule-making authorities on the spur of the moment. If a gas main blows a big hole in the road, and the Police won't let me go along and fall into it, what statute have they dug up for the purpose of curtailing my hard-won right to fall down holes? Or it is the personal whim of some Prime Minister?

I don't believe the Police need any statutory authority to close a street against anticipated terrorists; and if they allowed a Prime Minister to be blown up by way of showing how much they did need it, they would get a lot more from Parliament and public than a mere authority to close streets. Still, if we *must* have a statutory basis, what about Section 52 of the Metropolitan Police Act 1839, leaving out all the bits that don't apply to Mr. Fisk?

> It shall be lawful for the Commissioners of Police from time to time, and as occasion shall require, to make regulations for the route to be observed by all · · · persons · · · and also to give directions to the Constables for keeping order · · · in the immediate neighbourhood of Her Majesty's palaces and the public offices.

Luckily, on his own showing, Mr. Fisk was treated with scrupulous courtesy. Not this way, sir, please.

Police Review May 4, 1973.

One Day Myra Will Be Let Out

It says a lot for the prison service that in these difficult days it is not afraid of experiment. Taking Myra Hindley out of Holloway Prison for a brief airing was no doubt an experiment.

In view of the public horror that will always be evoked by the Moors murders, still a nightmare to most people, you could call it a pretty daring experiment.

The pattern of events in the rehabilitation of a prisoner, the decision to try something fresh as progress is recognised, the final "leak" and the inevitable hullabaloo, is a familiar one.

Every prisoner with a sentence of 18 months or more is "got ready for parole" from the day of reception into prison.

It's a long process, sometimes angrily resisted, but it doesn't usually include excursions from the prison with no specific destination or purpose.

But there is no reason why it shouldn't, in the case of a prisoner not known to be "escape prone." Prisoners going out to work from "pre-release hostels" are, accordingly, being "got ready for parole." They don't always get it.

Myra Hindley has now embraced, or rather has re-entered, the Roman Catholic faith. In this she has been helped by Lord Longford, her unofficial prison visitor, whose belief has always been (to my knowledge) that no one, absolutely no one, is so bad that redemption is impossible.

He says she is now a contrite and Christian woman, whose lifelong burden it will be to carry the ever-clarifying memory of a crime so frightful that only a handful of people, knowing who she is, will even speak to her.

Incidentally, when she gets parole, sooner or later, she will be subject to recall for the rest of her life. She will never be a free woman.

Now that we no longer put such people to death, and do not propose to keep, say, a 20-year-old girl in prison for 60 years or until she dies, what are we going to do with them? That is what we *must* face.

A prisoner serving a life sentence is considered by the Home Office "at an early stage," usually four years, to see whether parole may be possible within the following two (it seldom is).

More probably, after seven years the Parole Board may be asked whether it can fix a date, usually a year ahead, for provisional release. And that's pretty seldom, too.

If the trial judge has recommended a minimum period, his recommendation is valuable but not binding.

So, sooner or later, out they come. In mercifully rare instances they will commit another serious crime; and the only certain way to stop that is to let no one out, abolish parole, and go on building more and more prisons.

But we face the problem more bravely than that; and when you come to think of it, we absorb the occasional shock more sensibly than we did a few years ago.

The case of Graham Young, discharged from Broadmoor to resume his crazy poisonings of innocent victims, was not a "parole" case; it was the discharge of a mental patient. But the principle is the same.

The one way to prevent that is to keep Broadmoor patients in until they die; and of course build more Broadmoors to contain their fast-growing numbers. Does anyone advocate that?

Of course not.

A Myra Hindley is far less dangerous to society than society will now be to her. Since we haven't killed her, we have consciously and positively decided that she shall live; and that one day she shall live outside prison.

Live? What do we do to enable her to live? What we really need is a small army of Lord Longfords, though they needn't be peers, to help out the Probation and After-Care Service, to befriend the friendless, speak with the unspeakable, touch the untouchables. And to let the process go on quietly with no flash-bulbs, no excited telephonings, no headlines.

London Evening News September 14, 1973.

Dirty Work at the Crossroads

Thirty years ago on the roads of Britain you needed the instincts of a homing pigeon because all the signposts had been denuded of their little arms and fingers. That was because we were determined that German parachutists, once they were down and poring over their maps, wouldn't know how to continue their journeys. All the railway stations became anonymous, too, and in Oxford Street the London Estate Management Company had to paint out the word 'London'.

We have never recovered from all this. Indeed, when the signposts did get their limbs back, we missed a fine opportunity to drag them all into the twentieth century, especially at the dark intersections of minor roads, where to this day your headlights can illuminate no more than the pole on which, higher up in the darkness, there clusters all the information you are hungry for. These signposts were put up for people on horseback. They can still be read on a moonlight night by a man lying on top of a loaded haywaggon. But they don't belong in an age when no headlight may dazzle anyone 3ft 6in. tall and more than 25yds. away.

If you except, gratefully, those enormous green boards on the trunk roads, the more usual signpost is still designed by locals and yokels who, if you stop and ask them the way, conclude an irresolute response with, 'It's like this—if I was going to Biggleswade, I wouldn't *start* from 'ere.' It is usually bang on the corner you think you should have gone round, it bears eight place-names, and it is half-hidden by blackthorn. Having driven nervously past it, your attention riskily divided, you make a three-point turn and come back for another look. The name you want will not be there.

The local highway authorities make thousands of new traffic orders every year. Some of them concern signposting, and the discouragement of signposting by enthusiastic amateurs. This delegated and localised system gives full play to an inhospitable and infuriating chauvinism, which I will now illustrate.

Twenty miles from the town you want—let's call it Hogsville—you may see "Hogsville' on one of those big green boards. That will be your last sight of it. Eighteen miles later, after two or three nameless T-junctions, you will come to a diagram depicting an imminent roundabout, but the name you want will not be on it. Press on, and you will find a noice saying 'Town Centre'. What town? On again till you see a man leaning on a gate and ask him the way to Hoggsville. 'This *is* Hogsville,' he says pityingly.

Once you are in a town, you can start looking out for buildings that might be expected to carry the place-name: post office, railway station, bank, town hall, church. They will all be as delicately nameless as an Oxbridge college. Even if you suddenly see Hogsville Laundry Services, that doesn't mean you are in Hogsville: you are merely in a place that Hogsville knows about and whose shirts it is prepared to wash. But once you *have* got to the town centre, you will find a notice that says 'All Routes'. This means, "Whichever way you came in, clear out. You are not where you think you are."

The time for this parochial secrecy has gone. It dates back to the days of walled cities and the readiness to spy strangers. Let us have some cleaner work at the crossroads, proclaiming with clearly-printed eye-level notices that this is our town or village, and acknowledging at long last that today few of us go about on horseback carrying lanthorns.

The Observer Magazine, London, October 14, 1973.

The Dimbleby Lecture

One thing you are not supposed to do when asked to deliver a foundation lecture is to shake the foundations. But it was as though Sir Robert Mark had said "You would like me to do the Dimbleby Lecture this year? Say what I like? Tell you exactly what we think, or anyway what I think? Right: hold your hats on." And, as Lord Macaulay said, e'en the ranks of Tuscany could scarce forbear to cheer, though the Tuscan cheers were few and scattered, and you could hardly hear them above what ex-Commander Godfrey Duncan (in a brisk letter to the *Guardian*) called their "anguished screams". I hope someone is making a scrap-book of the news-headlines Sir Robert has provoked, and that if we do get a Royal Commission—or even a Select Committee—to overhaul the entire system of criminal justice, the frontispiece will be a tasteful montage constructed from them. Incidentally many a Royal Commission has been born of a public statement like Sir Robert Mark's, though never, so far as I know, by a lecture delivered to an audience of about 10 million.

For the time being, the result of it all is that we can now say in public that there are a few lawyers, both solicitors and barristers, who will cook up a defence if the money is big enough. There's never been any doubt about this; at one time I could have named six at least from each branch of the profession who were "bent'; and I knew that many magistrates, seeing one of them rise to his feet and introduce himself as "appearing for the defence", would at once say to themselves "*That* chap's guilty, anyway", whether in due course they could find him guilty or not. The overwhelming majority in both professions knew who they were and despised them. *But nothing was ever done about them.* A charge of conspiring to defeat the ends of justice could never have been more richly justified or better used, *pour encourager les autres.* But I don't think they ever made a lot of money at it. They never looked prosperous, and most of them looked seedy and ill-dressed. Legal aid must have given them an awful blow, and this new spate of publicity may have the effect of finishing them off.

I can endorse the truth of the quotation from the John Freeman *Face To Face* interview with Lord Birkett (wondering, at the same time, how Sir Robert Mark managed to dig *that* up?). Interviewing Lord Birkett in 1957, in a radio programme called *Frankly Speaking,* I asked him similar questions; and he said: "No man is so bad that he is not entitled to have his case properly presented." What did "properly" mean? Oh, within the rules laid down for the etiquette of the Bar. What did they say? Well, briefly, if a defending counsel *suspects* that his client is telling him lies, he is nevertheless bound to put to the court what the man says. If he is *quite certain* the chap is lying, then he should return the brief, i.e. wash his hands of the case altogether. In the hazy division between suspicion and certainty, integrity comes into operation. An elastic quality.

Police Review November 16, 1973.

May Their Tribe Increase

I got into well-deserved trouble lately when, having mentioned lawyers in a magazine article, I allowed myself the parenthesis: "May their tribe decrease". A tactical error, you will see at once. The kind of thing one might say to a group of lawyer friends over the top of a beer glass, but something to be kept within a tolerant circle to whom the remark is, at the very worst, the bray of a cheerful ass. You can be betrayed into such carelessness by much pre-recording for radio; which encourages you to talk unguardedly in the knowledge that things can be "edited out" before the broadcast. And even if the producer leaves in something you would have liked to say differently or not at all, well, it is as evanescent as the bath-water, gurgling away beyond recall as soon as the plug is pulled out.

Not so the printed word. I got a letter from a solicitor whom I don't know, to say that he was very distressed at "may their tribe decrease". And he added: "I am so used to snide comments about my profession in the media that a second skin had grown, but in your case I exclaimed '*et tu, Brute*'." What was needed, he assured me, was not a decrease in the tribe but "more and more men and women, of the best calibre, to serve the needs of the community". (Do you notice, by the way, that there is not enough of *anybody*? Not enough miners, bus-drivers, secretaries, policemen, plumbers, railway porters, jobbing gardeners, priests, teachers, daily helps. Perhaps too many burglars and babies.) Moreover there was "a more dangerous element in my unfortunate aside". Its effect might be to dissuade people from consulting a solicitor, which so often they ought to do at the earliest possible moment. "How often they come too late," he said, "and how often with the job cocked up by previously consulted amateur lawyers in their trade unions, the C.A.B., or the Press". How right he was. And if I was trying to adapt Leigh Hunt's poem, he concluded, the second line might be more poignant than the first:

Abou Ben Adhem (may his tribe increase)
Awoke one night from a deep dream of peace.

I wrote and apologised; abjectly enough to get away (I believe) on the rather contrived mitigation that "if your tribe decreased, it would be because we didn't need you any more, and we should all be getting on better with each other". I've always believed in the perfectibility of man, not as a winning post but as a kind of necessarily unattainable ideal; to be regarded, or expressed, as decimal-nine-recurring, always seeming within reach if you try, but never actually reached.

However, out of all this grew much conversation with other lawyers and with involved laymen; and when there began to emerge from it a fancy picture of the lawyer as a man conscientiously digging his own grave, the perfectibility concept took a sharp knock. The way you are shaping it, said the laymen, there won't be room for anyone else. What also emerged, though, was a revival in my own mind (where such a revival was overdue) of the urge to praise good lawyers. For what one of them wrote to me was ineluctably true, within my own experience: "There are thousands of solicitors who are *not* engaged in a headlong pursuit after the more lucrative kinds of work, but feel that all who knock on their doors are *clients*". In fact, he could have gone further. They often seem to feel that a client with a good cause, no money, and no hope of legal aid must be looked after more assiduously than anyone. I've lost count of how many cases I have propelled towards the offices of long-suffering lawyer friends; and have even forgotten the day when I decided that I need no longer cross the road at the approach of some solicitor who was a recent victim of this vicarious generosity. I've come to know about one form of legal aid that goes unhonoured and unsung: namely the detachment of an articled clerk to unravel some complex but small-time story of justice denied, and (for free) to come up with a suggested solution. Now that I bring myself to think of *that*, this is a happy piece to be writing and I'm glad of the trouble that brought me to it. Especially since, to quote another lawyer's letter, "one does get a bit frayed at the edges after coping with people's emergencies, when one subsequently sees them take their bit of conveyancing elsewhere".

No doubt there's the small voice of conscience in that wistful reference to conveyancing fees; and not long ago a very busy solicitor told me: "There's no doubt whatever that conveyancing costs are too high and it's all rather disgraceful." I could but remind myself, silently, of the hundreds of hours this particular man has devoted to lame ducks, whose lameness had to do with their ineligibility for legal aid.

I suppose that, if the tribe really increases enough, the day will come when anyone under police suspicion will go to a solicitor, just like a company chairman who has heard that the Department of Trade and Industry is making preliminary enquiries. "I've got a policeman coming to see me about a road accident. What do I tell him? I'd like someone to be with me. Can it be here?" Any hackles that rise at such a notion should never fail to go up when an off-beat financier places himself under the orders of the solicitor who, perhaps two years hence, will be defending him in court.

One truly interesting phenomenon is at present working havoc in places where goodwill to lawyers is most difficult to grow; and that is the constant preoccupation of the newspapers with the gigantic "estimated costs" of lawsuits that have excited public interest. One solicitor writes to me: "I always read with amazement that, in some case in London, costs have been estimated to be £30,000. So far as I'm concerned, that could be £300,000. It would be a lot of meaningless noughts." I know that some of these "estimates" have been wildly wrong, but lawyers could enhance their public esteem if they found some way of publicising (like the details of wills and bequests) what the costs really were, and why. Some of the lawyers' out-goings, like the astronomical cost of court transcripts, might be deflected, all in good time of course, to public funds. It might even transpire that one day we could really, and gratefully, adapt Abou Ben Adhem:

Long live the lawyers: may their tribe increase,
That all may share with them the Golden Fleece.

New Law Journal December 20, 1973.

Peaceful Picketing

The old Trade Disputes and Trade Unions Act 1906 spawned a fresh crop of judicial interpretations whenever there was a major strike, but it looks as though the Industrial Relations Act of 1971 will easily surpass it. When picketing has to be defined as 'peacefully obtaining" or "peacefully communicating" information, and "peacefully persuading" a man not to work, the legislators are obviously doing their best but the words have a strange air of unreality about them. And all that the Industrial Relations Act does is to concede (in Section 134) that this peaceful behaviour is not to be regarded as intimidation under the Conspiracy and Protection of Property Act, or any other Act or rule of law, and will not be treated as a tort or civil wrong. You might suppose, if a statute declares that no branch of the law can be used against you if you behave in a certain way, that you thus acquire a *right* to behave in that way. You would be wrong.

In *R. v. Kavanagh* (1974) a picket broke through a Police cordon at a London building site last March, to do some "peaceful persuading" on a coach driver who had a load of strike-breaking workmen. Peter Kavanagh had been fined £20 with £10 costs by the Lambeth magistrate for assaulting a Constable in the execution of his duty, and also for obstructing another Constable; and when he appealed to the High Court it was argued on his behalf that since he had a "right" to do some peaceful persuading, the Police were not acting in the execution of their duty when they sought to deprive him of it. "The essence of picketing," said his counsel (Lord Gifford),"as understood by trade unionists throughout the century, is that there should be *argument* between those on strike and those not on strike. A picket is not merely a demonstration. It involves the use of persuasive powers." Of course you can use persuasion by waving placards and shouting slogans, from behind a Police cordon; but that would not be argument; and without argument, trade unionists would be reduced (said Lord Gifford) to staging mass demonstrations.

Well, a *mass* demonstration, even on the other side of a Police cordon, might look remarkably like intimidation, which can certainly be achieved by numbers. But what the Lord Chief Justice decided, in Kavanagh's case, was that it is a fallacy to suggest that a picket has a "legal right" to approach a driver in order to speak to him. "It is inapt and misleading," said Lord Widgery, "to suggest that this legislation" (i.e. the Industrial Relations Act 1971, Section 134) "confers a positive right on the picket. It merely gives peaceful pickets immunity from prosecution for a criminal offence or a civil wrong, but it does not confer a right in the sense of an entitlement." The Police were justified in cordoning off pickets at the building site because they were apprehensive of a breach of the peace; their action in preventing pickets from approaching the driver was not illegal, and Kavanagh's appeal was accordingly dismissed.

We all talk confidently about our rights, but remarkably few of the things we do have ever acquired that status in law. We go on doing them until someone tries to stop us, and then we feel that a personal right is being infringed. I suppose a neat modern example is long hair. How many youths in recent years have asserted what they feel, and are often encouraged to feel, is a sacred right to have shoulder-length hair? They would search the law books in vain for its declaration. And if Parliament enacted that no man was to be criminally or civilly liable, under any statute or rule of law, for having long hair, not even that would promote long hair to the status of a lawful right. Similarly there's no more "right" to talk to anybody, including a coach driver with a load of strike-breaking workmen, than there is to have a Saturday-night bath. But a Saturday-night bath, which only gradually came to feel like a right, ended by being a sort of neighbourly obligation.

Police Review February 15, 1974.

Only Circumstantial

It's time to say another word or two in defence of "circumstantial evidence", which all the Police text-books for years have agreed in defining as "evidence, not of the actual fact to be proved, but of other facts from which that fact may be presumed with more or less certainty". It is supposed to be generally inferior to "direct evidence", e.g. the evidence of an eye-witness. Earl Jowitt's *Dictionary of English Law* admits, however, that it has "undoubtedly been found, in some instances, to produce a much stronger assurance of a prisoner's guilt than could have been produced by more direct and positive testimony". A recent report by the Community Relations Commission in Belfast was concerned with (among many other matters) complaints from Roman Catholics that the Police in two areas had "definite sympathies" with the paramilitary Protestant Ulster Defence Association. This report deleted all reference to such complaints from its final published version because, according to the chairman, they were based on "circumstantial evidence".

So they probably were, and they might have been totally unfounded, but Mr. James Flanagan, the R.U.C. Chief Constable, has been asked by Mr. Gerard Fitt, the Deputy Chief Executive, to promise that the missing sections will be examined. The evidence of eyewitnesses took a nasty knock during a recent television programme in this country called *The Evidence of Your Eyes*. Mr. Bernard Levin and the university lecturer Mr. Laurie Taylor staged a number of incidents (including a car-crash and a shooting episode) in front of a studio audience, and then tested the latter's immediate recollections of what had happened. The confident inaccuracy of their answers was positively frightening, although they knew in advance that they were to be shown the incidents and were presumably on their mettle to get everything right. The main virtue of "circumstances", as distinct from mental images retained by eye-witnesses, is that the circumstances can't tell lies, get rattled and confused under cross-examination, misunderstand questions, blurt out inadmissible things, or run away. As Napoleon said: "Circumstances? I *make* circumstances."

Police Review March 15, 1974.

Could do Better

I have been reading the 1974 Annual Report of the best Council for Civil Liberties we've got. For that matter, I suppose I've read every one of its Annual Reports since that remarkable man, Ronald Kidd, turned out the first one in 1934. In case you should wonder how the Council can put "Annual Report 1974" on the cover of something which is all about 1973 ("a year," it says youthfully, "which civil libertarians would have been better off without"), the answer is that you are lucky to have a date on it at all. The National Council for Civil Liberies has fallen into a habit of reprehensible sloppiness about dating its papers, pamphlets, and reports; and I offer my advance condolences to any research worker sitting in that British Museum limbo at Colindale in the year 2074, scratching holes in his head as he tries to date some of the NCCL's publications.

The year 2074? Will the NCCL be of interest for so long? Yes, because it has become socially, politically and deservedly important. If it didn't exist it would be necessary to invent it without delay. If it died, a successor would have to be organised at once. It makes the right people angry, and if it stopped doing that it would die like a withered limb no longer able to cause pain. But it often makes the wrong people angry, the people who wish it well and want to see its influence spread. Me, for instance. And it now has the backing, or at least the implied blessing, of a Parliamentary Civil Liberties Group which includes more than 120 well-known members of all political parties (I quote the figure, may I say defensively, from one of its undated pamphlets). Moreover, through its sawn-off affiliate, the Defence of Literature and the Arts Society, it has a list of sponsors distinguished enough to keep it permanently above the clouds like a hot air balloon. How many of these libertarian name-lenders are really satisfied that the NCCL always knows what it's talking about?

Its press relations work is very good indeed. It really can organise publicity—thanks, I doubt not, to a recent run of good General Secretaries, Martin Ennals, Tony Smythe and Martin Loney. Not that this should be difficult, for there will always be a wide open space in the media for attacks on the Home Office, the judiciary, the police, the prisons, and the law. Not only are they sitting targets, but they will go on sitting there all clustered together, so that a bullet bouncing off one pachyderm stands a good chance of embedding itself painfully in the next. And they never shoot back. I've often heard it said that the NCCL, in its press statements, its bulletins, and its annual reports is too fond of attributing base or corrupt motives to the servants of the law. The sad truth is that, in this imperfect world (where you often do find base and corrupt motives) it would never get any anywhere if it credited them with motives or loyalties that were lofty but misguided. Once as a member of a delegation to a Minister of Health (and he wasn't even a Tory) I approvingly quoted to him something the NCCL had been saying. He bristled and his eyes stuck out. "A noisy minority," he said contemptuously. I thought: "What the hell would be the use of a minority that made no noise?" As a member of many minorities and reformist movements, I've joined in the making of some very rude noises. But we all tried to ensure, before sounding off, that we were right on our facts and our law. What I'm saying is that the NCCL is careless about both.

And yet no-one seems to bother. How often do the newspapers, before they give willing space to it, get someone to vet the accuracy of what it says? It's a mark of this vigorous little society's *arriviste* success that a news editor would as soon detail someone to verify the statements of the Law Society or a judgment of the Privy Council. It's time someone at a much humbler level hurled a toy spanner into the works; and here it goes.

"The case of *Kamara*," says the Annual Report 1974, "resulted in the defendants being convicted of conspiracy to trespass, the existence of which offence came as a surprise to most English criminal lawyers." I must have met only the ones who weren't surprised, whether or not they were enthusiastic. Some legal men see the law of conspiracy to trespass as a possible way of discouraging the police from raiding, without a warrant, any house they deem urgently interesting; and that's a thought I venture to commend to the NCCL, which is well briefed on the futility of *suing* the police for trespass as a civil wrong. "Trespass is not, of course, a criminal offence," goes on the NCCL. No? Let them try telling that to the security people at atomic research stations, airfields, and dockyards; or even to the railway police. Lord Hailsham ("not content with destroying traditional rights of peaceful protest") is castigated for "extending the law of conspiracy" because, when he was Lord Chancellor, he observed that "all conspiracies to commit crimes are indictable, including conspiracies to commit offences which otherwise could only be dealt with by magistrates". Well, that's no extension of the law. Conspiracies to commit summary offences have long been indictable. So why blame Lord Hailsham (who might well be surprised, not to say embarrassed, to find me springing to his defence)?

On *Trial by Jury* the NCCL finds that Michael Zander's valuable bit of research on London jury trials shows that "the guilty do not, as has frequently been alleged, escape conviction." But what poppycock is this? Everyone knows that guilty men escape conviction, and the Zander report allows for it: the only controversy concerns how many, what proportion of those pleading not guilty on arraignment, and what proportion we can all regard as acceptable.

"In January 1974," says the section on Censorship, "a Divisional Court ruled that local justices were entitled to destroy 'obscene' books without even reading them. The judgment in this case was given by Lord Justice Edmund Davies, who was himself a member of the Longford 'Commission'." You see the implication about Edmund Davies, LJ? This must have been the case in which, in July last year, Lord Justice James in the Divisional Court turned down an Olympia Press appeal against a conviction by the magistrates at Stony Stratford. Six magistrates had had to read 36 books between them. Lord Justice James said there was no legal authority for the argument that every magistrate had to read every book. The Crown had agreed that none of the six magistrates had read all the 36 books, but said that every book had been read by at least two of them and that they had read several each.

"The NCCL played a key role in organising a campaign against the (Cinematograph and Indecent Displays) Bill," and "was successful in gaining a number of important concessions in the Committee Stage." Was it? However diligently you search the proceedings of the Standing Committee on this Bill, for important concessions wrung from an admittedly stiffnecked and ruthless government side, you will find only one, and that was the temporary withdrawal (for re-examination) of a clause that would have penalised film societies and *bona fide* cinema clubs. "The evils of this ludicrous legislation," says the NCCL, "were analysed in detail in NCCL's monthly 'Civil Liberty', and a full Parliamentary briefing was produced."

And you should have seen it. "A new hypothetical crime will be brought into the statute books," said the full Parliamentary briefing (I quote from the only one I've seen, which of course is undated), "where the individual or company has no way in advance of knowing whether he or it is committing a crime." What's new about that? Regrettable no doubt, and undesirable: but new? It has always been the case with obscenity trials, "unlawful possession" cases, manslaughter by negligence, defamation actions, a variety of others in which the offence waits for completion until the court pronounces its opinion. Even an allegedly "careless" motorist doesn't know whether he was culpably careless until some magistrate tells him he was (and he never believes it even then). "The Bill makes no provision for any defence, whether of merit or of public good." Merit and public good are the same defence, and the Bill *did* provide for it. The 1959 Act would have applied in full to cinema cases, and with it the "public good" defence. "Summary conviction with no right of appeal (*sic*) and unlimited fines on indictment:" but nothing in the Bill took away any right of appeal—can you imagine a Bill reaching committee stage if it said "It is hereby declared that no person convicted by magistrates under this Act shall have any right of appeal . . ."?

And by way of ending this Censorship section the NCCL publishes a photograph for which one man has already been fined under section 41 of the Criminal Justice Act 1925: the picture was "taken in court", and shows an Old Bailey judge and jury reading the evidence during the "Nasty Tales" trial. What sort of legal advice would allow such a gaffe as that, unless the intention were to invite another prosecution and do some public breast-beating? Here, at least, I don't want the dear old NCCL beating its fearless breast on my account. I want people in British courts protected against the press photographer, much as the NCCL wants people at political demos and in police stations protected against police photographers. Actually we all want pretty much the same kind of thing, in Benthamite terms. But the price of that kind of liberty now includes some invigilation of the NCCL itself, whose influential modern sponsorship could hardly rock this precious little boat without sinking it. I humbly offer the NCCL a motto for the current year's work: the greater the accuracy, the less the acidosis.

New Law Journal April, 1974.

Investigative Journalism

The Fourth Estate has suddenly expanded its boundaries and is having a whale of a time; powerfully sustained no doubt by the Press Council's pragmatic implication in the Lambton affair that 'nothing but success is an acceptable excuse', and by the occasional tip-off from the public-spirited about socialist land policy and slag-heaps. Mr

Harold Wilson's writs against the *Mail* and the *Express*, which a few years ago (whatever their motive) would have taken the 'Reclamation Affair' out of the news for a long cooling-off period, have instead provoked a torrent of news and comment which has swept the *sub judice* rule far out to sea. If it is ever salvaged by some future writ for contempt there will be great interest in how it looks and whether it can be made to sit up again. If not, there are vicious and sometimes crackpot organisations in this country which can expect trouble. They have a way of issuing writs at the drop of a hat: not because they mind about the hat but because once a writ is issued everything said about it is in breach of the *sub judice* rule. The public relations man got a mention of it into newspapers which seemed only too willing to shut themselves up, and the waters closed over it because the whole thing was too much bother. Or it was defamatory, or in breach of some tinpot copyright. At one time you could stifle any mention of a conviction in a magistrates' court by giving immediate notice of appeal. If you later abandoned the appeal (which was quite usual) you had to forfeit a £40 recognisance; but you had bought £40 of press silence and this might be cheap.

Generations of legal advisers had thoroughly frightened the newspapers about this kind of thing, but by the Fifties there were leading QCs who were telling the national dailies that they could safely be more adventurous. Eventually they got the Court of Appeal to admit, by way of highlighting the absurdity, that the mere issue of a writ made newspaper comment temporarily unlawful, one judge going so far as to doubt, tongue in cheek, whether you could even report that the writ had been issued. But then, just as everyone had come to accept that it was ridiculous, there came the Criminal Justice Act 1967 to say that the preliminary hearing by magistrates of a judge-and-jury case must not be reported (apart from names and a few such details) unless the magistrates specifically said it could. Still less, of course, may those proceedings be the subject of comment.

This is rather more important to the rich and famous than to the hoi-polloi, though for some time there seemed to be a belief in television studios that it didn't apply to television. For example in 1967, just before Dr Emil Savundra came up at the Old Bailey at long last for his fraudulent manipulation of the Fire, Auto and Marine Insurance Company, he was subjected to a kind of kangaroo trial in the *Frost Programme*. It was all rather nasty, and Lord Justice Salmon said it was reprehensible. But the *Frost Programme* was taking its cue and its courage from the *Sunday Times*, which had been gunning for Dr Savundra for some time and wondering publicly why he wasn't prosecuted. I don't know whether Mr Frost supposed that it was he who then brought about the prosecution, or whether Mr Harold Evans thought it wouldn't have happened but for the *Sunday Times*. If so they are both mistaken, though they may have hurried things along a bit, Savundra being big game and good copy. No one said all this was rather American, but that's what it really was; and it helped to illustrate why it can take months to empanel an American jury as the defence tries to eliminate jurors who have seen television programmes.

In 1972, when the Attorney-General got the High Court to stop the *Sunday Times* publishing its findings in the thalidomide case, the judges conceded nevertheless that the paper (or, I suppose, anyone) could publicly discuss the moral issues involved so long as there was no reference to the facts. 'There were,' wrote Harold Evans in the *New Statesman* of 8 March ('The Half-Free Press'), 'some vague and utterly impractical remarks about not wishing the press to be gagged by the mere issue of a writ'. But the gagging was done all the same, and on the whole it's a gag that comes into operation only when big money is involved.

Both these cases, Savundra and the thalidomide tragedy, illustrate the inequality of the legal aid system. A man like Savundra is sometimes under police and Board of Trade investigation for several years before he is charged, the Fraud Squad beavering away to build up a mass of evidence from which escape is impossible. The moment he knows of it (and here a sudden newspaper campaign can be a great kindness to him) he goes to his solicitor and thereafter acts under protective instructions. Those instructions will include the cold-shouldering of what is now rather nicely called investigative journalism. The ordinary man, with no solicitor to run to, will not get legal aid until he is in the dock; though it is fair to say that sometimes, when such a man *has* been thought to be worth a press investigation, a newspaper has come up with details which have stood him in good stead and have even got him off.

I want to take issue, however, with Harold Evans on one aspect of investigative journalism with which he seeks to comfort us all. "Let us not forget,' he says in one of his comments on the *sub judice* rule, 'that the individual who is named is protected, if innocent, by the law of libel.'As a statement of pious intention, that could have gone even further: the man is 'protected' even if he's guilty, for there are circumstances in which a newspaper (or anyone) can be prosecuted for telling the truth about a convicted man if it's not done 'contemporaneously' with the trial and for the public good. (And since the 1967 Criminal Justice Act we have known what contemporaneously means: 'as soon as practicable' after the proceedings.) But apart from pious legislative intention, what good is the law of libel to the ordinary man whose adversary is a newspaper or some other wealthy and insensitive pachyderm?

He can't have legal aid for libel proceedings, whether to prosecute or defend: nobody can. If he risks his money and wins, he can be hideously out of pocket when the court had decided which of his costs it is going to disallow. If he publishes the truth about a rich adversary and gets a writ for libel, he is on his own. I know a man with a criminal record who was blackmailed for years by members of a public authority in control of the job he had lawfully settled down to. Eventually he went in despair to the police and wrote down his story. He promptly received a writ for libel, and there began the fight of his life.

He came to see me at the *New Statesman* office and I took him to a solicitor, both of us wondering where the money would come from. The solicitor put an articled clerk on the job and asked her to sort it all out. She was so horrified at the story that she gave all her spare time to it for weeks; and finally, after endless court postponements, form-fillings, and rehearings, his powerful adversaries let go and paid money into court. He was lucky. He would need to be luckier if he had been traduced by a big newspaper: as a plaintiff, the protection he could expect from the law of libel, *pace* Harold Evans, would be a belly-laugh. It's even luckier for him that no one much cares whether he goes to sex-parties and is snooped on by Fleet Street cameramen serving what the Americans (and even the American judges) call 'the public right to know'.

'One thinks of W. T. Stead's documentation of the white slave traffic,' says Harold Evans. One does indeed. But you have to read the verbatim report of his Old Bailey trial to savour the real mercenary prurience, the muck-raking hypocrisy, of Stead's investigative journalism. It turned over a lot of flat stones in the formal Victorian garden, but its motives don't really belong in the same class as the work of the *Sunday Times* and its Insight team. It is true enough that, as Mrs Katharine Graham, chairman of the *Washington Post,* said in the last of the Granada Lectures that began with Harold Evans, 'the surest, simplest way to promote due process and equal treatment under the law is to report the ways the system works and does not work'. In the process, the newspapers have to comfort the afflicted and afflict the comfortable; but among the afflicted they can display all the altruism of the elephant among the chickens. Investigative journalism has, to my own knowledge, ruined some decent, obscure men. They may be expendable in the great cause of truth, but even that cause might be better served by extending legal aid for their protection.

New Statesman April 19, 1974.

The Bells

I was sorry to see Canon Douglas Rhymes in trouble about the noise from his bells at St. Giles's Church, Camberwell, because the Canon (and his recent predecessors) have the blessings of a great army of people among the poor, the homeless, and the afflicted. Still, among the afflicted was a Mrs. Devra Shifrin, who didn't like the church bells and—no doubt after some fruitless negotiation with the Reverend Canon—had taken out a summons against him under the Noise Abatement Act 1960. There must have been at least two other afflicted people, too, because she wouldn't have got a summons on her own. The Noise Abatement Act says that a noise nuisance is to be a "statutory nuisance" under the Public Health Act 1936 if, but only if, it aggrieves "any three or more persons each of whom is the occupier of land or premises, and is in that capacity aggrieved by the nuisance". The Canon would have got an "abatement notice" and then, if the bells went on ringing so as to be a nuisance, he would have been liable to a fine up to £20.

I hate bells; and have always been a bit ashamed of the emotion. I don't mind the "Bells Across the Meadow" kind of thing, because that can be as tolerable as a set of bagpipes three mountain-sides away, but I've tried to sleep in a Police section-house during the daytime on a Sunday, with church-bells challenging and drowning each other from 20 rival belfries. During the war I heard the famous bells at Bow Church, Cheapside, crash to the bottom of their splendid belfry when they were dislodged by a bomb, and I had to stifle the profane and unspeakable thought that, just occasionally, something good could come out of a war. Having made which declaration, I shall henceforth be a disqualified witness for anyone like Mrs. Devra Shifrin. "You don't like bells, do you?" I should be asked in court. "I mean, *any* kind of bell would be a nuisance to you?" Not the dinner-bell, I would say. "But if these bells, which are renowned for their beauty of tone throughout the world, were in some way abated by order of this court, you still wouldn't like them?" I should have to say no. And Mrs. Shifrin and her three fellow bell-baiters would be the worse off for having relied on me. Loud or soft, well played or ill, assorted or single, they are all a statutory nuisance. I don't see how anyone who loves music can love bells too.

Police Review July 26, 1974.

Photographing the Public

Have the Police any right to take photographs of people attending public demonstrations? There is a noticeable groundswell of public anger about this, and it is not stilled by any rejoinder that a Police camera, like any other camera, is merely a mechanical aid to vision and memory, an extension, so to speak, of the human eye. By that specious kind of reasoning, say the objectors, you could maintain that a secret bugging device is simply a hearing-aid. I remember that when an Old Bailey jury had just decided that *Lady Chatterley's Lover* did not offend against the Obscene Publications Act, B.B.C. cameramen toured the bookshops so that they could show us, on television news, the queues of men waiting to buy the suddenly liberated copies of the book. One man was so angry at being photographed in such a context (I think he said he was actually waiting to buy a copy of *Hall and Knight's Algebra*) that he wanted to sue the B.B.C. and its cameraman for assault. I never heard how he got on, but was it an assault?

The law has always caught up very slowly with these new-fangled things, and, after all, photography is little more than 170 years old. The common law still says it is an assault to cause personal discomfort to a man by shining a strong light on him, and the 1899 *Queensland Criminal Code,* which is quoted with approval by *Russell on Crime,* says it is an assault if a man "threatens unlawfully to project a light, heat, electrical energy, gas, odour or any other thing on to the person of another". So it is an assault to illuminate a man by flashlight for the purpose of photographing him, and he can lawfully resist the process—by turning his back, covering his own head with a raincoat, or pulling a funny face. How about photographing suspects in Police stations, which is engendering even more anger than the Police cameras at demos?

In the famous Scottish case of *Adair v. McGarry* (1933), which was a fingerprint case, the Lord Justice General said it was beyond doubt that when a man was legally arrested by the Police, they could "lawfully examine his person and his clothes for bloodstains and the like, or for any mark on his person which, according to their information, was observed when the crime was committed—without his consent and without any magistrate's warrant. Every man is entitled", said the Lord Justice General, "to the enjoyment of personal liberty, but he forfeits that right by committing crime." The trouble about this is that the man in the Police station may not have committed any crime, and the Police may be looking for bloodstains or other marks on a totally innocent person. Of course we always say that we are thereby helping the man to establish his innocence, and in fact going to a lot of trouble to establish it for him, but it's surprising how many people dislike that kind of help. No doubt this is why the common law has evolved no rules about this kind of thing, and why the Home Office has gone to the length of laying down a procedure only in relation to identification parades. In *Adair v. McGarry* Lord Sands added a few remarks about the common law and the inspection of Police station suspects. "There can be no common law rule about fingerprints", he said, "any more than there can be a common law rule as to whether a man may be X-rayed without a warrant to see if he has swallowed a watch or coin. . . . Is taking a man's fingerprints the same as examining his arms for tattoo marks, or making him put on his cap or overcoat for an identification parade? Or is it a serious invasion of his person or liberty, such as detaining him without any warrant beyond what is necessary, or shaving off his beard?" And Lord Sands actually went on, for the benefit of Scottish Forces but not, of course, of English ones, to say that

> an officer with an expert eye, looking at a man's finger tips through a hand glass, could tell (not accurately but with sufficient confidence to determine that it would be justificable to detain or release a suspect) whether his finger tips corresponded with a photograph of the print left on a window pane. Nobody, I think, will question the legitimacy of looking at the suspect's fingers, and requiring him to hold them up for that purpose. But it is said that one must not, without a warrant, adopt the much more satisfactory course of taking an impression, to ascertain whether there is any ground for detaining the man. This seems to be unreasonable.

That was 40 years ago, and no English court has yet said such a thing. But there are signs that it may well be an English court which decides on the legality of Police photographing.

Police Review September 13, 1974.

On Getting the Wrong Bank Statement

The Big Four Banks (Midland, National Westminster, Lloyds and Barclays) are now operating about 19 million indiviual bank accounts, and about 60 per cent of the customers' statements are put into envelopes by machinery. There have been recent reports that every week about 500 statements are sent in error to the wrong customers though it's fair to say that most of the errors are made by hand, at branches where "dispatch machines" don't come into it. A Midland Bank customer in London told the *Daily Telegraph* on 13 October that when he received his own bank statement recently it was accompanied by full confidential details of a total stranger's bank transactions. Inevitably this is being blamed on to computers, but a computer machine doesn't fold bank statements and put them into envelopes; that's done either by hand or by dispatch machines, and even the dispatch machines can only do what they are told, namely fold and envelope accounts in the order presented to them.

It would be easy to exaggerate the importance of 500 such errors in a total of millions, but the criminal possibilities are disturbing enough. To possess the details of another man's bank account is to be in a position, only too often, to blackmail him in a number of ways, to attack his credit-worthiness, to facilitate frauds, to cause private mischief in his family circle. For that matter, I once got a bank statement relating to a namesake whom I don't even know (and I wish he would move to another bank) which recorded an overdraft of such shocking dimensions that I had to go and lie down. Then I got up and compared his account number with mine, and the truth dawned. I was so glad to be able to send it scornfully back to my bank manager that its criminal possibilities never even occurred to me at the time. But they would occur to quicker-witted people, and we have all been warned.

Police Review October 25, 1974.

Red Faces in Somerset

Not every Police station charge-room has a "dock" in which to stand the prisoner while he is subjected to the formalities; but I know of one case in which a patrolling Inspector, discovering on a visit to a station that a man had been charged and put in the cells without actually standing in the dock, had him brought out again and charged "properly". He seemed to think the omission might be fatal to a conviction at the magistrates' court. For that matter, there is a deep-seated belief in many Police minds that the charge-room formalities are an essential part of the machinery of justice. But this superstition really came into its own in a recent case at Yeovil, details of which have been sent to me by a correspondent who tells me that "it has had the effect, with friends of mine who are Policemen, of either making them howl with laughter or turning their hair white".

On 13 November last year Mr. Robert Rees appeared before the Yeovil magistrates on a Public Order Act charge of using threatening behaviour at Yeovil Football Ground. He got a solicitor and, on a plea of Not Guilty, two adjournments. Finally on 6 December, after the Police evidence, his solicitor submitted that he had "never been charged" with the offence, and that the Police had not disclosed this omission in their procedure. So the "charging officer" was sent for, and while the court waited for him the solicitor (half-flushed perhaps, or tinted, with success) developed his remarks into a submission that there was no case to answer. There was an absolute obligation (he said, and I am only telling it to you as it has been told to me) on the part of the prosecution to prove by evidence that the defendant had been charged by the "charging officer" before his appearance in court. The magistrates retired with their assistant clerk, and came to the conclusion that the solicitor was right. They dismissed the charge; and inevitably they had to compile, in due course, a "case stated" for the prosecution's appeal to the High Court.

When it got to the Divisional Court (as *Rees v. Barlow*, 1974), the Lord Chief Justice asked the cogent question: "Was the fact of this man's being charged, or not charged, of any relevance at all? A charge is not always necessary. He could have been summoned." Answering his own question, he added that "with the man in court answering to the charge, the question of preliminaries in the Police station was irrelevant". Judgment allowing the appeal was delivered by Mr.

Justice Milmo, who said that the point taken by the defence was "thoroughly bad and ought never to have been taken. It should be recognised by members of the legal profession that these points take up time and money and do their clients no good." Lord Widgery remarked of the case stated that "this is absolute rubbish from start to finish", adding that the person who should pay the costs of the appeal was the solicitor who raised the point, but that unfortunately the court had no power to make him.

Police Review November 15, 1974.

Excusable Homicide

Once at a public dinner I heard the late Derek Curtis-Bennett, Q.C., who was almost equally esteemed with his more famous father for his knowledge of the criminal law, deliver an address on the law of homicide. I suppose it's 20 years ago, and yet he was already prophesying (as the Law Commission is now doing) that murder and manslaughter would eventually disappear as specific kinds of killing, to be succeeded by one all-inclusive crime of homicide. Then he invited questions from his audience and I ventured to ask him about something that had troubled me for a long time. I believe that if I found an intruder in my house at night I should try to hit him before asking any questions. (I keep a small Indian club for the purpose, though I have lately been favouring the idea that I might send my wife downstairs with it, leaving me free to plan further strategy.) Suppose I killed him, I asked Mr. Curtis-Bennett. Would that be excusable homicide? Beyond any doubt, he said firmly. The law would totally indemnify me. If it were otherwise the law would be "requiring me to give up my house to an adversary". I was uneasy about this, and asked him whether the intruder's entry didn't have to be felonious, or in pursuance of what was then called felony. Not at all, he said kindly; I could set my mind at rest.

I never did, actually. I notice that Kenny's *Outlines of Criminal Law* still says that in early law a homicide committed in self-defence was only "excusable" and not "justifiable", and quotes the Scottish case of *McCluskey v. H.M. Advocate* (1959) as showing that "to justify a plea of homicide in self-defence it is essential that the fatal resistance should have been made to save the accused's life" (i.e., to save my own life when I found the man in my house at night). It seems as though the law comes down somewhere halfway between these two doctrines, to judge from a case at the Old Bailey on 19 December.

Richard Fountain, aged 42, a schoolmaster who collects swords and daggers as a hobby, found that a man had "barged into his house". The man was drunk and angry, kicked a puppy across the room and was very aggressive and violent. Mr. Fountain, it seems, had opened the door to him in response to furious banging; but the press reports I have seen don't reveal whether they were known to each other. Having unavailingly asked the intruder to go, Mr. Fountain got one of his swords and "pointed it at him so that it was just touching his stomach. I wanted to frighten him. I didn't know that I had stabbed him," said Mr. Fountain in evidence, "I don't know to this day at which stage the sword went into him." But it did, inflicting a 7-in. stab wound of which the man died within minutes. (The man had "staggered on to the blade".) The D.P.P. decided to proceed on the full murder charge, with manslaughter as a possible alternative. And the jury's verdict was Not Guilty on both.

However, Mr. Fountain has had to wait since the episode took place, last July, until now to learn whether he had committed any crime. It must have been an unnerving six months. The club turns out to be mightier than the sword.

Police Review January 4, 1975.

Bail for How Long?

Once as a very junior station officer I got into a fearful row for releasing a prisoner on bail for 16 days, because that was the first convenient date for him to attend court after an impending visit to Algeria. He put up two good sureties and I felt quite comfortable about him. The feeling of comfort was dispelled when my seniors and betters came to examine the books; and I was sternly told that the maximum period for which the Police could release on bail was four days. No one could find chapter and verse for this and I was led to suppose that it was an impertinence to expect that anyone should. Privately, I never believed it, but kept my own counsel. I can't remember that the situation ever confronted me again.

But now I have a letter from a serving Police officer who asks me if I can suggest the origin of a local rule that "Police bail" must never exceed seven days; and he calls to my attention an answer given by the editors of the *Justice of the Peace* to a correspondent on 23 November last year: the questioner had said he knew of a local seven-day rule, but that in some areas "the Police bail to whatever date they think they will be ready to proceed". The J.P. saw no reason for a seven-day rule or any similar limitation. There ought to be no needless delay, but a defendant sometimes wanted time to get legal advice and prepare his case; and with regard to the fanciful possibility that the Police might bail to a date "many months or even years ahead", the J.P. thought that the High Court could be induced to provide a remedy for that.

I suppose it's odd that this has never happened, but a High Court application for (say) a writ of *mandamus* addressed to the Police might result—even if the application were turned down—in a judicial ruling as to the maximum length for which the Police should ordinarily release on bail. That is the only way in which the question is likely ever to be settled, for it is not sufficiently frequent or important to find its way into any Act of Parliament. As it stands, the Police have at their disposal a kind of prolonged "supervision and control order" which they never use.

Police Review January 11, 1975.

House-to-House Carols

My wife took a mini-bus load of children carol-singing, in aid of a registered charity. I said she ought to get a Police permit under the House to House Collections Act 1939, and it came in the form of a letter saying there would be no Police objection but that she ought to notify also the local authority. She preselected a number of fairly well-breeched victims and asked if they would mind having the carols projected at them. Since it's a rural district, where the householders have no experience of the repeated bangings on urban front doors heralded by two breathless lines about certain poor shepherds, they all said how nice it would be. And when it was all over, with the mountain of hot dogs consumed in our kitchen and the minibus returned to base, there ensued a great shaking of the collecting-boxes, which were obviously full and which (as you could see if you peeped through the slots) actually contained some paper money. My wife said she *must* open the boxes to see the result, and I said if she did I would dial 999. It was some time before she accepted that collectors were not allowed to open their boxes, but in the end the idea got through and peace was restored, if peace is the right word for a victory of rectitude over curiosity. Finally an official of the charity called, opened the boxes, accepted a cheque for the amount they contained, and took the empty boxes away. There hasn't been so much loose cash in the house since the last time I sold a selection of crowded-out books.

I was reminded of all this by the case of *Hankinson v. Dowland* (1974), 138 J.P. 795. A man was seen in the Duke of Wellington public house at Pendlebury, Lancs, collecting money in a box. The manager asked him for some details and learned that the collection was for the aged, homeless and under-privileged, the charity calling itself the British Direct Aid Group. No house-to-house licence was in force. A Police officer was called and the man was arrested. He had £15.49 in his pockets and £3.07 in the collecting box.

When he was charged with collecting without a licence, the magistrates rejected a suggestion that the prosecution must prove collection "from house to house" i.e. that there had been a collection in more than one place. They convicted him and he appealed by "case stated". In the Queen's Bench Division Mr. Justice Talbot recalled that "collection" was defined in the Act as "an appeal to the public, made by means of *visits from house to house,* to give, whether for consideration or not, money or other property". Giving this the strict interpretation it should have as a penal provision, he thought it was necessary to prove "either that the person charged was seen to go from one house to another, or that that was what he was about to do when he was found collecting at one house". Lord Widgery agreed (and so did Mr. Justice Melford Stevenson) that, although an unlicensed collector might be as much of a nuisance in the Duke of Wellington as he would be moving from door to door, he had collected only in the pub. So the appeal was allowed.

Police Review January 17, 1975.

Justice Asleep

Someone ought to write a book about sleep, magistrates, judges and juries. Sleep is the enemy of "open justice". I've always liked Emerson's reflection that "a sleeping child gives me the impression of a traveller in a very far country"; but a sleeping adjudicator gives you the impression of someone who doesn't give a damn, or would like to give one but is too tired. A magistrate rebuked a press reporter the other day, not so much for sleeping as for snoring; and as Mark Twain said in *Tom Sawyer Abroad*: "There ain't no way to find out why a snorer can't hear himself snore." The reporter roused himself and left the court.

Lord Justice Birkett once told me, in a burst of confidence which I suppose comes into the "now it can be told" category, that he had often been asked by his fellow judges on the bench to follow a case closely while they had a half-hour nap after the lunch adjournment—sitting on the bench beside him. Birkett never felt sleepy, and always believed a judge should try to *look* alert as well as being alert. During the war he was chairman of the 18B Committee hearing the appeals of people marked down for internment as having "hostile origins or associations". He always did the questioning himself. "That committee did some very cruel and wrong things", he said. "Working by majority, it sent many people to years of detention who were totally innocent and harmless." Once he was questioning a man who *had* for a time belonged to the Fascist movement. "Would you now tell my colleagues and myself why you changed your mind about Fascism?" he asked. "I will tell *you*, sir," was the reply; "it's not much telling your colleagues at the moment." Birkett looked along his line of colleagues. "They were all fast asleep", he said.

Police Review February 7, 1975.

"Midweek Special" on the Police

Did you see Michael Cockerell's report (B.B.C.1, 6 February) in the *Midweek Special* programme on the Police? I imagine a great many "worker Cops" will have missed it; for most of them would either be on late duty or night duty, in which case 10.20 p.m. is not their viewing time; or they would be on early turn, in which event they ought to have been in bed. But among those who did see it, once they had got over the sight of the Cadets and trainees squarebashing (a sight, I always think, to make the angels weep, though they may occasionally smile through their tears now that uniform trousers are—I suppose officially—braced three inches from the tops of boots) there may have been some who noticed Mr. Cockerell saying that C.I.D. men are trained to persuade all their prisoners to plead Guilty, and that they succeed in at least 90 per cent of their cases. (I *think* I've got that right, and should be relieved to get any correction.) This drew attention from the newspapers in advance notices about the press preview, no comment in any of the subsequent criticisms—which were a bit sparse anyway—and no angry letters to the press from champions of the free. Certainly it got no place in the long extract from the programme compiled by Mr. Cockerell for the *Listener* of 6 February. In that, Flying Squad men were quoted as saying that "if everything were done exactly in accord with the rules they would never arrest any criminals at all"; and unless this meant they would be too sulky to do any work it was an overstatement, for the majority of arrests involve no rule-bending whatsoever. But the bit about getting 90 per cent of all prisoners to plead Guilty ought not to go unnoticed, for it's the favourite theme-song of those who most disapprove of us.

Police Review February 21, 1975.

The Neglected Cat

Death or injury to a cat on the road was among the kinds of death and injury carefully excluded from Section 25 of the Road Traffic Act 1972 and its predecessors. I say "carefully" because there were attempts, in 1930, to get cats included among the animals whose misfortune must be reported to the Police (or to their owners). But the only animals held to qualify were horses, cattle, asses, mules, sheep, pigs, goats, and dogs; and I've always supposed that this was because those are the straying kind of animals, which, on the whole, cats are not. A cat is always going somewhere, not straying, and he usually keeps to the footpath. But Mr. Brian Sedgemore, who is Labour M.P. for Luton West, and who has manifestly never patrolled a night duty beat, thinks the Police are callous about cats, and he is asking the Home Secretary "to order the Police" (which he can't) "to get veterinary care for injured cats". Once, as a Constable, I called a vet to an injured cat myself, and he seemed none too pleased, though I assured him he could get his five bob from the R.S.P.C.A. It's still the metric equivalent of five bob, I notice. Is it perhaps time for an overhaul or is it true that the Police don't care enough about cats?

Police Review March 7, 1975.

"Don't Vote for a Jew"

It's too commonly assumed that breaches of the law about racial discrimination can be dealt with only by (or at the instance of) the Race Relations Board and must always go to a civil court. The Race Relations Act 1965 declared that anyone is to be liable to six months' imprisonment or a £200 fine or both (or, on indictment, two years or £1,000 or both) if, "with intent to stir up hatred against any section of the public in Great Britain distinguished by colour, race, or ethnic or national origins",

(a) he publishes or distributes written matter which is threatening, abusive or insulting; or
(b) he uses in any public place or at any public meeting words which are threatening, abusive, or insulting,
being matter or words likely to stir up hatred, etc.

The Public Order Act and its procedure (including power of arrest) would take care of the latter part of this enactment, but the "publishing or distributing" offence can only be prosecuted with the consent of the Attorney-General.

Well, the Attorney gave his consent in the case of Mr. Michael McLoughlin, the chairman of the British Movement, who had published election posters urging voters not to support Jewish candidates at the last General Election. On 26 March the magistrates at Bury fined him £150, and there is no indication at the moment whether he intends to appeal. But an interesting political fact about anti-semitism is that it is by no means confined to the sort of people who feel themselves at home in organisations like the British Movement, the National Front, etc. It must, presumably, have the approval of those who support the Soviet Union's anti-Israelite policy, to say nothing of those who swear by Marx and *Das Kapital*, for Marx was as anti-semitic as they come. The working classes of Europe didn't approve of Hitler (or not for long), but they very largely approved of his anti-semitism until they saw what it had led to; and some of them, even then, went on muttering that he "had the right idea". Anti-semitism is still rich soil for the pamphleteer and the poster-designer; and it should be the Police, sooner almost than anyone, who report Race Relations Act offences to the Attorney-General.

Police Review April 18, 1975.

Blue Angels

This was the heading chosen by the *Daily Express* for a reader's letter on 14 May. It told the story of two Policemen on the Kingston by-pass who helped the writer when his (her?) car broke down. "They not only tried to find the fault, they had the car towed away for me, called a mini-cab, and generally made the night more bearable." The letter is signed L. O'Mahoney, Guildford, Surrey; and that last bit raises the hope that L. O'Mahoney is a man. Have you ever noticed that when people write to the newspapers about Police conduct, it's usually nice conduct? When they want to condemn it, they write to the Chief Constable. I wouldn't have it otherwise, for this way round the happier kind of story gets two lots of publicity, one in the press and one on the chief Constable's desk. I once wrote to the Commissioner about two night duty Constables in the Old Kent Road, expressing my appreciation of their kindness, and got a courteous letter back saying how nice. But it might have been better to write to a newspaper.

I was driving home late at night with my wife (I think), and was unaware that my nearside front lamp had gone out. Two P.C.s stepped out into the road and made me stop. When I had lowered the window and expressed my shocked and innocent concern, one of the P.C.s told me to release the bonnet, while the other asked my wife for a hairpin. They proceeded to find the fuse-box, in itself a skilful operation since the vehicle dated from the Harry Tate period, and repaired the circuit by means of the hairpin. They then waved us on, and went back to the footway to resume their conversation. It seemed to me a neat little exercise in public relations, and of course it's the kind of episode one never forgets. On the other hand, a young woman of my acquaintance was recently a passenger in her mother's car when they were stopped by a traffic cop wearing the Nüremberg-type helmet and jack-boots which have unjustly earned them (in some circles) the name of Storm Troopers. I suppose the ladies' windscreen must have looked a little muddy. What was wrong, the Policeman wanted to know, with their windscreen *washer*? They didn't know that anything was wrong with it, or where it would be, or what kind of defect it might suffer from, believing that a washer was a flat metal ring. "It had better have some water in it", he announced, and proceeded to look. It had. Only a tiny drop, but just enough to absolve them from a charge under Construction and Use Regulation 26:

> Every motor vehicle which is required to be fitted with one or more efficient automatic windscreen wipers . . . shall be fitted with a windscreen washer capable of clearing, in conjunction with those windscreen wipers, the area of the windscreen swept by those windscreen wipers of mud or other similar deposit.

If there's even the smallest drip of liquid in your windscreen-washer reservoir, it is possible that your washer is in working order.

Otherwise not, and you are liable to a £50 fine. How many people know about this? Sooner or later someone will be "made an example of", by way of alerting us all. Perhaps, by telling this story, I shall have saved someone a £50 fine.

Police Review May 23, 1975.

The Clapham Omnibus

A mythical figure who is always making his appearance in the literature of the law, and is still referred to frequently by the judges, is "the man on the Clapham omnibus". In other words he's the plain citizen, the man in the street. A reader recently asked me when he was born, and perceptively suggested that he must at least belong to the days when you could go "up on top" of a bus and get the fresh air (or get wet through), because nowadays we should talk about the man "in" the bus and not on it. I'm not so sure about that, but I was very surprised the other day to see the phrase attributed (in a book preface) to Lord Devlin, who has said many useful things but certainly wasn't born when this one was coined. The first time I heard it used, longer ago than I propose to reveal, was when a judge was telling a jury that "reasonable doubt" was the sort of doubt that might affect the judgment of "the man on the Clapham omnibus", and I remember thinking that such a man might be calculating his chances of getting off without paying. But I've been looking into it, trying in fact to establish when the word omnibus was first used about a vehicle. This seems to have been 1829, when (according to the *Oxford English Dictionary*) "the new vehicle, called the omnibus, commenced running this morning from Paddington to the City". But it looks as though the "plain man" on it may have been the brain-child of Lord Bowen, who as Mr. Charles Bowen was in chambers in the eighteen-fifties with the future Lord Chancellor Herschell. Anyway in 1903 Sir Richard Henn Collins, Master of the Rolls, giving judgment in the case of *McQuire v. Western Morning News*, [1903] 2 K.B. 109, said that "the ordinary reasonable man" was "'the man on the Clapham omnibus', as Lord Bowen phrased it". And since the *Oxford English Dictionary Supplement* traces it to the *Journal of the Society of Arts*, 1857, it looks as though Lord Bowen, who wasn't a lord at that date, may even have said it from counsels' benches. What would he say today, in search of the some kind of image? Not the straphanger on the 7.45. More likely the 85th man in the bus queue, the one with no umbrella.

Police Review June 13, 1975.

Strangled Voices on the Air

Why on earth do we all put up with these distorted voices in modern radio and television news bulletins? It's the job of paid critics to grumble at this kind of thing. They say not a word about it, probably because they have long given up any belief that the broadcasting authorities will take any notice of them. The critics are very funny, snooty, malicious, sophisticated and enjoyable, telling us each morning why we had no right to enjoy some programme the night before; but they all seem totally deaf to *sound* quality.

'The Government of Malawi has decided that skirts may be 1½ millimetres shorter. Kevin O'Someone reports.' And there follows the sound of a man trying to speak while someone else is holding him by the throat against a wall. Why? If Malawi's leap into the unknown is thought to merit a place in the broadcast news, and the BBC man on the spot is ready to tell us about it, why can't he telephone his story an hour earlier so that it can be read, intelligibly, by someone in London? Answer: because, the BBC has told us, its far-flung correspondents (who are lonely out there) have to feel wanted and recognised; and it is also important that a man speaking from the top of Everest should sound like a man speaking from the top of Everest. Why, again? What on earth do they suppose has happened to our listeners' imagination, the improvised and notional scene-setting that has always inspired the best radio features, ever since the wartime ITMA?

It's not as if the man against the wall has the worst of it. After a few strangled introductory sentences he brings to us, in support of what he is probably saying, a man lying in a deep ditch with his head in a bucket. Sometimes even this man will then play us a recording made by someone who has caught his face in a washing-machine.

There was a time when all this would be read to us nicely by an Alvar Liddell,who would tell us, after the bit about skirts in Malawi, that 'our correspondent Kevin O'Someone has just reported that. . . .' But now, even when a current murder trial has finished for the day, we have to listen to a man who is sitting 'in our radio van outside the court'. Why, oh why? What does *that* add to the occasion? All the newspapermen are phoning their dispatches to their various news desks. Even if the second-quality voice in the radio van reaches us slightly before we can read the breathless news in the evening papers, so what?

If you compile a documentary for the BBC, with taped interviews, they will (rightly) turn down recordings that, though infinitely better than most of this stuff they inflict on you and me in their news bulletins, are not first class. But they use these atrocious recordings themselves so that you and I shall marvel, with the little cluster of sound engineers and studio assistants, that we are hearing for the first time in history the words of a man clinging under a freight car on the

Trans-Siberian Railway. Broadcasting really grew up in the 1930s. It's had its second childhood. Now that we know what clever grunts it can produce from men on the moon, can we get back to the superb sound quality we enjoyed before every kind of programme had to *sound* as cock-eyed as a stop-press column looks?

Observer Magazine September 28, 1975.

Verbals

I hear many suggestions among lawyers, and none among Policemen, that "verbals" should no longer be admissible in evidence. Verbals? Remarks made by an arrested person, or even by one of those public-spirited citizens who are always accompanying the Police to the station of their own free will. The idea (I gather) is that human speech is never to be trusted unless there exists, somewhere, a written account of it; or anyway that human speech is likely to be twisted as it goes into the ear of a Policeman, and that it is therefore important to be able to see what happens to it after getting in. No dictionary seems yet to have acknowledged this meaning for the word verbals. Every dictionary still believes that a verbal is "a noun derived from a verb", or some such thing: and they give no examples, though the deriving business has been going on (they say) since 1530. Hospitalise is a modern example, an ugly but (I suppose) useful verb derived from hospital. Journalists who write books about criminals and Policemen usually feel a need to end with a glossary, and some of these have their own definitions of verbals. Mr. Peter Laurie, for instance, in his book *Scotland Yard*, ends with a "short vocabulary of Metropolitan Police slang". This says: Verbals—a self-incriminating statement made to the Police after the arrest of a man, and given in evidence by them; verbals are often said to be manufactured by the Police; hence "to put the verbals on", or "to verbal up".

But if verbals were ever to disappear from the literature of crime, there would be some sad losses. Take Mr. Joseph Feldman, the New York lawyer whose Greenwich Village flat was found to contain more than 15,000 New York City Library books, valued at £60,000 (said the *Sunday Times* of 28 September). They were piled to the ceiling, they covered the stove, and they filled the bathtub and sinks. It took 20 men three days to remove them in seven trucks, which sounds like the ominous beginning of a "sample proportion" sum. And do you know what Mr. Feldman's "verbal" was? "I like to read."

Police Review October 10, 1975.

All in the Bag

The other day I had to listen to an altercation between two angry men outside the post office on Waterloo Station. One of them (like me) was waiting to post a letter while the other, who seemed to have about 20 letters for posting, was slowly distributing them among the London, Country and Abroad boxes, and seemed intent on crowding everyone out while he did it. The waiting man got impatient and posted his own during a brief lull. You'd have thought this was reasonable enough, but the man with the 20 letters resented it, possibly seeing it as a comment on his slowness. And there was a ridiculous row.

It would have been even more ridiculous if they had seen what I saw the very next day at Guildford post office. There the collecting postman scooped the contents of all the separate sections of the mail boxes into one mailbag, which must have meant that the sorting office staff would have to do all the sorting again. I notice that Mr. Eric Pearcey, who is secretary of the Post Office Users National Council, has told the *Sunday Mirror* (26 October) that he knows this has been going on and has complained to the Post Office about it. A post office official seemed to think it did, too, but not very much. "Most postmen", he is quoted as saying, "do put mail into separate bags when they collect it"; which is almost what you might expect. But it reminds me of an episode when, as a young Bobby, I was detailed by a Sergeant to stand by a "London and Country" pillar box in which the London section was full to overflowing—letters were sticking out of the posting slot. I was to wait there while the Sergeant telephoned the collecting office. During the wait a postman came along who knew nothing about it and asked me what was afoot. When I told him he tugged about 50 letters out of the London box and dropped them into the Country one. He had just gone on his way when the mail van turned up and its driver, finding nothing wrong, asked me for the explanation. When I had told him he said: "Well, couldn't *you* have done that, mate?"; and although the answer was that he didn't know my Sergeant, I felt a bit of a fool.

Police Review November 1, 1975.

Common Law Wife

No doubt the growing confusion about the true meaning of "common law wife" is one of the signs that the institution of marriage is shakier than it was. I believe the phrase came into general (and mistaken) use during the first world war, when it was realised for the first time that Great Britain was going to need conscription to replace the vast numbers of regular army men and volunteers being killed. And now when a modern government at war takes the breadwinner away from a household, it feels obliged to pay his wife an allowance; and because a lot of the conscripts were living with women who were not their wives, it was seen to be unfair that they should have no allowance merely because they had not gone through a form of marriage. What were these women to be called? Someone thought of the old phrase "common law wife", and thus they were christened.

But they are not common law wives, and sooner or later the misuse of the phrase is sure to cause trouble. A common law wife is one who has gone through an exchange of matrimonial vows in front of a priest or deacon, and not in the course of a church service or a register office ceremony. I don't know whether the phrase is properly used in relation to a Gretna Green marriage (in which, since 1856, one of the parties must have been resident in Scotland for 21 days immediately before the marriage—the Marriage (Scotland) Act 1856 put an end to the scampering across the border for a quick tie-up); or to that other adventure for elopers, the marriage on a merchant ship registered in England and carried out by a clergyman of the Established Church of England or the Church of Rome—not, incidentally, by the skipper, whose power to marry anyone is a popular myth. But it's nearly 200 years since you could get a common law marriage by the exchange of vows, unaccompanied by any form-filling, witnesses, or ceremony.

It seems that you can still marry in that way if you are in some overseas country which has accepted English common law (i.e. a present or former colony or dominion) and the local marriage laws are too primitive for you. Possibly those are now the only common law wives and husbands. I've always wondered whether the English criminal law now affords them its numerous protections and privileges—exemption from the law of conspiracy, non-compellability as witnesses, the law about rape, assault, coercion, privilege of communication, the killing of adulterers, and so on. Some of these questions might be more difficult to decide if the "common law wife" concept got out of hand, and the mere mention of them should be enough to suggest that the phrase has no place in the criminal law or in Police terminology.

Police Review November 21, 1975.

Minority is Always Right to Shout

If I had lived in London in the 1830s I would have gone often, I think, to St Paul's Cathedral, to hear that reverberating Canon the Rev. Sydney Smith praying for my immortal soul. And yet among all his wit and wisdom there stands out, to the embarrassment of disciples like me, the asinine pronouncement that the minority is always right. (Both Shaw and Ibsen cribbed it.)

Think of the minorities among us today, the flat-earthers, the National Front, the idiots who publicise the Protocols of the Elders of

Zion, the advertisers making the flesh creep about Joanna Southcott's box, the Maoists, the chaps with the sandwich boards proclaiming the end of the world. Whatever Sydney Smith had in mind, I reckon Ibsen and Shaw meant that the right-thinking are always in the minority. This is not at all the same thing, is more likely to be true, and is also why I like to think I'm a minority man myself, a Dissent man.

And yet any minority is almost certain to earn itself an adjective: noisy, vociferous, strident, crazy, reactionary, hippy. I went once with three other people to see a Minister of State about what we thought was a much-needed social reform; we were a deputation. And the Minister, sitting between two civil servants who plainly thought we were wasting everyone's time, told us we belonged to a noisy minority. Our spokesman asked him what would be the good of a silent one, but it wasn't the best moment for the question and the Minister took up the rest of our precious allotment of Ministerial time, or most of it, with an estimate of the noise that a decent and acceptable minority might make, while the two civil servants looked at their watches.

It must have been this kind of equation that gave rise to the new American concept of the 'silent majority', but that seems odd because the silent majority had always previously meant the dead. Today it has come to mean the great soft mass of the living who put up with things, who get on with their jobs, pay their fines, rates and taxes, spend 8½p on posting their letters, put their shaking fingers in their ears when Concorde goes over, wait two years for their hernia operations, sit through party political broadcasts, refuse to sign any kind of petition that would change something, and seek only the quiet life that no one, ever again, will get.

And thus emerges the theory that the only minorities that are 'right' are the massive ones, the only-just minorities that are pushing 49 per cent. I dissent from this. I find myself in agreement with some very tiny minorities indeed, and it is very often true that the smaller such minorities are the more noise they need to make, not less. Some of them will grow bigger and stronger on noise, and can lessen it as they come to maturity. Others will achieve little by noise: they must find other ways of making their voices heard. They know their enemies. They hate pop music, church bells, the cavernous hee-haw of ambulances and police cars, transistors on the beach, all this modern Academy of Music stuff which is so much better than it sounds, and the barking of other people's dogs.

Observer Magazine December 14, 1975.

I Saw Three Ships

As we come up to Christmas, the annual argument will break out again about the authentic words of the old carol *I Saw Three Ships A-sailing There* (every other caroller has a different version, and I've taken mine from the *Oxford Book of Carols* but won't argue with anyone). This year, to complicate matters, a lady has seen three flying saucers. She is Mrs. Maria Morrison, and she lives at Bath Street, Islington, on the 19th floor of a tower block. At 4.20 a.m. one morning last November she was awakened by a wind howling round the building, looked out to see in the sky a "circular craft with lights all round it and an orange light above" and aroused the whole family to watch. A smaller one came from under it, and then another one from the west. The big one was "much brighter than a star", and she saw an aircraft do a U-turn to avoid it. After half an hour the family went back to bed, but Mrs. Morrison stayed up "until they had all disappeared up into the sky".

"We've had no sightings reported to us" said the Police at King's Cross when asked by the *Islington Gazette*. How many Police Forces, I wondered, keep a "UFO Sightings Register", for reference when the great day comes? With tabular columns for time and date, size and direction of flight, numbers of little green men alighting to take soil samples, and so on? It would be a more romantic register than some that I've played a part in compiling. At one time people kept falling down open manholes, and we were required to take note of open manholes on our sections, recording the details in a little green book when going off duty. "Anyone got the man-'ole book?' we used to shout.

I've been credibly told that people have long been reporting to the Police (and not only the Scottish Police) that they have seen the Loch Ness monster. These miscellaneous sightings of the unexplained are reaching such a pitch that the Police will soon have to make a choice: take a full statement, with biography and fingerprints, or detain for self-protection under the Mental Health Act. Either would be wrong, if there *really* are saucers and a monster.

Police Review December 26, 1975.

Equal Opportunities

There are one or two legislative achievements about which I usually refrain from sticking my neck out, restrained by long experience of what can happen to it. But my heart was with the woman Police Sergeant who said on television last week that she was resigning from the Force because she thought the Sex Discrimination Act was daft—or rather that its consequences within the Police Service were going to be daft. My one regret was that when she was asked "But don't you *want* to be liberated?", she didn't say "That's an idiotic catch-phrase, I don't feel the need for any liberation". (But people are amazingly polite and tolerant with television interviewers, God knows why.) I'm all in favour of sex equality, especially equal pay for equal jobs—including, by the way, old age pensions at 60 for men as well as for women. But I have never believed that this kind of social rethinking can be imposed by law; I was even opposed, and still am, to the Race Relations Act.

The thing is, multitudes of people will be able to get round this Act by various devices, including the simple one of offering a wage that only an unattached woman would accept. And the ones who can't get round it will be taken to court and ordered by injunction to change their ways. Those who won't change will go to prison. And you know who will have to take them there? Right.

Police Review January 9, 1976.

Clearing the Books

I've been reading Ludovic Kennedy's new book, *A Presumption of Innocence.* It tells the story of Patrick Meehan and his conviction for the murder of Mrs. Ross at Ayr in 1969. Its purpose is to show that Meehan was wrongly convicted, and unlike any such book I have ever seen it begins with statements by five distinguished lawyers, all of whom appeared for the defence (including Mr. Nicholas Fairbairn, Q.C., M.P.), and all of whom believe Meehan to be innocent. If that's not sufficient to make people think, there is a pre-publication statement by Lord Devlin: "I know nothing about the case of Patrick Meehan except what I have read in this book. But", says Lord Devlin, "it is a very disturbing book. It needs to be answered, one way or another, if confidence in the processes of justice is to be maintained."

Meehan is a man with a bad (though not a violent) criminal record, and even so his record doesn't include a number of crimes for which, he freely admits, he has never been caught. This kind of man, let it be admitted, stirs up (in many breasts) less anxiety and urgency when it looks as though he has been wrongly convicted of something. I don't say that this has been the state of the Scottish Office breast about Meehan's case, and now that the facts are available for all to see I'm content to wait and watch. But one detail of immediate interest to the Police concerns the possible effects of "taking other offences into consideration".

At the age of 16 Meehan ran away from an approved school, committed another offence, and was arrested. To the Police he admitted not only that offence but others of which he was innocent, *in order to get sent to borstal.* "If you were committed to Borstal", he told Mr. Kennedy, "you could count on being released within one year. If you were returned to approved school you would remain there until you were 18—two years. The Police knew what it was all about, and were quite happy to clear their books." Now we all know that this is an established aspect of the T.I.C. system, and that men will frequently admit to crimes they really know nothing about, sometimes with an eye to the effect on the kind of sentence they will thus qualify for; though I should have thought it unusual for a lad of 16 to be thus sophisticated. But if ever the operation of the T.I.C. system were thoroughly investigated by a committee on the administration of the criminal law there would be some startling responses. It has been officially operated since 1922 and has never, so far as I know, come under any scrutiny.

Police Review January 16, 1976.

Common Law Lavatories

There was nothing very human about Barnsley's Market Council when it got to hear that one of its licensed street traders had been taken short one evening. The market was closed for the night, and all the premises had been locked. This included all the lavatories. So the belated street trader went up a side street and urinated. The rest of the story would delight the heart of any average television playwright. A security officer came along and saw what had been done; and his reaction seems to have been precisely that of the chief petty officer in the famous Bateman cartoon about the rating who had been seen to spit on the newly holy-stoned deck. ("And when I seen what 'e' ad done, sir, I says to 'im 'Good Gawd, I says, *wot 'as you done*'.") The matter was reported to the market manager, who felt that it was made worse by the fact that the street trader had been abusive when told he had done wrong. It reached the ears of the chairman of the Amenity Services Committee, and the following day the offender was told he was "no longer considered to be a suitable tenant of the council, and must give up his stalls and his pitch in the market". He appealed to the council, and failed.

So he took the matter to the Queen's Bench divisional court, asking for an order of *certiorari* quashing the council's decision; and failed again. On he went to the Court of Appeal, where the story was heard by Lord Denning (Master of the Rolls), Lord Justice Scarman, and Sir John Pennycuick, and you can make your own jokes about their names.

Barnsley's market was created by charter in 1249. The Appeal Court judges pointed out that by common law everyone had a right to sell and buy in an ancient market. Anyone who had been allocated a pitch or stall had a common law right to it. When Barnsley Council took over control of the market in 1969, it didn't acquire any right unreasonably to restrict public buying and selling; its right of control must be exercised "in accordance with the rules of natural justice". This hadn't been done because, when the council held its inquiry, the stall holder was not present and the market manager was. The Court of Appeal thought the appellant had been dealt with too harshly. Not only that, it was "unreasonable that in the circumstances the council should have power to inflict on a man of good character the grave penalty of banning him from his livelihood". So his appeal was allowed, *certiorari* was issued after all, the council's decision was quashed, and the question as to what happens when all the market lavatories are locked remains to be faced. It's not often that natural justice and a call of nature come face to face.

Police Review April 2, 1976.

Jurors at Lunch

Reading has a Crown Court which started life as a drill hall, and Mr. Justice Kilner Brown seems not to think much of it. Last week during a rape trial the jury had heard evidence from the victim, a girl of 17, when the court adjourned for lunch. The jurors went to the canteen, where, by what seems a very strange oversight, they lunched among a group of people which happened to include a witness for the defence in the case they were trying. The prosecuting counsel, Mr. Bruce Laughland, duly reported to the judge that the witness had heard jurors "expressing some views about the merits of the case" (*The Times*, 5 May); and the judge promptly discharged the jury altogether. "You are not to blame," he told them. The court should provide canteen facilities where jurors and witnesses could eat apart. "I hope the court administrators will note my remarks," said his Lordship. "Jurors and witnesses are the most important part of the system'.

Wildwood House, London, recently published a book called *Members of the Jury*, in which 12 men and women who have served on juries were asked to describe their experiences. Some of these had quite a lot to say about lunching and refreshment arrangements. (If I confess to being one of them, I can do so without plugging the book for profit, for my modest fee was an outright payment and no royalties.) But my jury went out and got its lunch at neighbouring pubs, and there, apart from any danger that witnesses might go there too—and who could stop them?—the jurors filled themselves with narcotic platefuls of steak and kidney pie, washed down with soporific mugfuls of beer. Back in court in the afternoon some of them accordingly went to sleep. This seems to me a lot more undesirable than letting them eat in the same room with witnesses. Now that I'm not eligible to serve any more, I maintain that jurors should be sustained on vitamin pills and (perhaps) tonic water.

But we were all outclassed by the juror at Dudley Crown Court last Friday, who (according to the *Daily Telegraph* of 8 May) nipped out of court to spend a penny and was not missed until he stumbled on the way back to his seat. Then everyone noticed him at the same time, including the judge, who told him to go away. The remaining 11 contained themselves.

Police Review May 14, 1976.

House to House Sponsors

A neighbour asked me recently why the Police don't control what she called the "growing menace" of demands for sponsorship of walks, rides, swims, knitting, and other forms of juvenile or feminine endeavour which encourage their participants to swell the number of people knocking at doors and ringing doorbells. She knew about the House to House Collections Act and Regulations, but she was sure that none of the children continually bringing her to the door had anything to do with official permits or licences. What brought it to a head was the loss of £14 raised by a "sponsored walk" about three years ago, and the local realisation that there was no real control over the money.

I forbore to tell her that not even the smallest of "sponsored walks", etc., is really exempt from the necessity for a Police permit: if all these enterprises applied to the Police for permission, existing Police departments for dealing with house to house collections would have to grow suddenly to about 20 times their present size. (The most recent one I've heard of was a "sponsored silence": the kids participating had to keep silent for two hours, and I heard later that one of them did, but is now making a reasonable recovery.) In the *Sunday Times* of 18 April, Miss Jean Watt, "a housewife living in Falkland, Fife", described how the registered charities collecting on doorsteps in Scotland have now been reinforced by "children requesting us to sponsor them with hard cash for knitting squares or swimming a length or walking a mile" (are the Scottish children softer or more modest than ours?); and she said the good causes are usually the funds of the local golf club or something similar. "Friends of mine," said Miss Watt, "have often moaned about being asked to give money to such causes, but they don't want to get a reputation locally for meanness so they give, time after time after time". She wants to see all forms of doorstep cash-collecting made illegal. It's begging, she says, however good the cause—it's gently blackmailing householders on their own doorstep. I know exactly how she feels and I'm not even Scottish.

Come to that, I wonder what our legislators would have done in 1824, when the Vagrancy Act first prohibited "endeavouring by the exposure of wounds or deformities to obtain or gather alms", if they had had to face our daily press pictures of leprosy, mutilation, emaciation and so forth in Third World countries? The distressing thing about these is the way they lose their impact by constant repetition.

Police Review May 28, 1976.

Academics on Crime

I don't go along with the growing attack on academic criminology. (Well, it seems to me to be growing, but one ought to be careful: it's so easy to discover and declare some growing evil, forgetting that what you've seen is some paragraph in a newspaper.) There is absolutely nothing to be gained by deriding "the academics" and pretending, or persuading oneself, that the only way to learn about crime is to join the Police Service. (It's equally silly to attack "do-gooders"—a phrase born of hate and ignorance, gaining nothing by being adopted, as it was recently, by a High Court judge in an outburst suggesting that only the judges know what is good for us. Among the do-gooders of history you find such names as Wilberforce, Elizabeth Fry, Bunyan, St. Francis, Buddha, and Christ himself. When I hear someone use the phrase "do-gooder" as a term of abuse, I write him off as a cretin.) But Mr. Ron Lewis, senior probation officer for Kent, has done us all a service in exposing some of the remarks made by "academics" (I wish I knew who they were) at crime conferences: "The concept of theft as an evil is a bourgeois one", "Delinquency is a function of the class struggle", "To ask a delinquent to give up offending is to ask him to give up his lifestyle". Can you beat those?

These observations came into the news because a probation officers' conference had been told by a professor of social administration that probation officers ought to divert thieves from the corner shop to the nearest Marks and Spencers, which "could well afford the loss". Baroness Phillips then pointed out in a letter to *The Times* (24 May) that honest people have to pay for what is stolen from shops, because such thefts "are as much an expense of shopkeeping as rent and rates, heat and light"; and she added that the £550 million shoplifted every year was equivalent to a Great Train Robbery every one and a half days. The shoplifting puzzle won't be solved by diverting the crooks to Marks and Spencers, whether because they "don't feel it" or because they've got good store detectives.

Police Review June 11, 1976.

One queue only, please

An elderly lady told me the other day that she was dissatisfied with the way the police dealt with assaults. "They just write your name and address in a book," she said, "and that's that. You never hear any more about it." It turned out that she had been waiting in a post office queue when another lady "deliberately" stamped on her foot. Since this was not the kind of stamp she was queueing for , there was a row, and a number of people joined in, from rival queues. Rival queues? Well, this is what it has come to: where you get several "counter positions" open, each having its own queue, you will also have queue-jumping, lateral sidling, artful manoeuvring, and shoppers trying to wait in three queues at once. This is natural enough, since you can often wait in one queue and see several others melt away before your very eyes. It's one of life's gambles; of course it ought not to entail having your feet stamped on by adversaries, but if it does the remedy lies with you, not with the police.

And the queue has now become so important to the orderly life that we ought to encourage it, as an aid to law and order. Actually we're better at it in this country than most of those struggling foreigners: try queueing for a bus in Paris and you'll find that, although queueing is supposed to be a French idea and has an untranslated French name, what you need in Paris is a sharp elbow and some rugby coaching. It's true that our *Oxford English Dictionary* quotes Thomas Carlyle as referring in 1837 in his *French Revolution* to "that talent of spontaneously standing in queue which distinguishes the French people", but it doesn't distinguish them nowadays even if it did then. It seems to have reached its final form here during the last war, when seeing a queue outside a shop and not knowing what it was for, you joined a shorter queue of people waiting to ask someone. The simple answer to the problem of rival queues, as in post offices, banks, big railway stations etc, is to insist on only one queue, from which the person at the head will go to the vacant counter position as soon as it's free. Some banks do it already, and have done it without their customer's feet being stamped on.

Police Review July 16, 1976.

Speaking as an ex-pig

"Why," asks an indignant correspondent, "are we now called pigs? And who started it? Does it have anything to do with George Orwell's *Animal Farm* or is it just a meaningless term of abuse?" Well, in 1873 it seems to have meant a plain clothes man, and in 1821 policemen were known as pigs or grunters; so I should call it a mark of unpopularity, and it's obviously far from new among those who dislike the police. Lord Russell of Killowen mentioned the 1821 usage when he was giving judgment in the case of *DPP v. Majewski* (1976), which concerned the effect of "self-induced intoxication" on a charge of assault (it was briefly reported here on 14 May this year). "When the police arrived," said his Lordship, "the appellant called them adjectival pigs, a word which has of recent years been revived as a reference to law enforcement officers, having been current in the early nineteenth century (see Pierce Egan's *Life in London,* 1821)." Lord Russell must have been interested enough in this pig-police comparison to look it up in the 13-volume *Oxford English Dictionary*, which gives the 1821 quotation. He said the appellant's use of it showed that he wasn't so drunk as not to know what was going on. He knew a pig when he saw one, and this "negatived lack of understanding".

I wish, on the whole, that we weren't called pigs, though it never happened to me when I was in the police service and though, in fact, I do rather like pigs. We have been called worse names, especially in America, the home of the poet Benjamin H. Burt; and since we are now at the peak of the silly season there may be some excuse for passing on to you, at some sacrifice of sobriety, what Burt said about the pig:

One evening in October, when I was far from sober,
And dragging home a load with manly pride,
My feet began to stutter, I lay down in the gutter,
And a pig came up and parked right by my side.
Then I warbled "It's fair weather when good fellows get together",
Till a lady passing by was heard to say:
"You can tell a man who boozes by the company he chooses."
Then the pig got up and slowly walked away.

Police Review July 23, 1976.

Missile season ends

And I'll tell you another hazard of rural England—village cricket pitches, like the one opposite my cottage, are usually smaller than the ones in urban parks. Now that the cricket season is (nearly) over I can heave two sighs, one of regret and the other of relief. Regret because I'm a vice-president of the club and take a benign interest in it, relief bacause my cottage windows have survived one more season. Driving a motor vehicle past this pitch is far more dangerous than most drivers realise—they even pull up here in the hope of seeing some good cricket. I suppose they're interested in bowlers (only once have I seen a windscreen smashed); or they may be foreigners. I share the feelings of a Mr Booker, whose apt address is Cricket Green Cottage, Hambledon, Surrey, and who got a ball through his window which smashed a china figure and cost him £100. According to the *Surrey Advertiser* of 14 September, the cricket club's insurance company wouldn't pay up because "the ball had left the ground" when the damage was done; and getting them to change their minds took two years and Esther Rantzen. I must find out whether there's a bye-law about propelling missiles to the common danger.

Police Review September 24, 1976.

Granny bashing

And yes, it really is being heralded as "the latest symptom of our sick society". Those are the words of a health visitor talking to the *Daily Telegraph* on 22 September, and he added that "attacks on elderly people living with relatives are now a major problem". When did they cease to be a minor problem? "It is only recently," said Miss Jean Maughan, Hertfordshire Area Nursing Officer, "that granny bashing has been recognised as something that can and does happen." How often? Well, she said, "I don't want people to get the idea that every old person living with relatives is being treated badly in this country" Good. "But we have had a couple of reports of this occurring."

And so a new social concern is born, a new class of wallopers takes its place alongside the bashers of babies and the batterers of wives. "Health visitors and community nurses," said the *Daily Telegraph,* "already on the alert for baby bashing, are now being urged for signs of granny and grandad bashing". It was time for something of the kind, some new revelation of what goes on behind the retina of the newspaper eye. Mugging, which took over the crime-front headlines for a year or two until it was suddenly identified as our old friend robbery with violence, has lost its pull and is no longer worth even a parliamentary question about what the police are supposed to be doing. Fewer bovver boots seem to be crashing into the faces of horizontal victims. Winkle-pickers (can't you remember winkle-pickers?) no longer pick holes in the bodies of citizens who have first been knocked down. But grannies—now there's a new line for you. Watch out for a new Home Office directive for those compiling Criminal Statistics: "Number of grandchildren, and whether frantic or loving". Grandparenthood has always been treated as a virtue in the mythology of crime, but we've kept no records of its treatment at home.

Police Review October 1, 1976.

Pound foolish

I remember a case in which a "novelty shop", on a popular royal occasion, proclaimed its mercenary devotion to the Crown by flying a Royal Standard from its first-floor window and offering for sale a cheap line in beer-mugs bearing the same design. Since there was (and there still is) a Home Office direction to the police that the Royal Standard, as "the personal flag of the sovereign", cannot properly be used without the Queen's permission, the manager of the shop was "asked to discontinue its use". He declined. "Why me?" he said. "Lots of other people are selling these, and I bought the flag from Webster's (a firm then famous as flag manufacturers). So he was visited by a more senior police officer, by way of applying pressure that could seem to be at once more tactful and more impressive. No good. Then he had a visit from a very senior officer indeed, who gave him the firm instruction that at least the flag over the shop was to be removed. He responded with the firm instruction that the very senior officer was to get stuffed. The Royal Standard remained where it was, being taken down the next day when the excitement was all over. From the police viewpoint, a highly unsatisfactory episode: and from that of the Home Office, who were duly informed, another one for the file. But there seemed to be no law that the police could invoke.

What can be done about the Ulster Weaving Company, which for many years has been printing £1 note designs on its tea-towels? This poser for the Bank of England has suddenly blown up at a time when the pound is being made to look specially defenceless, all over the world. Inflation is said to be responsible for the fact that the Ulster Weaving Company has lately added £5 note designs to the range. Every year it prints thousands, and they sell briskly in America, Australia and Europe. According to the *Daily Telegraph* (29 September) some Bank of England officials saw a girl wearing hot pants and "could not help noticing" (isn't that nice?) that the garment had a £1 note design. She had made the pants from a tea-towel, or possibly tea-towels. So the Bank of England wrote to the Ulster Weaving Company and said it must stop producing them. The company's chairman says that since the towels measure 30 inches by 20 inches, nobody will mistake one for a bank note. "They are based on the £1 note design," he said, "but they are marked 'Bank of Britain' and they have Britannia instead of the Queen." So the company will not stop making them.

Is this another case like that of the Royal Standard? Not quite. The Bank of England holds the copyright in its banknote designs, and *may* be able to convince a court (if it comes to that) about infringement of copyright. There seems less hope for the Bank in the Forgery Act 1913 — which has been mentioned — or in Section 38 of the Criminal Justice Act 1925, which penalises anyone who makes, or "uses for any purpose whatsoever", any document in any way resembling, or so nearly resembling as to be calculated to deceive, any currency or bank note". We must all hope, despite the worrying news, that it will be a long time before tea-towels, or even hot pants, are in circulation as banknotes.

Police Review October 8, 1976.

Drink and the Devil

I used to think that there were certain ways of dividing humanity, or anyway the British, into two opposing classes without any leftovers or "don't knows'. I realise now that if this were publicly asserted, there would emerge a non-aligned body of thinkers who wouldn't even know that they didn't know. Suppose you went in turn to the teetotallers and to those who, to put it at the lowest, like a little drop now and again, and asked them whether alcohol should be totally banned. There would be many don't-knows. Would they all be among the teetotallers? They would not. Among the moderate and uncertain tipplers, unable to make up their minds, there would be me.

This may in part be the legacy of a Band of Hope infancy: I believe I solemnly renounced Strong Drink when I was five. Anyway, from then on for many years, whenever I passed a pub door standing open on a summer's evening, the waft of booze from inside was as a poisonous exhalation from the jaws of hell. In a confused way it still is, though hell doesn't now seem so bad a place to go and sit down in. My parents (and theirs) had good cause to be terrified of alcohol, and in my childhood it was not only the Supreme Evil (at which no one ever laughed), it was the one you could identify in the streets and dumbly wonder about. The real tragedy about drunkenness, of course, and it has now been running for some thousands of years, is that it is often so funny. If drunken men were *never* amusing (I leave out drunken women because I don't see how they can be), always sickening and smelly, slobbering and angry, helpless and incontinent, obnoxious and hateful to everyone around them, would there be any breweries, distilleries, or vineyards?

The question has a sharper edge today because of the recurrent proposal to legalise soft drugs. Few people seem to doubt that cannabis, for example, does less harm than alcohol or cigarettes. Its addicts do not, because of it, commit murder, burglary, rape and grievous bodily harm. It is 46 years since a Road Traffic Act first penalised driving while under the influence of drugs as a separate offence from that of drunken driving. We still don't know from published statistics how many such drivers are unfit because of drugs, as distinct from alcohol. There's no doubt that some are unfit because of a deadly combination of both, a relatively new problem likely to militate powerfully against proposals for slackening controls of either. But since everyone recognises the role of alcohol on dulling the faculty of self-criticism, and nearly everyone knows about its powerful share in the causation of crime, is it not astonishing that drunken murder, drunken rape, drunken damage, drunken brutality are accepted as things we simply have to live with? Among the thousands of police 'crime reports' and parole board dossiers I have had to read, a majority, I swear, have reported the accused as saying 'Well, we'd all had a few drinks, and then . . .'

And the law has always faced two dilemmas about drunkenness. One is that punishment, and especially imprisonment, will have precious little effect on future thirst-quenching. The other is that juries and magistrates, trying cases in which a guilty mind must be proved or assumed, have to bear in mind that 'a drunken intent is nevertheless an intent'. The proper direction to a jury, said the Court of Appeal only last year (in *R.* v. *Sheeham and Moore*), is that 'the mere fact that the defendant's mind was affected by drink does not assist him at all, provided the necessary intention is there'. It is otherwise (now) if his drunkenness was 'involuntary', for the law may absolve an offender who has been plied with 'laced' drinks and doesn't know it. Such cases even further emphasise the helplessness of the law in dealing with drunkenness *post facto*; and encourage tentative and non-compulsive drinkers (like me) to think wistfully about preventive measures (for others).

Preventive measures of course abound in the various liquor licensing statutes, ranging through 'permitted hours', age limits, the status of clubs, what you may drink with or without a meal, what you may brew up at home, and what the grocer can sell. There is, however, one preventive measure which is strangely neglected, and its neglect seems to me of the same nature, having the same non-articulated motives, as the persistent silence about the effect of booze at scenes of violence like those at Notting Hill, Soweto and Cape Town. I refer to the common provision (in England it's Section 188 of the Licensing Act 1964) by which all the pubs in a threatened neighbourhood can be closed in advance of any trouble. Here it is:

> Where a riot or tumult happens or is expected to happen, any two justices of the peace for the county or borough may order every holder of a justices' licence for premises in or near the place where the riot or tumult happens *or is expected to happen* to close his premises for such time as the justices may order.

Why not, therefore, close all the pubs and liquor shops near football grounds and street carnival areas in advance of the occasion, as an alternative to waiting for them to be smashed in? The principle of compensation for aggrieved licensees is a long-established part of the licensing law, and the scope of the Compensation Fund could surely be so extended as to include suitable payments to pubs compulsorily deprived of a Saturday's business. The cost of that could hardly exceed the present liability of the ratepayers to make good all the shop fronts after riot damage. However it is astonishing (to others, I find, as well as to myself) how many magistrates and even justices's clerks have never heard of, let alone read, Section 188 of the Licensing Act – though it's much older than the Act of 1964, being then a re-enactment from 1910.

Nevertheless, it may well be the drunken driver who will slowly make it more difficult for all of us to get a drink, not just within 'permitted hours' but at any time. To take a recent example which could be the story of anyone tipsy at the wheel: at the Old Bailey on 1 September a motorist admitted killing a pedestrian while drunk and driving. He had had 'several beers and 12 gins and tonics'. His car mounted the pavement, ran down two married couples walking together, carried off one man on the car bonnet until he fell off unconscious, and dragged the other one's body, trapped under the chassis, into another street where he crashed. There have been criticisms of the leniency that gave him only six months, but even if it had been six years, or 16, the punishment could serve no purpose other than the attempt to assuage horror with revenge.

At the time I had a Dutch friend staying with me, and he was totally incredulous – I noticed that he would never drink anything if he was going to drive. In Holland the permitted blood-alcohol limit for drivers is now .005 per cent – five thousandths of a milligram. If you merely took a deep breath as you passed the open door of a pub, you could ingest enough alcohol to colour the crystals in a Dutch breathalyser. And the Dutch police have the power to stop and test drivers at random, that is to say without any pretence about prior suspicion. In this country, though the 80-per-cent level seems likely to stay, we are about to drop the pretence that we don't allow random testing, and the police are finding that wine-and-cheese parties in private houses, produce far more drunken drivers than pubs do. Why do I call it a pretence? Because there's always *something* a policeman can stop you for, such are the mechanical hazards of going around in a car or even on a push bike. And then you will notice that for part of the conversation his face is so close to yours that you can tell whether *he's* been drinking.

If I drank a lot, liked it, and meant to keep on, I suppose I should be angry at every new suggestion for liquor control. As it is, I think alcohol causes enough anguish, squalor and bereavement to outweigh all the synthetic bonhomie in what we called the civilised world. It also gives rise to much merriment and countless short periods in which, after all that worry, everything seems fine. It is this that makes me unhappy among the don't knows, and at the same time insulates me from those who proclaim, among all the human rights now being freshly discovered, the Right to Booze.

New Statesman October 22, 1976.

Truth in Advertising

On 15 October *Police Review* reproduced from *The Times* part of a full-page Whitbread advertisement which said "Generally speaking Whitbread landlords support the law" (which seemed to admit that some of them don't), "and we only wish the reverse was always true". The idea was to call attention to the amount of violence in pubs and to find out whether licensees (who were invited to fill in a questionnaire) were getting enough help from the police and the magistrates in relation to assaults on licensees. Then on 26 October *The Times* reported that magistrates had written a letter of protest to the Whitbread brewery company, repudiating the suggestion that magistrates are prejudiced against publicans. "It's perfectly proper," said Mr Joseph Brayshaw, secretary of the Magistrates' Association, "for sentence of the court to be criticised, but . . . if I were a shareholder of Whitbread I should want to know why the company was wasting money in this way". I can happily claim that Joe Brayshaw is an old friend of mine, and this makes it easier for me to recognise the rare occasions when he is talking through his hat. This is one. Why shouldn't Whitbread spend its money on calling attention to the vulnerable state of its licensees? I haven't got any Whitbread (or any other) shares, but if I had I would still applaud the use of my money to look after the chaps who were earning my dividends. The complaints about undue leniency on the part of magistrates dealing with assaults on licensees may be misconceived, though my own impression is that all too often the sentences suggest the indulgent reaction "Ah well, after all he was pretty drunk at the time". (No-one ever says it like this if the chap happened to be driving a vehicle.) But I have often wished the police authorities would take a regular full-page in one or more national daily papers and set out the police point of view that can't be put across in any other way.

So I now put it forward as a serious suggestion. A monthly, or even a weekly, full-page advertisement exposing and refuting the principal lies currently circulating about the police (there's never any shortage), and giving the facts; giving also the truth about police misconduct, and dodging no issues; telling the public what Shaw Taylor now tells them on television's *Police Five*; telling them also how to look after their property and personal safety, with examples of people who haven't been doing it. In the right hands, such a page could become the first attraction that every reader would turn to; the material for it, which news reporters spend their lives chasing after, is all there at the turn of a tap. What would it cost? Less than *Police Five* does, anyway.

Police Review November 5, 1976.

Illiterate Lorry Drivers

Once in pouring rain I was given a lift by the driver of a huge French eight-wheeled juggernaut, and our conversation, since his English was far better than my French, was conducted in English. After a mile or two he produced a delivery docket and asked me what was the best route to the address stated on it. He was on the right route when I left him, but I couldn't help wondering what I should have felt like if I were driving one of these monsters in France (or, come to that, driving anything in France) and unfamiliar with both route and language.

Yet we have a rather worse home-grown version of the same problem, in the presence on our roads of lorry drivers who are unable to read or write. I wouldn't have thought this possible until, quite recently, I met a self-employed builder who is totally illiterate and yet drives his own lorry and, somehow or other, conducts his business. On 5 November the *Daily Telegraph* published a letter from a Mr Alfred Garnett (I hope it wasn't the more familiar Alf choosing a new forum), who lives at Abergele, North Wales, relating an experience that tops all this. On the Colwyn Bay promenade he was stopped by a lorry driver who asked, in a broad Scottish accent, if he was on the right road for Aberdeen. "After ascertaining that I was not the victim of a leg-pull I suggested that he consult his map and offered my help. Further conversation elicited the fact that both the driver and his mate were unable to read either maps or roads signs. They were in fact totally illiterate." It turned out that the driver wanted Abergele, only a few miles away. But on 10 November another reader put the question that must have suggested itself to everyone. "How could these people possibly have passed a driving test," asked Mr F. Turnbull of Gosforth, "which requires the recognition of number-plates at a given distance, and how could they avoid being failed in the sections of the test dealing with the Highway Code? How, indeed, can an illiterate lorry driver be considered competent to maintain log-books or any other statutory written records?"

Somehow or other, they do. Perhaps the illiterate lorry driver, surviving all attempts to engulf him in "paper-work", has the same evolutionary hardihood as the turtle, the only animal (I'm told) to have stayed the same for 20 million years. But at a time when the emphasis is all on the *prevention* of offences we ought, surely, to be devoting more energy to the instruction of Aberdonians in the way to pronounce Abergele.

Police Review November 19, 1976.

Where-e'er You Walk

I want to finish on an off-beat note this week. It's about the policeman's walk, which in cinema and theatre has always been typified by an ultra-slow swinging of the arms, sending the left hand to the small of the back while the right hand comes round and touches the navel. It looks pompous, self-important, and threatening. Try it. What no one outside the police service seems ever to have realised is that it's the product of the two-miles-an-hour rate of walking. At that speed you simply can't swing your arms in the normal way, the way that gives you momentum and balance. The only other way to swing them is in unison, both arms going forward and backward together. If you watch any two men at, say, a weekend conference, strolling along a corridor deep in conversation, you will find that if their hands are not in their pockets, or carrying something, they will be swinging in unison. It makes them look like bears. Western newsmen and diplomats, most of whom only saw Stalin at conferences, saw him doing this, and all reported that Stalin walked like a bear. Fine, he was a Russian. But in a recent book Lord Avon (formerly Sir Anthony Eden) reports that this is the way Hitler walked, too. He's seen Hitler walking down a corridor deep in conversation with someone, and noticed that he swung his arms forward together. No doubt he did, for the length of a corridor, looking thoughtful and important. But he wouldn't have done it for eight hours on a beat. Come to think of it, he wouldn't have done anything for eight hours on end.

Police Review November 26, 1976.

Bottle Hunters

Round my way there are a lot of bottle hunters. They're a development of the current craze for collecting glass bottles of the kind used, say, a couple of generations ago. To be sought after by the antique dealers, and by those who sell things to antique dealers, an object doesn't have to be beautiful or even mildly pleasant to look at. It merely has to be breakable, and yet not broken: survival is all. You can see the truth of this when you look round our museums and treasuries of antiquities: some of the Roman and earlier artefacts are just damned ugly. In a Jermyn Street shop window the other day I saw a Roman jug, about the size of an egg-cup, which any child could make after ten minutes' instruction with a potter's wheel; or even without a potter's wheel. The price of it was £185, and I would wager that *someone* has bought it by this time, to stick on his mantel piece as something which has failed to get broken for 1,900 years. It may of course be broken by now.

Now that we are having so many plastic bottles, ugly old glass ones are enjoying a boom in market value. Accordingly, parties of youngsters (some of them no more than eight and nine years old) are rooting about in the rubbish dumps and, it is claimed, desecrating the countryside with the litter they thus distribute. There's a disused rubbish tip near a Surrey pub called the Half Moon, on the A3 between Milford and Thursley, where the bottle hunters are "worse than mere vandals—they are thieves" (I quote Mrs Pile, who is a Waverley Councillor and is also chairman of Witley, Surrey, Parish Council). "Thieving is going on," says Mrs Pile, "those bottles belong to someone". The treasure seekers smash six bottles for everyone they deem worthy of taking away, but those six bottles (*if* they belong to someone) are also stolen although left where they are. This particular dump is said to date from the first world war, when the Canadian Army was stationed nearby.

There's an organisation called the British Bottle Collectors' Club (not, please, to be confused with the British Bottlers' Institute) whose members only dig or rummage with permission, and always undertake to leave the dump exactly as they found it, which must sometimes be appallingly difficult. Presumably the bottles, and all their companions on a rubbish dump, the tins and tyres and bedsprings and broken baths and old lavatory seats, all belong to the man who allows the rubbish to be tipped on his land—usually to fill up a muddy and useless declivity. Accordingly if you dig up an old tobacco tin and walk off with it, not having asked him first, you are a thief. But if you *have* asked him whether you can keep anything you find and he says yes, the permission will hold good for a chest-full of diamonds. So it must be best to get it in writing.

Police Review December 10, 1976.

Drunk and Refusing to Stand

I remember a man being dragged out of the Memorial Hall, in London, by a constable who wanted to charge him with insulting behaviour at a public meeting. The evidence was going to be that the man refused to stand up for the singing of the National Anthem. A couple of older constables tried to square it all up and got the man released, whereupon he sat down on the pavement and it became clear that he was really too drunk to stand anyway. Thus the case moved out of the insulting behaviour class into the drunk and incapable one, and a fresh start was made. Now I read of a very similar episode at the close of a British Legion social evening in Berwick. One of the members, Mr Billy Simm, sat tight (you will see what I mean) while all the others stood and asked God to save our gracious Queen. In due course the committee unanimously agreed to ban him from the club, but then they readmitted him after allowing him to appear before them and explain his conduct.

That might have seemed all right to the club committee, but it did not have the approval of the steward, Mr Ivan Budworth, who applied his own private sanction the next time Mr Simm came to the bar for a pint. Mr Budworth told him he would never serve him with a pint again. The next development was that the club committee gave Mr Budworth the sack, and it then came out that Mr Simm actually *did* stand up for the Queen, but was too drunk to sustain the loyal posture and fell down again. "I have always stood for the National Anthem," he told the *Daily Telegraph* on 9 December, "it was just a question of being unable to stand".

I suppose the ability to stand up isn't the only faculty called into play when one is singing the National Anthem: there is also the gift of singing words without thinking about them, the survival-test of most of the drivel in the church hymnal. I have a regular correspondence with a retired procurator-fiscal in Argyllshire, who told me in his last letter: "I stand up when the National Anthem is sung, but I won't sing it. Why? Do you know the last verse?" And he quotes it:

God grant that General Wade,
Helped by thy gracious aid,
Victory may bring.
May he sedition crush
And like a torrent rush
REBELLIOUS SCOTS to crush—God save the King.

"As nothing would make me sing *that* verse," he goes on angrily, "nothing will make me sing the first. I suppose these days the English don't sing it?' Well, I never heard it before in my life, and suspect him of making it up. It's just the kind of thing these trouble-making Scots love doing. Can anyone help?

Police Review December 24, 1976.

Take that for Corruption

I've always thought that a thoroughly corrupt cop, as distinct from a not very resolute one caught up in a racket he sees no easy escape from, is an unlovely figure on the social scene. But into whichever of those two classes you sort the defendants in the recent Old Bailey trial, and whatever you think of pornography and extortion as running-mates, consider the sentences of 10, eight, seven and four years' imprisonment passed on the six police officers as against the normal modern sentences for vast financial fraud, for arson, even for attempted murder. Consider also, as Mr Justice Mars-Jones must have done, that they had all been waiting two whole years for this climax; and that whatever happens to a man in prison, and whatever his degree of subjective or inflicted suffering, nothing can add to the emotional impact of the original discovery—"That's it then; I'm caught, and I suppose I was bound to be caught sooner or later."

I hope it can be said without disrespect to the judge that these sentences, about which there has been amazingly little comment, are excessive even if they are meant to be exemplary. They will not in fact serve any exemplary purpose in a world in which a disgraced President of the USA can be given an outright pardon by his successor, without even facing a criminal charge or impeachment for corruption, and in which men bearing illustrious nmes throughout the world are exposed as million-dollar puppets of the Lockheed Aircraft Corporation, feathering their luxurious nests in the comfortable knowledge that this is the way of the world. It seems to me tht it's up in that stratosphere that exemplary punishment ought really to begin, if indeed it does any good at any level. It's the failed exemplars in the prisons who have bunged them full to bursting point.

Police Review January 7, 1977.

Trousers in Court

There will never be agreement about what kind of clothing is suitable for appearance in court, and the girl reporter who was recently ticked off by a judge for wearing slacks will not be the last. But in view of the fact that female shorthand writers are allowed to wear slacks on duty (an arrangement effected by their Association in consultation with the Lord High Chancellor of England, no less), we may be at the very beginning of an era in which all women will go to court in slacks and will get turned out if they wear skirts. Once in an Official Secrets Act case at the Old Bailey I saw an elderly witness stride to the witness box in a kilt. The judge looked at him for a long time over the tops of his glasses and then said slowly "Very well". No one knew quite what he meant by that. And now Miss Honor Tracy, the author (whom no-one would dare call an authoress) has written to the *Daily Telegraph* (28 February) to say that whenever men want to look *really* imposing they dress like women. Kings, peers, judges, clergy—all put on flowing garments to assert their authority. "Judges," she says, "go to the length of wearing an artificial hair-do reminiscent of the Dame in a pantomine. Imitation is the sincerest form of flattery". What matters is not what men say, it's what they do, says Miss Tracy. The judge who objected to the trousered girl reporter "wouldn't dream of appearing otherwise than skirted himself". But of course, as Miss Tracy knew perfectly well, she herself was quoting G. K. Chesterton, who said "When men wish to be safely impressive, as judges, priests or kings, they wear skirts. The whole world is under petticoat government". What no one has emphasised is that whenever men want their impressiveness to be absolutely splendid and awe-inspiring, as with City Sheriffs, Black Rod, and ambassadors accredited to the Court of St James, they go round in black knickers and silk stockings. No one ever orders them out.

Police Review March 11, 1977.

Close Proximity

"Do Lawyers go to some sort of a school," asks a correspondent, "where they learn all their jargon?" They don't in fact, they catch it from each other. My correspondent maintains that it's only lawyers who talk about "close proximity". ("Do you not know, officer, that my client was in close proximity to the vehicle throughout this time?") Close proximity means close closeness. They also say "oh-casion" for occasion and they even talk about an oh-casional licence—though they never seem tempted to say oh-portunity. I even knew one distinguished Counsel who used to say "close pro*mix*ity"; everyone told him about it, he always laughed, and he always went on doing it. His name was Lawrence Vine, and he went on to become Chairman of London Sessions, so it never did *him* any harm.

Police Review March 18, 1977.

Defective Public Clocks

Big Ben's prolonged sick leave has been causing world-wide concern. This is another way of saying that two people have written to me about it, one from Delhi and one from Adelaide, both of them complaining that they dont't like the inferior time-signal from St Paul's Cathedral which the BBC has been using in its World Services for many months past (For that matter, I don't like it myself much: St Paul's clock-chime has reminded me only too often, in the past, of the leaden slowness of night-duty hours.) Still, by the time this appears in print, Big Ben will at least be giving the right time once again—it stopped altogether on 4 April, allegedly because it had caught a glimpse of the next day's Budget Speech.

Some years ago there was a mild campaign to get all public clocks synchronised with Big Ben, one suggestion being that when a public clock, projecting over the footway, was telling the wrong time there could be a prosecution under the Police Acts for "setting up a projection from any part of a building so as to cause annoyance". If you reported an offending clock to the police, they would do the rest. Nothing ever came of it, and I'm glad, in retrospect, that the idea didn't come from the police. It seems to be true that Dent's, the clockmakers in Pall Mall, at one time received many calls from City clients to hurry a man along to put clocks right "as the police had warned them". A bluff, I should think, emanating probably from a constable who had been misled into losing half his refreshment-time. But where have all the public clocks gone? 27,000 of them were destroyed in London alone during the war, but it seems a bit pessimistic not to have restored them.

Police Reveiw April 22, 1977.

"Puts"

This is the word they write against a defendant's name in the minute book at the Central Criminal Court, Old Bailey. It means that he is pleading not guilty: he "puts himself on his country", a phrase that came into use when it was decided that trial by jury was probably better than seeing which side could kill the other first. At other Crown Courts they write on the indictment "*po. se.*", which means *ponit se super patriam*, and that's the same thing in Latin. I dig up this ancient truth because a lady social worker wrote to me last week to say that, in the course of an inquiry in the Public Office at the Old Bailey, she had noticed this word against the name of the prisoner she was interested in; and she wondered whether there was anything sinister in it? Her protégé was in fact a West Indian, and she could not rid her mind of the disturbing idea that the word "puts", which she only saw upside down as the Public Office clerk tried to help her by consulting the book, meant something racial. I managed to convince her that there were people who would see something racial in a black pudding, and I think she was reassured. I hadn't thought much about it before, but it does seem an odd word in the circumstances, surviving from such an involved historical context? Nothing will ever change it now, though.

Police Review June 3, 1977.

Snookered

I once undertook to play billiards for a pub team and then found that my opponent was to be a girl of about 19. She won with crushing efficiency and I was never quite the same again. Why should this be? If women had more access to the game they would probably demonstrate that gender is totally irrelevant. Snooker halls are now admitting women players, according to the Equal Oportunities Commission; and the landlord of the Wellington Inn at Broomhill, in Sheffield, faces a £50 compensation claim by Miss Gay Rice because she wasn't allowed to play snooker with some friends there. She was "horrified and angry", she told the *Daily Telegraph* (30 May). "I'm as good as the two male friends with me, and the landlord let *them* play". She hasn't got the idea. It's not being as good as men, it's the frightful danger of being better. The landlord said it was "a rule of the house", and his action is to be backed by the local licensed victuallers' association at Sheffield County Court on 16 June. Hope she wins.

Police Review June 10, 1977.

Answering Service

I have an irrational hatred of telephone "answering services". When I call a man up and hear a flat voice, like a speak-your-weight machine, telling me that he is "not available" and that if I want to leave a message for him I am to speak clearly, I often feel disposed to leave him a string of obscenities, to entertain him when he comes back, that could melt some of these new plastic telephones. But when you come to think of it, how could a man more clearly inform any inquiring burglar that the coast is clear? Much more positive than a ringing bell that gets no answer. Next time I get this response I shall say "Thanks: we are arranging a burglary at your place, and your co-operation is much appreciated. If you wish to record your opinion of this, please speak distinctly."

Police Review June 24, 1977.

Blasphemy

It's such an odd word that I wish I had the time to find out how it began. (The Romans called it *blasphemare,* the Greeks *blasphemeo*, and it seems to have a common origin with *blame*, or reproach.) About six months ago, someone thoughtfully sent me a photocopy of Professor James Pickup's poem *The Love that Dares to Speak its Name* and said that Mrs Whitehouse was after it. Well, I wasn't surprised, and in fact I thought the professor, who at 54 is one of our most distinguished poets, playwrights and interpreters of religious mystery, had gone clean off his rocker. Looking at the common law of blasphemy as it still stands, I couldn't see how any jury, unless you drugged them or got them all tight, could possibly acquit. In the *Daily Telegraph* of 13 July is was said that Professor Pickup had "left Britain for good because of the prosecution and now lives in Japan" (where, in fact, he has long-established academic associations). I should think he was wise, for he was as vulnerable to prosecution as *Gay News* or its editor. It was in the first place he who "published, or caused to be composed (or printed or published) a blasphemous libel", and the others took on from there.

Two questions remain to puzzle me, apart from the immaturity and craziness of the whole thing. First, why did so many lawyers and MPs complain that Mrs Whitehouse was using a "backstairs route" by going direct to a High court judge instead of to the magistrates? By reason of the Law of Libel Amendment Act 1888 she couldn't do anything else – she *had* to get permission from a judge in chambers before she could begin a prosecution, and she had to give notice to the other side that she was doing it. And the whole purpose of *that* provision is to protect the Press, not to create any Whitehouse short cuts. Secondly, who really *was* the prosecutor? The press as a whole reported that the prosecution had been "taken over by the Crown". Not so, says the Legal Secretary in the Attorney-General's Chambers, in a letter to *The Times* on 14 July. The case was "commenced and continued as a private prosecution". And "all cases on indictment are under the title *Regina v* the name of the defendant, but this does not mean that the Crown takes over responsibility for the proceedings in a private prosecution. The responsibility remains with the private prosecutor." I wonder if the intrepid Mrs Whitehouse knew *that?*

Police Review July 22, 1977

Sponsored Stunts

I seem to "sponsor" a lot of harmless little enterprises round my way, accepting that they are in aid of some charity. Only five or ten pence a time, amounting to a mildly reluctant bet that someone (usually a small girl) will be unable, after all, to walk, run, swim or ride from A to B, but knowing perfectly well that every such task will in fact be accomplished and that I shan't see my money again. I'm confident that all this money goes to its nominated charity, but what if it didn't?

On 25 August, Ian Hunter, aged 21, of Argyle Street, King's Cross appeared before Judge Bolland at Knightsbridge Crown Court on a charge of stealing £50, the proceeds of a "sponsored walk" in aid of the church fund at St Martin-in-the-Fields, London. Apparently he had done the walk, or convinced someone that he had, and then spent the money. This, said Judge Bolland, was not theft. The only document to support the charge was a list of sponsors. This did not bind the defendant to give the money to the fund. Accordingly he was found not guilty and discharged.

The case got a small report in *The Times* of 26 August and I saw it in no other paper (though it doubtless appeared locally), yet it seems important enough to have earned itself quite a splash, in view of the immense and mainly harmless development of sponsored events as a means of raising funds. It also provokes some disquiet about the disappearance of the old charge of "fraudulent conversion", which the 1968 Theft Act was supposed to have rendered unnecessary. If you can't prove the existence of "criminal deception" at the time of collecting the money, what offence *can* you prove? No prizes offered, but I'd like to have the answer ready for the next caller at my door.

Police Review September 9, 1977.

Eating in Public

I once wrote half a novel about a country in which the law required that all eating must be done in strict privacy. Being seen eating or drinking in public was treated as an outrage on decency. There was an enormous underground industry, run by food pornographers, in the printing of menus and cookery hints. I sent six chapters to a publisher and asked him if he would advise me to continue with it. No, he said. Luckily the deprived world of literature will never know of its loss unless it reads the *Police Review*. But now I read (in the *Daily Telegraph* of 15 August) that in Ocean Beach, New York State, the only thing you can eat in public is ice-cream. A bye law bans eating in public or carrying open containers of food or drink in the streets or on the beaches. The reason seems to be that Americans, just like us, simply will not put their crisp-bags and beer-cans in the litter bins provided. In this country, 90 per cent of the picnicking population throw their empties in the road, on the grass verges, or on the ground in parks and commons. The other 10 per cent chuck them on my front lawn. Two men and a woman have been arrested at Ocean Beach, one for eating a piece of cake, one for nibbling a chocolate biscuit, and one for holding a glass of water, *all in public*. A number of offenders have already been fined 25 dollars (£15) for similar outrages, and these are supporting the local shopkeepers in a campaign to get the bye-law rescinded and public eating made once more natural and unashamed. I thought I'd mention it, just by way of showing what litter can lead to. Ice-cream, by the way, is exempted because it's such an "American institution" that banning it would be wrong.

Police Review September 16, 1977.

"Now . . ."

It occurred to me the other day, listening with irritation to a radio interviewer beginning each question with "Now . . .", that some of these interviews ought to be recorded and played to police recruits and Police College students as a lesson in How Not To Do It. "Now, you are I believe a member of the So-and-So?" The "now" is the dimwitted ploy of the man filling up a form with someone else's answers. (I cannot understand why radio and TV interviewees are so docile and so damned polite. I suppose they're overcome with the flattery of being asked at all. You can count the really lively and prickly interviewees on one lot of fingers: John Osborne, Lord George Brown, Kingsley Amis, Clive Jenkins, a few others.) I once took a woman to the mortuary to identify the body of her husband, a street accident casualty. The coroner's officer began every question to the poor woman with "Now . . .", and never in my life have I wanted so much to hit anybody. I refrained because he was a very large coroner's officer and there was already one body on the slab.

Police Review September 23, 1977.

The Loved Ones

Years ago I was trying to find out why the judges so often said to a convicted sex offender: "It is not for me to suggest what should happen to you where you are going, but during the course of your prison sentence you will receive psychiatric attention". I was getting material for a radio documentary, and one of the people I went to see was the famous Dr Roper, then senior Medical Officer at Wakefield Prison. "It's nonsense," he told me. "Well-meaning nonsense.

Psychiatry hasn't a chance in a place like this, and even if it had, the whole prison attitude to the sex offender would smother it". And he went on to tell me something about child-molesters (as we called them then, paedophiles as we seem expected to call them now) that I've never forgotten. They were mostly harmless enough chaps, he said. The children they got involved with were their darlings, there was usually genuine tenderness in the relationship, and the offender was often betrayed into it. He allowed me to talk to one such man—who, far from being the dirty-old-man stereotype, was about 19 or 20. It became pretty clear to me, and Dr Roper certainly believed it, that this youth had been blackmailed by a couple of children, one of each sex, into having sexual intimacies and then rewarding them with money. Refusal would have meant that they told their parents about previous occasions. Dr Roper, a man far ahead of his time in psychiatric medicine, said he knew of no cure for the propensity and doubted the effectiveness of any treatment then known to medicine. "Whatever it may turn out to be," he said, "it isn't prison, what with the beatings-up and Rule 43 and the universal hatred".

Well the universal hatred has shown itself lately in a variety of forms, and I must say that the Paedophile Information Exchange has asked for it. You can't gain public acceptance for "child-molesting" by giving it a Greek monicker, still less by public campaigning and meetings. My dictionaries say that paedophilia is sexual love directed towards children, and the man who invented the word in 1911, Dr von Krafft-Ebing (he also came up with "paranoia"), clearly thought it was something curable. Any public meeting of paedophiles is sure to be attacked by the other form of child-lovers, vastly outnumbering them, whose emotional reaction finds expression in rotten eggs, soft fruit, and stinkbombs. I remember asking Dr Roper how he would feel about a man who was sexually intimate with one of the Roper children. "Interested," he said, "and it would be a rare chance to study the child. How would *you* feel?" I said I would feel like kicking the man in the pants, but I was younger then. At the moment we have no way of treating such people other than putting them in prison and hoping that they will come out different (which they won't). But if they think the law ought to be changed, their safest method of propaganda is to say so in the public prints, not on public platforms or by way of street marches. Are we going to have processions of paedophiles, with banners saying they love children?

Police Review September 30, 1977.

Interpreters

I believe the public, and especially the immigrant public, would be very surprised if they knew how our court interpreters are appointed. The text-books about the law and its practice are all very reticent about this, confining themselves to questions like admissibility and bias. (On bias, for example, there is the case of *R v Mitchell*, 1970, where the interpreter was actually in the employment of the victim of the alleged assault.) But who can say whether the interpreter put up in court is really good enough? No one in court really knows. He comes from a good firm, perhaps, a firm of interpreters to which the courts have had recourse for many years, and they can be trusted to supply a good man. But who says so? I used to know enough French to ask my way to Shepherd's Bush, and some of the French interpreters I've met in court have seemed pretty ineffectual to me. And if they deliberately *mis*-interpet the evidence in court, who finds out what they have done? They get a special mention in Section 1 of the Perjury Act 1911, as people liable to seven years' imprisonment when they are actually caught wilfully misleading the court, but how are they caught?

This is not to say that Mr Keval Kaila, who interpreted at Kent Assizes in 1970, wilfully misled the court when four Sikhs were sent to prison for grievous bodily harm; but in the Court of Appeal on 5 December these four men, having all finished their sentences, were found to be completely innocent when the case was re-opened at the request of the Home Secretary. Mr Keval Kaila had been the interpeter for the prosecution at their trial, and he later confessed that he had misled the court and that they were all wrongly convicted. The competence and integrity of interpreters have now become of more importance than ever before in this country, and the manner of their appointment might well be worth fresh examination.

Police Review December 16, 1977.

Canute was right

Beyond doubt, alcohol remains the supreme enemy of the crime prevention officer. The Rev Kenneth Lawton, who is the new general secretary of the temperance council of the Christian churches, goes so far as to say that alcoholism (and I think he means prolonged heavy drinking rather than the disease it can lead to) "has become the primary disease of the age and is increasing rapidly"; and the government is said to be planning a campaign in favour of moderate drinking. "Make alcohol freely available", said Mr Lawton to *The Times* on 12 December, "promote it, thrust it under the noses of housewives in supermarkets, and a frighteningly high proportion of the population will respond by setting out on a course of self-destruction . . . For wife-battering, football hooliganism, street mugging, car accidents, marriage breakdown, low industrial productivity, alcohol has to carry much of the blame".

I'm quite sure he is right. Not that he sees the solution in "instant religious conversion", which is "obsolete or at least irrelevant in a society without much interest in religion", or in Alcoholics Anonymous, which is "a self-rescue service for victims after the catastrophe has happened". He is mounting a campaign to produce a "drug-free culture", and he goes into action like a man who will move the Alps with a spoon. Well, that's a better image than the one in the headline he was given in *The Times.* "A few brave souls," it said, "with King Canute's faith, cry 'HALT' to a rising floodtide of alcohol". This is unfair to Canute, even though that murderous monarch has a phoney reputation as a man of great wisdom. When he told his courtiers to place his throne on the beach, he wasn't proposing to demonstrate how the tide would turn back at the royal command. That was what *they* had been telling *him.* His concern was to show them that they were a lot of flattering idiots and that he had got his feet wet. The Rev Kenneth Lawton is making a better start than that.

Police Review December 23 1977.

Historic Hole

When I was on the beat the various public utility authorities had discovered (or they may have copied it from Hitler) a simple cure for unemployment. They sent gangs of men round the big cities to make deep holes in the roadway, eat their sandwiches, and then go away. Just as the Nation's traffic was coming to a standstill we were all armed with little green notebooks in which we were to record every road hole (unattended or occupied), with the date of its appearance and guesses about its probable length of life. All this, when we went off duty, had to be transferred to a new tome called the Man-'Ole Book, though it bore other names whose ferocity increased with the struggle to get hold of it and sign off.

They will have to install this system at Bristol. In Royal Oak Avenue, the South West Gas Board dug a deep hole exactly a year ago, its object at the time, so far as can be recalled, being the installation of a new gas main. The hole is still there, forlorn and empty. "Work of a higher priority delayed the laying of this main," a Gas Board spokesman has told the press, "but we didn't think the hole was causing any inconvenience". This may mean that no-one from the Gas Board has fallen into it, but its place in Bristolian history has now been assured by the public-spirited action of Mr Jack Highfield, a local businessman, who assembled a small anniversary party round the hole last Wednesday week, stood a workman in the hole, and supplied champagne all round for what may turn out to be Entry No 1 in a Champagne Book of Records.

Police Review February 1, 1978.

Escape Me Never

And here's a story about a former Metropolitan magistrate, spoken by himself into my own tape-recorder about eight years ago and, for some reason I forget, never used until now. I hope he'll forgive its revival. It was Mr E R Guest, who so urbanely dispensed even-handed justice at West London Magistrates Court. "I was on my way to join my family on holiday," he said. "Driving patiently behind a long convoy of tanks near Lulworth. At long last I saw a chance of nipping past the lot. I pulled out and shoved my foot down, arriving abreast of the leading tank just as it swivelled abruptly to the right, on its own axis as these things do, and made for a camp entrance I hadn't seen. It brushed me off like a fly. I found myself in a crumpled version of my little car in the roadside ditch, still devotedly gripping the steering wheel. I was still recapping events when half a dozen enormous young tankmen lifted my wreckage back on to the road. Then while some of them gave me a billy-can of horrible tea, others scooped my car on to a GS wagon and bore it off to the nearest garage. And there, believe it or not, they had the spare parts to hand it back to me two days later looking as though nothing had happened".

A reminder that something had, in fact, happened came later in the form of a buff-coloured letter announcing the date of an Official Inquiry. Would Mr Guest care to be present? He hadn't the face to go. But the official report said in due course that the damage sustained by the leading tank amounted to "a scratch that had penetrated the second layer of paint". The damage to the West London Magistrates's self-esteem had penetrated deeper. But he got no summons and has never really understood why. Many a man is similarly perplexed (or makes out he is) when he does get one. Which of us can say, hand on heart, that he has never earned one? None. And you can include judges, policemen, priests, prime ministers, nuns, even motoring members of the Royal Family. If angels drove instead of hovering, you could include them too.

Police Review March 10, 1978.

"Borrowing" Shop Trolleys

Down my way you can often see supermarket trolleys (some people seem to call them push-baskets) abandoned in hedge-rows or pushed into ponds, though I expect you to believe that only a few of us behave like this. I thought at one time that the legislators could have helped by including these convenient little shoppers' mod-cons within the definition of "conveyance" in section 12(7)(a) of the Theft Act 1968, but that definition is carefully exclusive of any conveyance which has to be pushed or pulled by man. Not even a milk float is included, unless the driver can ride on it. Nor can this ingratitude to supermarkets be blamed on to the local children, for the trolleys can be taken away only by grown-ups who can pay their way at the cash desk. In nearby car-parks, there is usually a corner where the trolleys may be left for recovery by the management, and no doubt it's from there that the children take them.

Sainsbury's at Bretton, near Peterborough, have found that as many as 200 of them can "go missing" in one evening, and a fortnight ago a team of searchers found more than 100 abandoned in ditches and dykes. The result is that at Bretton, and no doubt the idea will spread, customers now have to leave £1 deposit at the check-out till, and can reclaim it at a kiosk in the trolley-bay provided for shoppers. Money governs all our ways. Even the burglar, said Bernard Shaw, has to pay for his jemmy.

Police Review March 17, 1978.

Ticket Touts

I know a man who has made himself rich by purchasing and selling coffee during the recent convulsions on the world coffee market. A decent man, he seemed a trifle uneasy when he told me why, at the age of 38, he doesn't need to work any more for the rest of his life: he was asking me what he could now do, as a volunteer, to make himself socially useful (and, I suppose, ease his conscience). I thought of him when I read about the unflagging determination of Mr Gwilym Roberts, MP, to force the Wembley and Wimbledon ticket touts out of business by means of "astronomical fines". "I would like to see these evil men fined so much," he told the London *Evening Standard* on 17 March, "that it would hardly be worth their while."

I don't much like the ticket spivs, or anyone else who battens on the entertainment industry, or seaside landladies and hotels who put up their charges in August because that's when they can make the money, or gamblers in commodity prices the world over. Bad luck to the lot of them. But why pick on the "ticket touts"? Mr Gwilym Roberts failed last year in an attempt to get a private member's Bill introduced to the detriment of ticket touts. This year he plans to use the "ten minute rule" to bring his Bill in again. Tickets for a cup-final, he says, which normally cost between £2.50 and £15, cost as much as £200 on the black market. It's the story of industry. Read some of the company balance sheets published in newspapers (you'll need a magnifying glass) and then ask yourself what's so different about a ticket tout. I suppose I'm against Mr Gwilym Roberts and his Bill mainly because he's out to create, selectively, one more class of criminals to swell the statistics and burden the police, leaving the really big swindlers untouched.

Police Review March 31, 1978.

Nothing but the Worst

Well, can the concoction of a series like Mr G. F. Newman's **Law and Order** (Thursdays 6-27 April BBC2) do any conceivable kind of good? I think it can; and before I come to the harm it will do, let me suggest its probable good effects, none of which I think Mr Newman intended.

If you believe that a significant number of people hate the police, hate the prison service, the lawyers and the courts, hate them enough to delight in any kind of devil's dance round authority, then a lot of people will have thoroughly enjoyed this series, and I'm in favour of people enjoying themselves in their own homes. They have also watched four plays in which the acting – especially if you look for naturalism, as I always do – has been of such consummate skill as to suggest or indeed to demonstrate that the cast themselves must have believed what they were portraying (it's a great help) and had been aching for a chance to let it rip. Perhaps that's good.

Then there is (I suppose) the need to show devotees or dupes of *Dixon of Dock Green* and of Ronnie Barker in *Porridge* (I belong among the second lot but not the first) that those two popular programmes present a false picture of cosiness. *Porridge,* in particular, is full of howling errors about prison life and administration, but they don't matter much because the scripts are so beautifully neat and Mr Barker possesses comic genius of such a rare quality.

But above all the *Law and Order* series will do good if it hoodwinks the sloppily quasicriminal (for example the tentative shoplifter) into a belief that prison is a hell-hole, and that all prison officers are dim-witted, shuffling slobs whose recreation is the infliction of suffering upon captives strong enough and defiant enough to keep coming up for more. You see, you can tell by the letters from 'Disgusted, Tunbridge Wells' that many people, as it is, believe prison to be a kind of holiday camp. This series may give them a salutary shock, jaundiced and phoney as much of it is – though every separate incident may well have happened somewhere at some time. Actually, if I had to choose between Mr Merlyn Rees's hospitality and Sir Billy Butlin's, I should go with Billy, but it would not be because of any fear that under the Home Secretary's protection I should be given successive periods of 56 days' solitary, beaten up, indecently assaulted by cretinous prison officers, and finally reduced to sycophantic conformity by massive injections of paraldehyde.

Now for the harm. These four plays are too bestial for fireside viewing. I have said that every single episode may have happened in real life somewhere, though I'm a bit dubious about one incident with the bent lawyers, which I'll come back to in a moment. I have actually known, and served with, one or two cocky detective officers who, like Mr Newman's cops, had the deportment of barrowboys, the manners of pigs, the morals of pimps and a greed for money that led them into many kinds of cruel extortion. They differed from the Newman cops in that they didn't chew gum or hurry aggressively about with their hands in their raincoat pockets and their heads wagging from side to side. They were also fools, unsure of themselves and heading for the disaster which they lacked the intelligence to foresee.

Next, there may now be an increase in the contemporary reluctance to report a crime to the police, encouraged by a belief that they won't do anything more than record it in a book or on the corner of a blotting pad. Who on earth would want to have anything to do with such a crew of illiterate spivs? Or have the smallest confidence in a body of mutually indulgent crooks officered by second-hand-car salesmen?

Already, to my certain knowledge, the Barlow image (which I think deplorable) has frightened off simple folk who, though they wouldn't know what the word meant, have accepted the recent torrent of police films as 'documentaries'. It's one of the oddest social effects of television to have developed the myth of police omnipotence and lack of scruple into a national malaise. The police themselves suffer from it as much as anyone, some of them actually believing in it.

And then the lawyers. Mr Justice Quigley, convincingly played as a meddling old fool by André van Gyseghem, would have got anybody off. For in real life the 'framed' villain Jack Lynn (marvellously played by Peter Dean) would have cake-walked it through the Court of Appeal. And would a barrister accept £2,000 from a 'villain', above the legal aid fee, to run a new line of defence? Alex Gladwell the bent solicitor (Ken Campbell) alternated in manner and diction between Noos-and-Standard and lottery promoter, and one wished there were someone to tell him that a bent solicitor doesn't *sound* bent, and that his managing clerk (Stanley McGeagh) shouldn't have looked and sounded like a bookmaker's runner. These were dents in the otherwise smooth verisimilitude; but in general I should think the legal profession will be as angry as the prison service about the whole series.

In the past few days we have had warnings from, among others, The Rt Hon Jo Grimond MP, Peregrine Worsthorne and David Howell MP about the danger they see in our growing disrespect for the law. They won't like Mr Newman's plays much. The BBC's own response to disquiet about them (which I should think is only beginning) is that there have been 'hundreds of portrayals of honest policemen in the past, and the portrayal of a dishonest one [*sic*] is a departure from the generality'. But this is a portrayal of a round dozen, every one of them a septic hoodlum without mercy, dignity, humour or future. What now? *Titus Andronicus* with a cast of baboons? No one would take that for a documentary.

Radio Times May 3, 1978.

Who Can Pull Teeth?

There's a pub in Birmingham city centre called *The Matador,* and its licensee is also a dentist, with his surgery some distance away in Hagly Road. Now you may think a matador is a man who kills bulls, but according to the dictionaries it is also a trump card. The General Dental Council, which has been leaving the licensee-dentist alone so long as he played his cards carefully, that is to say while he confined his advertising to saloon-bar gossip and personal recommendation among the drinkers, has suddenly trumped him because of a local newspaper article "drawing attention to himself as a consultant dental surgeon and a publican" (The Times, 11 May). He didn't write the article, but is said to have assented to its publication. So the disciplinary committee has struck him off the dental register.

Now why don't the police oppose the renewal of his publichouse licence? Can we really have our beer drawn by people who are known to draw teeth? Well, I don't know why but I have a feeling that a good dentist is quite likely to be a good publican, and *vice versa.* Once after a stay in America I wrote a newspaper piece over here and mentioned my surprise that American doctors were allowed to advertise their services in the press. There came an angry letter from an American doctor practising in Wimpole Street, asking me whether I was determined to do everything possible to damage Anglo-American relations and assuring me that the American medical profession did *not* advertise. So I sent him a copy of the *Los Angeles Times,* full of box advertisements like MIGRAINE? BRING YOUR POOR HEAD TO DOCTOR BLOOM, and DR CYRUS F BENSON, 3572 SOUTH AVENUE, CAN CURE EVERYTHING BUT AN OVERDRAFT. He didn't write again.

Incidentally, what about chemists who yank out teeth? These, says the Dentists Act 1956, may operate in an emergency when there is no doctor or dentist around, but they mustn't use any kind of anaesthetic. Anyone else who pulls out another man's tooth can be fined £1,000, which seems rather a lot if all the chemists are shut. There used to be a man in Petticoat Lane on Sunday mornings who pulled teeth out and sold second-hand dentures. He drowned the yells of his customers or victims by means of a very powerful hand-wound gramophone playing JUST ONE OF THOSE THINGS.

Police Review June 2, 1978.

Call the Whole Thing off?

Mr Robert Burchfield is editor-in-chief of all the Oxford English Dictionaries, and he thinks the Americans and ourselves will not be able to understand each other's lingo in 200 years' time. No doubt it would have been better if the French had hung on to America, for they keep a much tighter hold on their language, both at home and in their dwindling colonies. No-one seems to know who really discovered America, and Oscar Wilde asserted that it had several times been discovered before Columbus's day but had always been hushed up. But the news about the approaching death of Anglo-Americanism comes just as a New York friend of mine writes to ask me whether the Metropolitan Police District is a police "precinct" in the American sense, or a collection of precincts, or a part of some bigger precinct. I was going to look it all up and send him a decent sort of answer, but if it wouldn't be valid for more than 200 years I don't think I shall bother. As I understand it, a New York precinct is a sub-division of a county, and usually has its own police station; and if you want to know how it could come about that one American City could contain a lot of counties, you have pinpointed one of the reasons why the two languages, like the two countries, are gradually drifting further apart.

I've found that "precinct" can have different meanings according to how much you can afford to pay for Counsel's opinion. Section 41 of the Criminal Justice Act 1925, which prohibits the photographing of judges, jurors, witnesses, etc "in the precincts" of the court, doesn't define precincts, but in *Hayward's Criminal Justice Acts* the opinion is expressed that it "may include part of a highway in the immediate vicinity of the court building". This was what Lord Goddard decided it meant when, out in the street, the BBC took a newsreel picture of an Old Bailey defendant in 1956; and what Mr Justice Stable thought it meant when a freelance television cameraman snapped him leaving the Nottingham Assize Court in 1959. (In the latter case, the judge told the police to prosecute, the man pleaded guilty, and the Nottingham magistrates fined him £5 with three guineas costs.) Yet in 1956 Mr Gerald Gardiner, as he then was, got a man off at Bow Street by arguing that "precincts" couldn't possibly mean anywhere outside the court building: the precincts, he said, must mean the inside of the premises. I call that getting away with murder, and I was surprised the police didn't appeal. But Mr Gardiner went on to become Lord Chancellor, and that path is commonly strewn with unexpected arguments daringly put over.

Police Review July 7, 1978.

Softly Softly

Not far from where I live there's a junior detention centre at which my wife occasionally gives musical performances. Few of the boys are there for more than three or four weeks at a time. In their meeting hall (she tells me) they sit in utter silence, and they are marched in and out like miniature Guardsmen, watched by grim-faced officers who are loaded with keys on stout chains. Many of them, she finds, are back there time after time. "Wotcher Miss!" they say to her, cheerfully, when there's an opportunity to say anything at all, "I'm comin' out again Saturday". She asks me what it is all supposed to be in aid of. I don't know, but I wish it were possible for Mr Willie Whitelaw, for example, to go there perhaps ten or a dozen times, get to recognise the regular "recidivists", and then reshape his "short sharp shock" proposals. Is what these kids are getting short, sharp or shocking enough? If all these adjectives were stepped up, would we be getting any nearer what Sir David McNee so reasonably urges, namely that they should get a "sharp reminder that what they have done was wrong, and be left in no doubt what will happen to them if they do the same thing again"? Sir David's genuine concern is shared by all of us; but these boys know that what they did was "wrong" and they know what will happen if they do it again. I suppose the first thing to do is to ensure that, if the 1959 Children and Young Persons Act is not to be scrapped as an utter failure, the social welfare departments are provided with "community homes" for delinquent children, instead of the promise of community homes as soon as the country has achieved solvency, or a balanced budget, or the sunlit uplands, or something. People are always saying that the magistrates should make more "secure care orders", but what on earth is the use of that if there is no secure accommodation? The problem is not one of legal strength or stern resolution, it's now solely a question of resources.

Police Review July 28, 1978.

"BBC Bias"

If you put that in inverted commas it means that you don't really think the BBC are biassed but that somebody else is saying they are. Well, somebody always is; and sometimes with justification. I should imagine that Mr Desmond Wilcox, who is head of BBC TV Features (I hope I've got that right) is feeling that the BBC can't win, and the famous LAW AND ORDER programmes left me with the belief that he has stopped caring. I seldom write an angry letter, but I sent him one a few years ago after the presentation of a TV programme about the ill-treatment of old people in the geriatric wards of mental hospitals. I'd been much involved in its preparation, but it all began with a letter from four young nurses who were horrified at what was going on in the hospitals where they worked. The whole programme was finished (I thought) and neatly tied up; and then to my utter surprise Mr Wilcox brought on the then Minister of Health to say, in effect, that the nurses were liars and that the whole thing was a "smear campaign". It was fine to see the Minister defending his Department so vigorously, but he was misinformed, and a series of subsequent official enquiries and truly shocking reports showed everyone how sadly misinformed he was, prominent among them being the famous Ely Hospital report. But on that occasion, at least, Mr Wilcox was being shot at for being on the side of the Establishment.

So far as programmes about the Metropolitan Police are concerned, and Scotland Yard's reported withdrawal of facilities for documentary programmes "unless the producer first signs an undertaking to cut out 'undesirable' material", I shouldn't have thought there was much to withdraw but I can fully understand the withdrawal of it. I don't know what Yard facilities were conceded for LAW AND ORDER, but if I had made four programmes like those I shouldn't expect any more for quite a while. It was as if the BBC had decided to make a programme, say, about the Grenadier Guards, secured the regiment's co-operation, found a Guardsman with two left feet and a squint and then filmed a whole dressed-up company of squinting "extras" whose feet turned in. The prison scenes in LAW AND ORDER were filmed in Ireland, where the Dublin government makes an honest crust by letting off a disused prison to those whose business it is to entertain and brutalise us; but I can't imagine that the BBC, none too popular anyway at the Yard, were given any disused police stations to play with. I hope something good comes out of the BBC-Yard conversations, for there is goodwill and integrity on both sides, and a job to be done as well as feathers to be smoothed.

Police Review August 4, 1978.

Let's Go On Pretending?

One of the fattest volumes on my bookshelves is a bound-up copy of the *Minutes of Evidence to the Royal Commission on Police Powers and Procedure* 1929. It's the size of a church bible. At intervals through its pages of tiny print there appear, with some regularity, most of the recommendations made by Sir David McNee to the present Royal Commission on Criminal Procedure. Between the lines, all the way through, is the implication that if these "additional" powers can't be formally granted, then we shall have to go on behaving as though they had, with the same old explosions of well-founded protest and, as they finally go through the sound barrier, another Royal Commission.

That's all very well, and if we could always be sure of having policemen of the calibre and integrity of . . . well, I could name a couple of dozen paragons but I'll spare their blushes. If we had an ideal police service then Sir David's recommendations could be of enormous benefit to society. The crooks and spivs and swindlers now thumbing their noses would be caught and convicted much more often (Sir David, unlike so many of his contemporaries, says little about what should happen after that; it's not his business). But this perfect police service wouldn't last. It would gradually be supplanted by an organisation that wasn't really a "service" but a social command structure; and, little as the public seem to love us at the moment, we're a mutual admiration society compared with what that would produce.

All the same, Sir David is entitled to be fairly reported. He got "summarised" in some of the newspaper leaders in an unrecognisably ferocious stance; and none of the commentators seemed to have heard of existing police powers of "stop and search", or the numerous (and growing) exceptions to the so-called presumption of innocence, or the gaping loopholes in the Judges' Rules: they all sprang to the defence of the *status quo* as if these didn't exist. It's as if the Commissioner had written an *Honest to God* and leaked it to the Press before telling God.

Police Review August 18, 1978.

Mad or Bad

When I was a boy there seemed to be a lot of people in the streets, and even at school, whose behaviour was quite mad and who, as we tended to say in those days, "ought to be locked up". I always understood that 50 years earlier there were many families who kept one member shut away in a room because he was too dotty to be allowed out, and yet they didn't want him put away in an asylum. (Incidentally the word asylum has lost its original meaning: at first an asylum, was a hospital in which a mental patient could be "given asylum", i.e. shelter, from the primitive madhouses of earlier times.) Other families loyally looked after harmless defectives who, like Mr. Dick in *David Copperfield,* probably needed psychiatric treatment but got family love in its place.

Then there seems to have come a great locking-up of the mentally ill. The Lunacy Act of 1890 could now be enforced more rigorously because the mental hospitals were so much improved; and I can remember a time when the police power of detaining lunatics was being used freely against the harmlessly potty. If in those days you were a station officer and somebody brought in a so-called "wandering lunatic", you might have the gravest doubts whether the chap ought to have been interfered with at all, but you hadn't seen what the Constable saw and you could be committing a fearful mistake in discharging him on your own authority. You sent for a doctor. The crucial decision therefore was always that of the Constable who took the initial action, even though he might be half potty himself. And few doctors ever seemed to decide on the spot that the supposed lunatic ought to be allowed to go: they nearly always recommended a three-day detention order. I wouldn't mind betting that this procedure entrapped many a citizen who was saner than I am, even though that might not be saying much.

Now once again, and ever since 1959, the mentally handicapped are frequently to be seen in the streets and public places, because of the "open door" hospital policy introduced (with enormous enthusiasm, in which I certainly shared) by the Mental Health Act 1959. But many psychiatrists began to feel uneasy about this policy soon after it began, simply because there was no system of after-care for mental patients "in the community". The situation has steadily worsened.

It would take a lot to make me believe that a bad man is necessarily a madman, but a mad one is terribly likely to get into trouble with the law; and today this means that he is likely to go the rounds of "reception centre", prison, hospital-that-won't-admit-him, prison again, Broadmoor, prison, probation hostel, Grendon Underwood, prison once more, and so on until he is found dead somewhere. All this is understood at the Ministries concerned: they have been fed with research reports by the dozen which have exposed the whole miserable problem. But "now something has got to be done", urged Dr. David Tidmarsh at a London meeting of the National Schizophrenia Fellowship on 5 July. Dr. Tidmarsh is a consultant psychiatrist at Broadmoor Hospital, and he says that "the process by which the psychiatric services are rejecting the very patients who most need help has gone far enough. We should explain to the DHSS that our aim is not to empty beds but to use what resources we have to help as many patients as possible. . . . If a bed occupied by a chronic schizophrenic is emptied, it is a therapeutic failure and not a success if he ends up in a reception centre". Dr. Tidmarsh's address led to a suggestion "from the floor" that the Police should be adequately trained in the recognition of psychiatric problems – at least to the point of getting second opinions from doctors. In the tragic situation we've all been so busily engineering, no kind of training, for any branch of the social services, could be more important.

Police Review September 8, 1978.

No Whistling

I once saw in a town in the Potteries a posted copy of a by-law which prohibited singing and whistling in public places after dark. I'm not much in favour of street singing after dark, nor do I enjoy shrill and tuneless whistling. But have you noticed that whistling even by daylight seems to be dying out? All the ancient writers talk about whistling, especially as a symptom of contentment among the poor and the Sam Weller types throughout history. Newsboys, milkmen, postmen, sewermen, all the people you would think had so little to whistle about — they all whistled so melodiously that one could easily suppose that a whistling course was a part of their vocational training. I once used to hear an early-morning milkman who always whistled the *Overture to Figaro* as well as anyone could have done it on the variety stage: I used to roll over in bed and think of the *Dead March in Saul*. And look what William Cowper said about postmen in the *The Task*:

> He whistles as he goes, light-hearted wretch,
> Cold and yet cheerful; messenger of grief
> Perhaps, to thousands, and of joy to some.

Not any more. Whistling has gone. Except, it seems, in Burlington Arcade, Piccadilly, where the Arcade's Association is now once more enforcing the Regency laws which since 1819 have "disciplined public behaviour in the Burlington Arcade" (I'm quoting a letter from the Association's chairman in *The Times* of 22 July). Pedestrians, he says, are "not allowed to whistle, sing, hurry, or behave boisterously", and there are Beadles on duty to see that they don't, to "restore the old traditional restraints and values", and notices to this effect have now been posted at both ends of the Burlington Arcade. ("No hurrying, that man there: just a dignified walk please. Remember where you are.") And the chairman hopes that traders elsewhere in the West End will follow the Burlington example, with "measures calculated to restore good manners, if only for the admiration of foreign tourists, who, after all, do expect them of us." Well, they needn't expect any decent whistling nowadays; but they could help the police, and possibly the Beadles, if they kept a lookout for anyone hurrying in the vicinity of a smashed jeweller's shop window.

Police Review September 15, 1978.

Send for the Hypnotist

It is reported that the Los Angeles Police Department has set up a Society for Investigative Hypnosis, and that more than 40 Los Angeles policemen are learning how to do it. One of California's interesting citizens is a Mr Glen Bouck, a hypnotist of great experience who has often been called upon by the police to exercise his art (science, skill?) in the solution of crime puzzles; and he specialises in jogging the memories of rape victims, whose peculiarity (according to him) is that they repress unpleasant memories and need the aid of hypnosis in describing what happened. He seems to have found that it helps if he sits alone with them and holds their hands (watched, though, by a police video monitor). "Within a few years," the *Daily Telegraph* (26 September) reports him as saying, "the idea will have become widely accepted and used". So far, adds the report, not unexpectedly, everything discovered under hypnosis has to be corroborated by witnesses before the judges will accept it as evidence. Only so far?

Can you not imagine what a howl would go up in this country if this idea seemed to be catching on? And the headlines? THE THOUGHT POLICE ARE HERE. The question of admissibility would never reach the judges.

I think I should join the protesters. When the Hypnotism Act 1952 was in contemplation, I was sent to report on a professional hypnotist who was known to be performing for public amusement (or something) at a Butlin holiday camp. He asked a theatre audience of about 500 to put their hands on their heads and clasp their fingers tightly. "Now you will find you can't get them down," he said, "or a good many of you can't". And they couldn't. It was obvious, looking round, that about 100 or more were literally struggling to unclasp their hands and take them down. There was no pretence about it. He picked out about 20 of these oddly victimised holiday-makers and called them up on to the stage, where he sat them on chairs in a big semi-circle still with their hands on their heads. He told everyone else they could unclasp their hands, which they did. And then he required a selection of those on the stage with him to give each in turn a rapid account of their life history. One girl obliged with an autobiography that almost anyone would have preferred to keep dark, and the audience loved it. When she was recalled from her trance and had left the stage she genuinely disbelieved what was then repeated to her by her friends, and said it was a pack of lies. I had a meal with the hypnotist that evening, and he told me how he had "learned it all from a shilling text-book", admitting that anything said by a person under hypnosis, while it might be a revelation of some buried-away truth, was just as likely to be as fantastic as the dreams we all have in bed. Why is it supposed that the subconscious mind records nothing but the truth?

Police Review October 6, 1978.

Pies for Mrs Whitehouse

I have a friend in Brisbane who keeps me informed about the odder quirks of Australian behaviour. We disagree about Australians, whom he regards as barbarians (though he's Australian himself) and whom I rather like. He is angry this time because when our Mrs Whitehouse addressed a crowd of 1,000 at a Festival of Light rally in Brisbane City Hall, she was pelted with strawberry pies, or so the press described them. Seven men and two women have been charged with assaulting her by throwing them. Then she went to Sydney and repeated her attack on the pornography of Australia (which really merits her attention, though it is rather a long way to go), and was met with a further hail of pies. More charges of assault. The Brisbane team were clearly the better marksmen: The Sydney piemen missed her altogether because she ducked. I don't agree with Mrs Whitehouse much, but I know her to be a courageous woman with a fierce belief in human dignity; and I think she should not have pies thrown at her. But in particular, if those strawberry pies were anything like the ones I couldn't eat in Brisbane when some policemen took me for a kind of picnic, then they were not fit to be thrown at anybody. The charge ought to be Corrosive Fluid Throwing.

Police Review October 13, 1978.

False Hotel Registrations

There was a very interesting letter in *Police Review* on 13 October from Sergeant Gareth Jones of Llangollen, mainly about the value of identity cards. But he also thought the law should do something about the "Mr and Mrs Smith" lark in hotel registers. "Of course," he said, "nobody can do anything about such false entries," and he added that if national identity cards were issued "the hotel registration would become a positive assistance to us, instead of the joke it now is." It reminded me that earlier this year, writing in the *Justice of the Peace*, I expressed surprise that so few people seemed to know of the huge penalties now attached to this very common subterfuge, the temporary change of name for a hotel stay with a girl friend. Letters came in, some of them sounding anxious, and the *Daily Mirror* took it up. I had to produce chapter and verse, which of course I should have done in the first place; namely Regulation 4(1) of the Immigration (Hotel Records) Order 1972, made under section 4(4) of the Immigration Act, 1971. "Every person of or over the age of 16 years," it says, "who stays at any premises to which this Order applies" (and that includes hotels and lodgings, furnished or unfurnished) "shall on arriving at the premises inform the keeper of the premises of his full name and nationality".

And since any offence under this seemingly little-known Order is punishable under section 4 of the Act, I can only conclude that the maximum penalty – for everyone, not merely aliens – for inventing names in the hotel register is six months' imprisonment *plus* a fine of £500. It seems rather a lot, and reflects a stern official attitude to a firmly established national custom. After all, some of our legislators do it themselves, having, perhaps, been actually thus engaged when the Immigration (Hotel Records) Order 1972 was "laid on the table" of the House of Commons awaiting their approval. If I'm wrong about this, I hereby undertake to pay the sum of £500 to the International Society for the Preservation of False Names for Complaisant Girlfriends.

Police Review October 27, 1978.

What Do The Vandals Think?

One of the most horrifying things about vandalism is that it's a product of the human intelligence, one of the fruits of natural evolution. Animals rarely smash things up just for the hell of it; and sometimes when it seems that this is actually what has happened (as when a fox kills a dozen chickens in a run and leaves them lying around) it is probably obeying a blind instinct – and possibly hopes to return and collect the goods when things are quieter. In other words, vandalism isn't really "mindless". It should therefore be possible to find out the vandal's motives. When we say that his conduct is mindless, as (for example) Mr Callaghan did at the opening of the Home Office conference on the subject last week, we are really saying that we don't understand the sort of mind in which it goes on. This kind of thing *can* be done: one man who has done well at it is Mr Tony Parker, whose books reproduce tape recorded interviews (spreading over a period of months with each individual) with prisoners whose conduct has seemed just plain daft.

Another man who has been similarly engaged is Mr J A Walter, a sociologist who has recently published his findings after a three-year study of boys and staff at a residential school for young offenders in Scotland. The study was funded by the Social Science Research Council, as part of a research programme at Aberdeen University, and the book is called *Sent Away: A Study of Young Offenders in Care* (Teakfield Limited, Westmead, Farnborough, Hants). It drops right into the battle between the Laura Norder lobby and the prevention-cum-treatment enthusiasts. And "What do the children themselves feel?" asks Mr Walter. "If we want to understand delinquency and its treatment, we cannot automatically assume that agencies (and researchers) act purposefully and rationally, while delinquents are socially or psychologically determined". People are "not just pushed around by so-called social forces"; they are "more or less able to influence their actions, and therefore everyone's viewpoint must be taken into account if we want to understand why people behave the way they do".

And the people he looks at are not only the boys in the school and the staff who choose to work there, but other boys who don't qualify to go there, boys who "behave themselves". Why do they behave themselves? The common assumptions about them may be as faulty as those concerning the vandals. Beyond doubt the Home Office Committee will be swamped with books and memoranda for urgent reading (among the reasons that keep me off committees, this is second only to not being asked to serve on them); but this little book could well be the first on their list.

Police Review November 10, 1978.

Old Delusions Never Die

"Trial by jury itself", said Lord Denman in 1844 (he was giving judgment in the case of *O'Connell v The Queen*, "will be a delusion, a mockery and a snare." More than a century later it was abolished in Irish courts for terrorist cases, and even in this country you can see a growing tendency for judges to tell juries what "guilty" verdicts to bring in. It has always been accepted that a judge can tell a jury to acquit, on the ground that the evidence given by the Crown is not enough; and since he is the sole judge of law (as distinct from fact) it may seem logical that if the Crown's case *is* good enough and the defendant has offered no word of defence except the phrase "Not Guilty", then the judge should be able to tell the jury to convict. Mr Justice Mars-Jones did this in respect of one charge in the recent secrets trial at the Old Bailey, possibly thus reducing the jurors' deliberations from four days to three. But, said Lord Devlin in delivering the Blackstone Lecture at Oxford a few days later, this was wrong. "A judge can withdraw a case from the jury by directing an acquittal, but he cannot withdraw the question of guilt, even though this might result in a 'perverse acquittal'." Lord Devlin is renowned for his steadfast belief in the jury system: he thinks that the so-called perversity of juries is what justifies their existence. They play the role of the Disestablishment. In other words (not Lord Devlin's, of course) they are an immensely complicated and expensive method of cocking snooks at authority.

The same trial has seen yet another open and acknowledged attack on the so-called "randomness" of jury selection, an admission that we (like the Americans) go in for jury-vetting, except that we keep it a bit quiet. Apparently Mr Alex Lyon QC, when he was Minister of State at the Home Office in 1974, told the House of Commons that he was unaware that it went on. The present Attorney-General has recently said he knew it did in some cases, but that there seemed to be no record of it before 1948. I'm a bit surprised that there are any records of it at all, but to my own knowledge it was certainly going on in the Thirties. I can't see much against it. The pretence of "randomness" is pretty farcical anyway, to judge from the jury-summoning procedures operated in some parts of the country; and it seems to me better that a quasi-political prisoner shouldn't be tried by a jury of deadbeats, or a poet by a jury of illiterates. If a man called for jury service is a crook or lunatic, the summoning officer won't know. I belong to a rejected minority that wouldn't mind seeing the present jury system scrapped altogether, though I wouldn't now join a public procession about it, or chain myself to any railings. Actually what I would put in its place, namely a Judge with three or four qualified assessors, would still be a jury; and if it made people happy to go on calling it a jury, that would make me happy too.

Police Review December 1, 1978.

Commonsense and Cheerfulness

Some years ago the postman, an old friend, handed me a returned Christmas card and said I had fourpence to pay. The man I had intended it for had readdressed the envelope to me and written on the back: 'This is all a lot of bloody rot and I don't want nothing to do with it and you can keep it.' Remembering that the postman had not yet had his Christmas box, I rectified this and then told him that that was where the fourpence could come from. We went on to discuss the message on the envelope and he thought perhaps the best thing to do with something like that was to forget it. He proceeded, I believe, to forget it. But I couldn't do this because I knew the man to be in grave trouble, his Christmas message to me being among the minority that had been really thought out and carried some meaning. He has always maintained since that he's miserably ashamed of the episode, but I've often wondered how many people would, if they were really honest, write some such message on a proportion of their cards and whether, for that matter, there mightn't be a profitable line of business in cards conveying exasperated or insulting messages. 'I am a poor man,' said Mr Pooter, 'but I would gladly give ten shillings to find out who sent me the *insulting* Christmas card I received this morning.' You see? But the idea seems never to have caught on.

'There are some people,' wrote Robert Lynd in this paper one Christmas, 'who want to throw their arms round you simply because it is Christmas. There are other people' (he went on, just as you might have expected of him) 'who want to strangle you for the same reason.' If I had to take up a position with one faction or the other, I should be ill at ease among the stranglers. I like Christmas, enjoying it always with a resolute minimum of enquiry, a quite deliberately uncritical conformity nourished by the knowlege that so many people with great big intellects (or so they seem to me) allow themselves to do the same; and to enjoy themselves no end.

Nor does it matter where they are. As the Christmas of 1968 approached, I was just leaving Australia after a stay of some months.It was far too hot for me everywhere, and I was walking, if any walking *had* to be done, in the shadows of tall buildings, Yet the shop windows were being decorated with cotton-wool snowstorms, frost-covered Christmas trees, and toy cottages with icicles hanging from their roofs. The nativity scenes of course showed Arabs and date-palms, and the baby in the manger was naked. In Sydney, beach picnics were being arranged for Christmas Day, and they were all going to include roast turkey and pudding. I find now that to enjoy my own Christmas I need to get all that under control, relegating it to a series of tableaux visible only through little round windows in the mind. I always manage to do it.

But there is so much else that needs to be similarly straightened out.

Take Mr Pickwick and that heart-warming Christmas Day at Dingley Dell of which we think so fondly after a couple of brandies. Do you remember that? Then you are mistaken. You merely think you do. On Christmas Day, after a ghastly breakfast at which two medical students talk about human dissection, the whole Pickwick party goes to church, comes home to a meal which is merely referred to as 'a substantial lunch', and then goes to see Mr Pickwick fall through the ice while skating. He is rescued, is shrouded in borrowed shawls, and ridiculously trots home to bed. Then Sam Weller takes him up a dinner which is not even described. *That's* the famous Christmas Day at Dingley Dell. All the fun and games have taken place on Christmas Eve, and even that was all mistletoe and kissing, the whole party going to bed at midnight. No Christmas tree, crackers, turkey, plum pudding, gifts or carols. And no cards.

A Christmas card, in my own childhood, was a rarity and an ostentation. Someone, it was explained, was showing off. The following year one or two more people showed off, the quality of life was beginning to heave and change, and there had begun the long march towards the receding peak, an illusory ascent necessitating that every man, both he who bought and he who sold, should get a rise every year. And yet the first Christmas card had been commissioned in 1843 by Sir Henry Cole, whose other contributions to the fabric of our lives included the founding of the Public Record Office, the Great Exhibition of 1851, the Victoria and Albert Museum, the Albert Hall and the Royal College of Music. His card depicted a rustic-framed triptych, two sombre drawings of poverty flanking the highly coloured portrayal of a happy and prosperous family drinking port. It sold about 1,000 copies at a shilling a time; and no-one today outside the trade in antiques would look at it twice. Cole had an interest in furthering the development of the postal system, but his Christmas card idea was slow to dislodge the established custom of making 'cut-outs' of the kind that people kept in scrap-books. (Even I can remember that some Christmas cards were merely visiting cards pasted on to shaped and coloured bits of cardboard.) In 1870, the year of Dickens's death, the Christmas card industry was stirring and the post office was stirring it. Did anyone then suppose that, whatever the postal charges, the Christmas cards dispatched from and to this country alone would one day run into thousands of millions?

The truly significant thing, whether or not one finds it surprising, is that the commercially produced Christmas card has never yet attempted to breach the walls of religion or secularly benign sentiment. Birthday and even New Year cards have long since lined up with the saucy greeting from the seaside. The gruesome, the macabre, and the sick are acceptable for every anniversary but the birth of Christ, and the Christmas message makes its greatest concession in admitting a few funny men like Heath Robinson and Thelwell; but they have to be truly funny. Will anything or anybody now topple this gigantic structure, the Christmas card bonanza?. Will it last for ever? The Post Office couldn't stop the thing if it wanted to; and anyway its accountants long for Christmas as eagerly as children. 'We're sending no cards this year,' people tell each other, 'the whole thing's got out of hand,' and some of them buy space in a newspaper to warn their freinds what not to expect. The following year they are back on the old treadmill.

No doubt it may happen by the year 2,000 or 3,000 that on 25 December men will say to each other 'This used to be called Christmas: have another?'. But they will be vaguely celebrating *something*, just as they are now. Christmas took more than three centuries to get started, or anyway to be recognised by the Church of Rome as a Christian festival. If it now takes more than three centuries to lose (or freshly to disguise) its meaning, that seems as far ahead as anyone should dare to look. Gate-crashers who want to enjoy the Christmas they don't normally support can line up with that shrewd old ruffian Samuel Butler, who said: 'After all, what is the essence of Christianity? Surely commonsense and cheerfulness, with unflinching opposition to the charlatanisms of a man's own times.'

New Statesman December 22, 1978.

Very Well, I Was Wrong

I suppose if the weekly columnist had a patron saint it would be Walt Whitman, the 19th century American poet, who got into trouble with the censorship authorities by writing a long and boring book called *Leaves of Grass* but then secured immortality for himself by the following lines in *Song of Myself:*

Do I contradict myself?
Very well then I contradict myself.
I am large, I contain multitudes.

Lately there has been a considerable run of such admissions in Fleet Street. On 3 January there was the *Daily Telegraph* saying that for 20 years it had been wrong about government monetary policy and that Lord Thorneycroft (and Mr Enoch Powell) had always been right. (This is a bit alarming, for it suggests that no conceivable government will ever get it right). There was Lord Denning in *The Guardian* of 20 December saying "I am prepared to say, you see, that sometimes I am wrong". Lawyers say that Lord Denning is wrong more often than anyone else on the Bench, but that when he's wrong it is usually for the general benefit and most people hope the House of Lords won't over-rule him. It looks as though the Thoughts of Chairman Mao were all wrong (or most of them), and you can say the same about the

Warren Commission on the Kennedy assassination, which the Americans are about to denounce as a frame-up. It ought of course to be disturbing, but in a way it's most encouraging. For about ten years I answered the queries on what used to be called the *Law and Police Practice* page in this paper, and every so often I would get a letter saying "Why do these answers so frequently begin with the words 'In our opinion . . .'?" These letters came from readers who took the view that every answer must be either right or wrong, and that if the editor (or myself) didn't know which it was we ought to say we couldn't answer the question. Sometimes we would point out that even the Appeal Court judges often begin their judgements with "It is my opinion . . ."; and that if a solicitor puts up a legal problem to a barrister for the guidance of his client, what he gets back is headed OPINION. But it did nothing to pacify the chaps who expected a dogmatic answer.

Police Review January 12, 1979.

Long Conspiracies

My impression is that the editors of the *Guinness Book of Records* don't miss much in the way of new limit-breakers, but their present edition will not settle the dispute between Sir David Napley (Mr Jeremy Thorpe's solicitor), and Mr Peter Taylor QC who is prosecuting him on the subject of the longest-running unlawful conspiracy. It doesn't get a mention. Probably the longest will be found among the frauds perpetrated upon the British public, for example about the Road Fund (which doesn't exist) or *Magna Carta*, which says that justice mustn't be delayed, when it is already being prophesied that the Jeremy Thorpe case will last three months at the Old Bailey (why, for God's sake?). But Sir David Napley told the Minehead magistrates that there had never been a case in English law in which an alleged conspiracy had been said to stretch over nine years. Oh, yes there had, retorted Mr Peter Taylor, and Sir David's own firm had been involved in one of them. Sir David, he said, had "failed to check his facts". If the *Guinness Book* editors thought of taking it up, I would recommend them to seek out one or two ex-members of the City and Metropolitan Fraud Squad, who have worked on conspiracies that were festooned with whiskers. Perhaps the DPP's office would help them. Or they could look up the career of Mr Horatio Bottomley, MP, whose whole life was a conspiracy to defraud the public that unaccountably worshipped him. They could even start from the point that, as Bernard Shaw said, all professions are conspiracies against the ordinary man.

Police Review January 19, 1979.

Standing Witnesses

The Mansion House Justice Room in the City of London once had a justices' clerk (this was when such officials used to seem, and indeed deport themselves, like detached members of the Royal family) whose name was Sylvester Richards and who, because of his equine profile, was known to the rank and file as 'orses 'ead. I once heard him rebuke an elderly witness for leaning over the rail of the witness-box with his arms folded. "Stand up," he ordered, "and give your evidence properly". He hadn't chosen wisely. "I shall give my evidence in whatever posture suits me," said the incredulous witness when his breath came back, "and it would suit me much better if you had the courtesy to offer me a chair". He didn't get a chair, but neither did he change his position, though he henceforth received a little more deference from 'orses 'ead. Why don't we give our witnesses chairs? In an American court you seldom see a witness standing up, but it's quite rare to see one sitting in a British court. In the recent Old Bailey trial of Mr. Tom Keating for conspiracy to defraud by means of "forged" paintings, the lady who was the principal witness against him gave her evidence sitting down – and every press report I saw duly reported that she did. It was newsworthy. How often you hear counsel say to the Judge "My Lord, this witness is rather infirm – may he have a chair?" And the judge says "Of course", but what else could he say? We still seem to be tied to the dark ages in some aspects of our court design and procedure.

Police Review February 2, 1979.

PC in the Bar

I've been reading a long (well, it *seemed* long) and heavy-footed inquiry into American police corruption called *Scandal and Reform: Controlling Police Corruption*. Its author is Dr. Lawrence W. Sherman, of the School of Criminal Justice in the State University of New York, and its publishers the University of California Press, who value it at £10.25. It is a very thorough survey of corruption scandals in New York City, Newburgh (New York State), Oakland (California), and a town which is un-named because the scandal was too recent. It all makes a rather frightening story, which contrasts with corruption scandals over here in certain fundamental ways. For example an American policeman is quite often corrupt because he is acting on behalf of corrupt political masters, and it's simply the only way of keeping his job. But under the heading of corruption there comes, in this book, an account of US barkeepers supplying drinks for the man on the beat as a means of inducing him to sit around and discourage any hooliganism. I suppose that's a good idea from some points of view, even if it is hardly corruption – it's more like an unauthorised form of "private service". But it must operate best in a country where a seated policeman in a bar is quite a common sight – as he certainly is in many American cities. Over here the desire of any licensee who has a policeman on the premises is usually that he shall clear out as soon as possible; and I remember once dealing with a complaint from a licensee who said he received far too many closing-time visits from an Inspector-and-Sergeant team who were "trying to drive him out of business". They weren't, but his house had a reputation for punch-ups at closing time; and it was always a problem whether the frequent police visits had the effect of discouraging the non-punching kind of customer and perpetuating the very trouble that the police were trying to help him with. It seemed to be the kind of competition in which there can be no winners.

Police Review March 16, 1979.

Watching the Special Branch

Whatever the complexion of the government when the dust settles, the new Home Secretary is going to be pressed for more information about the Special Branch, which he will refuse to supply. Critics of the Branch, or perhaps I should say Branches (for their number is growing as more provincial forces perceive their advantages), are already armed with a battery of questions, mainly about "accountability" and about the jaundiced habit of keeping an eye on selected people who haven't really done anything wrong. There seems to be an unspoken assumption that no-one should be of interest to the police until he has sinned and that the police are not paid to have suspicions, only certainties. Here's an extract from *Security and the State 1978*, which is the collected annual volume of a political working group rather ambiguously known as *State Research*:

> Bulletin No. 5. THE SPECIAL BRANCH. In recent months there has been concern about the activities of the Special Branch and its immunity from democratic control. The latest statement by the Home Secretary, Merlyn Rees, made in reply to questions in the House of Commons, is unlikely to provide any reassurance on this matter: "The Special Branch collect information on those whom I think cause problems for the State" (*Hansard* 2.3.78).

(I hope he didn't say "whom", by the way, and if he didn't he is entitled to have the Stationery Office watched.) He could have added that the Special Branch also collects information on some people whom the Home Secretary knows nothing about, and would be falling down on its job if it didn't. But if you should be interested in what the Special Branch gets up to, you really ought to read the Bulletins of

State Research, which are published by Julian Freedman Books Ltd, of 4 Perrin's Lane, Hampstead. Don't expect anything impartial, and then you will be pleasantly surprised how impartial it can be, especially on matters like the Police Complaints Board. Of course it describes White Papers as "pitiful" and says that identity cards "would make Britain a police state in the true meaning of the term" (and I'm not kidding: that's what it really says, knowing presumably what a police state can be like). But if you read it carefully it contains a wealth of information about the job you are doing or failing to do, and its generally well-informed authors seem blissfully unaware that, if they got the Special Branch abolished tomorrow, the same work would still go on anonymously, leaving them with no-one visible to curse.

Police Review April 6, 1979.

Conduct Unbecoming

You must have some kind of catch-all clause in any law designed to control public behaviour. I've met a lot of people who find it hilarious that four men should be convicted of "breach of the peace" because they had jumped off the Clifton Suspension Bridge at Bristol and dangled at the end of "elastic ropes" (*Guardian* 2 April). They did it on April Fool's Day, and the evidence was that they leapt into the 200-foot gorge and bounced like yo-yos in their climbing harnesses on the end of elastic ropes secured to the central part of the bridge. Traffic on the bridge was held up for half an hour while the police "and other students" (students of what?) pulled them to safety. They were members (in fact one of them was President) of the Oxford University Dangerous Sports Club, and if you asked them why they went to the trouble of dangling dangerously over the River Avon they would presumably have said something like: "Well what else is there to do?" or "We've always wanted to bounce from that bridge, simply because it's there". Daft, of course, but how (I've been asked) could you call it a breach of the peace? To which I suppose the answer has to be that "the peace" is a guaranteed condition in which the bridges of this land (I'm now trying to think like a Judge in the Court of Appeal) have no Oxford graduates hanging from them, or, alternatively, that none of them shall be bouncing up and down like yo-yos. Our great seats of learning have a long tradition of this kind of thing, but it must be kept within, so to speak, bounds.

And section 91 of the Magistrates Courts Act 1952 prescribes the procedure for bringing such offenders to justice. We couldn't expect to find a statute saying that no person shall wilfully and without reasonable cause bounce at the end of any rope suspended from any bridge, etc. It all has to come within a general conspectus about the fitness of things, in the same way as conduct prejudicial to discipline or likely to bring discredit on the reputation of the force or of the Police Service. The four Bristol Bouncers admitted in court that they had committed a breach of the peace, and consented to be bound over to keep the peace for two years in recognisances of £100 each. The alternative they faced was going to prison for six months or until they made up their minds to sign. Perhaps this might be the better way to deal with the next desperadoes who climb up the Nelson monument in Trafalgar Square.

Police Review April 13, 1979.

What's Wrong with Youth?

During the current electioneering barrage about Laura Norder, Short Sharp Shocks, and Bring Back the Rope, we shall be hearing less than usual about police brutality and corruption because no-one has yet found a way of exploiting these for votes. So they'll be in cold storage for a bit, though there will be some references to a need for doubling police strength. (At ordinary times, with no elections in the offing, increasing police strength is nowadays seen as a method of increasing the crime figures – more police about, more crime smelled out.) But I've come across an authoritative statement of the trouble about young offenders, which I hereby pass on to any political party looking for a postscript to its election manifesto:

> The world is passing through troublous times. The young people of today think of nothing but themselves. They have no reverence for parents or for old age. They are impatient of all restraint. They talk as if they alone knew everything, and what passes for wisdom with us is foolishness with them. As for the girls, they are foolish and immodest and unwomanly in speech, behaviour and dress.

Wow. And the author is Peter of Ickham, who was writing in 1274, when we hadn't even got a Parliament. He was a church historian working then at the University of Paris. Later he came to Canterbury and became a monk. But the passage set out above came in an address he wrote at Worcester, seven hundred and five years ago. Of course according to Dean Inge of St. Paul's, these snippets of worldly wisdom began some time before that. Dr Inge seems to have discovered that Adam, offering Eve his arm after ejectment from the Garden of Eden, said "My dear, we live in an age of transition".

Police Review April 20, 1979.

Sherlock Holmes Revisited

I remember once telling an old friend that I was looking forward to the leisure for re-reading all the novels of Dickens. "Don't do it," he said. "Keep your illusions. Second time round, they're nothing like so good as you thought they were." Shocked, I decided not to wait for the leisure; and although they weren't *quite* so good (too much irrelevance, too many show-stopping yarns, too much apostrophizing, rather soppy heroines), most of the old magic was there, and more enjoyment than ever because, being 40 years older, I knew a bit more about the social history of the 19th century. Dickens was a miraculous writer who will survive any amount of revisiting.

But there are many novelists who wouldn't, many who keep reputations, in fact, precisely because no-one ever goes back to them. They survive on catch-phrases attributed to them – not always rightly attributed. "You know my methods, Watson," and "This should mean promotion for you, Lestrade:" those two phrases conveniently epitomize Holmes's attitude to his faithful stooge and to the haplessly cocksure police service, respectively. I had been promising myself for many years that I would one day re-read the much-loved Sherlock Holmes stories; and then recently I was asked to record *The Adventures of Sherlock Holmes* on tapes supplied by an organization producing "talking books" for the blind. I have come to know that this kind of reading calls for more concentration than reading for one's own pleasure; and from this special discipline, as applied to Sherlock Holmes, I have emerged a changed man. There now follows the Blasphemy of the Week.

These stories are badly written, careless about matching detail, skilful only in dressing up simple, everyday percipience to look like deductive genius, and culpably inaccurate concerning criminal law and procedure (even as they were in the 1890s). No publisher's reader today would let them through, and if they got through no critic worth his money would allow them to go unpanned. Was it because of this kind of thing, after all, that the first of the series ever to appear, *A Study In Scarlet*, was rejected by 34 publishers before Ward Lock & Company bought it outright for £25? For literary style and procedural accuracy, to say nothing about the criminal law, there are 50 "crimewriters'" today who leave Conan Doyle at the post.

Now while the law of blasphemy still survives, anyone who thus attacks so hallowed an institution is asking to be clobbered and had better be ready with shield and buckler, especially if he is alleging that the stories are not well written. Accordingly I begin with that special allegation, offering the following gems as showing (among other things) that Conan Doyle used words without knowing what they meant. In *A Scandal In Bohemia* there is a reference to the beautiful Irene Adler's place in Holmes's estimation. "In his eyes she eclipses and predominates the whole of her sex:" ("predominates" is intransitive: you can eclipse but you can't predominate other people. You can dominate them, but the beautiful Irene was not like that at all.) In the same story Holmes "loathed every form of society with his whole Bohemian soul . . . ;" and in *The Engineer's Thumb* Dr.

Watson "occasionally even persuaded him to forego his Bohemian habits so far as to come and visit us." But what does Bohemian mean if not society-loving? A Bohemian defies convention, but he's no hermit: he likes to have around him people who can see him defying it. There's no real fun in being eccentric without someone to watch.

In *The Noble Bachelor* occurs this pearl of English prose: "On ascertaining that his daughter had disappeared Mr. Aloysius Doran, in conjunction with the bridegroom, instantly put themselves into communication with the police." And then back to *The Engineer's Thumb:* "The sound of several footsteps were heard upon the stairs." In *The Speckled Band:* "I suppose," says Holmes, "that I am computing a felony" (in fact he was always compounding felonies, as the law then stood, but he never got into any trouble about it: luckily English criminal procedure hadn't yet gone in for compounderization). Incidentally he had trouble bringing *The Speckled Band* to a close: "Finally he walked over to the bed and spent some time in staring at it. Finally" (what, again?) "he took the bell rope and gave it a brisk tug." In *The Blue Carbuncle* Doyle commits one of the deadly grammatical sins still common today among better writers than he: "The Alpha Inn, which is a small public house at the corner of one of the streets which runs down into Holborn." (It's fair to say that there are still sub-editors who would alter this from "run down" to "runs down.") Can this be the man who wrote those classic stories *Rodney Stone, Micah Clark*, and *The Exploits Of Brigadier Gerard?* And would it be wiser *never* to revisit those? I find that hard to believe, but am unwilling to risk it.

It is in *The Blue Carbuncle* that Conan Doyle describes the eponymous precious stone as "treasure trove," which it certainly wasn't. Even when the great detective has Horner, the jewel thief, in his power he tells him to "Get out!" And later: "After all, Watson," he says, reaching up for his clay pipe, "I am not retained by the police to supply their deficiencies." This may have been as well, for Inspector Bradstreet (whose office is sometimes at Bow Street, sometimes at Scotland Yard), in presenting the case against Horner before the magistrate at Bow Street, gives evidence of a previous conviction although Horner is pleading not guilty and has elected for summary trial. (It's the previous conviction that decides the magistrate to commit him to sessions.)

In *A Scandal In Bohemia* Dr. Watson, as part of a thief-catching ploy, gives a false alarm of fire in a London street at a time when the LCC had just obtained a General Powers Act making it punishable to do so. (Not very important, but modern writers would have found out.) In *The Red-Headed League* Watson (at Holmes's instructions) carries his old army revolver at night in carefree defiance of the Vagrancy Act 1824: the Pistols Act 1903 was still some way off, but the Vagrancy Act would have made the good doctor a rogue and vagabond from the moment he stepped out of 221 Baker Street on to the pavement. Holmes, by the way, was carrying a hunting-crop with similar intent, an odd thing to find in the possession of a Bohemian who loathed company; and this, in due course, he did use on the criminal.

The theme of *A Case Of Identity* is really a story of forgery, personation, and attempted abduction, and yet Holmes agrees with the villain, having unmasked him, that his conduct is "not actionable" and that "the law, as you say, cannot touch you, yet there never was a man who deserved punishment more." There never was a man in real life who would have more surely got it. In *The Boscombe Valley Mystery* John Turner, the harassed old ex-bushranger from Ballarat, confesses to Holmes that he has murdered his blackmailer; and the great man merely says "Well, it is not for me to judge you," meaning go and sin no more. As for *The Copper Beeches*, if ever I'd had the skill and wit to devise that story, any publisher's reader would have been certain to tell *me* that Mr. Rucastle's daughter couldn't be living in Philadelphia and Nova Scotia at the same time. No-one told Conan Doyle about it; and the stories go through numberless reprints and new editions with all such errors uncorrected.

And there surely never was such a pompous cretin as Inspector Lestrade of the Yard, combining in one person an impenetrable stupidity, an unsinkable self-confidence, a taste for the expensive cigars handed to him now and then by a private eye who treats him with mocking contempt, and a chronic inability to convey to the Yard that it should either promote him or send him back into uniform. The best you can say for Lestrade is that Conan Doyle doesn't portray him as corrupt, or even corruptible, though in the 1890's there were plenty of real life exemplars he could have drawn on. Holmes himself, of course, is not corruptible, but then he seems to be doing the whole thing for fun. What does he live on? Do his adoring beneficiaries shower him with secret gifts? Does some grateful murderer pay the rent of No. 221? Irksome as he is to the Yard, is he nevertheless so valuable that he gets a Home Office subvention, concealed in the Secret Service Estimates?

Whew! This is where to stop. It is also time to step back into the ranks, wait for the heavens to fall, and enjoy these stories while it is possible; recalling that, as Sibelius so angrily said, nobody ever set up a statue to a critic.

Justice of the Peace April 21, 1979.

Photographing Mr Thorpe

A correspondent has asked me why it is that section 41 of the Criminal Justice Act 1925, which prohibits the photographing of participants in court cases as they enter or leave the court buildings, is "more honoured in the breach than in the observance." Jeremy Thorpe and wife and many other witnesses, says my correspondent, are being photographed every day as they arrive at and leave the Old Bailey, and there can't be any difficulty about enforcing the Act because the cameramen are obligingly photographing each other as they crowd round their victims, and the newspapers are printing pictures showing beyond doubt that the building is the Old Bailey.

Well, I can't resist first of all trying to rehabilitate this most misunderstood of all quotations – "more honoured in the breach than in the observance". It does *not* mean that a rule, law, custom or convention is being more often broken than obeyed. It's Shakespeare's Hamlet explaining to Horatio that the horrible din that has just broken out in the courtyard, guns and trumpets and guns going off as part of a "heavy-headed" drunken revel, is an old Danish custom which, in Hamlet's view, would be better discontinued than kept going. "Is it a custom?" asks Horatio. Hamlet says it is. "But to my mind," he adds, "though I am native here and to the manner born, it is a custom more honoured in the breach than in the observance"; why, that is to say, don't they pack it up? I suppose Parliament must have intended section 41 to be honoured when they imposed it upon us more than 50 years ago, but although it's flouted a thousand times a day there have been very few prosecutions – and most of those seem to have been ordered by judges. In 1956, for example, Mr. Justice Goddard angrily called attention to a BBC news-reel of a prominent Soho hoodlum known as Mr Jack Spot triumphantly leaving the Old Bailey after his acquittal. After which there were a few prosecutions, among them being one at Bow Street where the present Lord Gardiner, ex-Lord Chancellor, got a man off by arguing that the pavement outside the Court building wasn't its "precincts" for the purposes of the definition section ("photograph . . . made in the courtroom, or in the building or in the precincts of the building in which the court is held, or made of the person while he is entering or leaving the courtroom or any such building or precincts"). There was no police appeal against that decision, which accordingly went down in my private lexicon of decided cases under the respectful heading "totally daft". But I should have thought that if we now consider it more honourable to ignore section 41 than to observe it, the truly honourable thing to do is to scrap it.

Police Review May 25, 1979.

I Never Got Your Letter

Among the holiday reading I'm recommending to my jaded friends I have found no place for the Interpretation Act 1889, but it's not without relevance to the seaside postcards which, in due course, you will be swearing you didn't forget to send. For consider section 26: "Where an Act requires any document to be served by post . . ., then unless the contrary intention appears the service shall be deemed to be effected by properly addressing, prepaying, and posting a letter containing the document". And "*unless the contrary is proved*" (my own indignant italics) it is deemed "to have been effected at the time at which the letter would be delivered in the ordinary course of post". How on earth do you prove it never came? It might be a jury summons (which doesn't come by "recorded delivery"); or a bankruptcy notice, in pursuance of which, as you sit there on the sands, your creditor is selling you up; or any one of a dozen messages, comforting or alarming, to which you must respond or be punished or deprived.

The law has its own phrase for "I never got it". This is called a "negative averment"; and section 81 of the Magistrates' Courts Act 1952 puts upon the defendant the burden of proof. If the police say he has no driving licence or certain other kinds of qualifications, he has to prove them wrong; and that seems fair enough, when you consider the alternative. But the rural postmen round my way (I can safely disclose this, for they're unlikely to read the *Police Review*) have to cope with the fact that my neighbours and I live a very long way apart; so that if they get to my door still holding a letter which ought to have been delivered a quarter of a mile back, they shove it in among mine, hoping that I will re-deliver it. I actually did this for a time, but the virtue of it wore off, and I now stuff such letters into the pillar box next time I'm posting things. I'm pretty sure that my neighbours do the same, especially with *Police Review* printer's proofs. But such a thing is made no easier to prove by giving it an elegant name like Negative Averment.

Police Review June 15, 1979.

Do Not Spit

That is what you could read in buses, trains, trams and lifts when I was a boy. You didn't see it in churches, theatres, or museums, but you sometimes saw it on lamp-posts and street orderly bins in public places. A little before then it had always said "In the interests of the public health and the prevention of consumption" (which always seemed to me the same thing) "you are kindly requested to refrain from the objectionable and dangerous habit of spitting". I always refrained, but the "kind request" couldn't have been enough because, as I say, it was supplanted by the terser DO NOT SPIT, which was followed by the words PENALTY 40 SHILLINGS. Mr Callum Tod, who is employed as a labourer by the Edinburgh District Council and is 22, objects to the proposed Government cuts in Health Service expenditure, so when the Queen went to Edinburgh last week he ran in front of her car waving a copy of the *Socialist Worker*. This might not have been enough, of itself, to amend the Finance Bill, so he spat on the Queen's car as well. The crowd disapproved of Mr. Tod, whose shouts were drowned by theirs and he was arrested. At the Sheriff Court he was told to lodge £100 with the court as security for his good behaviour for a year, which must mean better and more discriminatory spitting. If he discriminates for the whole year, he will get his money back *with interest*. This is a kind of compulsory investment. If Mr Tod hadn't spat on the Queen's car, he might have lost all that interest. For one spectacular spitting effort, he gets what amounts to expert advice and help in the management of his money. I wonder what would have happened to him at Bow Street?

Police Review July 13, 1979.

Always Pick up Your Receipt

A neighbour of mine, an elderly widow who is looked after by her niece, telephoned me last week to say that the niece had been charged with shoplifting and that the whole dreadful business *must* be a mistake. Someone, she said, had put a packet of sweetcorn into the lady's shopping bag without her knowledge; and once she had passed the cash-desk and paid for half a dozen other things she *did* know about, a store detective asked her about the sweetcorn. "Sweetcorn?" she said, aghast, "I can't stand the stuff. What on earth would I steal *that* for?" But the supermarket people didn't know or really care how she felt about a sweetcorn; she might be stealing it for someone who did like it.The trouble was that she had no receipt to show that she had paid for anything. She never troubles to pick up these little curly printouts, she says; she has paid the money and got the goods and the transaction is over. (I believe the supermarkets could save themselves much trouble if they displayed notices, at least as prominently as the ones about thieves being prosecuted, urging all customers to accept the cashier's receipt and put it in with the goods they have bought.) In the event the charge against her was withdrawn, and I suppose she was lucky, though as it happens I would bet my very last coin that she was totally innocent – she's about as likely to go shoplifting as I am to go stealing aircraft. But she has decided (and so have I) always in future to pick up the cashier's receipt.

Anyway you have to wait long enough for it to give it almost the value of a certificate of discharge from custody. Not long ago I bought two dozen self-adhesive tiles, noted the price on them, got the exact money ready, waited in a long queue to pay for them, and then had to watch a young chap pumping a till-lever up and down 24 times while it added up my debt to the supermarket – and got it wrong. A supervisor had to be called to examine the till, and as this looked like being a lengthy operation he did my little sum on a paper bag lying handy. His answer came out the same as mine and I gave him the money which had been ready for so long. In the meantime I had missed my bus. But if I had known then what I know now I would (in the absence of a receipt) have kept the paper bag with the sum on it.

Police Review July 20, 1979.

And Nothing But The Truth

I've sometimes wondered, and have often been asked, who it was that originally devised the form of the witness's oath, by which any citizen of this land can be required to tell "the truth, the whole truth, and nothing but the truth". He may be doing it as a practising, pseudo, would-be or don't know Christian (swearing by Almighty God or, in some instances, by The Almighty Gawd), or he may be doing it as part of an affirmation, leaving out God but still invoking the three concepts of truth. I just can't find its origin, but it must have been someone with less confidence than the apostle St. James, who still exhorts the world from the *New Testament* (as witnesses hold him aloft in the right hand): "Above all things, my brethren, swear not, neither by Heaven, neither by the earth, neither by any other oath; but let your yea be yea, and your nay, nay."

I suppose that since St. James's time (he died in A.D. 62 as Bishop of Jerusalem) the truth has got more complicated. A witness swearing today to tell "the truth" might feel virtuous enough provided what he said contained no lies; so we require him to go on and tell the rest of it, the whole truth. And then, in case he wants to embellish it with a few fancy touches or begins to wander off into beliefs and opinions, we can remind him that he has sworn to tell "nothing but the truth". There are some people who would gladly abolish the whole thing as useless claptrap, and I can quite see why. But I don't believe it will be abolished until we are all so much less wicked that we all trust each other.

Police Review August 24, 1979.

Doppler and the Two-tone Horn

C. J. Doppler was an Austrian scientist (he died in 1853) who found out why it is that, if you stand on a railway bridge while a train goes underneath emitting a continuous whistle, the note of the whistle will seem to drop by a semi-tone when it has gone by and is rushing away from you. It's to do with the speed of sound (1100 feet a second), the number of vibrations used by the whistle (say 256 a second), and the resulting length of the sound waves reaching you (4.3 feet). Kids playing cops and robbers in the street don't know this, and when one of them, impersonating a patrol-car, arrives at the scene-of-crime, he lowers the tone of his hee-haw as he slows down on arrival. That's understandable, but you wouldn't expect the BBC to be unacquainted with the Doppler Effect when they are producing their innumerable crime plays. Yet their Z-Cars and other swoopers drop the half-tone *as they arrive,* not as they rush away. The effect is comical. It always sounds as if the police car so anxiously awaited by everyone has simply rushed by and is just not interested. Producers please note. It's one detail of police involvement that you could *infallibly* get right, and we could set it off against all the others.

Police Review August 24, 1979.

Trivia is the Greatest

The Press Council's 1977 report has only just come out (I wonder why?), and in it the chairman, Lord Shawcross, observes that there hasn't been much improvement in press behaviour about four things: sensationalism, violence, sex and trivia. And "the greatest of these is trivia" (sic). Trivia, goes on his Lordship in case you might have thought that was just grammatical defiance, "is perhaps a matter more involving the press, although anyone listening to the *Today Programme* on Radio Four can hardly find more trivia and vulgarity in 10 minutes anywhere else". From what I know of the Today Team, they probably know at least that "trivia" is a plural noun, and by the time I get this into print they will probably have had their little ho-ho about Lord Shawcross's English. But will they become less trivial? I doubt it; and since I always listen to them while I'm shaving and they help me to forget what a miserable daily scrape that is, I hope that they will continue to find room in their programme for the occasional trivium. I never forget that the whole lot of them are, after all, on continual First Relief or Early Turn, when ho-ho-ing can't be easy to put over.

Police Review August 31, 1979.

"Watch the Judge's Hand"

I don't know that I really thought this phrase had disappeared from the lingo of the criminal courts, but it hasn't: I heard it last week in a Crown Court which is so modern and spanking brand new in all other respects that it sounded like a Shakespearian phrase in a pop-song. It means that you mustn't give your evidence too quickly because the Judge, unlike the offical shorthand writer, is writing down what you say in a form that can be understood and nodded over by the Court of Appeal. The "Judge's note", as they call it, still takes precedence over all other records of a trial. Can you imagine anything more daft? A good many judges are afflicted by deafness (all right, impaired hearing), and few of them are speed writers. Now that we have, or *can* have, tape-recorded accounts of a trial as well as the shorthand writers' records, why on earth should a witness have to speak at what you might call Dictation Speed for Judges? I was once shown a judge's notes of a trial, and although wild horses wouldn't make me divulge his name (even if a wild horse could be found and induced to take any interest), I swear that the learned Judge had compiled a page of scrawl that he certainly couldn't read himself. Here's a suggestion. Give every judge a little tape-recorder, wired to all the microphones in court. Give him a key he can depress when he thinks something important is being said. Then at the end of the trial, while both counsel are making their interminable speeches which don't matter a damn to anybody, let one of the court typists transcribe the bits which his Lordship has seemed interested in. Then he can sum up from those.

Police Review September 28, 1979.

Knight of Mark Twain

You are now reading the words of a newly-elected Knight of Mark Twain, and if you are not impressed that makes two of us because I don't really understand it either. But last week I got a letter from Kirkwood, Missouri, telliing me that "in recognition of my outstanding contribution to modern publishing and World Peace" I have been "unanimously elected this day a Knight of Mark Twain". What on earth have I done? The letter's signed "Cyril Clemens", and since Mark Twain's real name was Samuel Clemens this must be Cyril carrying the ancestral banner. He edits the *Mark Twain Journal* (one dollar a copy) which is probably the journal of the International Mark Twain Society, and this sometimes bestows its Gold Medal on illustrious members. Winston Churchill got one, and I've received with my certificate of membership a copy of the letter that Winnie wrote from Downing Street in October 1943 expressing his pleasure. "It will serve to keep fresh my memory of a great American, who showed me much kindness when I visited New York as a young man". Until I get the Gold Medal I can be content with putting K.M.T. after my name, though this wouldn't have had the approval of the Great American himself. "All that I care to know", he once said, "is that a man is a human being, that's enough for me: he can't be any worse". I'll let you know when I get the gold medal, but between now and then I shall be working on the problem of what I'm supposed to have done for modern publishing and world peace. Should I be uneasy? (It was, after all, Mark Twain who said "The cross of the Legion of Honour has been bestowed upon me. However, few escape that distinction".)

Police Review October 5, 1979.

Block Capitals Please

I think I can remember when we were first required to use block capitals instead of our normal handwriting when putting our names and addresses on official forms; and if I'm anywhere near right, it was at about the time when handwriting began to be illegible. If you get a chance to look at some old police records, occurrence books, crime reports, and so on, you will see what I mean. In those days a man writing was like a man drawing or painting; he wanted others to know what he meant. When the nation's handwriting could no longer be understood by civil servants and others, someone had the idea that block capitals would always be safe. Pathetic illusion. Life is now so full of form-filling that the job has to be done at top speed, and block capitals done at top speed are even worse than modern handwriting. Which brings me to the subject of a nice letter I've had from a Dorset sergeant, who disagrees with me (I think) about my paragraph on 21 September headed *Killing a Wild Cat.* The man in my story was seen finishing off a wild cat by beating it with a stick, and whereas I had deplored the fact that the Protection of Animals Act 1911 couldn't touch him and "protected" only domestic and captive animals, the Dorset sergeant argues (in legible handwriting) that a wild cat becomes captive at the moment of capture. "There is no minimum period of time," he says, "which defines what is captive and what is not". Perhaps I ought to have mentioned at the time that in *Rowley v. Murphy* (1964), 128 JP 88, the Queen's Bench judges decided that a cornered stag, unable to escape for the moment, is not "in captivity" even though it is then taken and killed by its pursuers; and that in *Steele v Rogers* (1912), 76 JP 150, decided under an earlier Act called the Wild Animals in Captivity Protection Act 1900, a stranded whale waiting to float off with the incoming tide was held not be "in captivity or close confinement".

Normally I should send a personal letter to my Dorset correspondent as well as airing the matter above, but (a) I can't read his signature and (b) he has put his address in block capitals. Let us share the regrets and go halves on the apologies.

Police Review October 12, 1979.

Practical Penal Reform

Edgar Wallace wrote a book called *The Four Just Men,* a story about four international idealists who got tired of seeing notorious criminals acquitted or inadequately punished and worked out a system for inflicting the punishment themselves. Their last victim was a British cabinet minister (I think) whom they had warned that he was to die at noon on a stated day. The government took this very seriously, fortified the building and posted sharpshooters on surrounding roofs. But at noon on the predicted day the Minister slumped forward on his desk and died. In the edition I was reading the publishers offered a prize for the best solution of this mystery, suggesting absolutely none themselves. I never heard whether anyone got a prize.

Winchester Crown Court has just demonstrated what the attitude of English law would (and should) be to any such vengeful groups, though this time the four enthusiasts included one woman. Colin Jones and his girl-friend Jane had their flat burgled. The man eventually convicted of the burglary, Tim Shemeld, was dealt with at Portsmouth Crown Court on that and other charges, and got a nine months' suspended sentence. This failed to satisfy the burgled couple and their friends, and one day, with two friends called Paul and Gary Beckett, they sought out Mr Shemeld and administered what they felt was a more appropriate correction. They dragged him into a car, drove him to a wood, beat him up, blindfolded him and handcuffed him to a tree. In due course they all pleaded guilty to kidnapping and false imprisonment, adding in one or two "T.I.C.s" like shoplifting and theft, and all went to prison – Jones for 18 months, Jane for 12 months, Paul Beckett for 12 months and Gary Beckett to Borstal. I've never found out who it was that first said "You must not take the law into your own hands," but the idea at any rate must be about as old as settled communities and the earliest forms of law. Failure to conform to it is what eventually got the Krays and the Richardsons into their final ditch. But it may soon occur to somebody that it is being brought under increasing strain by the enormous development of "taking other offences into consideration". Nowadays the would-be prosecutors in "T.I.C." cases are not even asked whether they agree that their cases shall be thus disposed of. And indeed where there are several hundreds of them concerned with the treatment of one convicted man, it's difficult to see how they *can* be consulted.

Police Review December 21, 1979.

Justice Should be Heard, Too

Immediately after Christmas the daily columnist of *The Times* had a go at one of our Great National Problems which, for some reason, never gets into the open. He had paid a visit to the Lord Chief Justice's Court in the Royal Courts of Justice and tried to listen to what was going on. He found Lord Widgery inaudible (and who doesn't?). "Whole words and sentences", he said, "tailed into mumble. I wished at times I had an ear trumpet". Counsel were begging his Lordship's pardon frequently, and "they leaned to catch words like courtiers bowing to a sovereign". I suppose it's fair to pick on Lord Widgery as the Man at the Top, but nearly all the judges are the same—and they always have been. Not long ago I sat in the Recorder's Court at the Old Bailey during a murder trial, and I could swear that no-one outside the little rectangle of lawyers near the Bench could have heard the proceedings. It was like a whispered conspiracy, the object thereof being to defeat the irksome principle of "open court". At one point the Recorder must have said something important, for there was an instant rustle of activity all along Counsels' benches as papers were extracted from bundles, and as pairs of wig-crowned heads came close together in what might well have been some kind of conversation. "What did he say?" I whispered to a friendly usher. "No idea," he replied. "Can't hear him." I wondered how much the jury could hear.

Many, many times I have heard, or rather seen, judges summing up to juries when it has seemed almost past belief that the speaker could even hear himself. Once only have I heard a jury tell the judge, and it was after a whole morning's evidence, that they hadn't heard anything a witness had been saying. You hear a lot about "trained judges" and "trained lawyers", but in this country such training is non-existent. Our principle is what the Chinese used to call makee-learnee, you pick it up as you along. The one witness you can be pretty certain of hearing is a police witness in uniform (as soon as he graduates to the CID he begins to adopt the forensic mumble, feeling himself perhaps to be one of the Wiser Whisperers). Justice in this country is pretty nearly inaudible.

Now why should this be, in an age when electrical amplification is so utterly simple? In both Houses of Parliament the head-rest behind every seat is equipped with a little built-in microphone, so that no-one shall miss a word of what our prosy legislators are saying. If it is all that important to ensure a public audience for the speeches in Parliament, surely it can't be less salutary that we should be enabled to hear what's going on when our fellow-citizens are on trial for their liberty?

Police Review January 18, 1980.

Secret London

I suppose if a West-end club put up a brass nameplate saying what it was, or even exhibited a little card in the receptionist's window just inside the building, everybody would resign at once. It may be the same at Oxbridge colleges, whose identity everyone is expected to know by the light of nature; and it may be that, hidden away from the likes of us, there is some historical or sinister reason why we have to spend hours trying to find out which club or college is which. But streets are another matter. It's time I made my annual attack on the laziness, stupidity and/or indifference with which the Greater London Council (or somebody) defies the law and leaves London streets unnamed. This year the campaign has been started for me by a Mr Malcolm Rogers, to whom the *Sunday Times* allowed space on 27 January and whom it described as a musician and part-time van driver.

"For a city of such complexity," he wrote, "London must be the most inadequately signposted place in Europe". (I think he could have said in the world.) "Most streets in London, no matter how long, only have a sign at each end" (he's been lucky). "Arrive at any intermediate junction and you'll have to drive to the end of the street to find out where you are; or block up the street by stopping to holler at a passer-by. Why can't we follow the American example and have street signs at every junction?"

Thank you, Mr Rogers. If the government weren't so busy abolishing quangos I would urge the creation of another one, to go round reporting anonymous London streets, or anonymous streets anywhere. Or indeed writing up the names of streets with their own aerosol sprays, a benevolent outlet for the most popular modern form of vandalism. And while I'm about it I might as well get in my periodical moan about the English rural custom of still placing the arms on signposts where they've been for probably 1,500 years, on a level with the head of a man on horseback. The right place for them today is three feet from the ground and they should all glow brightly under headlamp illumination.

Police Review February 8, 1980.

Shorthand Pitfalls

I still use Pitman's shorthand a lot, and would use it even more if I could *always* be confident about reading what I've written. The combination of speed and accuracy displayed by the court shorthand writers has never failed to astound me, and their services are too often taken for granted. I'd better say that the same is true of the *Hansard* shorthand writers in the Commons and Lords, because my sister-in-law is one of them and she might get to know what I've been on about. But Mr Tam Dalyell, MP, who pronounces his name DL, discovered last week that a number of answers given to him by the Prime Minister had been inaccurately reported in *Hansard.* He discovered this by going to the House of Commons Sound Archive and getting a BBC recorded cassette of what the Prime Minister had actually said. There were at least six differences, one or two of them important. Nevertheless, said the Speaker of the House of Commons on 31 January, "I am not going to accept the BBC recording as in any way a check on *Hansard.* I am going to be guided by our *Hansard* reporters, on whose integrity we all rely and who will write down what they hear . . . The shorthand writing has been examined. There is a mistake in copying, a simple human error. I have no doubt it will happen again."

Now the Speaker is a man of power, and I tug my forelock. But even a man of power, elected to such an eminence by over 600 MPs, can occasionally talk rot. And it is rot to say that a microphoned recording cannot be a check on a shorthand writer. Now that we have the opportunity, in the courts of law as well as in the High Court of Parliament, to check shorthand notes against tape-recordings, we ought without hesitation to make use of it when the necessity arises. Here's an example. In 1960 I was commissioned by Penguin Books to compile a paperback about the *Lady Chatterley* trial at the Old Bailey. I got the official transcript of the five days' proceedings, all typed from the shorthand writers' notes. I had made notes of my own during the evidence of certain eminent witnesses, and I found that there were differences. Two of the differences were so vital that I wrote to the witnesses and asked them which of the two versions (setting them out side by side) was correct. In both instances the offical version was wrong. Years afterwards I said so in a magazine article and the magazine promptly received a letter from the offical shorthand writers' solicitors threatening action for libel. I produced the letters from the witnesses I had checked with, and that was the last we heard of it. I recall that the witnesses had been hopping mad about what they were alleged to have said in court, and they would have been only too willing to give evidence about it in a libel action. They probably still would. No tape-recording is infallible, but it's a bit less fallible than a statement typed from a hundred pages of shorthand, even when the typist and the shorthand-writer are the same person, which they seldom are.

Police Review February 15, 1980.

Pro Patria Mori

"MORI" really means, nowadays, Market and Opinion Research International. It sells its services to anyone who can afford them, finding out what we all think about each other or about the goods or services we prefer or hate. By the time you read this, you will be well aware that MORI has been inquiring, on behalf of the *Sunday Times*, what the British public thinks about its policemen. What, again? Indeed, and for the thousandth time. The results are presented on another page of this issue of Police Review. My own reaction to them is that I wish the enquiry had been commissioned by one of the organisations, or by a combination of them, which thrive on the smell of police corruption, and the sound of police jumping on the bodies of their prisoners. But then I suppose it would have been shelved.

But it reminds me that some years ago I was invited by Dr. Michael Young (as he then was—he's Lord Young now), and Peter Willmott of the Bethnal Green Institute for Community Studies, to do some additional recorded interviewing for a Ford Foundation research project. Most of it had already been done, by someone else who got ill. It was all about the process of growing up in Bethnal Green. In the course of a few months I accumulated hours of recorded chatter with voluntary victims in boys' clubs. They nearly all hated the police (they said). This was mainly because the coppers wouldn't them talk on street corners, but it was also because the coppers never believed that transistors fell from passing lorries. One boy told me that he would never dream of nicking anything except for his mother's birthday, or perhaps Christmas, and that the police were too thick to distinguish this from stealing. How did he know what policemen thought? "Well, my brother's just joined the police, you see. Decent job it is too, pension and all that." While we remain such a mixed-up nation, can't you see the scope for organisations like MORI?

Police Review March 28, 1980.

The Pigeon War

I knew an old Oxford City constable who never tired of relating how, under a street lamp at dusk, he was recording a few necessary details in his notebook when a pigeon, perched on the ladder-stay above his head, suddenly inserted a fullstop where none was needed. He ranked pigeons with burglars, rapists and hooligans. His father had been porter at one of the Oxford colleges, and because generations of pigeons had despoiled the famous architecture, had handed down from father to son a hatred of these otherwise stately birds. Now it has been found that peregrine falcons, which eat pigeons, have been nesting on the roof of the St Regis Hotel in New York, and that the New York Police, who like pigeons, have for the past forty years been shooting at the falcons to make them go away. Naturally enough the authorities at Wells Cathedral, reading about this in *The Times* (14 March), are excited about it because pigeons use the 13th Century statues on the West Front of the Cathedral as latrines and it is getting harder to recognise the statues. So Lord Waldegrave, who is President of an appeal fund to restore the West Front (at a cost of millions), is asking the New York Police to stop shooting their falcons and extradite them to Wells, Somerset, England. With two great police systems so much at variance, the time has come for Interpol to take a hand in the arranging of this.

Police Review March 28, 1980.

The Soft Answer

Biblical start this week. The *Book of Proverbs* has always seemed to me a *Book of Obscure Platitudes* (well, have another look at it), but Chapter Fifteen at least starts with one that ought to command universal agreement. "A soft answer", it says, "turneth away wrath, but grievous words stir up anger". No difficulty in believing that? And yet when the crunch comes, and we are at the receiving end of a volley of abuse, the soft answer is always difficult to fetch up. Human nature being what it is, there can be even greater difficulty in returning a soft answer when we are accused of a motoring lapse, and the manner of the policeman's accusation is what makes it easy or difficult. "Policemen are human," is the discovery reported by *The Guardian's* motoring correspondent on 21 April, "and provided they approach you courteously it pays dividends to respond in a similar manner". Now that seems to me muddled thinking. The time to be nice to a policeman, although it's the most difficult time, is when he's really nasty. Otherwise he will merely get nastier. No difficulty about earning the dividends when the policeman is being courteous.

But there is obviously something to be said for being voluble, if you are dealing with a member of one of those police forces which seek to save postage by giving their traffic warnings orally instead of by registered post. Mrs Doreen Gibson of Worksop, Notts, a meals-on-wheels driver, was told by a policeman that she might be prosecuted for speeding. But she didn't hear him because she too was talking at the time, and the constable (who must surely have been a single man) supposed that his words would get through to her nevertheless. The magistrates convicted her, and she appealed to the High Court by "case stated" on the ground that she hadn't been given the statutory 14 days' notice of intended prosecution, arguing that she was entitled to this because she hadn't been warned at the time of the offence. Quite right, said the Queen's Bench Judges. A warning which fails to get through is no warning at all. Conviction quashed. I suppose we shall never know what she was saying at the time of the oral warning, since there is no reason to suppose that this would get through to the police officer. But there is an atmosphere about the story which suggests that she wasn't employing the soft answer recommended in Proverbs 15.

Police Review May 9, 1980.

Police and the Embassies

Sooner or later, surely, the current contempt for the safety of embassies and diplomatic staff, and their increasing value as pawns in the kidnapping, hostage and blackmail industry, must lead to some pretty drastic revision of the 1961 Vienna Convention of Diplomatic

Relations. At present the police in this country, for example, can't forcibly enter a foreign embassy unless (it seems) the place is on fire or the head of the mission asks them to break in; which I suppose he might do if he'd lost his keys. So although a gang of armed murderers, or intended murderers, may be in occupation of the building, the lives of their intended victims are rated as less important than the building or its contents and the police are reduced to parleying, while the business of an entire urban district is brought to a standstill. It may well be that the gunmen have no intention of killing from the very start of the enterprise, but they have *announced* an intention to murder and it's part of their plan that the announcement be taken seriously. Any International Convention considering this growing problem could also consider the process by which an unprovoked atrocity becomes a "political" offence outside the scope of the Extradition Acts and Treaties. The position today suggests nothing so much as an encounter between a yob with an automatic weapon and an elderly gentleman dressed in breeches, silk stockings, buckled shoes and a velvet tunic and unrolling a parchment document from which to read out some dignified reproof.

Police Review May 10, 1980.

Look After the Victims

Ever since early Anglo-Saxon times, when organised Laura Norder began to deprive every man of his private right to retaliate against the criminal, the indifference of "the State" to the plight of victims has been cynical and atrocious. To the devastated victim the state has said: "Look, we've caught the man, we've hanged him" (or branded or whipped him, or mutilated him, or sent him to Botany Bay) "and you ought to understand that all this has been most expensive. Sorry about your property, and even perhaps your feelings, but what more do you suppose we can do?" Recently there has been more indulgence towards victims of bodily violence, but the burgled house-holder must still nurse his own grief.

Seven years ago the police at Bristol began working with the National Association for the Care and Resettlement of Offenders in a new "Victims Support Scheme". It advised on compensation, anti-burglar devices, medical help etc., and the rights of witnesses when there were prosecutions. Mr Charles Irving, M.P., who really started it all, now has the satisfaction of knowing that there are 65 similar organisations in the country, and that they have formed an Association of Victim Support Schemes with himself as its first President. The victim is losing his status as a propaganda missile, hurled at each other by the penal reformers and the hardliners. People are actually beginning to look after him.

Police Review May 23, 1980.

Scrap the Parole System?

A year or two ago I was a co-opted member of a Labour Party committee which was concerned with (among many other things) the simplification of the criminal law and procedure. At one meeting we were asked to prepare views about the value of the prison parole system, and since I had been a founder-member (so to speak) of the Parole Board it was suggested that I should contribute a special memorandum on the subject. In due course I recommended that the whole system should be scrapped, on the grounds that it caused more disappointment and heart-burning than its small results could possibly justify. The suggestion was frostily received, and we passed on to more worthwhile things. But now, I find, Mr David Thomas of the Cambridge Institute of Criminology is suggesting that the scrapping of the parole system has become a "high priority" (*Guardian,* 12 May). It must be replaced, he says, by a system of "predetermined remission, with the rest of the sentence suspended". Thus the judge fixing the sentence would be "making a decision with real consequences, not merely establishing the outer boundaries of a Parole Board's discretion". The thing is that the theory on which the parole system was founded, namely that a prisoner reaches a "peak" in his "training" at which he must be released unless he is to deteriorate, has been shown to be sheer poppycock.

Police Review May 30, 1980.

Bill of Rights

Depending on how long it is since you left school, you may well have forgotten that in this country we already have a Bill of Rights, though it seems to bring little comfort to those (including the Lord Chancellor) who are currently urging that we should have a better one. Our Bill of Rights is a statute passed by Parliament in England in December 1689 to ratify the conditions under which we had said to William of Orange: "All right, you can come and be King if you will put your signature to this list of conditions". The conditions included the demand that all jurors should own and occupy freehold property, that there should be no standing army in time of peace (I wonder what "peace" meant?), that all Protestants could carry firearms (no nonsense about police certificates) for shooting Roman Catholics, and that there were to be no "cruel and unusual punishments". They also said that every King and Queen must make a "declaration against Popery" and there are still idiots who regard this as the supreme requirement.

But Professor Henry Wade, QC, Master of Gonville and Caius College, Cambridge, has been explaining in his Hamlyn Lectures this year how difficult it will be to work out a Bill of Rights which no Parliament can ever over-rule. The usual idea is to give it an "entrenched" clause which will disable any future Parliament from changing or scrapping it. Professor Wade said that legal and constitutional experts believe Parliament is sovereign and can pass any law it likes, so that any Parliament could repeal such an "entrenched" clause or pass a law in conflict with it. But he had a solution to propose. Change the judicial oath, he said. Make the Judges swear that they will recognise the new Bill of Rights whatever Parliament may say or want, and "refuse validity to any Acts of Parliament, including future Acts, which conflict with it". They would thus be like the Supreme Court judges in America, who can over-rule Acts of Congress as "unconstitutional"; and the British Constitution would be what the judges thought it was. But where would this leave us? Parliament, by a resolution of both Houses, can sack the judges if it disapproves of them. Wouldn't it sack a judge who purported to be fulfilling his oath by undoing all its hard work in Committee rooms and its impassioned speeches in the Lords and Commons? God forbid (say I) that we should ever have a constitution that made it impossible to get rid of a judge, however he turned out. Think of old . . .

Police Review June 6, 1980.

Policeperson

It has happened at last. A correspondent has gravely suggested to me that sex equality in the police service can be achieved only by dropping the words policeman and policewoman. And he offers policeperson. He appears to be in all other respects sane. But I can see that this lunacy is spreading, and that, from the inane beginning of "chairperson" (there are already lots of chairpersons), there is developing an inconceivably daft game of oneuppersonship. In the last few years before he died, it was becoming a source of half-angry amusement to my old editor Dick Crossperson, who was member of Oxford City Council and referred to some of his fellow-councillors as alderwomen. He told me he had an old set of ivory chesspersons, two of which had been skilfully repaired in Banbury by the local handyperson, and so on. But the need for a word like man to include woman was forseen in 1810 by William Hazlitt, who said that "Man is the only animal that laughs and weeps; for he is the only animal that is struck with the difference between what things are and what they ought to be." Starting from there, it's a person-made dilemma.

Police Review July 26, 1980.

Trespassers will be Demoted

How many people can claim that by stepping over a threshold, or even across an imaginary line, they can completely change their status? That's what *you* can do. On one side of a doorway you're a constable. On the other you may be, unless you have invitation or other authority, as much a non-constable as if you had just got the sack. Of course there are officially happy countries where anyone, constable or civilian, can by crossing a boundary line change his status from terrified emigré to bullet-ridden corpse. But in this country no gas-man ceases to be a gas-man by forcing or tricking his way into a house, no rodent operative will by similar conduct cease to be a rodent operative. No judge, when he steps out of the Old Bailey at the end of the day, stops being a judge. In fact he can sign judicial papers for you at home, or even in the train. But, said the House of Lords in *Morris v. Beardmore* (*The Times*, 18 July), a trespassing constable ceases to be a "constable in uniform" within the meaning of section 8(2) of the Road Traffic Act 1972.

What the constable had done in that case (well, it was three constables led by a superintendent) was the sequel to a collision which took place at 10.45 p.m. at Walsall involving a car driven by Mr John Beardmore. After the collision he went home, and it wasn't until an hour and a half later that the police arrived at his house. His son let them in. Mr Beardmore was upstairs in his bedroom and declined to come down, although the superintendent five times sent the son up to call him. The message brought down by the son was that the police were trespassers (how could Mr Beardmore have known?) and that, by implication, they could regain their status as constables by going away. Nevertheless they went up to see him and required him to undergo a breath test. The breath he expended in rejecting this proposal seemed to the superintendent to smell of alcohol, so he arrested him. At the police station Mr Beardmore again refused a breath test and also declined to provide the usual specimen. The Walsall magistrates dismissed the charges against him on the ground that a trespassing constable is a non-constable, and the police appealed to the Divisional court by "case stated". They won their appeal and John Beardmore decided to challenge them in the House of Lords.

There the five Law Lords (Diplock, Edmund-Davies, Keith, Scarman and Roskill) unanimously held that the High Court had been wrong and the magistrates right. "In order to constitute a valid requirement," said Lord Diplock, "the constable who makes it has to be acting lawfully towards the person whom he requires to undergo a breath test at the moment that he makes the requirement. He is not acting lawfully if he is then committing the tort of trespass on that person's property, for section 8(2) gives him no authority to do so."

Lord Edmund-Davies put it more strongly, regarding the case as "one of great gravity". He found it "unthinkable that a policeman might properly be regarded as acting in the execution of his duty when he was acting unlawfully." If the police above all people, he said, "were seen to flout the law and were yet to be regarded as exercising powers granted to them by Act of Parliament," the result would be diminished respect for the law. The Law Lords seemed to feel that the Divisional Court had concerned itself only with "the common law rights of a motorist" (whatever they are), whereas the case was about the common law rights of a householder.

Police Review August 1, 1980.

Women do it Better

I'm not a feminist (I believe) and have always regarded the women's lib movement as slightly dotty, but in recent years the conviction has been growing upon me that, in the main, women make better magistrates then men. The evidence I can produce is not massive. It doesn't go beyond the fact that I know a lot of magistrates, and that among these the women are easy winners on the grounds of commonsense, freedom from prejudice, and determination to do the right thing if only they can. The pompous asses among them are all men. That's it – the women are not pompous! It's only lately that the probable reason for this has dawned upon me, after much thought. I now equate them with left-handers at cricket, golf and billiards. If you are a left-hander at any of those sports you don't go in for them in any big way unless you can see that you are going to be good. Left-handers are the pick of their lot, the cream of a normally inhibited minority. I suppose these reflections may have something to do with the fact that I recently saw a woman magistrate signing warrants with her left hand, and my own logic should mean that a left-handed woman magistrate can't go wrong. Of course now that I've committed this to paper two things will follow. I shall get letters telling me (not for the first time) that I don't know what I'm talking about, and I shall appear before a left-handed lady beak who will behave abominably and hand my licence for endorsement to a left-handed clerk.

Police Review September 12, 1980.

The Trouble They Took

A friend of mine who was born and lived in Budapest while it was still a desirable place to live in, and has been living in England since it wasn't, has just had his third burglary. While I was still offering apologies for the behaviour of my countrymen, he waved me to silence and assured me that "the behaviour of the police had made it all seem worth while". Why, what did they do? Catch the burglars within minutes? Oh no, they didn't catch anybody. Recover the property? No, they were just marvellous. It was "the trouble they took". They were round within minutes, they spent hours on the premises, they took flash-photos and fingerprints, they questioned neighbours, they measured up this and that, they were marvellous. Now, you have to make considerable allowances for the fact that these East and Middle Europeans have long been used to associating the policeman with the 3 a.m. knock on the door, he has been about as interested in their burglaries and losses as if he were a tramdriver or a customs man. But is there not something pathetic about this gratitude for a display of good intention? I learned later that the second of the three burglaries had been made the occasion for a tutorial demonstration for the benefit of three cadets; and of course the others might have been too. But similar stories from other victims of crime encouraged me to believe that people care more about what the police do *at the time* than about any consequences of what they do.

And now, as if to convict me of sooth-saying, there comes a report on this very subject in the July number of the *British Journal of Criminology* by research officer Mike Maguire of the Oxford Centre for Criminological Research. It is called *The Impact of Burglary upon Victims*, and it reports precisely the same sort of thing. "Those who praised the police." he says (and his research turned up a lot who didn't), "often did so in terms of "the trouble they took" over the case. Significantly, their satisfaction with the police was not affected by whether or not the burglar was eventually detected. . . . Victims were much less concerned with seeing an offender arrested than with receiving what they regarded as *the appropriate response to the incident*. In a state of emotional upset they had telephoned the police almost as an instinctive response." Less then ten per cent of them mentioned the hope that the offender might be caught. In fact I've found, among burgled neighbours, something like a hope that the burglars *wouldn't* be caught, largely because of the ensuing tedium and bother of several court appearances. The first thing they want is their property back (or the insurance money). The next is "an appropriate police response to the incident".

Police Review September 19, 1980.

Not Next to me Please

Somewhere in this country there are about two million ex-criminals who have turned the corner, seen the light, packed it in or found it didn't pay after all. We rub shoulders with them in the streets, buses, trains, pubs, sports stadiums. Because they don't bear some distinguishing brand-mark or have hooks instead of hands, we can't pick them out. If we could, most of us would object to their presence and join any organised demand that they be sent somewhere else. Where? Well, that isn't our business. When I lived in London I was asked by one of my nicest neighbours, who was wearing a pretty dress and carrying a clip-board, if I would please sign a petition to the Greater London Council protesting against the proposed use of a house in our road as a fostering home for children in trouble. I thought I chose the right language in which to decline, but she didn't speak to me again. The fostering home gave no trouble from the moment it was opened about a year later, and some years after that I found myself partly responsible for it as a co-opted member of the G.L.C. Children's Committee.

The villagers at Little Weighton, North Humberside, led by their parish council, are protesting about a proposal to use a two-acre small-holding as a place where offenders complying with "community service orders" can grow crops and make wooden bunks and outdoor tables, all the profits of their work going to the compensation of their victims. The parish clerk feared that the offenders will go into the village and either commit crimes or make plans for the crimes they propose to commit later. Humberside has had a Victim Support Scheme for about 18 months, looking after people suffering from the shock of burglary and other crimes, so there must be *some* local people who can see the need for new methods of tackling the aged problem of crime. Their chairman is the Rev. Peter Vowles, who believes the Little Weighton "victim compensation" plan is the first in the country. If so, I hope it's the first of hundreds, and that the parish council (and such villagers as are supporting it) will be the last to display organised prejudice at its worst.

Police Review October 3, 1980.

Rumpole

I suppose we are all Rumpole addicts, and many of us must know, in real life, seedy, waddling, puffing barristers on whom Mr John Mortimer QC may well have modelled his now famous Rumpole of the Bailey. Myself, I regard him with the affection and gratitude justly earned by Morcambe and Wise. But I wouldn't want to be defended by him. He belongs too firmly in the tradition of Sir Patrick Hastings, whose contemporaries called him Necessity because (they said) he "knows no law". Rumpole still talks of felony and misdemeanour as if those expressions had not been abolished years ago, he talks of "possessing housebreaking implements by night" as if the Larceny Act of 1916 had never been repealed, and in cross-examination he makes longish speeches which not merely shout down the witness who is struggling to answer, but also silence the judge who is ineffectually trying to stop the Rumpole flow. The week before last in his Radio Four version, as portrayed by that superb actor Maurice Denham, he was defending a schoolmaster on a "carnal knowledge" charge. [by the way the girl was just under 16 and provocative, but the poor devil got two years nonetheless.) Does anyone really talk about "unlawful carnal knowledge" these days? Even in the 1976 *Archbold*, where the Index still acknowledged the dear old phrase, it said "*See Sexual Intercourse*". The 1979 *Archbold* doesn't give it a mention. If no-one has yet founded a Friends of Rumpole Society, I hope it will be formed in time to get him a new *Archbold* for Christmas – so long as that won't change his character, which must be preserved at all costs.

Police Review October 17, 1980.

Victim Support Schemes

Last week at a public function I was talking to two men, each of them a man whose name is a household word, and each of them the kind of man who would be most unlikely, in the usual way, to be talking to the likes of me. I won't tell you who they were, because the story reflects adversely on their general intelligence and their awareness of what's going on around them; and they are both good men as well as rich ones, accustomed to forking out in support of good causes. To my astonishment I discovered that neither of them had *ever heard* of the 'Victim Support Schemes' now being formed all over the country, and they were most impressed when I described what these little organisations do. They were specially impressed with the idea of emotional 'first aid' given to burglary or mugging victims, the simple chore of clearing up a ransacked house, getting a cup of tea for a shocked and bewildered householder, arranging and advising about insurance and contacts with the local Crime Prevention Officer, alerting distant family members to the need for support and protection, and all the rest of it. At the time I was talking to these two innocents, there were about 70 Victim Support Schemes, some of them with government financial backing, and the whole thing started seven years ago when the Bristol Police began working with the National Association for the Care and Resettlement of Offenders (NACRO) in the setting-up of such a scheme in the Bristol area. (I shall now be told that it started long before that, and indeed I have an idea that Mr Charles Irving MP was doing it at Cheltenham, but the Bristol one was the first I learned about in detail.)

'Why on earth isn't all this publicised?' said one of my companions. 'I read the papers, listen to my radio, watch the telly quite often. But this is all news to me.' Well, there are people who haven't yet heard of the death of Queen Anne, but one of these two men was only recently the editor of a great British newspaper and he'd be bound to know about Queen Anne, though I didn't specifically test him. There must, however, be something lacking in the publicity accorded to the Victim Support Schemes, something which is not lacking in the news about police-station prisoners being hanged with their own braces, or suing for damages because their braces are taken away and they can't keep their trousers up. Why couldn't the Central Office of Information, for example, take time off from telling me in the middle of my television programmes to wear my seat-belt, and tell the public about the help available to them if and when they have the bad luck to be burgled?

Police Review October 24, 1980.

Crooks' Looks

The British Academy of Forensic Sciences publishes a glossy Quarterly called *Medicine, Science and the Law*. It has a highpowered editorial committee, and since the Academy was founded in 1960 its annual Presidents have included all the most illustrious criminological names you could think of. That being so, you might expect to read in its Quarterly nothing but the sort of articles which break off every few lines to say something like

$$2a\frac{d^2v}{dr^2} = \frac{dv}{dt}$$

Well, that one is actually to be found on page 117 of the April number for this year, and it illuminates an article called *Estimation of Postmortem Interval from Rectal Temperature by Use of Computer*, the joint work of five Japanese members of the Department of Forensic Medicine at Tohoku University, Sendai, Japan. I am reluctant to believe that you don't understand its perfectly clear meaning, though as a matter of fact I don't understand it either, and indeed its message to me, as always, is 'this is not for you, press on and find something written for the less gifted'. And forthright statements for the less gifted are not hard to come by. There is for instance a down-to-earth editorial about the growing and dangerous habit of glue-sniffing, which ends with the ingeniously simple suggestion that all such glues should be required by law to stink so horribly that sniffing them would be no longer a pleasure. (Yes, it *might* be difficult to enforce: 'It is my submission, Sir, that this highly efficient glue stinks badly enough to comply with the law, and I'm afraid I have to ask your Worship to take a sniff'. 'No, no, keep it away from me, I can smell it from here.')

But two men in the Department of Psychology at North East London Polytechnic have discovered that most crime is committed by the unintelligent, and they report their findings in a piece called *The Relationship Between Physical Appearance and Criminality*. They quote with enthusiasm Inspector Robinson's Police Review book, *Catching Criminals, Some Basic Skills* (1978). Inspector Robinson informs police recruits that when he is asked "How can you possibly say that a person looks like a criminal?', he usually says that when policemen talk about their ability to 'feel' or to 'smell' a criminal, what they are really talking about is the ability to see a criminal when they come across one. He even thinks they can state what kind of crime he goes in for. I'm in no doubt that there are policemen who can do this. Most small time crooks are dim-witted people trying to look intelligent with a special motive, and there has always been something about the faces of the poor that can give sudden alertness an appearance of active trickiness. It was the prophet Isaiah who denounced those who 'grind the faces of the poor', but it was the stony-hearted undergraduates in the Oxford Union who debated some years ago the proposition 'that the faces of the poor should be reground'.

Police Review November 21, 1980.

Noxious Self-Defence

There must have been some misgiving about the case against Mrs Caroline Farnejad, aged 28, who pleaded guilty (on legal advice) at West London Magistrates' Court when she was charged with possessing a 'prohibited weapon' for protection against attack (*The Times*, 5 December). It was an aerosol called a 'Sentinel Personal Protector', and her solicitor said it had been bought legally in the United States by a friend. The police witness said he was satisfied that it was for her own protection and not for offensive use. It seems that the effect of the spray would be to mark the assailant with a red dye, and by pleading guilty to the charge Mrs Farnejad has declared that the Sentinel Personal Protector is 'a weapon designed or adapted for the discharge of a noxious liquid'. I suppose it all depends upon what the legislators meant by 'noxious'. The dictionaries seem to agree that it means harmful or injurious and that it comes from the Latin *noxa* meaning harm. I suppose any kind of aerosol-propelled liquid or gas could be injurous to the eyes, at least in the sense of causing some temporary discomfort, but I wouldn't myself call that noxiousness. Even if it were it's a lot less noxious than a man who attacks women, and I should like to see every would-be rapist sprayed from head to foot with a dye that wouldn't come off until he was too old to bother, either about getting it off or about how it got there. I can't help wishing Mrs Farnejad hadn't pleaded guilty.

Police Review December 26, 1980.

Gresham's Law and Mrs Whitehouse

I've often thought that the state of literature, the stage, and the film industry (and even, I suppose, television) could be improved if there were a public organisation which, unlike the National Viewers and Listeners Association, existed to encourage the good instead of all this breast-beating about the bad. There's plenty of bad writing, plays, films and TV of course, some of it bad enough to stink. I go along with Mr John Mortimer QC, who thinks it would be 'highly inequitable that the talented should be permitted access to erotic fields' if the 'clumsy, talentless majority' were kept out.

Rotten scribblers, that is to say, must be allowed to scribble material that stinks. 'We should not only be able to defend to the death other people's right to say things with which we disagree; we must also allow them to do it in abominable prose'. The fear behind Mrs Whitehouse's organisation is the fear of a kind of Gresham's Law, namely that the bad will eventually drive out the good, just as a two-metal currency encourages the cheaper form to be used while the posher one is exported.

But we might in this matter take a lesson from Germany, where the Protestant churches present an annual money prize for films of quality shown at the Berlin Festival. The French government goes (rather riskily) further, putting a tax on pornographic films and using the money to reward films of artistic merit. I must say I can't think of any committee I would entrust with the job of classifying British plays or books as liable to a porno-tax, but I think the rewards of producing 'decent' literature, that is to say books, plays and films which don't stink, are pitiably small. That's how Mrs Whitehouse's organisation could usefully be supplanted by a society for the material encouragement of the good to the point at which it would begin to drive out the bad.

Police Review January 2, 1981.

On Leaving Out 'Not'

Some of our words are too short; too short, that is to say, for the job they have to do. You can often write a clear sentence in words of one syllable, and the sentence above was designed to prove it. But one word which is too short for its importance is 'not'. If it gets in where it doesn't belong, it does such a lot of harm. It got into my column in the issue of 19/26 December, under the heading Not Guilty By My Direction, which (for you won't remember) was about judges telling juries they must acquit. Two men had got off at Manchester Crown Court because prosecuting counsel had failed to turn up in time, and I said this was a piece of cake for them because they had intended to plead guilty anyway. This appeared in print, possibly because of pre-Christmas gremlins, as 'intended to plead NOT guilty anyway', thus making bilge of the whole thing. I cried. It reminded me that I once sent a police letter to a lady whose King Charles spaniel had abducted 4½ lbs of steak from a butcher's shop, and the letter was meant to say that prosecution was not being recommended. The typist left out the word 'not', and touched off a correspondence that swelled the file by 300%. I'm not pleading for long words, but we do need a longer word for implying negation, some word that simply *couldn't* get itself left out or wrongfully put in. And if you think I'm indulging in floccinaucinihilipilification, you can look that one up and see how wrong you are. (You'll find it in the *Concise Oxford Dictionary* and the *Guinness Book of Records*.)

Police Review January 9, 1981.

After Lunch on the Bench

At Weston-super-Mare a man has been tried twice for careless driving because he thought the lady chairman was asleep during the first hearing. When he appealed the judges said she should have retired from the case when the defending solicitor suggested it, but they made the rather surprising decision that the case must go back for a fresh hearing (*R v Weston-super-Mare Justices, ex parte Taylor (Daily Telegraph* January 30). On January 29, which was 18 months after the original trial, the man was retried by two magistrates imported from Bristol for the occasion. They found him not guilty. The lady chairman in the first trial had said in an affidavit that it was her custom to close her eyes and look down. (Mine too, but then I'm usually asleep).

I feel entitled to reveal that it was a much respected Appeal Court Judge who once (in my presence) told of a lady chairman at what was then called Quarter Sessions who fell fast asleep after lunch, sitting next to him on the bench. A girl was giving evidence in a rape trial, the prisoner being a lorry driver who had given her a lift. He had made a suggestion to her which she couldn't be persuaded to repeat in open court. Yes, she would write it down. The result was passed up to the Bench, the judge read it and, having carefully laid it in front of the slumbering magistrate, jogged her with his elbow. With a start she awoke and read it through. She turned and glared incredulously at the judge over the tops of her spectacles. 'Have you taken leave of your senses?' she hissed.

Police Review February 13, 1981.

From the Passenger's Seat

I know that lightning is alleged never to strike twice in the same place, but I've never believed it and a report in *The Times* diary on January 8 supports my scepticism. It concerned a man driving in France last summer in a British-bought Citroen with a right-hand drive. The police stopped him and passed a breathalyser bag through the left-hand window. The front passenger inflated the bag, handed it back, and was told the result was negative and he could proceed. I don't know whether the driver had been drinking or not, but I do know that an exactly similar thing happened to a friend of mine in this country last year. He was at the wheel of a left-hand-drive Renault and the lady sitting next to him was handed a breathalyser bag through the right hand-window. She blew into it and got the clearance when it had been examined. Both parties assure me that neither of them had been drinking, and indeed the driver is a teetotaller. But there's a moral there somewhere about the better side to sit when driving.

Police Review February 20, 1981.

By the Nine Gods

In my one-time bailiwick we used to have a justices' clerk who was known as Lars Porsena. This was because of his daily insistence that everyone giving evidence in 'his court' should take the oath properly. Lars Porsena (the title was the ancient Roman equivalent of Lord Porsena) was one of the heroes in Macaulay's *Lays of Ancient Rome*, in which the story of Horatius begins with:

Lars Porsena of Clusium
By the nine gods he swore
That the great house of Tarquin
Should suffer wrong no more.

There was no slovenly oath-taking in any court presided over by Lars Porsena – and I say 'presided over' because that's literally what he did, the magistrates toeing the line like everyone else. 'Stand up properly,' he used to say, glaring over the tops of his glasses. 'Take the Book in your right hand properly', 'Read that oath properly', and so on. I forget what happened about left-handed people or anyone whose right hand was missing. Incidentally he got a fearful jolt one day when a witness from Lazard's Bank, who must have been made of the same kind of stuff, asked him who he thought he was and thundered that he was quite used to taking the oath in court and would do it in the way that bound him. (I didn't see this episode myself, and have spent the subsequent years trying to visualise Lars Porsena's face at the end of it.)

It recurs to my mind because I've noticed that among recent

changes in the law there has appeared a provision which preserves the ancient custom of Scottish courts to make their witnesses extend their right arms while oath-taking. To the ignorant Sassenach, if only he were permitted to make jokes about the Scots, it looks like the Nazi salute: but in Scotland at least it's a dignified process, and even the judge, sheriff or magistrate stands up while it is done. In England we have recently begun taking a kind of antiquarian interest in the oath, and it all seems to suggest that we may one day get rid of it altogether. We have just repealed the Unlawful Oaths Act 1797, the Act under which six Dorset farm labourers (the Tolpuddle Martyrs) were sentenced in 1834 to transportation for swearing-in new members of a Lodge. They took their little oath with uplifted hands too, which must have seemed worse to the outraged authorities. But today, in section 3 of the Oaths Act 1978, it is expressly provided that

> *if any person to whom an oath is administered desires to swear with uplifted hand, in the form and manner in which an oath is usually administered in Scotland, he shall be permitted to do so . . .*

It may be that the repeal of the 1797 Act has come just in time to legalise the decision of the Northamptonshire Labour Party to make their candidates, in the May council elections, swear an oath of loyalty to the Labour Party, just to stop them going off and joining the new Social Democrats' group.

Police Review March 27, 1981.

Drink and the Devil

'There is no settled practice,' says Professor Glanville Williams in his *Textbook of Criminal Law* (p.418), 'on the question whether intoxication mitigates or aggravates an offence. Courts sometimes say the one, sometimes the other'. (And so they do.) 'Probably,' he goes on, 'the usual effect is to mitigate, since the judge hopes that the offence, if due to drink or drugs, was "out of character" and so is the less likely to be repeated if the defendant is given moderate punishment, or enabled to receive medical treatment'. The law, he says later, though it doesn't like drunkenness, has to recognise that it is relevant where it affects intention or recklessness.

I find that lately I've become a bit of a puritan about this, partly under doctor's orders. In this country we have already accepted the principle that being drunk makes dangerous driving worse. How long will it be before we line up with Mr Lev Smirnov, Chairman of the Soviet Supreme Court, who has just told a plenary meeting of the USSR judges that crimes committed in drunkenness should be dealt with more severely, not less severely, and that they should make wide use of their powers to prescribe enforced curative treatment for alcoholics? The Soviet authorities have admitted, at long last, that 'every second juvenile arrested' is drunk at the time of the offence for which the arrest is made.

I don't believe that we in this country have any idea of the part played in crime, not by 'drunkenness' (which is a vague enough term anyway) but by Dutch courage, by the effect of alcohol in dulling the faculty of self-criticism even in people who seem stone cold sober. I'd be glad to see Lord Avebury taken seriously in his recent accusations about tipsy MPs in the House of Commons. On April 6 he told an international conference on alcoholism that plenty of political leaders impair their intellectual capacity and their judgement by drinking too much (which they certainly do, and I've drunk too much in their company while they were doing it); and he added that 'records show that at the height of the Second World War there were times when Winston Churchill was paralytically drunk'. I don't know how reliable that is, and most people close to the Old Man are denying it, but it's the kind of statement which will get alcoholism into the headlines. I could once have named a dozen MPs who were all semi-permanently plastered, in or out of the House, or anyway functioning at an impaired level. But why don't we admit, as Lord Avebury has admitted (and he used to like a drink or two before he turned teetotal eight years ago) that drink-sodden minds are struggling with many of our top jobs and committing a vast amount of our crime? It's a question of literally staggering importance.

Police Review April 17, 1981.

Not Yet, Minister

I was delighted to see in *The Times* of April 22 a letter from Professor Glanville Williams urging that the Government should abandon the long-established habit of shoving committee reports into pigeon-holes and pretending they never happened. 'When a government asks busy and knowledgeable people,' says Professor Glanville Williams, 'to give their unpaid service on a committee,' it should act on the advice they duly give 'unless it sees sufficient reasons to the contrary'. And not only should the members then be told why their advice is being ignored – it should be the Minister himself who tells them, if only on the ground of courtesy, *and* he should listen to any comments they have to offer when they've been told. This would go a long way to dispel the belief that recommendations from Royal Commissions or Select Committees are commonly pole-axed by senior civil servants (my guess is that this is more than a belief).

If it turns out that Professor Glanville Williams has started something here, it may well prove also that the BBC's wickedly funny television programme *Yes, Minister* will have paved the way for it. On a recent Radio Four *Inside Parliament* programme (11.15 on Sunday nights), a House of Commons Select committee was questioning Mr Wille Whitelaw about *Yes Minister*. The committee obviously loved it and thought Mr Whitelaw should love it too. He loved bits of it, he said cautiously. Controlled enthusiasm, no actual falling about.

But if you don't hear the Radio Four *Inside Parliament* programme on Sunday nights (it's a bit late for a man on early turn) please let me commend it to you, if only as an antidote to the appalling exposure of *Today in Parliament*, with which the BBC is gradually establishing the Commons as a kind of cross between a Brixton riot and a Persian market. This must be doing irreparable damage to the parliamentary image, occasioning baseless fears as to the true value of what we still call democracy.

Police Review May 1, 1981.

Police Sirens

I'd made up my mind that (just to be different) I would have nothing to say about the Yorkshire Ripper, or the conundrums he has been setting for the jury, or the huge sums of money being paid out by the press to all the hangers-on who believe they have a story to tell about him, or whether a genuine madman can discuss his own madness and what the law will think of it; but Mr Michael Hutchison, QC, in a letter to *The Times* on May 1, has raised one aspect of it that won't get discussed elsewhere and deserves an airing. He quoted a news report to the effect that 'a police convoy with sirens wailing brought Sutclife to the Old Bailey,' and he went on to say 'we have to put up with enough sirens *necessarily* sounded in cases of emergency, and the authorities concerned should stop this gratuitous and now widespread practice when defendants are being driven to court'.

I don't know the history of this ear-shattering hee-haw or how it came to supplant the good old bell once used by police, ambulances and fire brigade vehicles alike, though I suspect that it takes its origin from some Common Market agreement ('all good Common Market citizens should make the same kind of filthy row in emergencies'). But while the television news-pictures of the Black Maria taking the Ripper from Brixton to the Old Bailey didn't bear out Mr Hutchison's complaint, or rather his endorsement of someone else's complaint – the sirens were making no sound in the pictures I saw – I feel emboldened to report that I myself regard the hee-hawing of all these vehicles as offensive in the extreme and have frequently wished them in hell, where they will probably blend perfectly with the general scenario. Gongs, sirens, and 'two-tone horns', forbidden to anyone else, are permitted as a fitting on fire brigade, salvage corps, ambulance and police vehicles, Forestry Commission vehicles on fire-fighting jobs, bomb disposal vehicles, Blood Transfusion Service cars, coastguard vehicles on rescue work, National Coal Board vehicles on rescue operations at mines, RAF Mountain Rescue Service vehicles dealing with crashed aircraft and other emergencies, and RNLI vehicles launching lifeboats.

But that's only when they can be 'fitted' (Motor Vehicles Construction and Use Regulations 1978, Reg. 29(5).) What about using them? Their use is permissible (says Regulation 118) *only* when

necessary or desirable either to indicate to other road users the urgency of the purposes for which the vehicle is being used, or to warn other road users of the presence of the vehicle on the road.

Nothing else. Does anyone really believe their use is confined to these purposes? If he does, let him come and sit in my cottage and nip to the window whenever one of these stentors goes by. More likely than not, he will find that the road is denuded of 'other road users' for as far as the eye can see, and he will conclude (as I concluded long ago) that the crew on the vehicle simply like making a row. Even so, he won't necessarily be right, for I've recently learned that there is not always agreement among the crews as to the amount and frequency of the din which is justifiable, and that hee-hawing enthusiasts have been sometimes told by their companions to go easy with the snorter. For my money, they could go a lot easier, making due allowance for my being in the ambulance with a raging appendix.

Police Review May 15, 1981.

Officiously to Keep Alive

Arthur Hugh Clough, who died in 1861, was not only a great theological scholar but also a wicked comic. He compiled what he called *The Latest Decalogue*, an up-dated version of the Ten Commandments. It included such directions as: 'Do not adultery commit: Advantage rarely comes of it', and 'Thou shalt have one God only: who would be at the expense of two?', and 'Thou shalt not steal, an empty feat, when it's so lucrative to cheat'. And one commandment said 'Thou shalt not kill, but need'st not strive officiously to keep alive.' This is the one that everybody remembers, lawyers particularly. It represents one of the gaps in English law. Professor Kenny, in his *Outlines of Criminal Law*, gives as an example the man who finds someone lying face downwards in a puddle, with mouth and nose submerged and unable to move. If the man watches him drown, lifting no finger to help him, he nonetheless commits no offence known to English law.

Last month at a lakeside holiday village north of Montreal a man named Jean Desjardins was reading a newspaper on the porch of his holiday cabin when he noticed that his wife swimming 100 yards from the shore, was drowning. So he went on reading. (The marriage had gone a bit stale, after 23 years.) A nine-year-old boy saw what was going on but was unable to swim so far. He rushed to his parents' cabin to tell them. But Mrs Desjardins had drowned, and her inactive husband was charged with murder. The judge reminded him that as he watched his wife drown, he had had on his porch a 20 ft length of rope with which he could have saved her, poor swimmer though he might be. 'You allowed her to die,' said the judge, 'but there is nothing the law can do. You cannot be punished for anything. Under the law as it is, it is not a crime to watch someone in distress and not render assistance. I would like to see the law changed, and this case may go a long way to doing that'. But the new widower walked freely from the court, and it *may* be that his story will reach the notice of our own Law Commission or the Criminal Law Revision Committee, for the law of Montreal is in this respect the same as ours. Quite a lot of people die because those in charge of them do not 'strive officiously' to keep them alive.

Police Review June 12, 1981.

No Sex Please, We're Romans

Whenever I see the criminal law in operation as a punisher in the field of sexual morality, I silently weep for it. I could line up with Mrs Whitehouse if she saw the cast of *The Romans in Britain,* Mr Howard Brenton's play, as a lot of idiots cavorting around starkers because they wanted to feel like randy Roman warriors, to be tut-tutted at as if they were three-year-olds making discoveries. But if there are no real privacies left in Mrs Whitehouse's world or mine (I think there are very few), they can't be restored by punishing playwrights and drama producers. That's the inexorable way of ensuring that the decencies get buried still deeper. The 1960 prosecution of Penguin Books for daring to publish *Lady Chatterley's Lover* earned that book millions of excited and then disappointed readers who would otherwise never have seen it.

The current prosecution of the National Theatre's director for staging the latest bit of limelit depravity could have the effect, whatever the jury's verdict, of herding into the theatres myriads of people who have been content to believe, hitherto, that they were boringly decent places and that the best you could get, in the way of dramatised odiousness, was to be had at home on the telly. Why, Mrs Whitehouse's campaign has even got the naked Roman warriors' photographs on to the nine o'clock news for all the world to see (and right idiots they looked, too). The criminal law's the wrong corrective, Mrs W.

Police Review July 10, 1981.

Where Have All The Uniforms Gone?

That is the plaintive last line of a letter in the *Daily Telegraph* of August 1. Its writer had seen an unkempt-looking man trying to force the garage doors of neighbours who were away on holiday, and challenged him. Oh, he was from the Gas Board and wanted to read the meter. He got no reply to his knocks on the front door. 'As a means of identification he brandished a book'. The good neighbour watched him for a while and saw that he went to other houses, where he was admitted with his book and was therefore probably all right. The next day the good neighbour, surely a crime prevention officer's dream, saw another unkempt man 'walking across my neighbour's garden and other gardens, not using the paths, and he turned out to be a postman'. And 'in neither case,' said the letter, 'was it apparent that these men were public employees. In these lawless days it would greatly help the public if such employees could be instantly recognised. Where have all the uniforms gone?'

Some years ago I did a series of BBC European Service broadcasts called *The Man in Uniform*, all about the various people who call at your door on missions connected with gas, electricity, water, mail, telephones, and so on. They all had a uniform of sorts — even the dustman. The idea (it wasn't actually mine) was that in this country, as contrasted with the benighted countries across the Channel, a helmet or a peaked cap was not something to be frightened of, and you could (for example) go up to a policeman in the street and actually speak to him without being arrested. A few years later a daily paper thought we could do a similar series for English readers — and then we realised that the title wouldn't do any more. It would have to be *The Man on Your Doorstep* because they didn't come in uniforms any more. (By the way, my postman has just called and handed me a letter through my ground floor window, afternoon delivery. It's very hot today. He's bare-headed and in open-necked shirt and braces, and good luck to him. If I were doing his job, which God forbid, I'd be similarly dressed except that the shirt would be more obviously St. Michael's.) But who can doubt that in this country anyway, a uniform is *some* guarantee of dependability? In a general way I'm against uniformity and regimentation, but might this not be an exception? I'm allowing for the fact that uniforms can be easily obtained and imitated, but even a peaked cap is *some* kind of reassurance. Nowadays not even a taxi driver bothers about that.

Police Review August 14, 1981.

Buttons and Bows

This time of the year, cricket nearly over, swallows beginning to pack their bags, is the period of conferences. As the seaside hotels lose their bed-and-breakfast holidaymakers, they fill up with great bodies of men and women who are willing to sit for long and heavy hours listening to delegates shouting at them from a long platform decorated with flowers.

'Conference maketh a ready man,' said Lord Bacon, without saying what it made him ready for, though he may have foreseen a growing national readiness to leap from the armchair and switch off the telly. Television has, in fact, ensured that a national conference, of scientists, theologians, boilermakers, politicians, teachers or lepidopterists, can now bore the pants off an entire nation instead of earning a standing ovation (or, more often, a crouching ovation) inside the hall itself for stentors who have at last decided to sit down. But this year, they tell me, conference delegates and audiences face a new problem. The lapel-badge industry has found a new way of boosting its sales.

Lapel buttons have seldom been big enough for anyone to read without coming close, and in recent years they have been growing larger. They have reached postcard size, and in the autumn the streets of Brighton, Blackpool and Scarborough are thronged with men and women wearing postcards declaring their names and allegiances. If you happen to live in such a town and you enjoy a tiny joke, you can now buy a postcard-sized badge saying something like GAY WHALES AGAINST RACISM, or I WAS A COPTIC MONK BUT MY HAIR KEPT GROWING, or even A WOMAN NEEDS A MAN LIKE A FISH NEEDS A BICYCLE. I haven't seen these, but a friend has sent me a specimen which says I ONLY TALK TO ANIMALS. Harmless enough, you might think, but some earnest delegates to the serious conferences are objecting and want something done about it. 'Wanting something done' always means done by the police. What should they do? 'Insulting behaviour'? Good old insulting behaviour.

Police Review September 18, 1981.

Hedging About Road Signs

Round my way the farmers have taken their cue from the local authority (ie, saving money left and right), and have happily left their hedge-trimming to look after itself. It doesn't look after itself, with the result that, even where there's a roadside footpath, you are continually stepping out into the roadway to avoid being scalped by overhanging holly or blackthorn. Prudent and resourceful walkers go equipped with a pair of secateurs. A specially urgent outcome of all this is that white lines are buried under creeping undergrowth and speed-limit signs are engulfed in privet, elm and ivy. So are a lot of the route-markers, and the number of lost motorists increases week by week.

It seems to be the same in Northamptonshire, where a motorist succeeded, on September 17, in getting a speeding conviction quashed on the ground that a 30 mph sign was covered — *by grass*! My local 30 mph signs are too high up for the kind of grass we can grow round here, but we are doing our best with every other kind of vegetation; and the coming winter, when the leaves are down, will probably reveal a lot of once-familiar commands we've forgotten all about. Still, it occurs to me that if the local council wants to save money it could also save much ill-temper (and possibly lives) by moving all the road signs to positions where they simply *can't* be covered in vegetation. It would be a one-off expense for the ratepayers.

For example, in 1976 Essex County Council suddenly found that all its 30 mph signs had flat-topped threes, and didn't conform either to the Highway Code or to the Traffic Signs (Speed Limit) Regulations and General Directions 1969. They had to be changed to round-topped threes, because they *could* otherwise be mistaken for fives. There were 2,000 threes to be altered, and it cost the ratepayers (who were very fed up about it) no less than £40,000. But it seems to me that having figures the wrong shape is less dangerous than having figures which no-one can even see; and that if it's worth while to spend £40,000 on changing the tops of 2,000 threes, you could justifiably spend quite a lot on putting the threes where nature couldn't obliterate them. But I doubt that my local council will read this.

Police Review October 2, 1981.

The Gas-filled Room

On September 26 there was a report in *The Times* about a man found dead in a gas-filled room at the top of a four-storey house in Orlando Road, Clapham. He had been lying dead there for 10 months, although the neighbours had complained of the smell of gas and the 10 months' rent (at £20 a week) had presumably gone unpaid. When at last the police were called they couldn't be sure that gas was still coming from the unlighted gas fire — it was turned on but the room was so full of gas that (for all they could tell) the supply might have been turned off elsewhere. The Gas Board said it was trying to find out why nothing had been done about unpaid gas bills. There should be an interesting inquest.

But I relate the story here because it recalls the fate of an old colleague of mine who, as a sergeant, was called to investigate a very similar situation. He managed to spring the lock and push the door open. There were thousands who wished he hadn't: he was a popular chap and a good friend of the community. The gas was of the lighter-than-air variety and had built up downwards, so to speak, until the only space clear of gas was the 12 or 18 inches at floor level. In the room was a gas-driven refrigerator with a pilot-light at the bottom.

The pushing open of the door was just sufficient to press the mass of escaped gas down to meet the pilot-jet and there was a huge explosion, killing the sergeant instantly. Of course we all said, with the grief and wisdom of hindsight, that you should never push open a door into a gas-filled room. You should never go in by the door at all unless it opened outwards. If it didn't you should smash a window and get the windows open.

I mention it here because I've recently come across a belief that the modern North Sea gas is *heavier* than air and that an escaped mass would build upwards from the floor. It isn't and it wouldn't. Its behaviour in this respect is precisely the same as that of the old gas, and I have taken the trouble to telephone the Gas Board to make sure.

Police Review October 9, 1981.

Speaks With An Irish Accent

I'm rather interested in the decline of Spoken English, because I am quite certain that the London kids I played with in my several elementary schools were more agreeable to listen to than their descendants are. No one seems to care a damn about this. Children are taught the pronunciation of French and German, and given fanciful ideas as to how the Romans pronounced their Latin, but no one now tries to tell them how to pronounce their own language. So what is happening is that a dreadful, flat, lazy, aitchless, glottal style of English is spreading outwards from London throughout the Home Counties and will eventually engulf the whole country. Why? Why not start teaching English as a *spoken* language? The trouble is, you would have to start with the teachers, who nowadays instruct their little victims in the very accent I'm moaning about.

There was once a special kind of confidence trickster (he may be still around, I don't know) of whom the Police Informations always said 'Speaks with an Irish accent'. What was this? Cork, Dublin, Londonderry? They could hardly be more different, English being the common speech origin of all those fine cities. I happen to believe (though many people would be glad to shoot me down) that the best English in these islands is spoken in Dublin, but is that the *'Irish* accent'? After the terrorist outrage at Chelsea Barracks, Scotland Yard asked that people — especially landladies — who had noticed recent arrivals with 'Irish' accents should tell the police about them. This is really most unfair in its implications, and probably counterproductive. The *Ulster* accent is much more like Lowland Scots, and anyway is nothing like the Irish accent known to the British public through such heroes as Terry Wogan, Val Doonican and Frank Delaney. A police appeal giving examples of the RC Belfast voice might produce much more helpful leads. As it is, the blonde girl portrayed so imaginatively by the police artist might well be another Dr Rose Dugdale, with an English public-school and pony-club accent. Somehow these drawings and photofits and cloth-eared reactions to 'accents' are becoming a specially expensive kind of red herring. Think of the Yorkshire Ripper and his supposed Sunderland accent on the famous tape-recording. That must have cost a few lives? The study of local accent ought to be in every CID syllabus.

Police Review November 27, 1981.

Merry Village Chime

No doubt the Western world is divided into two great classes of citizens, those who love church bells and chiming clocks (headed by Sir John Betjeman) and those who hate 'em. I'm among the latter. I've spent totally sleepless nights in French, German and English village hotels on account of town hall clocks which banged out the quarter-hours throughout the night. To me all bells are discordant anyway, because their notes run into each other (no check-action), and every set of bells I've ever heard included at least two which were out of tune in the way that constricts the throat. Their sole claim to redemption lies in the fact that, when on night duty, you could usually tell when it was time to go in for refreshments.

So I mourn for Mr Colin Thompson, the landlord of the Red Lion at Twyford (whose pints I have sampled), because in a desperate effort to get some sleep he sought a County Court injunction to stop the quarter-hour chimes of the church clock of St Mary's, Twyford, Bucks, between 11 pm and 8 am. This seems to me a modest proposal, speaking as a man who would gladly see the ghastly things banned altogether like sonic booms or hooters on stationary vehicles. But Mr Colin Thompson was opposed in court by a succession of old gaffers who told the judge that the bells had rung out all their lives, they loved them, a chiming clock was 'a comforting sound at night', poor Mr Thompson 'must be neurotic if he can't sleep through it', and turning the chimes off 'would upset the whole village.' The vicar clinched it by saying that his parishioners were 'angry and afraid' (!). Not a rational thing, he said. It was something 'deep inside people's hearts.' So the bells clang on, and Mr Thompson has lost a lot of money in legal costs. I'm sending him a small cheque, inspired to some extent by the fact that when I go (as I occasionally do) to our small village church to hear my wife play the organ voluntaries, the opening one is often inaudible because a rope-tugging fanatic is bang-bang-banging away with a toneless bell which means nothing to anyone — and certainly calls no one to prayer.

Police Review December 4, 1981.

Corrective Ridicule

We pride ourselves, as a nation, on the humanitarian nature of the punishments we inflict on our lawbreakers, and in 1688 we made William III put his signature, as a condition of becoming king, to a so-called Bill of Rights. This is the document which says that 'there shall be inflicted no cruel and unusual punishments'. The same phrase appears in the American Constitution and in the 1950 European Convention on Human Rights. No one seems to know what the phrase really means. In 1968 the U.S. Supreme Court outlawed the death penalty as a cruel and unusual punishment, after using it for 250 years. The Council of Europe has ruled that the infliction of the birch in the Isle of Man (where they want to go on doing it) is a cruel and unusual punishment. No international court has yet ruled, or so far as I know been asked to rule, that detention in our crammed and stinking local prisons is a cruel and unusual punishment; but this may be because so many occupants of the local prisons are not being punished at all, but merely locked up while we find out whether they have done anything wrong. They are being subjected, that is to say, to a cruel and unusual regime of non-punishment; and so far this hasn't been condemned.

But if we are content with a system which can treat its social captives like that, and can *then* turn them loose in a finger-pointing and scornful society, how can we pretend that it would be retrograde to punish offenders by ridicule? Katharine Whitehorn suggested in *The Observer* of November 8 (and I think she was being serious though with Miss Whitehorn you can never be all that sure) that bottom-pinchers should be 'made to parade round a typing college with placards saying "I can only get my kicks by pinching bottoms" '. The law, she thinks, would be much less of an ass if it could find ways of making a man make an ass of himself. After all (she recalls) in the Middle Ages you put someone in the stocks for mildly bad behaviour, and everyone could come and throw eggs at him. The trouble was, people came and threw bricks, just as if a man in the stocks was a Brixton policeman. The village constable had to stand by and ensure that only non-lethal missiles were thrown . . . But maybe we ought to be more honest about this business of ridicule. It would be a good beginning to admit that the whole criminal process contains a strong leavening of ridicule already; and take it from there.

Police Review December 11, 1981.

Wrongs of Finders

'There are many decisions, hard to reconcile,' says the new *Oxford Companion to Law*, 'on whether property found in public places, or in private premises, belong (sic) 'to the finder or to the occupier of the premises.' I've fallen out of love with the *Oxford Companion to Law,* which at first I greeted with great enthusiasm, and here it is actually suggesting that found property *belongs* to finders and occupiers — it belongs to no one other than the owner. But everyone must agree, at any rate, that the decisions as to *lawful custody* and contingent ownership of found property have been in a mess for years, certainly since *Bridges v Hawkesworth* (1851), which said that goods found in a shop, though given up by the finder to the shopkeeper so that the find may be advertised, may be recovered from the shopkeeper by the finder. Subsequent decisions have tended to concern themselves with the question whether the article was found in the 'public' or 'private' part of the shop (eg on which side of the counter), with endless possibilities for argument about shop geography.

So I suppose we should welcome *Parker v British Airways Board (The Times,* December 23), which has added to the existing mass of law the surely important consideration whether the shopkeeper (or other occupier) has shown 'any intention to exercise control over the building' and the things which may be found in it. Mr Alan Parker, one of Heathrow's posher passengers, was in the International Executive Lounge at the airport when he found a gold bracelet on the floor. He seems to have known enough about the law of 'finders' rights' to be aware that the bracelet was his as against everyone but the true owner, but that he must take steps to find the loser. He had already been through Customs and Security to reach the lounge, and must have had a first class ticket and boarding permit. It seems likely that his flight had just been called and he was pushed for time. Anyway, said Lord Justice Donaldson in the Court of Appeal, 'he gave the bracelet to an anonymous British Airways official instead of to the police', supplying also his name and address and asking that the bracelet be returned to him if not claimed. British Airways proceeded to sell it for £850.

Mr Parker sued them in a county court and was awarded the £850 plus £50 interest. Believe it or not, British Airways appealed. In the Court of Appeal Lord Donaldson pointed out that, among all the conflicting previous decisions, there wasn't one which was binding on the Court of Appeal and that Court therefore had 'the right and the duty to extend and adapt the common Law in the light of established principles and the current needs of the community'. The Appeal Court judges found that Mr Parker had acted with absolute honesty, had a full finder's rights and obligations, discharged them by handing over the bracelet, and had not had his entitlement displaced by any assertion of entitlement by British Airways. (It would have been different if he had been a British Airways employee.) And as the true owner had never come forward, it was (said his Lordship) 'a case of finders keepers'. Lord Justice Eveleigh and Sir David Cairns agreed. I don't know whether they left it at that (the *Times* report stops there), but as I understand it Mr Parker will *never* become anything more than the 'keeper' unless and until the loser comes forward and relinquishes ownership. But the law has certainly been clarified, and it has been done by the always agreeable spectacle of awarding the verdict to David while Goliath still lies on the ground.

Police Review January 8, 1982.

Rape and Normality

Anyone who has the gall to write a weekly column like this, and who pretends to keep it topical, learns to give 'topical' a wide meaning and keep quiet about current news stories until they have worked themselves out. One exception, of course, is the English climate. Last week I chose to write about snow and by the time I got into print the snow had all gone. If I now add some kind of postscript to the Great Rape Season, I shall not be implying that the rape has all gone. Like all other crimes in the annual criminal statistics, rape maintains a mysterious constancy. Roughly 1,000 rapes every year in England and Wales, and so it has gone on for a very long time. The annual figures for every sort of crime are so similar that the statistical tables look like symmetrically patterned wallpaper, and I've never been able to understand how the qualified statisticians in places like the Home Office can look at them without laughing. But they can and do, and people like you and me are supposed to accept them as valid and reliable.

But at any rate we know what to think about parliamentary allegations like the one wrapped up in the question put to the Prime Minister on January 26 by Mr Nigel Fisher, Tory MP for Surbiton: 'Is she aware of the public concern about the increasing number of offences of rape?' The only increase is in the space given by Press and broadcasting editors to their rape correspondents, which in turn is brought about by some particularly asinine judicial decisions and some specially horrific examples of the crime. Ministers are bullied by circumstances into short-term promises about fresh legislation, with their inevitable sequel — an obscurely reported backing-down, as when a 90-minute meeting of Ministers at Number 10 on January 26 was followed by an announcement that there would be no legislative changes, and in particular no mandatory sentences for convicted rapists.

No doubt it was an instance of Sods' Law that the famous BBC programme 'POLICE' went out in the middle of the current excitement, and that particular example of police interrogation has been justly described by Mr John Duke, Chief Constable of Hampshire, as a 'blatant, inept, Star Chamber performance . . . offensive to any fair-minded person, inside or outside the service'. (It wasn't offensive, by the way, to Mr Peregrine Worsthorne of the *Sunday Telegraph,* who usually gets in more common sense to the square inch than most of his contemporary pundits. The girl, he wrote on January 24, 'took it in her stride — indeed, the final sequence saw her laughing and flirting with one of her "persecutors"; and the suave sympathy and polite circumlocution so beloved of the middle class might well have embarrassed her far more acutely than crude directness, which seemed in fact to put her surprisingly at ease'.)

As it is, the uproar itself will have had a better effect than any kind of legislation, and among the good effects will be a new line of thought, or whatever it is that goes on between their ears, on the part of those men who maintain that rape is quite impossible. I suppose they can visualise no kind of victim other than a woman violently struggling, kicking and screaming, and could never imagine the helplessness induced by terror or even insensibility. These men still exist and they move about among us, taking up room, eating valuable food, filling in public opinion forms, and voting.

Police Review February 5, 1982.

Escape From Custody

Last November I had a letter from a senior constable (he in now within 18 months of retirement) who was facing disciplinary charges as a result of losing a prisoner. He assured me that he didn't in the least mind if I identified him in print, but it turned out that I minded more than he did. I wrote nothing about his case at the time, and propose to write nothing now except to say that he was merely cautioned. But his case raised the general question of liability for escaping prisoners, and I found that there was much divergency of police practice. I met a chief constable, for example, who thought it was barbaric to punish anyone for escaping or attempting to escape, since the desire to regain one's freedom is a natural instinct and shouldn't be denied. During the war, he pointed out, British officers were expected to escape from their internment camps if they possibly could. If an escape was to be punishable in anyone, the person punished ought to be the custodian — policeman, prison officer, escort, etc.

But the fact remains that escaping from lawful custody is one of the few remaining Common Law offences, and so is 'negligently permitting a prisoner to escape'. It is also one of those offences (legal purists like to pretend they don't exist) which requrie the defendant to prove his innocence. 'It is not necessary to prove negligence on the part of the constable,' says Hale's *Pleas of the Crown:* 'the law implies it'. If there was no negligence, if the prisoner got away by force or was rescued by others, and the constable pursued him but lost him, all this has to be proved by the defence.

I was reminded of all this by a case that came from Jamaica to the Privy Council on January 25 *(Dillon v The Queen, The Times* January 26). The appellant, a police constable, was on duty at the central police station in Kingston, Jamaica. Two prisoners got away and the constable was convicted of negligently permitting their escape from lawful custody. For complicated local reasons there was a doubt whether their custody was in fact lawful, and the Privy Council allowed the constable's appeal. The odd thing was that, in stating the law on the subject of escapes, Lord Fraser of Tullybelton said there was no room for presumptions in favour of the Crown. 'If there were to be a presumption,' said his Lordship, 'that any person in custody was there lawfully, the scales would be tipped in favour of a *fait accompli* in a way which might constitute a serious threat to liberty'. The prisoner also committed an offence in escaping. And it would be contrary to fundamental principles of law that the burden should be on a prisoner to show that he was *not* lawfully detained. The fundamental principle seem a bit kinder to the prisoner than to his captor.

Police Review February 12, 1982.

The Use of 'Up'

I once knew an insurance clerk named Upp, Stanley Upp, and he prided himself on the fact, or belief, that he was unique. Then one day on a visit to Montana he found another Upp family. The less credible part of his story, I suppose, is that he married a girl called Celia Down. I read the other day that Mr Wilfred Wright, attending the annual dinner of the Institute of Petroleum last month, found himself next on the guest list to a Mr Wrong. It reminded me that when I was a PC and stood on parade waiting for dismissal at the end of a day's duty, it was customary for the man nearest the street door to call out the names of stragglers coming in, the men for whom we were all impatiently waiting. Names were important here. 'Turner up,' they would shout, and 'Roper up, 'Stringer up, 'Sender up, 'Holder up'. Sometimes the parade was convulsed. Finally — 'Tickler up,' and this was too much. 'DISMISS!' roared the station officer prematurely.

Police Review February 26, 1982.

Handcuffs

On February 12 in this column I was holding forth about the injustice (as I saw it) of punishing people for trying to escape from custody. I've never been able to understand why it is that more people don't try to escape, though I'm glad they don't. More than once I've actually seen a man who has been arrested waiting patiently (and unheld) for a police car door to be unlocked, or leaning against a wall while some less docile accomplice is being subdued by the arresting officers. They could have nipped off with a very good chance of getting clean away. But no; they chose instead to stand by like frogs awaiting consumption by a caged snake. The discussion brought me a number of letters, the main burden of which was that the onus was indeed upon the captor rather than the captive, but that more use ought to be made of handcuffs. And among the handcuff supporters there was a strong feeling that the prisoner's hands ought to be manacled behind his back, not in front where he could use them almost unhindered.

There is also a general astonishment that neither force orders nor the Home Office 'Consolidated Circular to the Police on Crime and Kindred Matters' can be found to have given much attention to the use of handcuffs. There is the classic language about the decision whether to handcuff 'depending on the circumstances of the particular case, as for instance the nature of the charge and the conduct and temper of the person in custody', and there is the injunction that handcuffing 'should not be resorted to unless there is fair ground for supposing that violence may be used or an escape attempted'. One of my correspondents says that 'two men would now probably be still at liberty but for having gone opposite ways round a lampost' (they were handcuffed together and hadn't done their forward planning), and that 'only a few days ago a police officer was badly injured by a handcuffed prisoner sticking a needle into his eye after asking for a light for a cigarette'.

Other readers think there has been a revival of the handcuff in recent years, and that this *may* be a by-product of the renewed police attention now being given to 'insecure premises'. Formerly, when beatsmen got around on foot and found how forgetful were shopkeepers and businessmen in leaving their street doors unfastened, handcuffs were used as a substitute for padlocks and the occupiers on arrival in the morning had to wait until a policeman with a handcuff-key could be dispatched to the premises and let everybody in. But you would think handcuffs had been around long enough now to have evolved quite a mountain of instructions as to use. According to the *Oxford English Dictionary* they were known as handcuffs as early as 1663, and that's a century before Dr Samuel Johnson compiled *his* famous dictionary — which doesn't even give them a mention. Today the *Encyclopedia Britannica* says you can call them manacles, shackbolts, shackles, gyves or swivles. What a subject for a Bramshill thesis!

Police Review March 19, 1982.

Using the Wrong Statute

It was the inimitable A. P. Herbert who, in his *Misleading Cases,* reported the prosecution of a man who had flung himself from a bridge into the River Thames. Speaking from memory, I think he was charged with obstructing the navigation of an inland waterway, polluting the River Thames, throwing a missile to the common danger, and discharging rubbish into a public watercourse. The magistrate discussed the use of statutes for purposes which had not been present to the minds (if any) of the legislators. I once invoked this story in the course of a seminar for station officers, as illustrating the danger of stretching Acts of Parliament further than they were designed to go. But I never did it again — one chap retained only the idea that someone so worthless as to attempt suicide was simply throwing rubbish away.

But the ingenious use of ambiguous clauses has a long police history. One of my earliest recollections is of seeing a van driven along a busy street with a long rope trailing behind it on the carriageway. I was being 'shown round' by an elderly constable. he seized my arm. 'There you are, young shaver,' he said 'See that? Know what that is? Causing an unnecessary obstruction'. Two current cases have been illustrating the scope for imagination in the framing of charges. One of them, of course, is Mrs Whitehouse's prosecution of the National Theatre for staging *The Romans in Britain.* At the time it seemed to be a contempt of court to mention this anywhere outside the Old Bailey swing doors, but it was quite safe enough to say that Mrs Whitehouse wanted to establish an incident in the play as an 'act of gross indecency' under the Sexual Offences Act, and thus to by-pass the difficulties, if any, which might get in the way of a prosecution under the Theatres Act 1968. Another is the case of *Parkin v Norman, Valentine v Lilley, The Times,* March 13, in which two men had been convicted under the Public Order Act 1936 of 'insulting behaviour whereby a breach of the peace was likely to be occasioned'. The insulting behaviour consisted in the usual gestures of anatomical pride in a public lavatory, but the difficulty was that in each case the recipient (target, or spectator) was a police constable placed there as a kind of captive audience. Could these officers be 'insulted' by what had happened? Could anybody? 'The Public Order Act,' said Mr Justice McCullough in the Divisional Court, 'does not make it criminal to use *offensive or disgusting* behaviour whereby a breach of the peace is likely to be occasioned. It requires *insulting* behaviour. What then is an insult? An insult is perceived by someone who feels insulted . . . The appellant's conduct was aimed at only one person, who he hoped was a homosexual'. It was unrealistic to say that the police officer could feel insulted, said his Lordship — a bit unrealistically, it seems to me. But the convictions were quashed. When the Nottingham Crown Court had dismissed the first appeals, it had obviously treated the word 'likely' as meaning 'liable'. That was wrong. Liable, it seems, means no more than 'possible' and can still include the improbable. *Police Review* March 26, 1982.

Broken Windows

I hate vandals, these brainless smasher-uppers who get their pleasure from destruction and the promotion of rage and misery. Hating them, I would normally be prepared to agree with almost any kind of extreme treatment that society might hand out to them. But given time to cool, I know in my bones that the utmost severity of punishment will leave the problem as it was. The broken window is the sign that a neighbourhood is on the way down. Well, not one broken window but three or four close together. You could almost say that a minor rash of broken windows is proof that there are no police foot patrols. Is that the same as saying that 'getting the men back on the beat' is the way to reduce crime?

Well, apparently not, in any sense that will be reflected in the statistics. In *The Atlantic Monthly* for March 1982 there is a report on *The Police and Neighbourhood Safety* for which the editors have actually chosen the heading *Broken Windows*. In the 1970s the State of New Jersey carried out a 'Safe and Clean Neighbourhoods Programme', to see if it could improve the quality of life in 28 chosen cities. It involved, among other things, taking the police out of their patrol cars and assigning them to walking beats. Police chiefs were sceptical. Foot patrol, they said, reduced police mobility and weakened headquarters control. The lower ranks agreed, but for different reasons. It was hard work, it kept them outside on rainy nights, it had been used as a form of punishment, and it never paid off. Five years later, the Police Foundation in Washington published a survey. Foot patrol had not reduced crime rates, and no one was surprised. But residents in the 28 cities felt more secure, *believed* that crime had been reduced, and had slackened their own measures of crime prevention. (For one thing, they went out a lot more.) They thought more of the police. The police thought more of them. Was everyone fooled? Not at all. The level of public order had been raised. Drunks and addicts, loafers and beggars, loiterers and molesters, had been almost eliminated. Noisy teenagers kept quiet, or quieter. It was found, or rather confirmed, that if a window is broken *and left unrepaired,* many surrounding windows will soon be broken. 'One unrepaired broken window is a signal that no one cares, and so breaking more windows costs nothing'. Get a window repaired at once, and vandalism is far less likely.

There's a great deal more in the *Atlantic Monthly* article which is worth attention, but who will see it in this country? Bramshill, perhaps. The thing is, it completely establishes the case for more foot patrols, if only on the basis that much of the current criminal violence springs from excitement and fear, from street dereliction, muck, and neglect. Neighbourhood self-respect is a thing beyond price.

Police Review April 2, 1982.

The Romans in Britain

Well, at least when you start work under a headline like that, everyone will know that you are not going to write about the Romans in Britain, a period of history combining long straight roads, tessellated pavements, big marble bathrooms and utterly barbaric cruelty, but about Mrs Mary Whitehouse and recent sexual cavortings at the National Theatre. I think Mrs Whitehouse is, in this instance at least, greatly misjudged. Typically, the *New Law Journal* for March 25: 'Mrs Whitehouse claimed that by bringing the prosecution she had "proved an important legal point". What that point was is far from clear'. On the contrary it was clarity itself. She had proved that an Old Bailey Judge would be ready to tell a jury that indecency between men on the stage could be 'gross indecency' for the purposes of the Sexual Offences Act 1956 if there were other people around to witness it. I have to confess that I don't see how he could direct them otherwise. I suppose Mrs Whitehouse would have been able to see (if, for example, she reads the *Daily Telegraph,* which had a field day on the subject as if the Judicial Proceedings (Regulation of Reports) Act didn't exist) that to prolong the trial beyond that point would merely fill the papers with muck and add nothing much to her success.

The whole trial was possible because the Theatres Act 1968, in a half-hearted (or even artful) show of protecting stage plays, had said, in section 2(4), that no one producing an obscene play was to be prosecuted 'at Common Law'. This, following the absurd example of the Obscene Publications Act 1959, had left any possible *statutory* prosecution wide open. It was a government gambit which had outraged the promoters of the 1959 Bill — amongst whom were Mr Roy Jenkins, Mr Norman St. John Stevas, and Lord Birkett, all of whom angrily felt that they had been sold down the river. And so they had.

Police Review April 9, 1982.

The Knock on the Door

I don't profess to know how 'street mugging' can be reduced, though I have certain rather boring ideas on the subject and I believe that heavier and nastier punishment will merely make the punishers feel happier. Correction: delete 'merely'; it may be very important to make *someone* feel happy about this ghastly and perennial problem. Nobody does at the moment. But there has lately emerged a possible way of ascertaining just how many people *really* feel frightened to go out at night, by comparison with those (if any) who write to their MPs and say they are, and those called up by the writers of blood-curdling articles in the Sunday papers. Dorothy Cameron, an SDP candidate in the recent local council elections, told the *Daily Telegraph* on May 5 that, having knocked on about 3,000 doors while she was canvassing, she was disturbed at the difficulty of getting people to come to the door at all. They 'look through their spy-hole,' and 'with much sliding of bolts and pulling of chains, gingerly open the door and peep through the few inches between the door and the frame'. So do I actually, but not because of muggers in the streets, or even because of political canvassers (by the way, I wonder if the latter have *ever* done themselves any good?). Before I fling open my door at night, I like a glimpse of the chap outside, though I refuse to believe I'm doing anything new. But Dorothy Cameron draws a cogent lesson from it. We are closing our eyes, she says, to the gangsters who have invaded our streets, 'creating an unpublicised curfew'. The politician at the door is being told, in effect, 'You're not going to do anything for us. We're not voting for any of you'. This is, she finds, the catchphrase of the 1982 election, and we must mount 'a positive programme to clear the streets of vicious gangsters. It would cost,' she has discovered, 'less than the price of one Harrier Jump Jet.'

That's a highly topical comparison, but I believe she underestimates our native skill in spotting a political canvasser through the net curtains. We don't want to go to the door unless it's an exciting TV personality or someone whom the press have been building up as a blackguard of untold unfamy. But if Dorothy Cameron fights again, I hope her election manifesto will disclose just how the money we spend on a Harrier could clear the streets of muggers.

Police Review May 21, 1982.

On Losing Your Pension

'If it wasn't for the pension,' an old sergeant used to say to me, 'you'd never get a policeman to stand for five minutes'. I supposed he was right, but the pay in those days was pretty poor, unemployment wasn't much better than it is today, and the insurance companies and finance houses hadn't yet thought up all these marvellous schemes for the provision of private pensions and annuities. As things have developed, it may not be long before some thoughtfully determined policeman, disenchanted with the terms of his pension rights and the 'rateable deductions' he will be paying out before he gets any pension, will demand the right to opt out of the whole pension scheme and accordingly suffer no deductions from his pay. (His application will certainly be turned down, but that will be merely the first, and the most predictable, of his hurdles.) 'I can buy a better pension than this,' he will explain to the man on the next beat; and he will attach to his application copies of several current private schemes that offer him more money for less sacrifice. None of these, he will point out, though he will do it in the humble language which alone will get him any consideration in such a revolutionary context, will take any interest in his private life or hold over him any threats about scrapping his pension if he does this or that. He will probably concede, by way of showing that he has really studied his subject, that 'occupational pension schemes' must not now, by law, contain forfeiture provisions which are harsher than those in the State pension scheme. And he will point out that if he divorces his wife or parts company with her, they won't grab all the money and tell him that's the end. He might, who knows, fight his case all the way to the House of Lords and make police pensions history.

A few years after I left the police service I got a letter from a police solicitor saying that if I went on writing the kind of thing I was then producing (I had just been holding forth about a case of injustice) the question of my pension 'would have to be considered'. Since the idea, I judged, wasn't that it should be increased, I took no part in the correspondence, deeming it unworthy of encouragement. But it would be nice to think that such threats could no longer be made, however empty.

Police Review June 4, 1982.

Good Police Guide

May I suggest that some citizen, fired by whatever it is that fires Mr Egon Ronay, who tells us every year which are the good hotels and restaurants and which are the rotten ones, could earn himself a place in the Hall of Fame by compiling annually a guide to the good and the rotten police forces? Mr Egon Ronay has reported this year that the Ritz Hotel in Piccadilly is no longer one of the best hotels in the world. He doesn't say it's one of the worst, but as a result of lunching there recently he was so shocked by its lapsed standards that he sent a long report to its management. The management, like all managements except my local licensee, takes Mr Ronay very seriously. 'We shall go all out,' says the general manager of the Ritz, 'to get back into his favour.'

Now what a marvellous idea. If someone started a GOOD POLICE GUIDE, praising here and cursing there, wouldn't the bad police forces feel challenged and eager to get back into favour? No doubt some forces would refuse to be sampled or tasted. In which event they would appear in ROLPH'S GOOD POLICE GUIDE as 'Declined to co-operate: unable, therefore, to recommend'. I would have to say the same, of course, about The Ritz, which would probably refuse to serve me my customary ploughman's — I am uncertain because I so seldom go there. But people don't like being left out of these things for too long.

Police Review June 18, 1982.

On Not Renewing a TV Licence

Not long ago two men called at my door and said they would like to talk to me about my television licence. They were much smarter-looking than I am, and could, I thought, have been oil executives or perhaps upper-crust bookmakers. Their politeness was oddly terrifying. 'Not again?' I said. 'I get this every year, though we usually do it by correspondence. You write and tell me you have no record of my having taken out a licence, I write back and tell you its number, you lose the letter, we both write again, and then it's all right for another year.' This time I got out the licence and showed it to them, whereupon their politeness was, if anything, intensified.

But I didn't know that they apply the same pressure on people like justices' clerks. Mr D. C. Swift of the Justices' Clerks Office at Peterlee in County Durham has written to tell *The Times* (June 14) that the magistrates at Peterlee receive forms to be filled explaining why their court has no television licence. These were ignored for some time, but eventually one of the forms was completed with the observation that 'though we are public servants, we don't find time to watch television at the same time as conducting magistrates' courts.' No more questionnaires were received, says Mr Swift, but he may be crowing too soon. He hasn't yet had his call from the two well-dressed men.

Police Review June 25, 1982.

Freethinkers in the Witness Box

I knew a special constable who once caused a sensation, when he gave evidence in a magistrates' court, by refusing to take the oath. The magistrate (as the law requires) asked him why. He was a Freethinker, he said, and actually made it sound as if it had a capital 'F'. That meant that the oath wouldn't be binding upon him. Up jumped the defending solicitor at once to object. The constable must have taken the Oath of Allegiance on joining the Special Constabulary, he said, and there could be no reason why he shouldn't be properly sworn now. The justices' clerk pointed out that a police officer didn't swear an oath of allegiance, he 'solemnly and sincerely declared' that he would 'well and truly execute the office of constable' etc. So the special constable and Freethinker was allowed to use the same kind of language in 'affirming' how true were the words he was about to give in evidence.

But the incident touched off quite a brisk correspondence in the newspapers. Why should a Freethinker be recruited into the police service? Why shouldn't he? How free was a Freethinker? (Some of the Freethinkers I knew at the time seemed about as free in their thinking as a modern Maoist.) Then someone started counting up the atheists and agnostics in the House of Commons, a surprising number, and irreverent citizens began wondering what went on in the minds of such men during House of Commons Prayers, and at State funerals and weddings etc. Why, it came out that they even stood as godfathers to each other's children. It all got so involved and disturbing that editors put a stop to it, and we all got on with our formerly untroubled business of being believers, atheists and agnostics, shuffling through the religious occasions which seemed inescapable if we valued our jobs, and feeling it must be in some way justifiable to do this because old so-and-so did it. What no one seemed to suggest was abolishing the oath and telling witnesses that they might go to prison if they told lies.

Police Review July 2, 1982.

Those Without Sin

I've always been interested in Liberia, the negro republic founded by America in 1821 for freed American slaves, and in the ideals of the Rev Mr Gurley, who gave it the brave name of Liberia as befitting a new country of the liberated. Since then its chief function seems to have been the registration of ships which aren't fit to be registered anywhere else, even if it didn't actually invent the 'flag of convenience'. But its latest eruption into the news reveals a sorry state of affairs among its policemen. Two senior policemen convicted of corruption were sentenced to death, and Liberia's military ruler, Samuel Doe, ordered that the firing squad must comprise only policemen who could swear that they had never succumbed to corruption themselves. They couldn't find one. So President Doe sacked the Minister of Justice and the Commissioner of Police, and the local papers talked about 'the woman taken in adultery' and the crowd which was busily preparing to stone her to death when Christ suggested to them that the first stone should be thrown by a non-sinner. The two convicted police chiefs have gone back to their jobs, and Liberia's two million liberated citizens, who have grown used to corruption as a way of index-linked public salaries, may have started considering whether something less than the death penalty might after all be more suitable in what we call the Prevention of Corruption. Come to think of it, it's a search for the sinless which has lately been complicating our own efforts to improve our jury system.

Police Review July 16, 1982.

Everyman a Criminologist

Someone described me once in the public prints as a criminologist, which I'm not. I threatened to sue him, but he said he could prove it. Probably it's the determination not to be one which has always hindered my understanding of those long boring articles in the criminological literature, all wandering bits of algebra and huge lists of behavioural problems made to look like rural bus timetables. Strong, clean-living policemen are sent to Bramshill and subjected to this kind of thing for many months on end. Why? Is it not possible to present current thinking on the problem of crime in language that we can all understand?

It is. It has just been done by Mr Martin Wright in a book called *Making Good,* published (with a foreword by Barbara Wootton) by Burnett Books, 17/21 Conway Street, London W1, at £5.95 in soft covers or £12.95 in hardback. A truly excellent book. It will enable us all to recognise that we are all criminologists, all involved in the search for some rational alternative to the daft and despairing system by which, having caught our criminals, we set about the business of making them worse. 'In the search for a society in which people harm each other as little as possible,' says Mr Wright, 'and as much as possible of the harm is repaired, the radical question is whether a system that is primarily penal is the most effective and just that we can devise.' His answer of course in No, otherwise he wouldn't have asked the question, or written the book. He is neither a hardliner nor a softie. As Barbara Wootton says, he has succeeded in producing a penological proposal which has not already been flogged to death. It's a carefully worked out scheme requiring the offender to make amends to his victim, 'the person most overlooked in the current debate,' as well as to society, for the damage he has caused.

Necessarily, such a book must first describe in some detail what we are doing already. And to read all this, in Mr Wright's easily digested prose (it's a beautifully written book), is to realise the utter hopelessness of it all, the blinkered, compartmentalised futility, and to marvel once again that despite all the reformist campaigns and the seminars and conferences and political promises, *nothing* changes, or anyway improves. The prisons are worse than they were 50 years ago, crime is more frequent and more nasty, all our energy is expended in what has been called the punitive obsession. Here's a book, and a scheme, that an intelligent 10-year-old child could understand and approve. I wish every citizen could be provided with a copy and, if necessary, an intelligent 10-year-old to read it to him.

Police Review July 23, 1982.

Glaring at the Jury

Broadcasting House, London, is no longer big enough, even though it's one of those corridor deserts in which you can get lost and frightened. So the BBC is going to build itself a new one across the road, first knocking down the Langham Hotel, which would be in the way. But the BBC is not going to ask the architectural profession to submit competitive plans. It will ask architects to submit *ideas,* setting out the various considerations which, in their opinion, a plan for the new building should reflect. I marvel that this should be seen as an innovation. An architect's is an exciting job, and most of the excitement comes from trying to foresee all the problems which will confront the new building's occupants, thinking out the new ones which inevitably occur to the occupants as you go along, and adding a few which neither of you has ever thought of before.

The people who design criminal courts have never seemed to me very clever, and one of their worst failures has at last been getting some promising publicity. This is the almost universal habit of seating juries exactly opposite the public gallery, and also providing seats in court for witnesses who have already given evidence. For centuries, or anyway for as long as we have had juries, our hapless jurymen have been herded into an exposed cage like crooks into an Alabama identification line-up. Most of them don't want to be jurors at all, and in particular don't relish their spotlight prominence in the court room. What is important is that they shall be able to see, not so much that they should be seen. It has recently been found that they resent being 'stared at' from the public galleries, that fists have been shaken at them, and that they have been embarrassed (not to say influenced in their decisions) by the behaviour of witnesses who remain in court after giving evidence. I must say I've seen this happen myself, especially the gestures of disbelief and derision sometimes displayed by spent witnesses — and police witnesses at that.

Lately there has been an 'anti-nobble' security reorganisation in the seating at some Old Bailey courts; and, according to the *Daily Telegraph* of July 13, 'the moving of juries from their benches to seats *under* the public galleries meant a frantic furniture upheaval'. Extra tables and chairs were still being moved around on July 12 'when the courts were due to begin their day's proceedings'. One 'regular defence lawyer' (Rumpole?) was said to have described the rearrangement as 'melodramatic' and another said the whole thing was like Piccadilly Circus. But it's something the architects should have thought of, long years ago.

And now that events have at last inspired the necessary sense of courtroom purpose, can we hope that future designs will recognise that the principle of 'open court' means that the public shall be able to *hear* what's going on, not merely to observe the backs of the barristers' wigs and the way they hitch up their gowns as a preliminary to whispering some specially searching question? In a sensibly designed courtroom, the public seats would be in the middle, and the barristers would have to talk over the occupants' heads in addressing witnesses, judge, or jury. At the moment the lawyers are arranged in a little huddle around the clerk of the court, where they mutter to each other confidentially, inaudible conspirators.

Police Review July 30, 1982.

Do You Know Who I Am?

There's a long-cherished story about a Lord Mayor of London who (because he was a very small and spherical Lord Mayor) used to go jogging on Southwark Bridge in the evenings to get his weight down. In the evenings it was a deserted bridge, ideal for jogging Lord Mayors who wished to jog unobserved. Unhappily, because it was a deserted bridge it was also suitable for people who wanted to go over the side and end it all. So there was a 'Southwark Bridge Patrol', 8 pm to 1 am, for the purpose of discouraging would-be suicides and making life a little easier for Thames Division (as it then was). Late one evening an alert constable saw a little round man take off his overcoat, throw it across the back of a seat, revealing himself in singlet and running shorts, and start running. The constable started running too. 'What's the idea?' he asked the angry jogger when they met. With a huge effort of patience the Lord Mayor explained. 'That's it', said the PC. 'Just about what I thought. Now what about a nice cup of tea? Then we can sort out who you really are when you're not being Lord Mayor of London. Come along then'. Sad to say the station officer, who was much younger, was no better acquainted with his Lordship, and looked at the fuming little man in shorts with undisguised scepticism. Luckily for him he saw no reason why his Lordship shouldn't use the phone, and by this means there was soon assembled a group of high functionaries who were able to smooth the feelings of all present except one. The exception was the Lord Mayor, who took a long time to get over it and illustrated, yet again, that a sense of humour is what you use for laughing at other people's misadventures, not at your own.

I was reminded of him the other day when a solicitor friend of mine was driving me into town and inadvertently went into a one-way street at the wrong end. A policeman saw him, asked him where he thought he was going, and rather riled him. 'I'm an officer of the Supreme Court' said my companion rather unnecessarily. 'Tipstaff?' said the policeman. 'I am a solicitor' he replied frostily. 'Ah, well, that seems to leave you no excuse, does it?' The colloquy went on and got rather embarrassing. But oh, I could have told him that these declarations of rank and importance are, in the modern jargon, counter-productive. Better to remain nobody, except perhaps when you are an illustrious and unlikely jogger at an improbable place.

Police Review August 13, 1982.

Holes in the Road

Mr Patrick Jenkin, Secretary of State for Industry, wants to overhaul our ancient Telegraph Acts so that they can look as if they belong in the area of cable TV, microwave and satellite broadcasting. He makes it seem that the telegraph pole is doomed. I don't mind this. I have a pole right in front of my house, and until about 10 years ago the Electricity Board paid me a shilling a year for what they called 'wayleave', a kind of rent for the bit of my land it stood up in. For some reason they have stopped paying this, and because it was only a shilling I have let them get away with it. (Also I thought they *might* have discovered that I had never really been entitled to the bob a year, and they could have put me in my place by suing me for countless bobs stretching far back into the past. As a sleeping dog, The Law is all too easily aroused and can be very nasty if the moment is not well chosen.)

The existing Telegraph Acts say that poles should not be placed where they can spoil the view from a mansion, but that has never helped me much. However, they also govern the digging of holes in the roads for the laying of underground cables, and this has long been a major concern of the police, who are supposed to satisfy themselves that the men doing the digging, or sitting in the holes eating their sandwiches, are fully-paid-up hole-diggers and not dim-witted practical jokers. (Well, the latter is not unknown.) There are still police divisions where the location, and indeed the duration, of holes in the road have to be recorded in special little books (the one I remember was known as the 'man-ole manual'), and the elimination of at least one hole-digging battalion can but lighten the total load of police duties. All power, therefore to Mr Patrick Jenkin and his new Statute, for it will repeal, it seems, more than 12 Telegraphy Acts.

Police Review September 3, 1982.

Helping Police With Their Inquiries

Some years ago, many years I suppose, newspaper editors decided that the English libel laws were so fierce that you couldn't safely say 'the man was later arrested', you had much better say 'a man was later arrested'. Then even that acquired risky possibilities and almost anyone arrested became a man 'helping the police with their inquiries'. No one seemed to mind that you could equally describe a condemned murderer on the scaffold as a man 'helping the executioner with his duties'. Now I have a letter from a man who has had, he tells me, 30 years of CID work, asking me if I know who this helpful chap is. 'I may have convinced many prisoners,' he says, 'that they should help the police, but rarely do we get a man who presents himself and eagerly insists on helping by way of a confession'. Well, but do the papers say the man is 'eagerly helping the police with their inquiries'? If I'm a prisoner of war about to be shot, and have been ordered to dig my own grave, I dig it because it defers the moment of shooting and allows time for the impossible reprieve to come through. And unquestionably I am 'helping' my captors. But not eagerly?

However, my correspondent says it riles him to read in the papers, when he is dealing with a difficult case plus a difficult prisoner, that his prisoner is 'helping' him. 'A man is being questioned by the police,' he says, is nearer the mark, 'but it seems that the media think they are assisting us in some way by not mentioning questioning'. There is indeed a fog of misunderstanding about the propriety and scope of 'questioning', and editors may well suppose that if they report an arrest or detention as a 'questioning' they will expose the police to some unjustified attack in the courts. It is as if the police, having arrested a suspect were expected to say to him, 'Now all you have to do is sit there and look straight to your front. Don't say *anything*. If anyone asks you a question, you are entitled to complain, and on request you will be supplied with a form for complaining on'.

'Helping the police', etc, is one of the more hilarious euphemisms infesting the fringes of the law. Not long ago a well-known High Court judge went into a police station to produce a road traffic document. While he was there, a tremendous din arose in an adjoining room where a platform was being erected for a police concert; shouting, oaths, and the echoing whang of about six large hammers. 'Someone helping the police?' said his Lordship approvingly.

Police Review September 11, 1982.

Police on the Floor

Some people are natural-born hecklers, and probably heckle the midwife immediately on arrival. Others, me for instance, do not heckle but listen, even if the listening is done angrily and with throbbing veins. The police now do it at Federation meetings, and I would have thought it was one of the intended functions of a Police Federation that its members should be able to heckle their speakers, even (or perhaps specially) politicians and Home Secretaries. After all, they clap and applaud at other times, and the speaker waits while they do it, looking round benignly. Mrs Thatcher thought the recent behaviour of a Metropolitan Police audience was 'disgraceful', and letters to the press have since been busily explaining that the booers and slow-hand-clappers were not really representative of their mates. Mr John Newman, who is secretary of the offending Metropolitan branch of the Federation, told the *Daily Telegraph* on October 22 that Mr Whitelaw 'fared no worse than he does in the House of Commons, and he was loudly clapped a number of times'.

Should we ever have been allowed to hear on the radio that zoological feeding-time uproar in the House of Commons? Without that, we could have gone on pretending to each other that our elected leaders were dignified tribunes of the people, measured and 'gentlemanly', wise and restrained. Added to their self-destructive performances on *Today in Parliament*, we have their apparent eagerness to appear on television, even if it entails being browbeaten and insulted by a Robin Day. (The *Radio Times* stoutly published a sheaf of letters after Mr John Nott, Minister of Defence, stalked out of that carefully and painfully humiliating interview, the tone of which was set by Mrs Veronica Blake of Chepstow: 'Noted as Sir Robin Day is for hard questioning, this time he exceeded even his own talent for rudeness'). Mr John Naughton in *The Listener* (October 14), who sees Robin Day as 'an oleaginous old prune', looks forward to the time when more interviewees will upset the BBC applecart by refusing to participate further. But even he has discovered that one 'academic', told that the fee for an interview was £35, the following day sent his own eager cheque for that amount to the BBC Television Centre by post. Even if the arclights have made would-be actors of us all, that only means that booing merely looks ill-mannered on a vastly bigger scale than it ever did before. What does a Federation meeting gain by allowing the newsmen to come in? Without them, it could boo with total freedom.

Police Review November 5, 1982.

Handbills

I get the impression that a growing number of people don't even know what a handbill is — 'printed notice circulated by hand' says the *Concise Oxford Dictionary*. But even more people seem unaware that, in central London at any rate, it is unlawful to distribute handbills without the approval of the Commissioner, who has power (under the Metropolitan Streets Act 1867) to control their 'form and manner'. If ever you have been in some town like Athens or Rome at election time, when the street corners are ankle-deep in leaflets bearing the names and photographs of candidates, you will remember what an uncontrolled freedom to chuck handbills about can do to a beautiful city. Your refusal (and everyone's refusal) to accept the handbills thrust under your nose by thousands of swarthy enthusiasts will have resulted in their gaining access to first-floor windows from which the handbills can come floating down in fluttering clouds.

I am grumbling about this because the other day in a walk down Oxford Street I was offered, I think about a dozen times, handbills urging me to try a sauna bath somewhere near by. I didn't want a sauna bath, having not yet fully recovered from the last one, which was about 10 years ago. The footways were littered with similar injunctions, thrown down by people who didn't want a sauna bath. And now I notice that Mr Keith Waterhouse, whose misadventures are recorded twice weekly in the *Daily Mirror,* reports on January 24 that recently in Earl's Court he was 'treated as a receptacle for enough handbills to paper a wall with. Their subjects ranged from the inadequacies of the present Iraqui leadership to a sale of carpets, from the opening of a new cocktail bar to the fact that Jesus lives . . . Leaflets advertising the latest disco are thrust upon old ladies of ninety, while respectable middle-aged columnists' (I hope I come in there) 'are handed gratuitous advice on where to go for pregnancy tests'. And Mr Waterhouse calls for a return of the sandwichboardman, so that we shall all be able to 'absorb all these messages without being unwillingly converted into a perambulating dustbin'.

Of course the sandwichboard-man would need the Commissioner's approval, too, anyway in so central an area as Earl's Court. At one time he used to grant this kind of authorisation pretty freely, and the streets were full of hungry men in flat caps carrying sandwich-boards proclaiming that 'The Wicked Shall Descend into Hell' or that an American evangelist called Judge Rutherford had discovered that 'Millions Now Living Will Never Die'. These got a passing glance from the doomed populace hurrying by, but sometimes a new play or a new cough-cure or a new embrocation for horses would be thus proclaimed by about 50 sandwichmen in single file, a saturation advert. If these walked on the footway they were a nuisance, and if they walked in the gutter they had to keep on sauntering round parked vehicles and causing an obstruction to traffic. So the sandwichman has all but disappeared.

Police Review February 4, 1983.

The Cross of King Arthur

King Arthur seems to be about as real as Dick Turpin and Winnie the Pooh. This is because when the Romans had gone home, late in the Fourth Century, and the Saxons had chased the Britons into the Welsh mountains, there ensued two centuries of utter chaos of which we today know absolutely nothing. 'Between these points,' says the historian G.M. Trevelyan, 'there stretches a great darkness'. So the mythmakers have bunged it full of romantic characters, the most popular one being King Arthur. I discovered his spuriousness about two years after someone had debunked Father Christmas for me, and have never recovered my trusting nature.

Some people survive this kind of thing. Mr Derek Mahoney is a 50-year-old archaeologist who lives at Enfield, Middlesex, and who in 1981 dug up a seven-inch leaden cross, inscribed in Latin, in the grounds of a mansion belonging to Enfield Borough Council. This, he said, was King Arthur's legendary 'Glastonbury Cross', so called because the monks of Glastonbury Abbey had found it in the 10th century in what they called the tomb of King Arthur. From this point in the narrative it becomes difficult to guess who is kidding whom, but at least Mr Mahoney took his lead cross to the British Museum and asked them how he should store it. I don't know what they told him, but he took it away and buried it again.

Then the Borough Council wanted it. It's ours, they said, because it was found on our land after we had dredged the lake. And they got Mr Justice Croom-Johnson to order that Mr Mahoney must give it up. When he persistently refused the judge, unavoidably I suppose, sent him to prison. Moreover, he got the maximum contempt-of-court sentence of two years, which of course he can bring to an end at any time by revealing the whereabuots of his little lead cross. The Enfield councillors seem determined to get it, even though the British Museum has declared it a seventeenth century fake (how do you fake something which is phoney already?). And Mr Mahoney, who can't be said to have stolen the cross from anyone, made a further brief appearance before the same judge on December 26, when the Official Solicitor suggested that he might perhaps be released as 'there was no reasonable prospect that he would ever hand over the cross'. Not at all, said the judge. 'In view of his attitude, I don't think this is the time for him to be released from prison.' So he has gone back. He probably won't read this, but his best course now is to give the Official Solicitor an exact description of some spot where the cross will NOT be found, and then swear blind that someone else has got at it, probably the Enfield Council Works Department.

Police Review February 11, 1983.

Destruction by Newspaper

'I'm all for freedom of the press, but . . . ' And that's the opening of most comments on the Right of Reply in the Media Bill, which failed at its second reading on Friday February 18 because there weren't enough MPs in the Commons to give it a proper hearing. Even the Home Office Under-Secretary, Mr David Mellor, said it. 'The general idea,' he told the Commons, 'must at first sight seem to have a good deal to commend it — BUT, in the Government's opinion, it would be highly undesirable if this Bill were to become law'. And this was because (as always) freedom of the press must be seen as 'one of the fundamental features of a democratic society'.

And it includes the freedom to get hold of a little man, totally unable to defend himself against whatever stream of lies (for he won't get Legal Aid in a libel action), and utterly destroy him. Sometimes a trade union has financed a libel action for one of its members, and sometimes the Police Federation has found the money to vindicate police officers pilloried for the sake of a good story. But huge numbers of people are quite defenceless in such circumstances, and they will look in vain for redress to the Press Council. Oh, the Press Council may well denounce the offending newspaper, and the offending newspaper will (probably) publish the denunciation, but by then the damage has been done and is usually irreparable. Indeed there are newspapers to which a rebuke from the Press Council, which can never be more than a slap on the wrist, is gratefully accepted instead as a shot in the arm. The *Daily Telegraph* on February 19, gleefully rubbing its hands over the temporary eclipse of this Bill, published an editorial which, it seemed to me, almost wickedly misrepresented its scope and purpose. But it promptly published two letters that said so (on February 23) from Mr Frank Allaun, MP, who had introduced the Bill, and from Sir Derek Walker-Smith, QC, MP, who drafted and sponsored it. That's press freedom, and in my experience the *Telegraph* has never closed its columns to criticism. What Mr Allaun and Sir Derek are after is the publication of false statements followed by refusal to withdraw them (or to publish the truth) when they are proved to be untrue. It doesn't seem to do much good to point out that France, West Germany, Canada, Denmark and many other countries have long had laws like the one now contemplated. 'We're not interested in what other countries do,' is the usual response, 'we're talking about England, the home of democracy'. But those countries enjoy remarkable press and radio freedom. The classic instance of official and press injustice to an individual, and its subsequent redress by the compulsory publication of the truth, is that of Captain Alfred Dreyfus, convicted in 1899 in France on a false charge of betraying military secrets and imprisoned for many years on Devil's Island. When the Court of Appeal in Paris finally vindicated him it ordered that its verdict be posted up in Paris and published not only in the *Journal Officiel* and five other Paris newspapers but also 'at the public expense' in 50 provincial newspapers of his own choosing.

Our newspaper proprietors are expressing the intention, and apparently the belief, that the press will in this matter now set its house in order. All the signs are that this is growing less, not more, likely. Mr Allaun's Bill, or someone else's, will sooner or later pass into law. And then its title will begin to appear as a heading to letters which begin 'I am directed by the Chief Constable to ask that you will take an early opportunity to publish, not less conspicuously than your news item of . . . . ' I'll believe it when I see it.

Police Review March 4, 1983.

Fair Cop Guv

Now that I've committed myself to the stated belief that villains don't *really* say 'It's a fair cop guv', I receive almost daily proof that they do, though my informants seem ready to believe that the phrase may be imitative, picked up from books or from the telly. Actually I don't derive much comfort from this, because nearly everything we say is imitative, picked up from somewhere — that's how a language is learned. But the examples that readers are sending me are nice. Familiar to most of us, of course, is 'That's all right constable, I'm a councillor — I'll have a word with your inspector'. Grrr. One with special implications is that which begins (unprompted) 'I was proceeding along the road in a southerly direction . . . ' There is an unusual but authentic-sounding story about an evening punch-up in a mining village called Newbridge, Gwent, when two constables, an elderly sergeant, and a dog handler (with dog) were trying to disperse a crowd of 60 drunken youths, who were waiting outside a club for the second half of a fight begun earlier in the evening. One youth barked at the police dog, and the dog's response got things going again. In answer to a charge of drunken and disorderly conduct, the barking youth replied: 'The Bible says do unto others as they do unto you. He barked at me, so I barked at him.' I didn't know the Bible said that, but they know their Bible down in Gwent. From Grays Inn Road comes the story that two men discovered *in flagrante* in a quiet part of King's Cross Railway Station said 'It's all right officer, we're old school friends'. I still believe this to be a potentially rich vein of British social history. More please.

Police Review March 11, 1983.

I Cannot See You Mr Sharpe

One day at the Old Bailey I witnessed a scene which seemed to me to have been scripted by someone like Noel Coward for performance by elderly halfwits. The judge in No. 1 Court was Mr Justice Finlay (who was, by the way, a renowned eccentric, and who spent much of his time during a trial walking up and down the Bench with his hands behind his back, like Felix the Cat). He had just adjourned the court for the weekend (it was a Friday) and was halfway to the mysterious door through which judges disappear when their day's work is done. At that moment there burst into the court a frantic little figure which some of us recognised as that of a junior barrister called Mr Sharpe, who was short, thin, white-haired, long-chinned, and pointed of face. He was wearing neither robe nor wig. 'My Lord,' he called out, 'if I might detain your Lordship one moment longer-'. The judge stopped and looked at him with painful incredulity. 'This court is adjourned,

Mr Sharpe,' he said coldly. 'But my Lord, this is a matter of-'. The judge continued: 'Moreover,' he said, 'I cannot see you, Mr Sharpe'.

I didn't know, but this meant that Mr Sharpe, since he was not wigged and gowned, was not technically or professionally visible to a judge. He simply wasn't there. 'My Lord,' shouted Mr Sharpe as the judge resumed his majestic exit, 'this is a matter concerning the liberty of the subject'. As a matter of fact it was about a defendant who had just been 'put back' on bail but whose surety had suddenly died. An acceptable surety had been hurriedly found, and it was Mr Sharpe's job to get the judge's approval (or he seemed to think it was—I had my doubts later). 'I do not understand,' said his Lordship, 'why you did not say so at once'. But he came back at once, and actually sat down. The application was heard, and bail confirmed. For me, it was an unforgettable lesson in the supreme importance (in the courts) of 'the liberty of the subject'. But it was also a comic illustration of the tradition that an unrobed barrister in court is 'invisible' ('I cannot see you, Mr Sharpe'). Many a case had to be put back, on some pretext or other, where the true pretext was that 'my clerk hasn't brought my robes.'

And it happened again the other day in a West Midlands Crown Court, with a different sequel. Counsel was once again unrobed, having (as with Mr Sharpe) had no time for togging up, and he apologised abjectly for his nakedness. 'It's all right,' said the judge. 'Let us not bother. I may even hear you better without your wig.' Is this a giant step forward, or a lapse into barbarism?

Police Review April 8, 1983.

Flung into a Cell

A man with a criminal conviction, who is suing the West Midlands Police for unlawful arrest, has told the *Daily Telegraph* (April 4) how he was taken to Birmingham Road Police Station and 'flung into a cell'. It's a phrase that has always interested me—abstractly, for I've never seen a real case of cell-flinging. Most people, of course, don't much like going into their police cells, and their reluctance has to be reflected in something a little more expressive than 'Mr Jones was shown into a police cell,' even though, if the public did but know, that's a lot closer to what happens than 'flung'. Before I joined the police service and saw how people got into their cells, I tended to accept this flinging business as I had accepted the historical assurance that Mary Queen of Scots was flung by her sister into prison. Scepticism must, I think, have begun to assert itself after the appearance of that moving work, *The Yellow Peril* by Hoo Flung Dung. By that standard, I suppose, the Birmingham policemen who flung their man into his cell were themselves flung on duty at the beginning of their day and given a conditional discharge at the end of it. The whole idea may stem from the old Roman custom with rioters: flog the rank and file, and fling the ringleaders from the Tarpeian Rock.

Police Review April 15, 1983

'Neither a Borrower . . .'

Charles Lamb reckoned, as so many wits have reckoned, that the human species is composed of two distinct races, the men who borrow and the men who lend. (Long after him, Chesterton said that we are divided into two distinct races, those who believe we are divided into two distinct races and those who don't. It's an old rhetorical device, and in recent weeks the British have been giving a frenzied illustration of it.) Myself, I think Lamb was wrong, because we all borrow and we all lend. Particularly, we're all money lenders, though we prefer to call ourselves investors, and even though a good many of us never invest more wildly than a little in the Post Office Savings Bank and about 10 premium bonds. But moneylending must have been thought to be a dirty word, for it's now called consumer credit. The old Moneylenders Act of 1927, which enabled you to recognise a moneylender when you saw one (and ask to see his licence), has been succeeded by the Consumer Credit Act of 1974. I've been studying this, and have to report that I simply can't make head or tail of it.

I tried because of the warning issued last week by Sir Gordon Borrie, director-general of the Office of Fair Trading. He told the horrifying story of a couple who borrowed £50 to set up a home, and who didn't realise that they had signed an agreement to repay it within one year. They must have been paying interest at about 400% per annum, for they had paid off £102 at the end of the year and 'still owed £98'. The moneylender, sorry, consumer credit executive, gave them two options. They could be taken to court over it, or they could borrow more money to get them over the hump. They borrowed more money on the same terms, and then a year later faced the same old problem. It went on for 25 years, and 'this year,' says Sir Gordon Borrie, 'they owe £2,500 including interest, and they are still paying £10 a week'. Which will get them nowhere. Why aren't the sharks prosecuted? Have a look at the Consumer Credit Act and see where you would begin.

Police Review July 22, 1983.

Lending Weapons

Here's a problem. I possess a powerful bolt-cutter, big enough to get me arrested if carried incautiously in the street. Under its twin-lever persuasion, its jaws go through quarter-inch steel bolts as if they were cow-parsley stems. Once I lived in a rented house whose front garden (about the size of a kitchen table) was protected from something or other by a row of vicious-looking spiked railings. I hated these, wanted to get rid of them, and sought the landlord's permission, giving him a poignant account of his legal position if someone (especially me) got impaled on them. He consented, and I beheaded them all with my bolt-cutters. Then a neighbour's child *did* get impaled on some similar railings at a municipal recreation ground, and he wanted to borrow my cutters to make sure it never happened to anyone else. So I lent them to him, with the proviso that I knew nothing of his intentions. (Offence?) Recently I saw in the *Sunday Times* (July 7) a photograph of some similar railings at Doncaster, accompanied by a letter denouncing them and all devices like them. They are Victorian barbarities, every bit as wicked as mantraps and spring-guns, which the law specifically forbids. I would say it's the job of the police, as 'protectors of life and property', to warn these spiky landowners of their responsibility. To put it no higher, it might be the police who got impaled.

Police Review July 29, 1983.

Wrong Court

I usually refrain from capping other people's stories, mainly because I like my own to remain uncapped, at least until I'm out of earshot. But here goes. At the Law Courts in the Strand on July 28 the Lord Chief Justice, Lord Lane, presented the British Empire Medal to the retiring Chief Office Keeper, who in 37 years had climbed to that dizzy eminence from the post of 'night-cleaner', being successively stoker for the judges' rooms, messenger, usher, and head usher. The *Daily Telegraph* of July 29 extracted from him a story about his ushering days. He once led his judge into the wrong court. 'Silence', he boomed, and then realised (surely a bit late?) that he had interrupted a trial, where another judge was in full session.

At the Old Bailey I could always see the possibility of some such thing, and nursed a private grievance that it never happened. And then at last it did. Nearly all the courts had adjourned for lunch, but not Court Two. Suddenly the door on the judge's bench was kicked open and there staggered in a diminutive uniformed attendant carrying a pile of law books from the library. There were so many that the bearer's head, using his chin to keep them in position, was tilted too far back for him to see anything. Inevitably, as he turned, he dropped the lot and they shot all over the carpeted floor of the Bench. It was only then that he discovered that a trial was in progress. The judge was the recorder of London, Sir Gerald Dodson, who never even smiled at anything. And he laughed aloud, from sheer joy, holding up both hands to invite the whole court to join in, which it did. It made my day.

Police Review August 12, 1983.

Cricket Hazard

When my father was a young soldier at Shorncliff Camp he was walking past the cricket field while an officers' match was in progress. Someone hit a six, and the ball came down vertically on the crown of the paternal head. He was in no doubt as to what had happened but decided, with the speed and resolution which have made the Rolphs what they are, to walk on as if it hadn't. Arriving at the canteen, he collapsed and was then off sick for three days. This family saga has always discouraged me, not merely from walking close to village cricket matches but from playing in them. No such inhibition afflicted Hampshire's Robin Smith on August 11, for on this very day when his brother Chris was opening for England against New Zealand at Lords (his first ever Test match) and getting out for a tragic duck, Robin knocked up 150 at Southampton and, while doing so, put a ball through Mrs Iris Clarke's kitchen window 120 yards away. Angrily she pinched their ball. 'If they break my windows,' she said, 'I spoil their silly cricket'. Hampshire Cricket Club won't pay for the window. 'We were here before any flats,' they say. What would *you* do if they all came into your station, Mrs Clarke with the ball in her handbag and all the cricketers arguing angrily? I think I should remind the players what their game has long been a synonym for.

Police Review August 26, 1983.

Decline of the Public Loo

And while on the subject of local authorities and their shortcomings, a subject dear to all ratepayers, it's opportune to inquire what's happened to the so-called 'public convenience', the good old 'gents' and 'ladies'. It's a feature of what everyone is now calling 'inner city decay' that many of these one-time havens are now closed to the public they once seemed to welcome, secured with heavy chains and padlocks. What is going on in them? Are they museums, shrines of some sort, Ministry of Defence outposts? What do their former custodians suppose is happening to the comfort, or (more urgently) its relief, that they were once happy to further? Was it really the modern craze for 'economy at all costs' that led to the redundancy of all those underground Dans?

Lesson from New York. In recent months the *New York Times* has been up-braiding the Police Department for not being sufficiently tough with people 'using the city's streets as toilets'. Now it is receiving angry letters asking 'Where *does* one answer the call of nature?' And it transpires that the owners of new office buildings are providing public loos 'in return for the right to build extra floor space'. Community Board Five, for example, has succeeding in getting public toilets installed in the lobby of the Fisher Building. The Olympic Towers have some already. The Equitable Life Assurance Society, which is building a new place next to its old one on Sixth Avenue, is installing six 'public rest rooms' under the lobby of the new buildings. In this country, many of our big hotels and office blocks are providing this facility without intending to. It looks as though our local authorities know about this, and are exploiting it to do a bit of rate-saving by stealth.

Police Review September 2, 1983.

Neighbourhood Watch Schemes

If you are angered by your newspaper, you can screw it into a ball and hurl it across the room. This is difficult with a television set. Worse, you can't even write to it, tear it across, or cancel your order. And yet, compared with press reporters, its interviewers are sometimes maddening. They have established a custom by which every new proposal, every innovation, every attempt to redress some social wrong, every plan for changing something has to be treated as if it were the product of an idiot mind. All the questions addressed to the innovator, the supporter, the enthusiast, have to begin with the words 'But surely . . .' The next question will then begin 'But don't you think that . . .' Astoundingly, no one ever replies 'Of course I don't, you scatterbrained twit, this is something I've been working on for years'. I find that I'm not alone in marvelling that so much television and radio interviewing of this kind has become hostile and often even offensive. It wasn't always thus, and for once in a way I do know what I'm talking about.

All of which has been sparked off by the TV and radio interviewing of citizens and police officers concerning the Metropolitan Police schemes for establishing 'neighbourhood watches'. (I suppose it wouldn't do for police interviewees to hit out in the way I've suggested, but anyway the policemen I've seen interviewed on the matter were restrained, courteous and convincing.) It's as though the microphone wallahs have been briefed to 'send the thing up, make it look silly, get the weak spots, show the public that we're not hoodwinked—there's someting funny going on here'. What's the best line? Snooping! That's it. Nation of snoopers. 'Don't you think the police are asking you to act as a lot of snoopers, spying on your neighbours? Informing on each other, as if you were frightened Jerries trying to put each other away under the Nazis?' The neighbourhood watch schemes have nearly got through this stage. The next one will be ridicule. *Courage, mes braves.*

Police Review September 2, 1983.

Cockroaches

I have never much liked cockroaches. I can't remember when it was that we all stopped calling them blackbeetles, but they are the same chaps. And I confess to feeling a bit sorry for the Café Royal when it was fined £675 for having them on its premises, even if it was a trifle mystifying to read that £50,000 costs were awarded against Westminster City Council for bringing the prosecution. What seemed especially interesting was the angry protest that illustrious caterers like the Café Royal, Trust Houses Forte, Brooks's Club etc are being 'singled out' for persecution, by way of 'making an example of the famous'. In the days when I was searching premises at night, hot (or cold), on the scent of breakers-in, I was often appalled at the hordes of cockroaches to be seen in some of the smartest and most exclusive restaurants, City Clubs and institutions. And I bet any urban policeman can say the same. To say nothing of rats. I can't imagine who would have dared to prosecute any of these sanctums, but there were frequent prosecutions of little Italiano caffs and pull-ups for the same kind of thing. Mr Bryan Denyer, who as director of environmental health for Westminster City Council is the man behind these disturbing disclosures, seems to me to be operating at the right end. But if ever he feels like applying for membership of a West End club, he can expect to be blackbeetled. Perhaps, with all that he is now discovering, he won't really feel like applying.

Police Review October 7, 1983.

Impossible Takes Longer

Twenty years ago, nay 10 or even five, it would have been seen as a sign of complete mental breakdown to suggest that complaints against policemen should be investigated by anyone other than policemen. I've always thought it was a possibility, though not necessarily promising any improvement in results. For some years it has seemed to me a conceivable way of satisfying the critics, at least for a time, that is to say until everyone could see that matters were either (a) no better than they used to be or (b) worse. I once suggested it at a committee meeting within the sacred portals of the Home Office, mentioning as examples the (then) Post Office Investigation Branch, the S.I.B., the

Board of Trade inquiry officers, and the Customs and Excise men (newly active on the trail of VAT dodgers). It would have needed an H.M. Bateman to depict the horrified incredulity of the committee and its chairman. Did I know, someone inquired, what Sir Robert Mark had said about the idea of non-police investigators? I did, and was unmoved. Well, moved but not transplanted. I simply couldn't then believe, and still can't, that this is a nation of such fools that it couldn't find out what is going inside its police service if it really tried.

And now we have this extraordinary chumming-up of the NCCL, the Law Society, and the Police Federation saying, in effect, 'OK, you all keep on about the iniquity of allowing the police to inquire into their own misconduct — set up your own organisation and have a go'. The Law Society have been in favour of it for a long time. They put it up to the Royal Commission on Criminal Procedure, and then worked out a scheme. The Federation was interested, seeing it as a possible way of silencing all the moaners. The Association of Chief Police Officers, with justifiable caution, gave it an experimental shove. Even the Home Office withheld its fire (though some Home Office sniping has been heard since). So now we have a proposal for an 'independent investigation force' centred within the Police Complaints Board, reporting to an independent Complaints Tribunal. If such an investigation force comes into being, it will inevitably call to mind Bertrand Russell's plea for a second police force to monitor the behaviour of the regular one. He never got so far as to consider whether, in due time, the second force might need a third to keep an eye on it. But he only lived to be 98.

Police Review October 21, 1983.

Psychiatry in Court

You often hear it said, among people who go much to weekend conferences, that their true value lies in what happens *between* lectures and the awful 'reading of papers', what happens in bars and corridors, over pints and pipes. The much lamented death on October 27 of Professor T.C.N. Gibbens of the Institute of Psychiatry, who must have been about the best-loved man in the whole varied world of criminology, has reminded me of two episodes. The first was when I drove him back to London from a conference (concerning I know not what) at the Cambridge Institute of Criminology, and got him to talk about his job and about, in particular, the exasperating experience of giving evidence as a forensic psychiatrist in court. And the second is the recent psychiatric argument at the Old Bailey on whether Dennis Nilsen, the thoughtful-looking clerk who admits to having killed 15 men and 'thinks there may have been a lot more', was suffering from a 'severe personality disorder' within the meaning of the Homicide Act

1957. The psychiatrists on one side said yes, those on the other said no. Which leaves the man in the street to suppose that they will say what they're paid to say.

The forensic psychiatrist, said Professor Gibbens as his pipe gradually filled the car with smoke (it was Player's 'No Name'), is always looked upon as if he dealt in absolutes. He is expected to say whether a man is mad or not mad. I suggested that every man is slightly mad. He preferred Bernard Shaw's view that every man is slightly sane. But he wondered that any psychiatrist would ever consent to give evidence in court, when he considered the obloquy and ridicule to be met with there. Had he ever encountered ridicule himself? Well, not really, they always seemed rather kind to him personally. (In the witness box he always sounded *interested* rather than over-confident, admitting readily that there were other lines of current research that might invalidate what he was saying, and winning adherents all round. He looked a little like a younger Clive Brook.)

He would have been the first to say, of the Nilsen case, that the evidence of mental disorder (in the conventional view) was that he killed people, while the explanation of the mental disorder is also that he killed people. 'Psychiatry has emerged from the Nilsen trial,' said a *Times* article on November 5, 'as from the Sutcliffe trial, with mud on its face. The law has come out of the contact with psychiatry looking a bit of a clodhopper'. Beat that. But try, also, to think up a formula that will save future juries from so absurdly impossible a task, and forensic medicine from serio-comic exploitation.

Police Review November 18, 1983.

Aged Shoplifters

In the present-day shoplifting context (I nearly said contest), not much sympathy is extended to the shops, especially when they are as big as Woolworths, But in a recent case concerning Woolworths, it seemed that the prosecution had decided to 'offer no evidence' on no other ground than that the accused party was a lady said to be 76. This was the case in which, to the indignation of the press and somebody in the House of Commons, a London judge had announced that if the trial had been proceeded with he would have made the prosecution pay the defendant's costs as well as its own. (The press reports didn't say whether or not this would have depended on the old lady's acquittal, but I suppose it would.) Another lady, Mrs Daphne Gaywood, wrote to the *Daily Telegraph* (November 23) from Portscatho in Cornwall to say that she was 78 and would like to know whether she now had immunity to go and help herself. I'd been wondering the same thing, since I'm getting on too. As Christmas approaches, I am watching this situation closely. There seems such a lot to buy.

Police Review December 2, 1983.

Denning's Digest

'Short sentences are best and verbs are optional'. So said Mr Simon Brown, Treasury counsel, at the farewell ceremony for Lord Denning in the Court of Appeal of July 30 last year. I've just been reading his Lordship's latest (but I bet not his last) book, *The Closing Chapter* (Butterworths, £10.50, or softcover £6.50). And like his other books, indeed like his judgements, it serves two purposes. It comes as a kind of (strictly selective) *Poor Man's Halsbury*, and it helps to explain why it was inevitable that Lord Denning should become a Professional Character. What would happen to any manuscript like this if it were written by a nobody? If the publisher thought he saw some reason for accepting it, for example the feel of a pistol on the back of his neck, some editor told to 'prepare it for publication' would proceed to muck it up. His Lordship emerges as the Denning we all think we know and uneasily love, the plain man's champion, the scrutiniser of the small print. The trouble is, he quotes too many House of Lords decisions without telling us what they were about. We're supposed to know. Law students, I suppose, will know. Or will they? The judges, he says, are not allowed to know many vitally important things when they are making decisions. Recalling the ruling that a Sikh boy couldn't wear his turban to school, he repudiates the press headline DENNING thwarts commons. He and his brother judges didn't know the facts, he says. *Hansard* ought to be available to them, so that they could find out what Parliament really wanted (and many people have argued for this, always in vain). But this Sikh turban case is a long story, and not even Lord Denning's *Listen With Mother* style of telling it can rescue it from turning into a bore. The book as a whole needs no such rescue — it's a benign, bumbling essay in sheer commonsense and plain English. The judges find a 'lacuna' in the law, he says. What's a 'lacuna? A gap. Then why on earth don't they say a gap? The implication is that they have an inherited desire to bewilder and impress the layman, unaware that millions of laymen already know that a lacuna is not some kind of mountain goat. I believe there are people who rejoice that Lord Denning is no longer Master of the Rolls. But I bet most of them are lawyers.

Police Review December 9, 1983.

On Being Late

My own police service began at a time when all probationer constables belonged to a feckless generation which was in urgent need of a sharp lesson. This was to be delivered by the sergeants, who had been divinely appointed for the job. Discipline was the thing, iron discipline. It would get this old country back on its feet, and the feet that would make the biggest impression were those of policemen. If you were to get the full benefit of this treatment, you must start the day promptly and punctually. Therefore Being Late for Duty was the cardinal sin. No excuses were listened to. If you were not there at the shout of 'Fall In', you were late, and you were for it. After some years this began to soften a little, and in the Discipline Book there might sometimes appear the excuse 'Up all night with dying child'.

I recall seeing a juror arrive 10 minutes late for a part-heard trial at the Old Bailey. He clambered, panting convincingly, to his seat while prosecuting counsel was just warming to his closing speech. The judge appeared not to have noticed him and the trial went on. But at the next pause in counsel's speech the judge said 'May we know why that juror was late?' The Clerk told the poor man to stand up. Why was he late? Circumstances over which he had no control whatever, he said. 'May we know what they were?', said the judge (it was the Recorder, Sir Gerald Dodson). 'My Lord, I am not in a position to tell the court,' said the juror, a white-haired man with a long face. The face had gone white too. 'Indeed?' The Recorder began warming up. 'Do you know that you face a heavy fine if your explanation is not acceptable?' He did, he said, and he must accept whatever was in store for him. But whether his explanation would be acceptable or not, he was unable to give it in open court. There was a little legal dialogue about the possibility, indeed the propriety, of clearing the court for the occasion. Everyone knew this wouldn't happen, and it didn't. The Recorder could have told the erring juror to stand down, but he didn't do that either. In fact he did nothing more, apart from telling counsel, rather testily, to get on with his interrupted speech. In the more lowly and primitive parts of the building, theories were circulated, and bets taken, about the probable reasons in the secretive juror's heart. But we never found out.

Police Review December 23, 1983.

Postscript

And that, surely, must be enough. There are thousands more, but it's probably better that they should stay there. I decided to finish with 'On Being Late' because lateness, and especially the fear of it, have done much to shape my life, though not in the sense of getting me everywhere early. I have read that the aphorism 'Better late than never' originated with Noah's reassurance to the Zebra, which had understood that passengers were expected to present themselves in alphabetical order. There are people who are late on principle, like the man in *The Picture of Dorian Gray* who held that punctuality is the thief of time. But time and lateness have been hovering over this self-selected cluster of articles, and I have the best of reasons for being glad that it is done.

C.H.R.

INDEX

2.65 Hamlet